Prospects for Monetary Unions after the Euro

CESifo Seminar Series
Edited by Hans-Werner Sinn

Inequality and Growth: Theory and Policy Implications
Theo S. Eicher and Stephen J. Turnovsky, editors

Public Finance and Public Policy in the New Century
Sijbren Cnossen and Hans-Werner Sinn, editors

Spectrum Auctions and Competition in Telecommunications
Gerhard Illing and Ulrich Klüh, editors

Managing European Union Enlargement
Helge Berger and Thomas Moutos, editors

European Monetary Integration
Hans-Werner Sinn, Mika Widgrén, and Marko Köthenbürger, editors

Measuring the Tax Burden on Capital and Labor
Peter Birch Sørensen, editor

A Constitution for the European Union
Charles B. Blankart and Dennis C. Mueller, editors

Labor Market Institutions and Public Regulation
Jonas Agell, Michael Keen, and Alfons J. Weichenrieder, editors

Venture Capital, Entrepreneurship, and Public Policy
Vesa Kanniainen and Christian Keuschnigg, editors

Exchange Rate Economics: Where Do We Stand?
Paul De Grauwe, editor

Prospects for Monetary Unions after the Euro
Paul De Grauwe and Jacques Mélitz, editors

Prospects for Monetary Unions after the Euro

edited by
Paul De Grauwe and
Jacques Mélitz

CESifo Seminar Series

The MIT Press
Cambridge, Massachusetts
London, England

MIT Press books may be purchased at special quantity discounts for business or sales promotional use. For information, please email special_sales@mitpress.mit.edu or write to Special Sales Department, The MIT Press, 55 Hayward Street, Cambridge, MA 02142.

This book was set in Palatino on 3B2 by Asco Typesetters, Hong Kong and was printed and bound in the United States of America.

Library of Congress Cataloging-in-Publication Data

Prospects for monetary unions after the euro / edited by Paul De Grauwe and Jacques Mélitz.
    p.   cm. — (CESifo seminar series)
Includes bibliographical references and index.
ISBN 0-262-04230-4 (alk. paper)
1. Monetary unions. 2. Euro area. I. Grauwe, Paul de. II. Mélitz, Jacques. III. Series.
HG3894.P76   2005
332.4'566—dc22   2005043898

10 9 8 7 6 5 4 3 2 1

Contents

Contributors   vii
Series Foreword   ix

1 **Introduction**   1
Paul De Grauwe and Jacques Mélitz

2 **The Eastward Enlargement of the European Monetary Union**   7
Michele Ca' Zorzi and Roberto A. De Santis

3 **Structural Reforms and the Enlargement of Monetary Union**   31
Carsten Hefeker

4 **The Endogeneity of the Optimum Currency Area Criteria and Intra-industry Trade: Implications for EMU Enlargement**   55
Jarko Fidrmuc

5 **Exchange Rate Volatility and the Decline of Employment Growth in the CEE Economies**   77
Ansgar Belke and Ralph Setzer

6 **The Influence of Productivity, Demand, and Regulated Prices on the Real Bilateral Exchange Rates of Four Accession Countries**   127
Ronald MacDonald and Cezary Wójcik

7 **The EMU Effect on Trade: What's in It for the UK?**   155
Alejandro Micco, Guillermo Ordóñez, and Ernesto Stein

8 Output Smoothing in EMU and OECD: Can We Forgo the
   Government Contribution? A Risk-Sharing Approach   187
   Carlos Fonseca Marinheiro

9 On the Implications of a Unilateral Currency Union for
   Macroeconomic Volatility   225
   Roberto Duncan

10 Regional Currencies versus Dollarization: Options for Asia and
   the Americas   263
   Felipe Larraín and José Tavares

11 An Output Perspective on a Northeast Asia Currency Union   289
   Yin-Wong Cheung and Jude Yuen

12 Have a Break, Have a ... National Currency: When Do Monetary
   Unions Fall Apart?   319
   Volker Nitsch

   Index   347

Contributors

Ansgar Belke
University of Hohenheim

Michele Ca' Zorzi
European Central Bank

Yin-Wong Cheung
University of California, Santa
Cruz

Roberto A. De Santis
European Central Bank

Roberto Duncan
Central Bank of Chile

Jarko Fidrmuc
Austrian National Bank

Carlos Fonseca Marinheiro
University of Coimbra

Carsten Hefeker
Institute of International
Economics, Hamburg

Felipe Larraín
Pontificia Universidad Catolica,
Chile

Ronald MacDonald
Strathclyde University, Glasgow

Alejandro Micco
Inter-American Development
Bank, Washington, DC

Volker Nitsch
Free University of Berlin

Guillermo Ordóñez
Inter-American Development
Bank, Washington, DC

Ralph Setzer
University of Hohenheim

Ernesto Stein
Inter-American Development
Bank, Washington, DC

José Tavares
Universidade Nova de Lisboa

Cezary Wójcik
Warsaw School of Economics

Jude Yuen
University of California, Santa
Cruz

CESifo Seminar Series in Economic Policy

This book is part of the CESifo Seminar Series in Economic Policy, which aims to cover topical policy issues in economics from a largely European perspective. The books in this series are the products of the papers presented and discussed at seminars hosted by CESifo, an international research network of renowned economists supported jointly by the Center for Economic Studies at Ludwig-Maximilians University, Munich, and the Ifo Institute for Economic Research. All publications in this series have been carefully selected and refereed by members of the CESifo research network.

Hans-Werner Sinn

1 Introduction

Paul De Grauwe and Jacques
Mélitz

The introduction of the euro is a milestone in the history of international monetary relations. Until the late 1980s few observers would have bet on the success of monetary integration in Europe. Yet today monetary union is a fact of life in Europe.

One of the more remarkable aspects of the process of monetary integration in Europe is that it started at the end of the 1980s at a time of widespread skepticism, if not hostility, about the project among economists. The skepticism about monetary unification was very much influenced by the theory of optimal currency areas, as Robert Mundell pioneered it. Mundell's analysis of the problem was Keynesian. According to it, the exchange rate is a variable allowing for more flexibility in a world of rigid prices and wages and immobility of labor. In the late 1980s, these rigidities were seen as endemic in Europe. If so, Europe was certainly not the place where monetary unification should be introduced. Remarkably, though, politicians pushed through the whole process of monetary integration against the advice of most experts.

Experts change their minds. Two factors have contributed to the turnaround, one of which speaks poorly about expert opinion. First, the monetarist counterrevolution that became popular during the 1980s and 1990s stressed the futility of monetary fine-tuning, and warned that countries engaged in such monetary activism would experience an inflation bias and macroeconomic instability. From the perch of this new theoretical outlook, relinquishing one's own monetary policy instrument did not appear to be as costly as before. Central bankers were also early converts to the new monetarist conventional wisdom, in particular in Europe. Consequently, rather than forces of opposition, they became important promoters of monetary integration in Europe.

The other factor that contributed to the change of mind—the one that casts doubt over expert opinion—is the very progress toward monetary union. There had been an element of *realpolitik* in the skeptical attitude of the experts. They believed that the reform would never take place. After all, had not the proposition of monetary union in Europe first been mooted in the Werner report in 1970 and had it not been allowed to stay in limbo for the better part of two decades afterward? However, at some point monetary union began to be seen as something inevitable, as something that was written in the stars. At that point, professional opinion largely rallied in its favor.

There can be no doubt that the mere existence of European Monetary Union has changed economists' outlook about monetary union. The purpose of the conference organized by CESifo in Venice in July 2003 was to take stock of the new insights into monetary union that economists have brought since their change of heart. How does the profession think today about the desirability of monetary unions in general, and of monetary unions in other parts of the world? Does it make sense to start monetary unions in Latin America and in Asia? How desirable is it to enlarge the existing eurozone and to include the United Kingdom and central European countries? What are the likely problems of transition in case of such an enlargement process? How does the existence of a monetary union affect the workings of the "real economy," in particular, the labor markets? Does a monetary union give the right incentives to introduce structural reforms in the labor markets? What is the role of capital markets and the government budget in insuring against asymmetric shocks? These are some of the questions analyzed during the conference. Some interesting debate and new insights resulted.

Issues of enlargement loomed large during the conference. The first five chapters testify to this. In chapter 2, Michele Ca' Zorzi and Roberto De Santis develop a model to analyze how the enlargement of the eurozone to admit the central European countries will affect its workings. Not surprisingly, they find little effect on the inflation rate in the eurozone as a whole. Nonetheless, the new member countries may experience a higher rate of inflation because of structural reasons linked to the Balassa-Samuelson effect. In general, new entrants into the eurozone will bear a considerable impact on their macroeconomic developments at home.

How will enlargement affect the trend toward labor market reforms in the eurozone? Carsten Hefeker argues in chapter 3 that the enlargement will increase the incentives to introduce these reforms in the present members of the eurozone. But the opposite may happen among the prospective new members.

Much of the early skepticism about monetary union was also the result of thinking in a static context. According to a static analysis, if the conditions for a monetary union are not satisfied beforehand, countries should not join. Frankel and Rose added a dynamic dimension in our thinking. They argued that even if the right conditions for monetary union are not present, a monetary union in itself might generate these conditions. They called this the "endogeneity of the optimum currency criteria." In chapter 4, Jarko Fidrmuc tests the empirical validity of this hypothesis for the likely new members of the eurozone in central Europe, and confirms the hypothesis. This would seem to be good news, particularly for the prospective members that still hesitate about entry.

The latter countries may also want to take a look at chapter 5 written by Ansgar Belke and Ralph Setzer. These authors find empirical evidence that exchange rate volatility in central European countries lowers employment growth and raises unemployment rates. The authors conclude that the new entrants in the European Union should join the eurozone as soon as possible.

The next chapter by Ronald MacDonald and Cezary Wójcik contains a lot of information about the transition process of the central European countries into the eurozone. Among the problems these countries face is the fact that their relatively high productivity growth may require a higher rate of inflation than the rest of the eurozone. The authors find this Balassa-Samuelson effect, as it is known, to be large for the central European countries. This would not necessarily be a cause for concern after these countries were well ensconced inside the eurozone. But it could be problematic during the transition period because of the Maastricht convergence criteria concerning rates of inflation and the exchange rates in the interim. Thus, unless a liberal interpretation of the convergence criteria takes place, the central European countries could face serious obstacles to entry into the eurozone.

The early skepticism of economists vis-à-vis monetary union was also inspired by a lack of evidence that stable exchange rates stimulated trade. Most econometric evidence seemed to suggest that a move toward a regime of irrevocably fixed exchange rate would promote trade only to a limited extent. Then came Andy Rose. Using panel data, he uncovered very large effects of monetary unions on trade. Merely belonging to a monetary union could triple the size of trade flows among members of a monetary union. The first reaction of the economics profession was one of disbelief. A whole spate of econometric efforts to check up followed. As a result, the quantitative importance of the effect of monetary union on trade flows has been revised substantially downward. However, the idea of a significant positive effect stands. This is also the conclusion of Alejandro Micco, Guillermo Ordóñez, and Ernesto Stein in chapter 7. Applying a modified methodology to the same sort of panel data used in the earlier Rose studies (by controlling for bilateral pairs), they find that the European Monetary Union has already added 8 to 16 percent to trade among the member countries in the short period since the system began. Interestingly too, even without joining, the United Kingdom has benefited thus far from some added trade with the members. In effect, the trade advantages of monetary union are therefore not confined to the membership. Yet Micco, Ordóñez, and Stein also estimate that membership would have added another 7 percent to the United Kingdom's international trade with everyone.

There is now a large consensus among economists that a monetary union works better if insurance mechanisms are in place to deal with asymmetric shocks. One relevant insurance mechanism concerns transfers through an upper level government budget; another comes from integrated capital markets. Much research focuses on the contribution of these two mechanisms to smoothing asymmetric shocks. The consensus view is that both mechanisms are relatively strong in the United States but weak within the eurozone. Chapter 8, written by Carlos Marinheiro, confirms this view. The author finds that risk sharing through government budgets and capital markets is relatively weak in the eurozone compared to the United States. This is true despite evidence from other sources that the members of EMU have gained considerable ability to borrow from one another in the last decade or more. The so-called Feldstein-Horioka puzzle (concerning the link between domestic investment and domestic saving) has weakened in Western Europe. Still there is little doubt of the desirability of strengthening the risk-sharing mechanisms in the eurozone so that member countries hit by temporary misfortunes relative to the rest do not feel disaffected from the system as a whole.

One outstanding result of monetary union in Europe is a fresh impetus to thinking about monetary unions in other parts of the world. The next three chapters deal with the desirability of monetary unions in Latin America and East Asia. In fact there is a basic alternative to the sort of monetary union that has arisen in Europe: dollarization or the mere adoption of the US dollar and abandonment of a national currency. This can be regarded as monetary union of sorts too (of a unilateral kind). But, even if so, the contrast with the European model is important. Chapter 10 by Felipe Larraín and José Tavares is interesting in focusing precisely on the choice between dollarization and the collective form of monetary union in Europe. Their basic conclusion is that South America and Central America would both benefit more from dollarization than regional monetary union of the European sort. By contrast, East Asia would benefit more from regional monetary union. These results obtain from an analysis and a comparison of the different degrees of trade integration and real exchange rate volatility in the two cases.

In chapter 9, Roberto Duncan focuses instead on the choice between the status quo and dollarization in the particular case of Peru. As a relevant feature, Peru exhibits significant dollarization, even as things stand, because of currency substitution by individual households and firms. In order to treat the issue, Duncan simulates a dynamic general equilibrium model (rather than relying on econometrics, as Larraín and Tavares do). Given an explicit utility function, he raises the question of which system would yield higher welfare. According to his model, the answer depends heavily on differences in the volatility of output and prices. While acknowledging some significant opposition in the literature, he comes out guardedly in favor of the status quo.

For Larraín and José Tavares, the basic impediment to monetary union in the case of East Asia is political. This view receives confirmation from Yin-Wong Cheung and Jude Yuen in chapter 11 on the potential for a monetary union between China, Japan and South Korea. The authors find a relatively high degree of correlation between output behavior in these three countries and a common business cycle. The basic economic precondition for a successful union is thus satisfied. However, for political reasons, the monetary union of this particular trio of nations is hard to imagine.

The diehard skeptics about monetary union will find comfort in the fact that many monetary unions have broken apart in the past. In the last chapter of this conference book, Volker Nitsch analyzes the episodes of dissolution of monetary unions and looks for an explanation. Using a panel data of 245 country pairs in which a common currency broke up in about half of the cases over the 1948 to 1997 stretch, he finds little sign that the usual factors stressed by the theory of optimum currency areas have much power in explaining the dissolutions. Instead, the big influences are political breakups and large inflation differentials. This last influence gives pause: it clearly reflects the wide presence of monetary unions between countries with weakly integrated economies in the sample (e.g., as is true for most monetary unions between ex-colonized and ex-colonizer). Otherwise, of course, monetary union itself would exclude the scale of the inflation differentials in the sample.

Much research about the desirability and the optimal functioning of monetary unions remains to be done. There is still so much we do not know. Yet we believe that this conference book adds significantly to our knowledge and will be a valuable reference source in future research on this fascinating subject.

2 The Eastward Enlargement of the European Monetary Union

Michele Ca' Zorzi and Roberto A. De Santis

2.1 Introduction

It is one of the aims explicitly set out in the Treaty establishing the European Community that economic cohesion be strengthened through the ultimate adoption of a single currency, excluding any form of positive or negative discrimination among the member states (the equality of treatment principle). The Treaty also identifies among the goals of the Community, the need to promote sustainable and noninflationary growth, assigning to the Eurosystem the primary objective of preserving price stability (the price stability principle).

In this chapter we make an attempt to assess these objectives, by studying the impact of EU enlargement on inflation and output upon the inclusion of new member states (NMs) in the European Union (EU), ten in May 2004 and two more expected in 2007. We use a simple modeling framework that refers to the standard time inconsistency literature initiated by Kydland and Prescott (1977), Barro and Gordon (1983), and Rogoff (1985) and recently applied to the case of currency unions by Lane (2000), Alesina and Barro (2002), Berger (2002), Gros and Hefeker (2002), and Ca' Zorzi and De Santis (2004).[1]

To examine the currency union issue, we developed a general specification of the model that allows differences in the countries' economic structures (see Ca' Zorzi and De Santis 2004). The model generalizes Lane (2000), Berger (2002) and Gros and Hefeker (2002) by introducing a deterministic and a stochastic component to the real exchange rate. This approach is useful in the context of enlargement, as it is consistent with the empirical and theoretical finding that currencies of new NMs tend to appreciate as a result of the catching-up process (Grafe and Wyplosz 1997; De Broeck and Slok 2001; Frait and Komarek 2001; Halpern and Wyploz 2001; Kovacs 2002; Égert 2003).

The model assumes three phases. In the pre-Maastricht phase, steady-state inflation depends on the monetary policy framework adopted in each country. With a flexible exchange rate, steady-state inflation in NMs will be higher, the less credible the monetary policy framework and the flatter the Phillips curve. In the case of a currency board regime, however, inflation is partly imported from the anchor country and partly determined by the real exchange rate appreciation process. The model is also consistent with the view that the currency board regime may be suited to countries that need to enhance the credibility of their monetary policy framework, but it poses a number of risks if country-specific supply shocks are deemed to be likely.

In the Maastricht phase, the model assumes that the inflation requirement of the Treaty determines a radical change to the way inflationary expectations are formed, consistent with the rapid achievement of the nominal convergence objective. At the same time the process of appreciation of the real exchange rate in NMs exerts an upward pressure on the nominal exchange rate of these NMs.

In the enlarged monetary union phase, the model suggests that average inflation in the enlarged euro area is not affected via the credibility channel or via the real exchange rate appreciation process, provided that the monetary policy framework is unchanged. Enlargement in this case simply results in a different distribution of inflation across countries, with a deflationary impact on the euro area.

To gauge the magnitude of the effects, this analytical framework is then applied to ten NMs and the euro area. Several alternative scenarios are considered, in order to account for the uncertainty over the pace of the real appreciation process in NMs and over the parameter values of the model.

The main insights of the numerical simulations can be summarized as follows: The impact of enlargement on steady-state inflation of the current euro area is limited, if participating countries are weighted on the basis of their nominal GDP and if the upward pressure on the real exchange rate is postulated to be in line with most estimates of the Balassa-Samuelson effect. However, the deflationary impact on the euro area is more sizable if NMs are weighted in terms of purchasing power parities and if a stronger real exchange rate appreciation process is assumed.

With regard to shocks, the results depend on whether they are symmetric or country-specific. If supply shocks are symmetric, the response of inflation and output in the enlarged currency area is very similar to that of the euro area before enlargement, while the response in NMs is sensitive to the slope of the Phillips curve. In the event of either country-specific supply shocks in NMs or real exchange rate shocks, the response of inflation and output is found to be small in the enlarged currency area but sizable in the NMs, irrespective of the slope of the Phillips curve.

The remaining sections of the paper have been structured as follows: sections 2.2 and 2.3 describe the model for NMs and the euro area; section 2.4 examines the consequences of the Maastricht phase under the hypothesis that entering in the exchange rate mechanism is fully credible; section 2.5 explores the consequences of the enlargement of the euro area from both the point of view of the NMs and the euro area; section 2.6 presents the benchmark of the model, and simulates the impact of institutional changes as well as of supply and real exchange rate shocks; finally, section 2.7 provides the main conclusions.

2.2   Independent Monetary Policy

Consider a static n-country Barro-Gordon (1983) model, defined by a set $(a = 1 \dots n - 1)$ of NMs and the euro area n. The objective function of the central bank in each country $(i = 1 \dots n)$ is based on the assumption that monetary authorities dislike departures of actual output and inflation from their respective optimal values. Thus they minimize a quadratic loss function of the following type:

$$L_i = \tfrac{1}{2}E[(y_i - y_i^*)^2 + \beta_i(\pi_i - \pi_i^*)^2], \tag{1}$$

where y_i denotes actual output, y_i^* desired output, π_i actual inflation, π_i^* the bliss point, and β_i weights the cost of inflation relative to that of output.

Define $\kappa_i \geq 0$ as the degree of distortions, market imperfections or technological gap that prevents countries from achieving their maximum potential convergence vis-à-vis the euro area (Beetsma and Jensen 2003; Berger 2002). This parameter in the present framework will be referred to as the "convergence gap." We assume that the difference between desired output, y_i^*, and the natural rate, $\bar{y}_i$, is a fraction ϕ_i of the convergence gap, κ_i, where the coefficient $0 \leq \phi_i \leq 1$ measures to what extent monetary authorities wish to converge faster than the natural rate would allow for. In the extreme cases, if $\phi_i = 0$, the convergence gap does not have any influence on the monetary policy-making process, so $y_i^* = \bar{y}_i$. If on the contrary $\phi_i = 1$, the convergence gap entirely feeds into the monetary policy response, $y_i^* = \bar{y}_i + \kappa_i$. In the case of the euro area we assume that $\phi_n = \kappa_n = 0$; thus $y_n^* = \bar{y}_n$ holds always.

On the supply side, the deviation of output from its natural level, $\bar{y}_i$, is positively related to unanticipated inflation:

$$y_i = \bar{y}_i + \alpha_i(\pi_i - \pi_i^e) + \varepsilon_i, \tag{2}$$

where π_i^e denotes expected inflation and α_i the output elasticity to inflation surprises or the inverse of the slope of the Phillips curve; $\varepsilon_i \sim IID(0, \sigma_{\varepsilon_a}^2)$ is white noise.

Events unfold as follows: The private sector forms expectations on prices, conditionally on the information available at that time. The output shock is realized and, finally, monetary policy is set. Monetary authorities therefore dispose of an informational advantage with respect to private agents. The game is solved by backward induction. Since y_a^* is higher than the natural rate $\bar{y}_a$, the standard time-inconsistency problem of monetary policy arises.

Monetary authorities minimize the objective function (1) subject to (2). Replacing (2) and y_i^* in (1) and differentiating with respect to π_i determines the reaction function of the central bank as a function of inflationary expectations:

$$\pi_i = \frac{\beta_i}{\alpha_i^2 + \beta_i}\pi_i^* + \frac{\alpha_i^2}{\alpha_i^2 + \beta_i}\pi_i^e + \frac{\alpha_i}{\alpha_i^2 + \beta_i}\phi_i\kappa_i - \frac{\alpha_i}{\alpha_i^2 + \beta_i}\varepsilon_i. \tag{3}$$

Imposing rational expectations on (3) yields the inflationary expectation of the private sector

$$\pi_i^e = \pi_i^* + \frac{\alpha_i}{\beta_i}\phi_i\kappa_i, \tag{4}$$

which in turn replaced in (3) yields realized inflation:

$$\pi_i = \pi_i^* + \frac{\alpha_i}{\beta_i}\phi_i\kappa_i - \frac{\alpha_i}{\alpha_i^2 + \beta_i}\varepsilon_i. \tag{5}$$

The inflation variance is equal to

$$\sigma_{\pi_i}^2 = \left(\frac{\alpha_i}{\alpha_i^2 + \beta_i}\right)^2 \sigma_{\varepsilon_i}^2. \tag{6}$$

To derive ex post output, replace (4) and (5) in (2). Then

$$y_i = \bar{y}_i + \frac{\beta_i}{\alpha_i^2 + \beta_i}\varepsilon_i,$$

while the output variance is equal to

$$\sigma_{y_i}^2 = \left(\frac{\beta_i}{\alpha_i^2 + \beta_i}\right)^2 \sigma_{\varepsilon_i}^2. \tag{7}$$

Given (5), the inflation differential between NMs and the euro area is

$$\pi_a - \pi_n = \pi_a^* - \pi_n^* + \frac{\alpha_a}{\beta_a} \phi_a \kappa_a - \frac{\alpha_a}{\alpha_a^2 + \beta_a} \varepsilon_a + \frac{\alpha_n}{\alpha_n^2 + \beta_n} \varepsilon_n. \tag{8}$$

In steady state the inflation differential between NMs and the euro area is wider the larger the difference between π_a^* and π_n^* and, if $\phi_a > 0$, the larger the distortion κ_a.

The analysis also allows us to get an insight on what are the determinants of the nominal exchange rate. Let us assume that the real exchange rate of the euro vis-à-vis NMs' set of currencies is determined by factors exogenous to the model.[2] Although this restriction is not a necessary feature of the model, both theoretical and empirical considerations suggest that, owing to the catching up process, NMs' currency are bound to appreciate in real terms.[3] The nominal depreciation of NMs' currencies vis-à-vis the euro, defined as $\hat{e}_a = \pi_a - \pi_n + q_a + \eta_a$, is therefore equal to

$$\hat{e}_a = \pi_a^* - \pi_n^* + \frac{\alpha_a}{\beta_a} \phi_a \kappa_a + q_a - \frac{\alpha_a}{\alpha_a^2 + \beta_a} \varepsilon_a + \frac{\alpha_n}{\alpha_n^2 + \beta_n} \varepsilon_n + \eta_a,$$

where $q_a < 0$ is the deterministic component of the real exchange rate appreciation of NMs and η_a is a shock to the real exchange rate with zero mean and constant variance. In other words, NMs' currencies are expected to depreciate in nominal terms, whenever the steady-state inflation differential is larger than the real exchange rate appreciation, which is due to the catching-up process.

2.3 Currency Board

Estonia, Lithuania, and Bulgaria have chosen to adopt currency board regimes.[4] How are inflation and output to be affected in this case? Under the assumption of a fully credible regime, the value of the inflation rate does not ensue from an optimization program.[5] By fixing the exchange rate, $\pi_a^{CB} = \pi_n - q_a - \eta_a$, and by using (5) to determine π_n, the NMs' inflation rate is found to be equal to

$$\pi_a^{CB} = \pi_n^* - \frac{\alpha_n}{\alpha_n^2 + \beta_n}\varepsilon_n - q_a - \eta_a. \tag{9}$$

Under a currency board, inflation in NMs depends on both the impact of shocks affecting the euro area and on real exchange rate movements determined by the catching-up process. It should be noted that inflation no longer depends on supply shocks affecting NMs. This is because a pure currency board implicitly prevents the monetary authorities from stabilizing them. The output equation becomes in fact the following:

$$y_a^{CB} = \bar{y}_a + \varepsilon_a - \frac{\alpha_a \alpha_n}{\alpha_n^2 + \beta_n}\varepsilon_n - \alpha_a \eta_a. \tag{10}$$

If supply shocks are symmetric and $\alpha_a = \alpha_n$, the impact on inflation and output is the same as for the euro area. By contrast, if supply shocks affect only country a, there is no response in terms of stabilization by the monetary authority, and hence inflation remains unchanged whereas output absorbs entirely the shock, ε_a. Foreign shocks may also have sizable effects on the domestic economy. This can be seen for example by the positive relationship between the variances of inflation and output in the NMs and the variance of supply shocks in the euro area, $\sigma_{\varepsilon_n}^2$:

$$\sigma_{\pi_a^{CB}}^2 = \left(\frac{\alpha_n}{\alpha_n^2 + \beta_n}\right)^2 \sigma_{\varepsilon_n}^2 + \sigma_{\eta_a}^2 + 2\frac{\alpha_n}{\alpha_n^2 + \beta_n}\sigma_{(\varepsilon_n, \eta_a)},$$

$$\sigma_{y_a^{CB}}^2 = \sigma_{\varepsilon_a}^2 + \left(\frac{\alpha_a \alpha_n}{\alpha_n^2 + \beta_n}\right)^2 \sigma_{\varepsilon_n}^2 + \alpha_a^2 \sigma_{\eta_a}^2 - \frac{2\alpha_a \alpha_n}{\alpha_n^2 + \beta_n}\sigma_{(\varepsilon_a, \varepsilon_n)}$$

$$- 2\alpha_a \sigma_{(\varepsilon_a, \eta_a)} + \frac{2\alpha_a^2 \alpha_n}{\alpha_n^2 + \beta_n}\sigma_{(\varepsilon_n, \eta_a)}.$$

Another interesting aspect is that a priori at least, it is not possible to say whether inflation is lower under a currency board regime or under flexible exchange rates.[6] Average inflation under the currency board regime (9) is lower than that under the flexible exchange rate regime (5) if the real exchange rate pressure is sufficiently contained, in other words, if $-q_a < \pi_a^* - \pi_n^* + \alpha_a \phi_a \kappa_a / \beta_a$. This regime therefore appears particularly suited to countries that need to enhance the credibility of their monetary policy framework, whereas it poses a number of risks if country-specific supply or real exchange rate shocks are thought to be likely.

2.4 Maastricht Phase

Following accession, new member states participate in the EU coordination of economic policies and, to the extent to which they have reached a sustainable level of convergence, are expected to join the euro area provided they satisfy the criteria set out in the Maastricht Treaty.[7] The implications of the Maastricht criteria on inflation and output can be seen in the light of the present modeling framework. We assume that the policy makers decide to proceed with a rapid process of nominal convergence to bring the inflation differential down to the level required by Maastricht, π_λ. We also assume that this strategy is fully credible, as the payoff is deemed to be sufficiently high. Then $\pi_a^M = \pi_n + \pi_\lambda$. By using (5) to determine π_n, we have inflation and output in NMs reducing respectively to

$$\pi_a^M = \pi_n^* - \frac{\alpha_n}{\alpha_n^2 + \beta_n}\varepsilon_n + \pi_\lambda, \tag{11}$$

$$y_a^M = \bar{y}_a + \varepsilon_a - \frac{\alpha_a \alpha_n}{\alpha_n^2 + \beta_n}\varepsilon_n. \tag{12}$$

Examining finally what determines the nominal exchange rate appreciation, we find that

$$\hat{e}_a^M = q_a + \pi_\lambda + \eta_a.$$

While the inflation criterion is by assumption satisfied, there would be some upward pressure on the nominal exchange rate if $-(q_a + \eta_a) > \pi_\lambda$, which would have to be dealt with in the context of the exchange rate mechanism. It is useful contrasting this result to the currency board solution (9). In the latter case it is the inflation criterion that is not satisfied when $-(q_a + \eta_a) > \pi_\lambda$.

It can easily be shown that in the case of Maastricht supply shocks are stabilized in the same way as for currency boards. However, the variances of inflation and output differ, as in the case of Maastricht the nominal exchange rate absorbs real exchange rate shocks[8]:

$$\sigma_{\pi_a^M}^2 = \left(\frac{\alpha_n}{\alpha_n^2 + \beta_n}\right)^2 \sigma_{\varepsilon_n}^2,$$

$$\sigma_{y_a^M}^2 = \sigma_{\varepsilon_a}^2 + \left(\frac{\alpha_a \alpha_n}{\alpha_n^2 + \beta_n}\right)^2 \sigma_{\varepsilon_n}^2 - \frac{2\alpha_a \alpha_n}{\alpha_n^2 + \beta_n}\sigma_{(\varepsilon_a, \varepsilon_n)}.$$

2.5   The Enlargement Phase

We now turn to consider the case where NMs join the monetary union, with the objective of monetary policy being represented by

$$L_u = \tfrac{1}{2} E[(y_u - y_u^*)^2 + \beta_u (\pi_u - \pi_u^*)^2]. \tag{13}$$

Inflation, output, and the natural output in the enlarged currency union with n countries are expressed as a weighted average between the amounts of respective inflation and output rates in the euro area and in the NMs: $\pi_u = \sum \varphi_i \pi_i$, $y_u = \sum \varphi_i y_i$ and $\bar{y}_u = \sum \varphi_i \bar{y}_i$, where the weights φ_i are interpreted as the size of country i relative to the enlarged currency area. The inflation differential between any NM and the euro area is equal to the sum of the deterministic and stochastic components of the real exchange rate appreciation: $\pi_a^U - \pi_n^U = -(q_a + \eta_a)$.

Likewise the difference between desired output and the natural rate is defined as $y_u^* - \bar{y}_u = \phi_u \kappa_u$. The timing of events is unchanged and the game is solved as before. Replacing π_u, y_u and y_u^* into (13) and differentiating it with respect to π_n^U determines the reaction function of the central bank as a function of inflationary expectations. By imposing rational expectations one can derive expected inflation. Finally the equilibrium outcome is achieved by replacing expected inflation in the reaction function, which yields

$$\pi_u = \pi_u^* + \frac{\alpha_u \phi_u \kappa_u}{\beta_u} - \frac{\alpha_u}{\alpha_u^2 + \beta_u} \left[\sum_i \varphi_i \varepsilon_i - \sum_a (\alpha_a - \alpha_u) \varphi_a \eta_a \right], \tag{14}$$

$$\pi_n^U = \pi_u^* + \frac{\alpha_u \phi_u \kappa_u}{\beta_u} + \sum_a \varphi_a q_a - \frac{\alpha_u}{\alpha_u^2 + \beta_u} \sum_i \varphi_i \varepsilon_i$$

$$+ \frac{1}{\alpha_u^2 + \beta_u} \sum_a (\beta_u + \alpha_a \alpha_u) \varphi_a \eta_a, \tag{15}$$

$$\pi_a^U = \pi_u^* + \frac{\alpha_u \phi_u \kappa_u}{\beta_u} - q_a + \sum_a \varphi_a q_a - \frac{\alpha_u}{\alpha_u^2 + \beta_u} \sum_i \varphi_i \varepsilon_i - \eta_a$$

$$+ \frac{1}{\alpha_u^2 + \beta_u} \sum_a (\beta_u + \alpha_a \alpha_u) \varphi_a \eta_a, \tag{16}$$

where $\alpha_u = \sum \varphi_i \alpha_i$.

Provided that the NMs' real convergence objective does not influence monetary policy, namely $\forall a$, $\phi_a \kappa_a = 0$, then $\phi_u \kappa_u = 0$, the monetary policy framework remains invariant (i.e., $y_u^* = \bar{y}_u$) and expected inflation at the steady state is $\pi_u^e = \pi_u^*$. It is also noticeable that expected inflation in the enlarged currency area is not affected by anticipated developments in the real exchange rates of NMs' currencies. However, aggregate inflation is affected by real exchange rate shocks if $\alpha_a \neq \alpha_u$. To be more precise, a negative shock to η_a would have a positive (negative) impact on inflation if the slopes of the Phillips curves of NMs are on average steeper (flatter) relative to the euro area. For example, an unanticipated increase in nontradable prices in NMs by causing a temporary appreciation of the real exchange rate, $\eta_a < 0$, would increase aggregate inflation if the output elasticity to inflation surprises in NMs is on average smaller than that in the euro area, (i.e., $\alpha_a < \alpha_n$). This implies that if the transmission mechanism of monetary policy differs among member states, shocks to relative prices, whether or not the consequence of a relative productivity shock or a change in world demand for domestic goods affects aggregate inflation in the currency area.

To highlight any potential effect of a departure from the current monetary policy framework in the euro area, we also examine an additional case where monetary policy in the enlarged euro area would account for the desire of NMs to converge in real terms. In this case $y_u^* = \varphi_n \bar{y}_n + \sum \varphi_a y_a^*$. As a corollary it can easily be shown that $\phi_u \kappa_u = \sum \phi_a \kappa_a$, which would imply a positive inflation bias, potentially threatening the price stability mandate; see (14). It also highlights how the inflationary impact of enlargement is neutralized if ϕ_a is equal to zero.

In addition to the impact on average inflation, this framework allows us to get an insight on the distribution of inflation. Average inflation will be higher in NMs than in the original euro area, following the assumption that NMs are characterized by an appreciating trend $-q_a$. Inflation will be higher in those NMs appreciating the most relative to the average appreciation of the region, $-\sum_a \varphi_a q_a$.

Output in the euro area and NMs is represented by the following set of equations:

$$y_u = \bar{y}_u + \frac{\beta_u}{\alpha_u^2 + \beta_u} \left[\sum_i \varphi_i \varepsilon_i - \sum_a (\alpha_a - \alpha_u) \varphi_a \eta_a \right],$$

$$y_n^U = \bar{y}_n + \varepsilon_n - \alpha_n \frac{\alpha_u}{\alpha_u^2 + \beta_u} \sum_i \varphi_i \varepsilon_i + \frac{\alpha_n}{\alpha_u^2 + \beta_u} \sum_a (\beta_u + \alpha_a \alpha_u) \varphi_a \eta_a,$$

$$y_a^U = \bar{y}_a + \varepsilon_a - \alpha_a \frac{\alpha_u}{\alpha_u^2 + \beta_u} \sum_i \varphi_i \varepsilon_i - \alpha_a \eta_a + \frac{\alpha_a}{\alpha_u^2 + \beta_u} \sum_a (\beta_u + \alpha_a \alpha_u) \varphi_a \eta_a.$$

The equations derived for inflation and output suggest the following: after a real exchange rate shock, inflation and output co-move in every country. At the union level, however, aggregate output and aggregate inflation move in opposite directions, as monetary authorities tend to offset the inflationary (or deflationary) impact of the shock. Say φ_a is a small number. Then the impact of a country-specific shocks, ε_a, is almost entirely reflected in terms of changes in the output of country a. A real exchange rate shock, η_a, has sizable effects in country a, with inflation and output moving in the same direction. It is interesting to note how both types of shocks have a limited impact on the euro area. Conversely, if a shock takes place in the euro area, ε_n, the effects on NMs are sizable. Given the closed form solutions calculated in the previous section, it is relatively straightforward to derive the variances of inflation and output in the enlarged euro area:

$$\sigma_{\pi_u}^2 = \left(\frac{\alpha_u}{\alpha_u^2 + \beta_u} \right)^2 \left[\sum_i \varphi_i^2 \sigma_{\varepsilon_i}^2 + \sum_a (\alpha_a - \alpha_u)^2 \varphi_a^2 \sigma_{\eta_a}^2 + \Phi \right],$$

$$\sigma_{y_u}^2 = \left(\frac{\beta_u}{\alpha_u^2 + \beta_u} \right)^2 \left[\sum_i \varphi_i^2 \sigma_{\varepsilon_i}^2 + \sum_a (\alpha_a - \alpha_u)^2 \varphi_a^2 \sigma_{\eta_a}^2 + \Phi \right],$$

where $\Phi = 2 \sum_{i \neq j} \varphi_i \varphi_j \sigma_{(\varepsilon_i, \varepsilon_j)} + 2 \sum_{a \neq b} (\alpha_a - \alpha_u)(\alpha_b - \alpha_u) \varphi_a \varphi_b \sigma_{(\eta_a, \eta_b)} - \sum_i \sum_a \varphi_i (\alpha_a - \alpha_u) \varphi_a \sigma_{(\varepsilon_i, \eta_a)}$.

Therefore the variances of inflation and output depend on four factors. First, they are a positive function of the variances of supply shocks in each member country. These variances, however, are weighted by the square of the share of the size of each participant to the union. A relatively high variance of shocks in one country may therefore have a limited impact on the union insofar as this country is not too large.[9] Second, they are an increasing function of the variance of the real exchange rate, $\sigma_{\eta_a}^2$. The impact will be greater the more the participants to the common currency area differ in supply structure, as measured by the wedge $\alpha_a - \alpha_u$. In the specific case where the slope of the aggregate supply is the same ($\alpha_n = \alpha_a$), the variance of inflation and output of the currency union is not affected by the stochastic fluctuations of the real exchange rates. Third, they depend positively on the degree of correlation among supply shocks, $\sigma_{(\varepsilon_i, \varepsilon_j)}$. This is quite intuitive, since the more closely supply shocks are correlated, the less they are likely to offset each other. Four the variance of inflation and output in the currency union depends on $\sigma_{(\eta_a, \eta_b)}$ and $\sigma_{(\varepsilon_i, \eta_a)}$. Under the hypothesis that $(\alpha_a - \alpha_u)(\alpha_b - \alpha_u) > 0$, it increases if $\sigma_{(\eta_a, \eta_b)} > 0$. This implies, for example, that if NMs are characterized by the same slope of the Phillips curve, then the variance of inflation and output increases if η_a and η_b are positively correlated.

2.6   A Numerical Exercise

The analytical framework developed in the previous section is applied to the euro area and ten NMs (the eight central and eastern European countries that recently joined the European Union plus Romania and Bulgaria, which are expected to join in 2007). The analysis aims at providing an insight on the size of the impacts of institutional change and of supply and real exchange rate shocks under alternative scenarios.

2.6.1   The Benchmark

Table 2.1 shows the benchmark dataset, which constitutes a baseline from which we depart to account for the uncertainty over the parameter values. We compiled quarterly data from 1997 until 2003 from a variety of sources, including Eurostat, the European Central Bank (ECB) and the International Financial Statistics (IFS) of the International Monetary Fund.

In choosing the sample period for this analysis, there is clearly a trade-off. The longer the time span considered, the more one underestimates the impact that in the last decade structural reforms and recent changes in the monetary policy framework of NMs have had. The shorter the time span, the more one runs into potential distortions of the results due to changes in cyclical conditions. We have therefore opted for a compromise solution, by computing sample averages and applying in some cases a limited degree of judgmental assessment.

We decided to exclude data before 1997, since before then NMs experienced a sizable fall in output while inflation stood at relatively high levels. Both of these aspects do not seem representative of the current situation, as the initial phase of restructuring is over, while the monetary policy framework of many countries has changed remarkably since then. Taking averages over the sample period gives us a first

Table 2.1
Benchmark values (%)

| | Inflation (π_i) | Output (y_i) | Convergence gap (k_a) | Real exchange rate (q_a) | Weights | | β_i $(\alpha_a = 3.2)$ | β_i $(\alpha_a = 1.6)$ | β_i $(\alpha_a = 0.8)$ |
					GPP in euro	GDP in PPP			
Bulgaria	5.5	4.1	4.9	-3.7	0.2	0.6	—	—	—
Czech Republic	4.1	2.8	2.6	-3.6	0.8	1.9	1.60	0.80	0.40
Estonia	4.9	5.8	1.2	-3.0	0.1	0.2	—	—	—
Hungary	9.7	4.1	2.0	-4.3	0.7	1.5	0.39	0.20	0.10
Latvia	3.4	6.2	1.9	-2.7	0.1	0.2	1.60	0.80	0.40
Lithuania	2.2	5.3	2.3	-5.9	0.2	0.3	—	—	—
Poland	7.1	3.6	3.4	-1.9	2.3	4.2	0.97	0.49	0.24
Romania	39.9	4.3	3.9	-6.1	0.5	1.8	0.16	0.08	0.04
Slovak Republic	7.5	3.5	2.7	-5.0	0.3	0.7	0.72	0.36	0.18
Slovenia	7.3	3.7	1.5	-1.3	0.3	0.4	0.41	0.21	0.10

Source: Authors' data elaboration based on 1997 to 2003 data from Eurostat, ECB, and IFS.

representation of the benchmark.[10] This procedure is clearly rough, and it is also clear that convergence is a dynamic process whereby the parameters of the model may continue to change. Therefore the benchmark is only a starting point and various alternative scenarios must be considered to get an insight of the magnitude of the effects.

The first two columns report average inflation and output growth of NMs. As explained above, we interpret these numbers as expected inflation and the natural rate of output respectively, which are needed to compute β_a and κ_a. In the third column we report κ_a. This measure is proxied by taking the difference between the growth rate, which allows a rapid convergence, and the natural rate of output. Rapid growth is here defined as the rate necessary for NMs' per capita GDP to catch up twenty percentage points as a percentage of euro area per capita GDP in the next ten years.[11] Finally, in this numerical example, we assume that π^* is equal to 1.5.[12]

In the fourth column we have computed the average real exchange rate appreciation of the euro vis-à-vis the currencies of NMs over the same sample period (HICP based). In the fifth and sixth column, we report computed GDP weights both in nominal terms and PPP.

With reference to the slopes of the Phillips curve, we have set $\alpha_n = 1.6$, hence making the implicit assumption that output is more responsive than prices in the euro area. Some recent evidence supports this hypothesis. For example, a recent empirical study by van Els et al. (2003) presents evidence on the monetary transmission mechanism for the euro area by way of four alternative methodologies, which are (1) a vector autoregressive model, (2) a structural model for the euro area, (3) an aggregate of euro area national central banks structural models, and (4) a macro model estimated by the National Institute of Economic and Social Research. All four empirical approaches suggest that if the time horizon spans over two years, the output response to changes in monetary policy is between 1.8 and 6 times larger than the price response. Less clear-cut is the result if the horizon spans over three years, as the output response is, depending on the model, in the range between 0.4 and 1.9 times the price response. Therefore the value we chose for the slope of the Phillips curve implicitly collocates our time horizon in the range between two and three years after the shock.

As for the slopes of the Phillips curve in NMs, we are not aware of any major attempt in the literature to estimate the Phillips curves for all countries on a comparable basis. Because of this uncertainty we decided to conduct a sensitivity analysis by considering three alternative values for α_a, making the assumption that the responsiveness of output relative to prices is twice as great as in the euro area ($\alpha_a = 3.2$), the same ($\alpha_a = 1.6$), or half ($\alpha_a = 0.8$).

β_a is then computed so that the observed value of endogenous variables constitutes the equilibrium of the numerical model:

$$\tilde{\beta}_a = \frac{\alpha_a^0 \phi_a k_a^0}{\pi_a^0 - 1.5},$$

where the tilde represents the computed parameter, while the nil denotes the initial value of the associated variable. The results are reported in the last three columns of the table, under the assumption that $\phi_a = 0.5$. A relatively high parameter β_a suggests that the inflation rate has been kept at a relatively low level in those countries relative to the level of the structural parameter κ_a. It is higher in the case of Latvia because this country has been pegging its exchange rate to the IMF Special Drawing Rights since 1994, a strategy that has been consistent with low average inflation. This case is not explicitly modeled in the current setup, but it is indirectly captured via a high β for this country. Bulgaria, Estonia, and Lithuania have adopted a currency board regime. Therefore β cannot be computed in their case, as they are "importing" the credibility of the euro-area monetary framework. As far as the euro area is concerned, the lack of an inflation bias breaks the link between β and π^e. Therefore the cost of inflation relative to that of output of the euro area can only be computed by taking the relative variance between inflation (6) and output (7): $\tilde{\beta}_n = \alpha_n^0 (\sigma_y^0 / \sigma_\pi^0)^{1/2} = 1.66$.

2.6.2 Scenarios

The model developed in the previous sections allows us to examine a number of scenarios assessing the impact of enlargement. In table 2.2 we start by reporting the first set of simulations in the pre-Maastricht phase, which can be seen as the benchmark.

The ratios $\hat{\pi}_i / \hat{\varepsilon}_i$ and $\hat{y}_i / \hat{\varepsilon}_i$ measure the responsiveness of inflation and output to a 1 percent positive supply shock. For example, in the case of the euro area we find that inflation falls by 0.38 while output increases by 0.39 percentage points. To get some insights on NMs, we repeat the same exercise in succession for the three different values of α_a. If the supply structure of NMs is the same as for the euro area, meaning $\alpha_a = 1.6$, then NMs with flexible exchange rates stabilize supply shocks sizably more than countries with currency boards.[13]

Table 2.2
Pre-Maastricht phase: Impact of symmetric supply shocks on inflation and output (percentage points)

	$\alpha_a = 3.2$ $(\hat{\pi}_i/\hat{\varepsilon}_i)$	$\alpha_a = 3.2$ $(\hat{y}_i/\hat{\varepsilon}_i)$	$\alpha_a = 1.6$ $(\hat{\pi}_i/\hat{\varepsilon}_i)$	$\alpha_a = 1.6$ $(\hat{y}_i/\hat{\varepsilon}_i)$	$\alpha_a = 0.8$ $(\hat{\pi}_i/\hat{\varepsilon}_i)$	$\alpha_a = 0.8$ $(\hat{y}_i/\hat{\varepsilon}_i)$
Bulgaria	−0.38	−0.22	−0.38	0.39	−0.38	0.69
Czech Republic	−0.27	0.14	−0.48	0.24	−0.77	0.38
Estonia	−0.38	−0.22	−0.38	0.39	−0.38	0.69
Hungary	−0.30	0.04	−0.58	0.07	−1.08	0.13
Latvia	−0.27	0.14	−0.48	0.24	−0.77	0.38
Lithuania	−0.38	−0.22	−0.38	0.39	−0.38	0.69
Poland	−0.29	0.09	−0.53	0.16	−0.91	0.28
Romania	−0.31	0.02	−0.61	0.03	−1.18	0.06
Slovak Republic	−0.29	0.07	−0.55	0.12	−0.98	0.22
Slovenia	−0.30	0.04	−0.58	0.07	−1.08	0.14
EU-12	−0.38	0.39	−0.38	0.39	−0.38	0.39

Carrying out a sensitivity analysis across the three different values of α_a, we find that the steeper the Phillips curve is in NMs (hence the smaller α_a), the higher the impact of supply shocks is in terms of NMs' output and, when $\alpha_a > \sqrt{\beta_a}$ as in this case (see table 2.1), in terms of inflation. For countries adopting a currency board, the higher impact is instead reflected in output terms only.

In the Maastricht phase, NMs experience a process of nominal disinflation. As we discussed earlier, in response to supply shocks, the impact on inflation and output becomes basically the same as for the three countries that have a currency board. Conversely, real exchange rate shocks cannot be stabilized under the currency board, but they are fully absorbed by changes in the nominal exchange rate under Maastricht.[14]

Turning to the case of enlargement, the loss function of the euro area is modified to account for the new countries participating to the currency union. As monetary policy takes account of the state of the economy in the enlarged monetary union as a whole, the weight of each country depends on its GDP share. As it can be seen from table 2.3, we aggregate countries using either nominal GDP in euro (to capture the weight of NMs in the enlarged euro area today) or GDP in PPP (to capture the weight NMs will progressively get closer to as the catching up process continues). Both scenarios assume that the common monetary policy is characterized by the same preferences as before enlargement, namely $\beta_u = \beta_n = 1.66$.

Table 2.3
Enlargement phase: Deviation of inflation from average inflation in the currency union
($\phi_u = 0$, in %)

	$q_a = -1.5$	$q_a = -3$	q_a
GDP in euros			
Bulgaria	1.4	2.8	3.5
Czech Republic	1.4	2.8	3.4
Estonia	1.4	2.8	2.8
Hungary	1.4	2.8	4.1
Latvia	1.4	2.8	2.5
Lithuania	1.4	2.8	5.7
Poland	1.4	2.8	1.7
Romania	1.4	2.8	5.9
Slovak Republic	1.4	2.8	4.8
Slovenia	1.4	2.8	1.1
EU-12	−0.1	−0.2	−0.2
GDP in PPPs			
Bulgaria	1.3	2.6	3.3
Czech Republic	1.3	2.6	3.2
Estonia	1.3	2.6	2.6
Hungary	1.3	2.6	3.9
Latvia	1.3	2.6	2.3
Lithuania	1.3	2.6	5.5
Poland	1.3	2.6	1.5
Romania	1.3	2.6	5.7
Slovak Republic	1.3	2.6	4.6
Slovenia	1.3	2.6	0.9
EU-12	−0.2	−0.4	−0.4

Let us suppose that the desire of NMs to converge faster does not affect the Eurosystem monetary strategy. Then $\phi_u = 0$, and expected inflation in the enlarged euro area would remain constant. Under the alternative (upper bound) hypothesis that $\phi_u = 1$, the rise in expected inflation in the enlarged euro area would be between 0.15 and 0.39 percentage points, depending on the weights and the slopes of the Phillips curves.

As we found in section 2.5, the distribution of inflation across countries depends on the real appreciation and size of each NMs. To gauge the size of the impact in the first two columns, we assume that q_a ranges, in line with most estimates of the BS effect (Halpern and Wyploz 2001; Kovacs 2002; Égert 2003), between 1.5 and 3 percent, while in the third column we assume that q_a is equal to the average pace of appreciation between 1997 and 2003 (see table 2.3).

The numerical results indicate that the impact on steady-state inflation of the current euro area is limited (between 0.1 and 0.2 percent) if participating countries are weighted on the basis of nominal GDP. The deflationary impact on the euro area is instead more sizable (between 0.2 and 0.4 percent) if GDP of NMs are weighted in terms of purchasing power parity. The size of the impact is clearly also an increasing function of the pace of real exchange rate appreciation in NMs. As shown in table 2.1, in the period under review the average appreciation of the real exchange rate was stronger than the 3 percent threshold in six NMs out of ten. This does not mean necessarily, however, that the trend will continue to prevail over the long term, since it may partly be a reflection of the undervaluation phase that characterized the early years of transition. Nevertheless, it underscores how a stronger pace of appreciation than suggested by the BS may prevail over a relatively long period of time. Indeed, seven years of data are not sufficient to net out the possible impact of cyclical factors. The case of Poland is indicative, as the annual rate of real exchange rate appreciation has dropped from above 6 percent per annum between 1997 and 2001 to less than 2 percent between 1997 and 2003. To summarise, this analysis has shown how the impact on the current euro area is limited if the upward pressure is postulated to be in line with most estimates of the BS effect. The deflationary impact on the euro area might be instead more sizable if NMs are weighted in terms of purchasing power parities and a stronger real exchange rate appreciation process is assumed.

How would the new currency area be affected by symmetric supply shocks? For the enlarged euro area, as a whole the results are robust irrespective of the values of α_a (see table 2.4). Indeed, the impact on inflation and output in the enlarged currency area in response to symmetric shocks is similar to those of the euro area before enlargement. The effects for NMs are much more similar to the case where they would adopt a currency board regime than that of flexible exchange rates. This is not surprising, considering the relatively low weight of NMs in the aggregate measure of inflation and output. As was the case for currency boards, inflation and output stabilization in NMs is thus sensitive to α_a. In particular, when $\alpha_a = 3.2$, a positive symmetric supply shock on the enlarged euro area would have a considerable impact on output in NMs.

Table 2.4
Enlargement phase: Impact of supply and real exchange rate shocks on inflation and output (%)

		Symmetric supply shock				Country-specific supply shock				Real exchange rate shock		
		NMs	EU-12	Enlarged euro area		NMs	EU-12	Enlarged euro area		NMs	EU-12	Enlarged euro area
GDP in euros												
$\alpha_a = 3.2$	$\hat{\pi}_i/\hat{\varepsilon}_i$	-0.38	-0.38	-0.38	$\hat{\pi}_i/\hat{\varepsilon}_a$	-0.02	-0.02	-0.02	$\hat{\pi}_i/\hat{\eta}_a$	-0.92	0.08	0.03
$\alpha_n = 1.6$	$\hat{y}_i/\hat{\varepsilon}_i$	-0.20	0.40	0.37	$\hat{y}_i/\hat{\varepsilon}_a$	0.94	-0.03	0.02	$\hat{y}_i/\hat{\eta}_a$	-2.93	0.13	-0.03
$\alpha_a = 1.6$	$\hat{\pi}_i/\hat{\varepsilon}_i$	-0.38	-0.38	-0.38	$\hat{\pi}_i/\hat{\varepsilon}_a$	-0.02	-0.02	-0.02	$\hat{\pi}_i/\hat{\eta}_a$	-0.95	0.05	0.00
$\alpha_n = 1.6$	$\hat{y}_i/\hat{\varepsilon}_i$	0.39	0.39	0.39	$\hat{y}_i/\hat{\varepsilon}_a$	0.97	-0.03	0.02	$\hat{y}_i/\hat{\eta}_a$	-1.51	0.09	0.00
$\alpha_a = 0.8$	$\hat{\pi}_i/\hat{\varepsilon}_i$	-0.38	-0.38	-0.38	$\hat{\pi}_i/\hat{\varepsilon}_a$	-0.02	-0.02	-0.02	$\hat{\pi}_i/\hat{\eta}_a$	-0.96	0.04	0.02
$\alpha_n = 1.6$	$\hat{y}_i/\hat{\varepsilon}_i$	0.70	0.39	0.41	$\hat{y}_i/\hat{\varepsilon}_a$	0.98	-0.03	0.02	$\hat{y}_i/\hat{\eta}_a$	-0.77	0.06	0.02
GDP in PPPs												
$\alpha_a = 3.2$	$\hat{\pi}_i/\hat{\varepsilon}_i$	-0.37	-0.37	-0.37	$\hat{\pi}_i/\hat{\varepsilon}_a$	-0.04	-0.04	-0.04	$\hat{\pi}_i/\hat{\eta}_a$	-0.82	0.18	0.06
$\alpha_n = 1.6$	$\hat{y}_i/\hat{\varepsilon}_i$	-0.18	0.41	0.34	$\hat{y}_i/\hat{\varepsilon}_a$	0.86	-0.07	0.04	$\hat{y}_i/\hat{\eta}_a$	-2.63	0.29	-0.06
$\alpha_a = 1.6$	$\hat{\pi}_i/\hat{\varepsilon}_i$	-0.38	-0.38	-0.38	$\hat{\pi}_i/\hat{\varepsilon}_a$	-0.05	-0.05	-0.05	$\hat{\pi}_i/\hat{\eta}_a$	-0.88	0.12	0.00
$\alpha_n = 1.6$	$\hat{y}_i/\hat{\varepsilon}_i$	0.39	0.39	0.39	$\hat{y}_i/\hat{\varepsilon}_a$	0.93	-0.07	0.05	$\hat{y}_i/\hat{\eta}_a$	-1.41	0.19	0.00
$\alpha_a = 0.8$	$\hat{\pi}_i/\hat{\varepsilon}_i$	-0.38	-0.38	-0.38	$\hat{\pi}_i/\hat{\varepsilon}_a$	-0.05	-0.05	-0.05	$\hat{\pi}_i/\hat{\eta}_a$	-0.91	0.09	-0.03
$\alpha_n = 1.6$	$\hat{y}_i/\hat{\varepsilon}_i$	0.69	0.39	0.42	$\hat{y}_i/\hat{\varepsilon}_a$	0.96	-0.07	0.05	$\hat{y}_i/\hat{\eta}_a$	-0.73	0.14	0.03

To examine the impact of country-specific shocks, suppose that an identical shock takes place in all NMs contemporaneously and that no shock occurs in the euro area. The impact of a scenario such as this on the enlarged currency area would be quite limited (see table 2.4). But on the countries subject to the shock the impact would be very large, irrespective of α_a, as the degree of output stabilization turns out to be extremely small.

Table 2.4 allows us also to get some insights on the impact of real exchange rate shocks. Here again the impact on the enlarged euro area is in general limited (while the sign is ambiguous as it depends on $\alpha_a - \alpha_u$) and it tends to be rather large for the NMs. For example, an unexpected real exchange appreciation in NMs would result into higher inflation and a temporary boost to NMs' economies,[15] whereas it would have only a small deflationary impact to the current euro area.

In summary, shocks persisting after enlargement may be problematic for the new entrants, and to a smaller extent for the union. Therefore, in assessing the implications of euro area enlargement, the issue of the endogeneity of shocks is a crucial one. The greater the fall is in the variance of supply and real exchange rate shocks after enlargement, the stronger is the positive impact on welfare for both NMs and the union. Indeed, it is striking how many countries currently participating in the euro-area monetary union, including those with a relatively low GDP per capita, have observed in the course of the 1990s a sizable fall in the variance of inflation and output. Monetary union and the associated process of convergence may well have been important factors behind these developments.

2.7 Concluding Remarks

In this chapter we attempted to assess the economic implications of an enlargement of the European monetary union to include new member states (NMs) within a simple analytical framework.

In the Maastricht phase, the inflation requirement of the Treaty determines a radical change in the way inflationary expectations are formed, consistent with the rapid achievement of the nominal convergence objective. In other words, the convergence gap no longer feeds into the inflationary expectations' mechanism.

After enlargement we find that there is no impact on average inflation in the enlarged euro area via the credibility channel, provided that its monetary policy is unchanged, and via the anticipated real exchange rate appreciation. Enlargement in this case simply results in a different distribution of inflation across countries. We also find that unanticipated shocks to the real exchange rate will affect aggregate inflation if the aggregate supply structure differs from one participating country to the next. In general, the cost of an enlarged monetary union for each member would depend on the slopes of the Phillips curves of all members, the size of its economy, and the variance of country-specific supply and real exchange rate shocks.

The model is applied to ten central and eastern European NMs and the euro area. The results of the numerical simulations critically depend on the relatively small size of NMs. For the euro area the impact on steady-state inflation is limited if participating countries are weighted on the basis of their GDP in national currency and if the upward pressure on the equilibrium real exchange rate is limited. However, the deflationary impact on the euro area is more sizable if we assume a strong appreciation of the real exchange rate and if NMs are weighted in terms of purchasing power parity. The simulations also confirm that the major impact on inflation and output stabilization are borne by the NMs, and only to a much smaller extent by the euro area and the enlarged currency union. Sensitivity analysis also indicates that the impact of symmetric shocks on inflation and output in the NMs critically depends on the slope of the Phillips curve. In particular, if the transmission mechanism of monetary policy differs among member states, real exchange rate shocks affect union wide inflation.

It should be emphasized that an enlarged monetary union would, in itself, have several positive effects: it would strengthen economic cohesion, reduce risk premia, facilitate foreign direct investment, and encourage technological progress. Clearly, the simplified setup employed in the present study entirely omits these important aspects. Finally, this modeling framework may also be extended to include fiscal issues, as the delegation of monetary policy could not entirely solve the time inconsistency problem on the fiscal front.

Notes

We would like to thank Fabio Comelli for his invaluable research assistance. We also thank Frank Smets, Oreste Tristani, Fabrizio Zampolli, and an anonymous referee for valuable comments and suggestions. The opinions expressed herein are those of the authors and do not necessarily represent those of the European Central Bank. All errors are the authors' responsibility.

1. As in the papers by Lane (2000), Alesina and Barro (2002), Berger (2002) and Gross and Hefeker (2002) we have adopted a static approach. It should be noted, however, that Clarida, Gali, and Gertler (1999) have shown how to extend the single-country discretionary case with rational expectation to a dynamic framework maintaining the typical results of the Barro-Gordon setting. The model becomes more complex due the persistence parameter of the AR(1) process, which characterises the supply shocks.

2. Alesina and Barro (2002) generalize the one good model to allow countries to produce different market baskets of final goods by introducing a random error term, which was taken to be serially independent with zero mean and constant variance and to be distributed independently of countries' supply shocks.

3. Whenever countries successfully catch up, productivity growth tends to be higher in the tradable than in the nontradable sector. Under a standard set of assumptions this implies that successfully catching up countries face a real exchange rate appreciation vis-à-vis trading partners (Balassa 1964; Samuelson 1964).

4. Estonia and Lithuania also joined the exchange rate mechanism II (ERM II) on June 28, 2004, while maintaining the currency board arrangement in place, as a unilateral committment.

5. See Alesina and Barro (2002) for a more in-depth analysis of currency board regimes.

6. Cukierman et al. (2002) found evidence that transition economies with currency boards do not necessarely post lower inflation rates.

7. This institutional framework was re-iterated on a number of occasions by the President and Governing Council Board Members of the ECB. See, for example, Central Banking (2001, *Interview: Otmar Issing*, volume 11, pp. 28–29).

8. This section does not fully account for the implications of the exchange rate mechanism, which only allows some degree of exchange rate flexibility.

9. The strength of the impact thus depends on whether $\sum \varphi_a^2 \sigma_{\varepsilon_a}^2$ is high relative to $(1 - \sum \varphi_a)^2 \sigma_{\varepsilon_n}^2$.

10. In the case of the Czech Republic and Romania, we have restricted the sample for GDP from 2000 onward in view of the severe downturns at the beginning of the sample period. In the case of Bulgaria, although the currency board was introduced in July 1997, very high inflation persisted for almost one year longer. To get a representative trend for the dynamics of output and inflation in this country, we have considered data starting from 1999.

11. Sensitivity analysis on the convergence gap parameter has been carried out. The overall results suggest that the scenarios are robust for any plausible values of κ_a.

12. We have also carried out an alternative numerical exercise, which assumes that π^* is higher in NMs. Under this hypothesis the credibility channel would play a smaller role in explaining the inflation differential with respect to the euro area. Therefore the inflation and output responses to shocks would be numerically different in the flexible exchange rate regime. The other numerical results here—in particular the case of enlargement—would remain unchanged.

13. Bulgaria, Estonia, and Lithuania's response is identical to the euro area, only when the supply structure is the same.

14. The model makes the simplyfing assumption that shocks are sufficiently small to be accommodated within ERM II.

15. The negative effect on competitiveness, which may offset the positive impact on output growth, is outside the scope of this model.

References

Alesina, A., and R. J. Barro. 2002. Currency unions. *Quarterly Journal of Economics* 117: 409–36.

Balassa, B. 1964. The purchasing power parity doctrine: A reappraisal. *Journal of Political Economy* 72: 584–96.

Barro, R., and D. Gordon. 1983. A positive theory of monetary policy in a natural rate model. *Journal of Political Economy* 91: 589–610.

Beetsma, R. M. W. J., and H. Jensen. 2003. Structural convergence under reversible and irreversible monetary unification. *Journal of International Money and Finance* 22: 417–39.

Berger, H. 2002. The ECB and euro-area enlargement. *IMF Working Paper*, no. 175.

Ca' Zorzi, M., and R. A. De Santis. 2004. Currency unions and the real exchange rate. *Economics Letter* 85: 23–27.

Clarida, R., J. Gali, and M. Gertler. 1999. The science of monetary policy: A new Keynesian perspective. *Journal of Economic Literature* 37: 1661–1707.

Cukierman, A., G. P. Miller, and B. Nyapti. 2002. Central bank reform, liberalization and inflation in transition economies—An international perspective. *Journal of Monetary Economics* 49: 237–64.

De Broeck, M., and T. Slok. 2001. Interpreting real exchange rate movements in transition countries. Bank of Finland, *BOFIT Discussion Papers*, no. 7.

Égert, B. 2003. Assessing equilibrium real exchange rates in CEE Acceding countries: Can we have DEER with BEER without FEER? A critical survey of the literature Oesterreichische National Bank, *Focus on Transition* (2): 38–106.

Frait, J., and L. Komarek. 2001. Real exchange rate trends in transition countries. *Warwick Economic Research Papers*, no. 696.

Grafe, C., and C. Wyplosz. 1997. The real exchange rate in transition economies. *CEPR Discussion Paper Series*, no. 1773.

Gros, D., and C. Hefeker. 2002. One size must fit all: National divergences in a monetary union. *German Economic Review* 3: 247–62.

Halpern, L., and C. Wyplosz. 2001. Economic transformation and real exchange rates in the 2000s: The Balassa-Samuelson connection. *Economic Survey of Europe* (1): 227–39.

Issing, O. 2001. The euro area and the single monetary policy. *International Journal of Finance and Economics* 6: 277–88.

Kovacs, M. A. 2002. On the estimated size of the Balassa-Samuelson effect in five Central and Eastern European countries. *National Bank of Hungary Working Paper*, no. 5.

Kydland, F., and E. Prescott. 1977. Rules rather than discretion: The inconsistency of optimal plans. *Journal of Political Economy* 85: 473–90.

Lane, P. 2000. Asymmetric shocks and monetary policy in a currency union. *Scandinavian Journal of Economics* 102: 585–604.

Rogoff, K. 1985. The optimal degree of commitment to an intermediate monetary target. *Quarterly Journal of Economics* 100: 1169–90.

Samuelson, P. A. 1964. Theoretical notes on trade problems. *Review of Economics and Statistics* 46: 145–54.

van Els, P., A. Locarno, B. Mojon, and J. Morgan. 2003. New macroeconomic evidence on monetary policy transmission in the euro area. *Journal of the European Economic Association* 1: 720–30.

3 Structural Reforms and the Enlargement of Monetary Union

Carsten Hefeker

3.1 Introduction

After European monetary union (EMU) has successfully started with twelve countries, the next major task is enlargement. Currently it seems likely that all ten new members will join the European Union in a few years time.[1] The question is whether all these countries can be considered sufficiently close in economic structure to join monetary union as well. This applies not only to the entry criteria stipulated in the Maastricht Treaty but to structural economic features.

While the Maastricht criteria for entry are nominal criteria, most of the literature on monetary unification stresses the importance of similarity of economic structures for the success of a monetary union (e.g., see Fidrmuc and Korhonen 2001). But this literature usually takes the economic structure of the countries as given, without taking into account that economic structures change over time (Frankel and Rose 1998). The obvious question thus raised is When might a candidate country be appropriately reformed to be admitted and willing to join an existing monetary union?

The timing of enlargement has been addressed in a paper by Martin (1995) who, however, takes the convergence of the accession economy as given. He addresses the question of when a monetary union with low distortions would admit a converging economy. Endogenous structural reforms, in turn, have been analyzed by Ozkan et al. (1997) and Beetsma and Jensen (2003). In these papers the candidate country must decide whether to undertake sufficient reform to be admitted to the union. It can gain from joining due to the high level of distortions that results in relatively high inflation. Monetary union is a convenient way to solve this problem. By construction, in Beetsma and Jensen (2003) the candidate always wants to join but the present members decide unilaterally about admission. In Ozkan et al. (1997) the country decides whether to fulfill the entry criteria.

The present chapter aims to bring these various aspects together and extends them in several ways. In contrast to the existing literature, it allows for economic distortions in both countries. Most of the present members of the monetary union need to carry out structural adjustments themselves and the question is whether these are speeded up or slowed down by enlargement. I also allow for asymmetric shocks that constitute a potential reason for the candidate country to remain outside the monetary union, even if joining would be possible (see Hefeker 2003). Hence both countries have to agree to enlargement.[2]

In focusing on the economic reforms interacting with the choice of the monetary regime, the present study qualifies earlier results concerning the interaction between monetary union and structural reforms. Calmfors (2001), Sibert (1999), and Sibert and Sutherland (2000) have argued that labor market reforms are less likely to be pursued by member countries if they interact with the inflation bias problem in monetary policy. As the latter is automatically reduced by monetary union, there is less incentive for a government to implement structural reforms. By exporting part of the inflationary pressure negative spillover effects on the other country arise.

This result, however, need not hold in general. By introducing reform needs in the present member states as well, it turns out that monetary union with a high distortion country increases the incentives to implement reforms. Thus enlargement will lead to more reforms in low distortion countries. This implies that the negative results of monetary union on structural reform efforts derived earlier have to be qualified. It also means that current member states could benefit from an early enlargement of the monetary union. At the same time new members with high distortions will have less incentives to pursue reform policies. An enlargement of monetary union could hence lead to polarization instead of convergence between old and new members.

The chapter is structured as follows: Section 3.2 presents basic indicators of the state of structural reforms in the accession countries and explains why governments are so reluctant to implement reforms. Section 3.3 introduces the model and derives monetary policy decisions in each country (group). Section 3.4 determines, depending on the monetary regime, the amount of structural reforms in the monetary union and the accession country. Section 3.5 analyzes under what circumstances the enlargement of monetary union is possible. Section 3.6 concludes.

3.2   Structural Reform Policies

3.2.1   Need for Structural Reforms

Compared with the situation from which they started, most of the candidate countries for enlargement have made considerable progress.[3] However, as table 3.1 and figure 3.1 show, in many respects there are still quite significant differences to the European average, most clearly with respect to unemployment and current account deficits. In some cases the inflation and budget deficit criteria are also violated (table 3.1). More broadly, a summary index of convergence puts all of the candidates listed here at a position below the EU average (figure 3.1).

While GDP growth rates are not surprisingly higher than in the European Union, higher unemployment and larger shares of agriculture and industry in GDP point to the still ongoing process of structural adjustment, which is also evident from a relatively large public sector. In particular, the large share of agriculture in some economies implies large fiscal requirements to subsidize and phase out this sector over time. Moreover large current account deficits suggest that some of the countries are vulnerable to current account and currency crises. A weak banking system in addition suggests potential problems in the future because there is a considerable amount of nonperforming loans, which could affect public finances (Gros 2000). It is by now well known that some of these indicators reflect the danger of a currency and banking crises (Tornell 1999). Another danger is that, although tax rates are comparable to Western European ones or even above (World Bank 2002), the transition economies in some cases often show significant fiscal deficits (Svejnar 2002). One reason for this can be seen in an ineffective tax systems and a large underground economy (Burda 1998). Large deficits might have negative implications for monetary stability and give rise to currency attacks.

Finally, more qualitative evidence supports the impression that many new members, in preparation for enlargement, have introduced labor market regulations and laws that could be problematic for employment. Many of them are comparable to those in EU countries (Burda 1998; EBRD 2000) and the OECD (1999a) sees the level of labor market regulation in some of the further developed transition even above those in older EU members.

Table 3.1
Structural convergence indicators (2003)

	EU average	Bulgaria	Czech Republic	Estonia	Hungary	Latvia	Lithuania	Poland	Romania	Slovakia	Slovenia
GDP growth	0.8	4.5	3.0	4.5	2.9	6.8	8.9	3.7	4.9	4.2	2.3
Unemployment	8.8	13.2	10.3	10.0	5.9	10.6	12.5	20.0	7.2	17.4	6.7
Inflation (CPI)[b]	2.1 (2.7)	2.3	0.1	1.3	4.7	2.9	-1.2	0.7	15.4	8.5	5.6
Fiscal balance[a,b]	-2.7 (-3.0)	0.0	-7.9	0.8	-5.7	-1.9	-1.9	-4.8	-2.3	-7.2	-1.9
Government debt[a,b]	70.4 (60)	60.7	25.5	5.1	54.9	16.3	25.3	51.0	24.1	45.2	32.1
Current accounts deficit[a]	0.5	-8.2	-5.1	-15.4	-6.7	-9.6	-5.8	-2.2	-6.0	-1.2	0.0
Exchange rate[b,c]	(+/-15)	-0.4	-3.9	-1.6	-9.0	-12.7	0.4	-21.6	-26.7	-6.2	-4.7

Source: Deutsche Bank (2004), EBRD (2004), and EU Commission (2004).
a. As share of GDP.
b. Data in parenthesis are reference values.
c. Exchange rate vis-à-vis the euro.

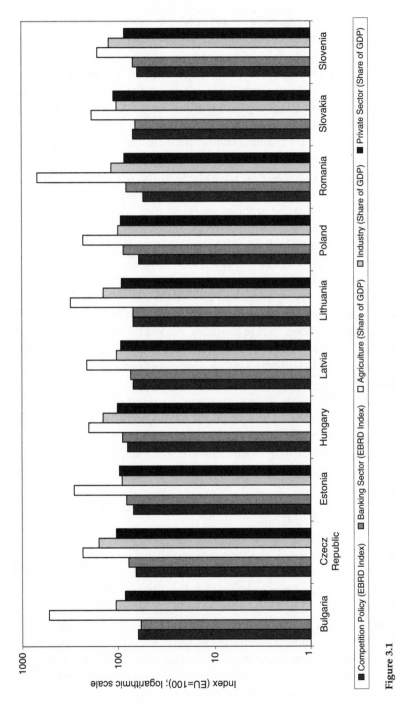

Figure 3.1
Convergence indicators for accession countries (data from Deutsche Bank 2002).

This evidence clearly reflects the need for more structural reforms in candidate countries. Especially the governments' large fiscal needs for restructuring and social expenditures could have a negative influence on monetary policy. The same applies to high unemployment. The higher these structural problems are, the more likely it is that they will ultimately lead to an expansive monetary policy and thus pose a problem for the monetary integration process.

However distorted the candidate countries might be, there is considerable evidence that the current members of EMU have a need for structural reforms themselves. Distortions in the labor market, mainly held responsible for high unemployment in western European countries, and distortions in product markets, like excessive regulation, seem to be the major problem so that most of the current members need to provide more reform efforts in labor markets to realize their economic potential (Siebert 1997; OECD 1999b). Figure 3.2 shows that almost all of the EU-15 are very slow and hesitant to implement the changes that have been proposed by the OECD to increase the efficiency of national labor markets. Based on the coding by Eichengreen (2002), figure 3.2 shows that of the labor market reforms recommended by the OECD, members countries have not implemented on average more than a third (with the United Kingdom implementing some 70 percent and Luxembourg even moving in the opposite direction).[4]

Despite reform needs in candidate and member countries alike, the overall amount necessary seems still to be larger in the candidates for EMU because reforms are required in almost all areas. Therefore I will use the stylized fact that candidates are more highly distorted than older members, even if this might not be literally true for all candidate countries.

3.2   Resistance to Reforms

Despite the undisputed need for structural reforms, both types of countries are often slow to implement recommended reforms. In the older member states labor market reforms with respect to employment protection, hiring and firing costs, working and overtime regulation, and high payroll taxes and unemployment benefits are not implemented, while the new member states are often slow in restructuring their economies from agriculture to modern industries and services and in reforming their banking systems. The preparation for EU membership often times even involves introducing a comparable degree of

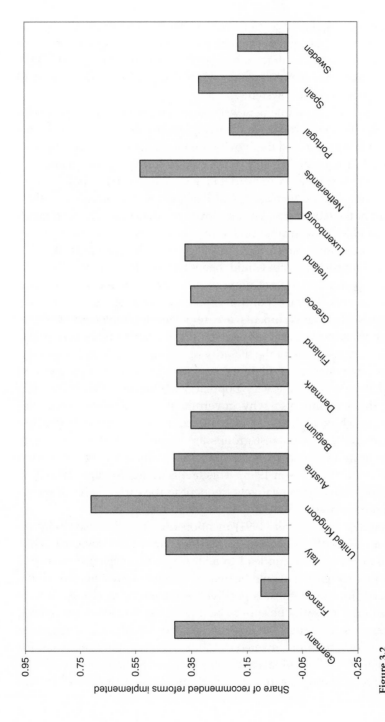

Figure 3.2
Labor market reforms in the EU-15 (data from Eichengreen 2002 and OECD 1999b).

labor market regulation as in the older member countries (Boeri 1997; Burda 1998), while generous unemployment benefits, together with high payroll taxes, constrain the growth of employment (World Bank 2002). It therefore seems that transition does not necessarily lead to less distorted economic systems.

The resistance to implement necessary reform measures is surprising if one assumes welfare-maximizing governments, but is less surprising if it is recognized that governments are also and often foremost interested in maximizing and preserving political support. Saint-Paul (1996, 2000) explains in great detail why labor market policy is, in general, not welfare increasing but designed to the benefit of only a segment of the labor force. The employed insiders (mainly union members) are able to determine policy to a large extent because they are well organized and have access to policy makers. In contrast, the unemployed outsiders who would benefit from deregulation have no lobbying power and are not numerous enough to overcome the interests of insiders. From a political-economic point of view, it is thus no surprise that governments are reluctant to implement welfare-increasing labor market reform, even at the price of more unemployment, as it risks to offend the majority of voters.

Since labor market regulations, such as minimum wages and employment protection, are very popular with the majority of the electorate, this explains also why governments in transition economies have put such regulations in place. Moreover, as transition progresses, the more and better interest groups are organized and begin to gain increasing influence on economic policies, pushing for their preferred type of regulation (Olson 1995). This fact is an additional explanation why reform have been relatively frequent in the early phases of transition and have become harder to implement over time.

Fernandez and Rodrik (1991) mention one further reason why reforms are difficult to implement and are often even reversed. They show that uncertainty can lead to a status-quo bias even if all agents are aware that reforms would be overall welfare improving. Even if the expected gain from reform is positive for the entire economy, individuals cannot necessarily be sure to be among the winners from reform, thus resisting reforms if their expected individual gain is negative. Since a reform not implemented cannot reveal that it is overall and for the majority of individuals positive, there is a bias to support the status quo if enough agents are uncertain about their personal gains from reform. Implemented reforms that were expected to make the majority better off may fail to fulfill this expectation and be consequently reversed, thus explaining why a reversal of reforms can sometimes be observed. Disappointment with reforms, in general, or a change of government with different constituents can hence rationalize the mixed experience in Europe with reforms and their reversal.

The major problem with reform policies is therefore that with agent heterogeneity, and that there are winners and losers of reform policies, even welfare increasing reforms cannot be implemented if enough individuals must fear to be worse off after reforms. Political support maximizing governments will in this case tend to shy away from implementing too many and too radical reforms in order not to lose too much political capital.

3.3 Monetary Policy with and without Monetary Union

3.3.1 The Basic Model

Consider two countries, one (labeled H) where the level of structural distortions is relatively high, while the other (L) has relatively low structural distortions. This captures the presence of strong asymmetries between the existing monetary union and the candidates for enlargement that section 3.2 has demonstrated.

Each government determines the amount of structural reform implemented in each period, and the monetary authority sets monetary policy. Both interact with a private sector that rationally forms expectations about the rate of inflation the central bank will set in response to the economic situation. The timing in every period is (1) the amount of structural reforms is determined, (2) inflation expectations are formed, (3) shocks occur, (4) monetary policy is set, and (5) output is realized. I assume that the governments are Stackelberg leaders vis-à-vis the central banks, but that they play Nash against each other.

It is assumed that structural reforms are time independent; thus distortions in a period are influenced by structural reform in that period (see Beetsma and Jensen 2003). This is not as unrealistic as it might seem at first sight. Unemployment benefits, minimum wages, or tax rates are often adjusted by a government on a yearly basis. Moreover changes in the governing party might involve changes in these areas too. Often incoming governments turn back the reforms that the previous government has implemented. This has happened in countries in

Eastern Europe and also in countries like Germany, Italy, and France where, with a change in government, formerly implemented reforms have been taken back.[5]

With these assumptions, output in country i is

$$y_t^i = \pi_t^i - E[\pi_t^i] - s_t^i + \varepsilon_t^i, \qquad i = L, H. \tag{1}$$

The (log of) potential output is normalized to zero and actual output can be increased through monetary surprises $\pi_t^i - E[\pi_t^i]$, with π denoting inflation and E the expectations operator. Output is affected by country-specific exogenous supply shock ε_t^i that captures the influence of asymmetric business cycle developments.[6] All shocks have an expected value of zero, constant variances, and are uncorrelated. Last, $-s_t^i < 0$ denotes the presence of distortions in the economy. As indicated above, this can be due to the presence of strong employment and production regulation in the economy or a distortive tax system. The higher these distortions are, the more is the current output below potential output.[7]

Distortions per period are

$$s_t^i = k^i - c_t^i, \qquad i = L, H. \tag{2}$$

There is a given level of structural distortions k^i that can, however, be reduced through structural reforms c in period t. Structural reforms are specified very broadly because different countries have different needs for particular structural reforms, depending on their economic situation. One might therefore best think of the variable c_t^i as a vector of policies that can be implemented to reduce distortions in the economy.

Government preferences are identical for each period. Utility (in logs) for the government is

$$v_t^i = -\{b(y_t^i)^2 + (\pi_t^i)^2 + \gamma(c_t^i)^2\}, \qquad i = L, H. \tag{3}$$

The government in each country aims to minimize differences between actual and potential output and to minimize deviations of inflation from zero. Structural reforms are (politically) costly because they hurt certain interest groups or voters. As argued above, although reforms are output increasing, governments are under pressure from insiders to protect their rents, and individual uncertainty about the consequences of reform leads to reform resistance in the electorate (Fernandez and Rodrik 1991). The more reforms are executed, the more potential losers there are and the higher the political costs for the government.

All parameters in the utility function are set equal across countries in order to abstract from gains or losses arising through monetary unification that are simply due to differences in preferences (e.g., see Berger et al. 2001). All governments have the same interest to avoid inflation and are also equally reluctant to implement structural reforms. Hence all aspects discussed below are due to structural differences between the economies.[8]

3.3.2 Monetary Policy before and after Monetary Union

The central bank has preferences very similar to those of its government, but without being particularly interested in the achievement of monetary union nor being concerned with the implementation of structural reforms.[9] Since the central bank has no influence on structural reforms or on the decision of enlargement, these factors have no influence on its optimal policy. Moreover I am not interested in conflicts between central bank and government, so I have equalized the utility weight parameters for central bank and government. The period utility of the central bank is then

$$u_t^i = -\{b(y_t^i)^2 + (\pi_t^i)^2\}, \qquad i = L, H. \tag{4}$$

Monetary policy is set after the government has decided upon structural reforms and after a possible shock to the output occurred. By assumption, the central bank has full control over the rate of inflation. If we take expected inflation as given and impose rational expectations, the equilibrium rate of inflation is

$$\pi_t^i = bs_t^i - \frac{b\varepsilon_t^i}{1+b}, \qquad i = L, H. \tag{5}$$

The central bank, if unable to commit to a different policy, will respond to a high degree of structural distortion with an increase of the rate of inflation and will also partly stabilize the shock ε_t^i. Given rational expectations, the public will expect inflation of bs_t^i, so this systematic component of monetary policy has no output effect (Barro and Gordon 1983).[10]

In a monetary union, policy is determined by the common central bank, a merger of the formerly separated monetary authorities. The common central bank's per period utility function is assumed to be

$$u_t^{CC} = u_t^L + \varphi u_t^H, \tag{6}$$

where the accession country is likely to receive a smaller weight than the current members of the EMU, thus $\varphi < 1$ (Hefeker 2003).

Again, the central bank takes expectations as given when choosing the optimal rate of inflation. It reacts to structural distortions in both countries, where the relative weight φ determines by how much developments in accession countries are taken into account. Then inflation is

$$\pi_t = \frac{b(s_t^L + \varphi s_t^H)}{1 + \varphi} - \frac{b(\varepsilon_t^L + \varphi \varepsilon_t^H)}{(1 + \varphi)(1 + b)}. \tag{7}$$

3.4 Structural Reforms under Autonomy and Monetary Union

The central bank's reaction is taken into account by the government when it determines how much structural distortion should be reduced. The incentive for the government to reduce structural distortions is twofold. It would increase output directly, and it would reduce the central bank's incentive to increase output through inflation. Without the political costs of reform, the government would therefore abolish distortions completely.[11] Because of their political costs reforms will be limited.

I begin with monetary autonomy in the two countries. Governments optimize (4) with respect to c_t^i and subject to (7). This leads to

$$c_t^i = \frac{\beta k^i}{\gamma + \beta}, \qquad i = L, H, \tag{8}$$

with $\beta \equiv b(1 + b) > 0$. Because distortions are given as $s_t^i = k^i - c_t^i$, the level of distortions is

$$s_t^i = \frac{\gamma k^i}{\gamma + \beta}, \qquad i = L, H. \tag{9}$$

Structural reforms and distortions after reforms have been implemented are only determined through national distortions and preference parameters with national monetary policy.

Structural reforms in the two countries are no longer independent in case of monetary union. Subject to (9), both governments optimize (4) with respect to c_t^i. This yields

$$c_t^i = \frac{k^i[\beta^i(\gamma + \beta^j) - \chi^2] + \gamma \chi k^j}{B}, \qquad i, j = L, H, \quad i \neq j, \tag{10}$$

with $\beta^L \equiv b(1 + b/(1 + \varphi)^2) > 0,\quad \beta^H \equiv b(1 + \varphi^2 b/(1 + \varphi)^2) > 0,\quad \chi \equiv \varphi b^2/(1 + \varphi)^2 > 0,$ and $B \equiv (\gamma + \beta^H)(\gamma + \beta^L) - \chi^2 > 0.$ Notice   that $\beta > \beta^i$, and that $\beta^L > \beta^H$ if $\varphi < 1$.

This leads to distortions of

$$s_t^i = \frac{\gamma}{B}\{k^i(\gamma + \beta^j) - \chi k^j\}, \qquad i, j = L, H, \quad i \neq j. \tag{11}$$

Equations (10) and (11) show that the introduction of monetary union creates spillovers between the two members. How are economic policy and structural reform in the two countries affected through monetary union? (The derivation of the results can be found in the appendix.)

Result 1   The extension of monetary union to a high-distortions country will induce more reform in the low-distortions country and thus reduce distortions if k^H is sufficiently larger than k^L. The impact on the rate of inflation for country i depends on the difference between k^H and k^L and the size of φ.

Result 2   By entering monetary union, structural reform efforts in the high-distortions country will fall and distortions will increase. The rate of inflation for the country will fall if its distortions are sufficiently larger than those in the low-distortions country.

Because of its inflation aversion the low-distortions country wants to avoid that high distortions in the new member country increase common inflation. To lower the incentives for the common central bank to increase inflation, it will lower its distortions. Extension of the monetary union thus leads to more structural reforms in low distortion country, which is in contrast to the result derived for symmetric countries by Calmfors (2000) and Sibert and Sutherland (2000). With symmetric countries and Nash behavior all perceive they can export part of the inflationary consequences of distortions, which leads them to reduce structural reforms in the monetary union. With asymmetric countries instead, some countries are aware they import inflationary pressure and increase their reforms to counter this effect. Therefore enlargement has positive output and employment effects for low-distortions countries.

The influence of enlargement on inflation in the low-distortions country is not certain because there are two conflicting influences on the central bank. While the inclusion of the high-distortions country increases inflationary pressure, more reforms in the low-distortions country reduce this pressure. The net effect on inflation thus depends on the influence of the high-distortion country on common monetary policy. If it is large inflation in current member states will increase.

Reform policies in the high-distortions country follow the reverse logic. For this country inflation is automatically reduced when entering monetary union, and hence incentives to reduce structural distortions fall. The rate of inflation will decrease because the common central bank cares less for developments in single countries and because the increased reform efforts in the other member country additionally reduce pressure on the common central bank.

The monetary union thus creates spillovers of reform policies between member countries. Those who import inflationary pressure will increase their reform efforts; those who export inflationary pressure are able to lower their reform efforts.

The strength of these results depends to a large extent on the relative weight of the high-distortions country φ. If the new members have a decision weight close to zero, they do not influence the common monetary policy and the spillover effects on the current members are zero. The question of relative weight will therefore be of great policy importance and probably trigger a debate about the appropriate weight of accession countries (see Berger 2002; Hefeker 2003).

In general, comparative statics show $\partial s_t^H / \partial \varphi < 0$ and $\partial s_t^L / \partial \varphi \gtreqless 0$. For the high-distortions country, a large weight means the central bank will react strongly to its high distortions. To avoid the strong inflation reaction, more reforms must be implemented, which is why the degree of distortion in that country will monotonously fall in its relative weight. This is not the case for the low-distortions country, though. High distortions in country H mean a strong inflationary pressure on the central bank and thus a potential increase of inflation. This is an incentive to lower distortions. In this case, and if k^H is sufficiently larger than k^L, distortions will go down in the low-distortions country. An opposite influence is exerted by a large weight for the high-distortions country because then the government of the low-distortions country knows its policy has only little influence on the common rate of inflation. It can reduce reforms without having to fear more inflation, while a reduction of distortions would be nearly inconsequential for inflation. A sufficient condition for the first influence to prevail is $k^H > 2\varphi k^L$.

A relative weight of zero for the candidate country may also reflect one of two cases that are prominently discussed for transition countries on their way to EMU. It may reflect a unilateral peg, such as a currency board (as in Bulgaria and Estonia), or full euroization, meaning the introduction of the euro as a means of payment in the domestic economy (which is the case in Montenegro).[12] Several observers have argued that such a "hard peg" can give more credibility to monetary policy and lower expected inflation. These benefits have to be weighed against the costs in terms of the forgone possibility to stabilize shocks and the loss of a lender-of-last resort.[13] For some of the candidates for enlargement, it has been argued that the benefits of full euroization will clearly dominate the costs (Gros 2000).[14] Whether this will indeed occur will depend on how reform incentives are affected by euroization, an outcome that is usually overlooked in the debate about exchange rate regimes for transition countries.

Therefore the question is what effects such an extreme regime will have on reform policies in the two countries. For simplicity, I only consider the case of a full eurozation because it is more credible than a currency board and thus directly comparable to monetary union. In this case the situation for the low distortion country is the same as under monetary autonomy. The expected rate of inflation for the pegging country in turn is determined by distortions in the anchor country $\pi_t^H = bs_t^L = (b\gamma k^L)/(\gamma + \beta)$.

The strategic decision of setting structural reforms would now be different because the rate of inflation is exogenous for the government, thus making it no longer the Stackelberg leader in its relation with the central bank. This leads to $c_t^H = (bk^H)/(\gamma + b)$ and $s_t^H = (\gamma k^H)/(\gamma + b)$ and therefore to the next result:

Result 3 Compared with monetary autonomy, under eurozation reforms efforts fall and distortions increase in the high-distortions country. Inflation is lower than under monetary autonomy. Distortions increase even more than under full membership in the monetary union.

Inflation will fall when monetary policy is tied to the low-distortions country because there is less incentive to inflate for the central bank. This implies that structural reform efforts fall because the danger of high inflation vanishes. They fall even more than under the monetary union because the government has no influence on the rate of inflation and therefore no incentive to implement reforms, whereas with full monetary union and $\varphi > 0$ there is some influence on the central bank's policy.

3.5   When Is Enlargement Possible?

Under what circumstances could the enlargement of monetary union be achieved? As is argued above, this would require that both countries agree to enlargement. The current members must be convinced that it is in their interest, and the same applies to the candidate country. Since monetary union will have different implications for the two countries, it is not sure, however, that both will agree to enlargement at the same time.

Computing expected government utility under monetary autonomy (A) and monetary unification (MU) and comparing utility levels gives the condition for $E[u_t^i(MU)] > E[u_t^i(A)]$ that must be fulfilled to make enlargement possible. (See the appendix for details.)

The positive effect from monetary union for the low distortion country is the reduction of structural distortions induced by enlargement. This has to be compared with the costs of monetary union. First, the country suffers from a potential increase in inflation due to the fact that the common central bank will take care of the structural distortions in the new member country. Whether inflation does increase compared to the case of monetary autonomy depends, as derived above, on the size of this impulse (and hence the level of distortion in the new member) and by how much this influences the monetary policy of the common central bank (and thus on b and φ). It is, as derived above, also possible that the overall rate of inflation will decrease, which would make monetary union more attractive for this country. Second, the government will be negatively affected because it is forced to pursue more reforms than under monetary autonomy. This, as argued above, can be politically costly for the government if the population is averse to reform policies.

Depending on the relative weight that the government assigns to these various effects enlargement might be welcomed or not. It is more interesting, however, to see what is the main structural influence on a country's decision. The most interesting influence for the decision to agree to enlargement is the amount of distortions that the candidate brings into the union since highly distorted new members bring the most pressure on the central bank to increase inflation and thus also the most incentives to reform. It can be shown (see the appendix) that the positive output effect prevails and that an increase in distortions in the new member leads to an increase in net benefits for the low distortion country.

Likewise one can derive the condition when monetary union is attractive for the candidate country. It profits from monetary union because the inflationary response to distortions in the economy is lower under monetary union and the overall rate of inflation for that country will fall if its distortions are relatively large (see result 2). The government also profits because structural reforms are lower and therefore lower political costs from reform arise. This implies that a strong resistance to reforms makes enlargement attractive. The candidate also benefits, since the structural component of inflation falls; thus a strong inflation aversion is beneficial for enlargement. A high concern for output, instead, would mean that monetary autonomy is preferred. Again, it is mainly a question of relative preferences whether joining the monetary union is attractive for the candidate country.

For the candidate as well it might be interesting whether it enters a union that is characterized by high distortions itself or not. The appendix shows that the accession country will lose interest in monetary union the higher the distortions in the low distortion country are. Because a high value of s_t^L implies a relatively high rate of inflation, the country could gain less in terms of lower inflation from entering the union. In addition the level of reforms would not fall by much.

Both countries would simultaneously suffer if the shocks are strongly asymmetric because a common central bank would then be forced to react to shocks in both regions, which would, if shocks are not positively correlated, lead to more output and inflation variance than an autonomous monetary policy (see Berger et al. 2001). Both, however, might also have similar noneconomic interests in enlargement. They might expect noneconomic political gains from enlargement that overcome any economic costs of enlargement. For the present monetary union, for instance, it has often been claimed that it was pursued mainly for political reasons (Wyplosz 1997).

Because the effects of EMU on distortions, output, and inflation have opposite signs for the two countries, an extension would be agreeable for both if the preference parameters that measure the influence of these effects on utility have intermediate values. Countries that are predominantly focused on inflation, output, or structural reforms are likely to resist enlargement more than countries that value positive and negative effects of enlargement more equally. Therefore, if countries have different preferences for employment, inflation, and resistance to reform, it might be easier to find support for enlargement among the member states and candidates for the larger EMU.

An interesting thought experiment would be to assume that the aversion to reform is different in the two countries. Assume that the low-distortions country is less averse to reforms than the high aversion country, $\gamma^H > \gamma^L$. This might actually be one reason, apart from higher initial distortions because of the legacies of central planning, why the level of distortions is different in the first place. In this case the candidates will resist reforms even more and be willing to accept more unemployment in order to implement less reforms. Through the creation of monetary union, these countries can reduce their reform efforts even more, while the low distortions countries implement more reforms. Thus different degrees of reform aversion can lead to a further polarization concerning reforms between high and low distortions countries and not to convergence as advocates of an early monetary union (so-called monetarists) tend to argue (see Eichengreen 2002 for that debate).

3.6 Conclusion

The chapter derived the influence of an extension of monetary union on structural reform efforts in accession countries and older member of EMU, and argued that one can expect more structural reforms to be undertaken in the older member states after enlargement. In this respect an early extension of EMU to accession countries may be desirable in terms of necessary structural reforms and add to the expected gains from trade integration (see Baldwin et al. 1997). In as much as more reforms can be politically costly for governments, this is at the same time one explanation why the extension of EMU is made conditional on the convergence of candidates and member states. Then an extension will have comparatively little influence on reform policies in current member states, although at the price of forgone positive output effects.

By contrast, extension will most likely result in a slowing down of reform efforts in the joining countries, but those countries are very likely to gain from extension in terms of lower inflation. Only if the gains in credibility and reduction in inflation more than outweigh the negative output consequences of a slowdown in economic reforms, those countries will be interested in an early enlargement.

The main logic behind the argument developed here is the relation between structural distortions and monetary policy. Labor market distortions and high unemployment exert pressure on monetary policy, and this connection is affected by the change in the monetary regime, thus creating important spillovers between countries with high and low levels of distortions. In this sense the model captures the essential argument behind the Maastricht Treaty and the entrance criteria to the EMU that suppose a relation between monetary policy and fiscal and structural policies. Otherwise, there would be no need for such criteria. The Maastricht criteria and regulations have been created to deal with spillovers as they have been described here, although most of the literature has so far been focused on fiscal policies instead of reform policies more broadly and the so-called real convergence.

Therefore it is an important result of this chapter that enlargement can lead to more polarization rather than convergence between old and new members. A positive conclusion, however, and somewhat in contrast to the official EU position, is that an early extension of monetary union could bring benefits for both groups of countries. It is often overlooked that a full monetary union could not only ensure more credibility and monetary stability for new members of the European Union but be an engine of reform in current member states.

Appendix

Comparison of Reform Policies

Result 1 Comparing (9) and (11) shows that the condition for distortions in the low-distortions county to be reduced, $s_t^L(A) > s_t^L(MU)$, where A and MU denote the case of monetary autonomy and monetary union respectively, is $k^H > k^L[(\gamma + \beta^H)(\beta - \beta^L) + \chi^2]/\chi(\gamma + \beta)$. Although $k^H > k^L$, the multiplier on the RHS is larger than one, because $(\gamma + \beta^H)(\beta - \beta^L) + \chi^2 > \chi(\gamma + \beta)$ can be rewritten as $(\gamma + b)(1 + \varphi) - [b^2(1 - \varphi^2)]/(1 + \varphi) > 0$. This is clearly fulfilled for $b < 1$ (or if $\varphi = 1$).

Likewise the comparison of inflation in country L before and after monetary unification, yields that $\pi_t^L(MU) > \pi_t^L(A)$ if $\varphi k^H > k^L \cdot \{[(1 + \varphi)B]/[(\gamma + \beta)(\gamma + b)] - 1\}$. The multiplier is positive for $b < 1$, but smaller than one if $(\gamma + b)[1 - b - \varphi^2(1 + b^2)] + 2b^2(1 + \varphi) > 0$. Hence, depending on the difference between k^H and k^L and the size of φ, inflation may increase or decrease.

Result 2 The condition for $s_t^H(MU) > s_t^H(A)$ is $k^H\{[(\gamma + \beta^L)(\beta - \beta^H) + \chi^2]/[\chi(\gamma + \beta)]\} > k^L$. Since $k^H > k^L$ and because the multiplier on the LHS is larger than one, this condition is fulfilled.

The comparison of inflation before and after monetary unification for country H yields that $\pi_t^H(A) > \pi_t^H(MU)$ if $k^H\{[(1+\varphi)B]/[(\gamma+\beta) \cdot (\gamma+b)] - \varphi\} > k^L$. The multiplier on k^H is positive and inflation in country H will fall if k^H is sufficiently larger than k^L.

Result 3 The condition for $s_t^H(E) > s_t^H(MU)$, with E denoting euroization, is $k^H[(\gamma+\beta^L)(\beta^H - b) - \chi^2] + k^L\chi(\gamma+b) > 0$ and always fulfilled.

Comparison of Government Utility

To simplify, I restrict the considerations of asymmetric shocks to one country and set $\varepsilon_t^L = 0$, $\varepsilon_t^H = \varepsilon_t$ in what follows.

The low-distortions country will agree to enlargement if

$$b[(s_t^L(A))^2 - (s_t^L(MU))^2] > b^2 \left[\frac{(s_t^L(MU) + \varphi s_t^H(MU))^2}{(1+\varphi)^2} - (s_t^L(A))^2 \right]$$

$$+ \gamma[(c_t^L(MU))^2 - (c_t^L(A))^2] + \frac{b^2\varphi^2\sigma^2}{(1+b)(1+\varphi)^2}$$

with $\sigma^2 = E[\varepsilon_t^2]$.

Defining $E[\omega_t^i] = E[v_t^i(MU)] - E[v_t^i(A)]$, it follows that $\partial E[\omega_t^L]/\partial k^H = k^L[(\gamma+\beta^H)(\beta^L - b) + (\gamma+b)^2 - \chi] + k^H(\gamma+b)[\varphi(\gamma+b) + \chi] > 0$.

Similarly the condition for $E[u_t^H(MU)] > E[u_t^H(A)]$ is

$$b^2 \left[(s_t^H(A))^2 - \frac{(s_t^H(MU) + \varphi s_t^H(MU))^2}{(1+\varphi)^2} \right] + \gamma[c_t^H(A)^2 - c_t^H(MU)^2]$$

$$> \frac{b^2\sigma^2}{(1+b)(1+\varphi)^2} + b[s_t^H(MU)^2 - s_t^H(A)^2].$$

Moreover $\partial E[\omega_t^H]/\partial k^L = k^H[(\gamma+\beta^L)(\beta^H - b) + \varphi(\gamma+b)^2 - \chi^2] - k^L(\gamma+b)[(\gamma+b) - \chi]$, which is positive if k^H is sufficiently larger than k^L.

Notes

I am grateful to Florin Bilbiie, to the participants of the CESifo-Summer Institute on Monetary Unions after EMU (Venice, July 21–22, 2003), and to one referee for helpful and constructive comments.

1. Estonia, Poland, Hungary, Cyprus, Slovenia, the Czech Republic, Latvia, Lithuania, Slovak Republic, and Malta joined the European Union in May 2004. Bulgaria, Romania, and Turkey are applicants to join later.

2. Although EMU is an integral part of the *acquis communautaire* that countries accept when joining the European Union, it is unlikely that countries can be forced to join EMU, as the Swedish example shows.

3. This is documented in Fischer et al. (1997), European Commission (2000), Deutsche Bank (2004), and World Bank (2002). Continuous monitoring is provided in the EBRD's annual *Transition Report*.

4. Figure 3.2 is based on data provided by the OECD (1999b). Each reform measure receives two points. Implementing the recommendation fully gives two points; partial implementation gives one point. No response receives zero, and opposite reaction gives minus one point. The graphs shows the relation between points demanded and received.

5. Modeling persistent reforms would make no qualitative difference. It would mean that distortions decline over time, thus reducing the incentives to pursue further reforms. Even persistent reforms would never lead to a fully distortion free economy.

6. I abstract from common shocks because with identical shocks monetary union does not distort the optimal response for individual countries and are thus irrelevant for the decision to join a monetary union.

7. With the assumption that purchasing power parity holds, there is no influence from trade on output because the real exchange rate is constant.

8. I discuss below what happens if governments have different degrees of reform aversion.

9. Actually one can expect central banks to place a negative value on the achievement of monetary union. Bureaucracy theory suggests that they are interested in maintaining their independence. One might also expect that central banks are in favor of reforms because this relieves the pressure to reduce unemployment with monetary policy. I abstract from both complications.

10. Delegating monetary policy to an independent central banker with lower preferences for output stabilization than the government could lower this systematic inflation but lead to more output fluctuations (Rogoff 1985). The first-best situation could be reached by setting distortions to zero, which is politically not feasible, however.

11. The equations below show that $s_t^i = 0$ whenever $\gamma = 0$, independent of the monetary regime.

12. See, for example, Ghosh et al. (2000) and Eichengreen (2002) respectively on the relative merits of such arrangements.

13. Calvo (1999) argues there are ways to retain a lender-of-last resort even under dollarization.

14. Euroization is legally not compatible with the Maastricht Treaty, since it precludes that conversion rates be set by the Council of Ministers. For ways around this problem, see Buiter and Grafe (2002).

References

Baldwin, R., J. Francois, and R. Portes. 1997. The costs and benefits of Eastern enlargement: The impact on the EU and Central Europe. *Economic Policy* 24: 125–76.

Barro, R., and D. Gordon. 1983. A positive theory of monetary policy in a natural rate model. *Journal of Political Economy* 91: 589–610.

Beetsma, R., and H. Jensen. 2003. Structural convergence under reversible and irreversible monetary unification. *Journal of International Money and Finance* 22: 417–39.

Berger, H. 2002. The ECB and euro-area enlargement. IMF Working Paper 02/175.

Berger, H., H. Jensen, and G. Schjelderup. 2001. To peg or not to peg? A simple model of exchange rate regime choice in small economies. *Economics Letters* 73: 161–67.

Boeri, T. 1997. Labour-market reforms in transition economies. *Oxford Review of Economic Policy* 13: 126–40.

Buiter, W. H., and C. Grafe. 2002. Anchor, float or abandon ship: Exchange rate regimes for the accession countries. *Banca Nazionale Lavoro Quarterly Review* (221): 1–32.

Burda, M. 1998. The consequences of EU enlargement for Central and Eastern European labor markets. *EIB Papers* 3: 65–82.

Calmfors, L. 2001. Labor market reform and monetary union. *Journal of Labor Economics* 19: 265–89.

Calvo, G. 1999. On dollarization. Mimeo. University of Maryland.

Deutsche Bank Research. 2004. *EU Monitor* No. 12, January. Frankfurt: Deutsche Bank.

EBRD (European Bank for Reconstruction and Development). 2004. *Transition Report Update*. London: EBRD.

Eichengreen, B. 2002. When to dollarize. *Journal of Money, Credit and Banking* 34: 1–24.

European Commission. 2000. *Enlargement Strategy Paper*. Brussels: EU-Commission.

Fernandez, R., and D. Rodrik. 1991. Resistance to reform: Status quo bias in the presence of individual-specific uncertainty. *American Economic Review* 81: 1146–55.

Fidrmuc, J., and I. Korhonen. 2001. Similarity of supply and demand shocks between the euro area and the CEEs. Bank of Finland, BOFIT Discussion Paper 2001/14.

Fischer, S., R. Sahay, and C. A. Végh. 1997. How far is Eastern Europe from Brussels? In H. Siebert, ed., *Quo Vadis Europe?* Tübingen: Mohr (Siebeck), pp. 97–122.

Frankel, J. A., and A. K. Rose. 1998. The endogeneity of the optimum currency area criterion. *Economic Journal* 108: 1009–25.

Ghosh, A., A. Gulde, and H. Wolf. 2000. Currency boards: More than a quick fix? *Economic Policy* 31: 269–335.

Gros, D. 2000. One euro from the Atlantic to the Urals? *CESifo Forum* 2: 26–31.

Hefeker, C. 2003. Federal monetary policy. *Scandinavian Journal of Economics* 105: 643–59.

Martin, P. 1995. Free-riding, convergence and two-speed monetary unification in Europe. *European Economic Review* 39: 1345–64.

OECD (Organisation for Economic Co-operation and Development). 1999a. *Employment Outlook*. Paris: OECD.

OECD (Organisation for Economic Co-operation and Development). 1999b. *Implementing the OECD Jobs Strategy: Assessing Performance and Policy*. Paris: OECD.

Olson, M. 1995. The secular increase in European unemployment rates. *European Economic Review* 39: 593–99.

Ozkan, F., A. Sibert, and A. Sutherland. 1997. Monetary union, entry conditions and economic reform. CEPR Discussion Paper 1720.

Rogoff, K. 1985. The optimal degree of commitment to an intermediate monetary target. *Quarterly Journal of Economics* 100: 1169–90.

Saint-Paul, G. 1996. Exploring the political economy of labour market institutions. *Economic Policy* 23: 263–315.

Saint-Paul, G. 2000. *The Political Economy of Labour Market Institutions*. Oxford: Oxford University Press.

Sibert, A. 1999. Monetary integration and economic reform. *Economic Journal* 109: 78–92.

Sibert, A., and A. Sutherland. 2000. Monetary regimes and labour market reform. *Journal of International Economics* 51: 421–35.

Siebert, H. 1997. Labor market rigidities: At the root of unemployment in Europe. *Journal of Economic Perspectives* 11 (Summer): 37–54.

Svejnar, J. 2002. Transition economies: Performance and challenges. *Journal of Economic Perspectives* 18 (Winter): 3–28.

Tornell, A. 1999. Common fundamentals in the Tequila and Asian crises. NBER Working Paper 7139.

World Bank. 2002. *Transition: The First Ten Years*. Washington, DC: World Bank.

Wyplosz, C. 1997. EMU: Why and how it might happen. *Journal of Economic Perspectives* 11 (Fall): 3–22.

4 The Endogeneity of the Optimum Currency Area Criteria and Intra-industry Trade: Implications for EMU Enlargement

Jarko Fidrmuc

4.1 Introduction

The introduction of the euro and the progress of several new member states of the European Union raised a general interest in the optimum currency area (OCA) theory. However, the countries participating in a currency area face the benefits and costs of the common currency. The benefits are directly related to transaction costs in the countries' bilateral trade. Therefore countries with intensive trade relations are likely to gain relatively more from the monetary integration. In addition, as Frankel and Rose (1997, 1998) hypothesize, business cycles become more similar across countries having intensive trade links. The Frankel-Rose hypothesis is supported by cross-sectional estimations of the relation between the correlation of business cycles and trade intensity among OECD countries between 1959 and 1993. Both Fatás (1997) and Hochreiter and Winckler (1995) show that a common European business cycle has been emerging as predicted by the endogeneity hypothesis of OCA criteria.

Nevertheless, there remains considerable doubt whether there is a causal relationship between trade links and the correlation of business cycles in the involved countries. Kose et al. (2003) find only weak evidence for the hypothesis that increased trade and financial flows have increased the synchronization of business cycles. Kenen (2000) notes that the correlation of business cycles may increase with the intensity of trade links between these countries, but he argues that this does not necessarily mean that asymmetric shocks are reduced as well. Moreover Hughes Hallett and Piscitelli (2001) show that a currency union may increase cyclical convergence, but only if there is already a sufficient symmetry in the shocks and institutional structure across the countries. Their findings thus support Krugman's (1993) discussion of the implications from the US currency union for the economic monetary union (EMU) in Europe. In Krugman's view, trade liberalization facilitates increased specialization according to comparative advantage of countries and possibly a divergence of business cycles in the EMU.

Furthermore Frankel and Rose's work lacks a stronger relation to trade structure.[1] The trade links between countries could explain the similarities of business cycles, just as the intra-industry trade they use in their argument. The particular effects of trade on the convergence of business cycles should depend on the degree of industrial specialization that is induced by the integration.

However, Helpman (1987) and Hummels and Levinsohn (1995) find that trade specialization plays a lesser role for trade among developed economies. In these works, a majority of trade is observed within the same industries (the so-called intra-industry trade). This result suggests increasing correlation of business cycles between these countries. Therefore in this chapter I test the OCA endogeneity hypothesis, using bilateral levels of intra-industry trade between OECD countries in the 1990s. I show that intra-industry trade induces the convergence of business cycles between trading partners, while there is no direct relation between business cycle and trade intensity. As a result the OCA endogeneity hypothesis can be confirmed. However, this finding also underlines the role of the specialization in trade.

In this chapter I also consider whether the central and eastern European countries (CEECs) should introduce the euro as soon as possible after accession to the European Union (EU), or whether they should do so at a later stage. I address this issue by applying the endogeneity hypothesis of OCA criteria to eight transition economies—Czech Republic, Estonia, Hungary, Latvia, Lithuania, Poland, Slovakia, and Slovenia—that joined the European Union in May 2004. I look at the degree of trade integration, the shares of intra-industry trade, and the convergence in business cycles to CEECs and EU countries to predict the degree of business cycle harmonization of CEECs with EU countries in the medium term. This approach reflects the Lucas critique in so far as it considers possible structural changes during the accession of the CEECs to the European Union and the EMU. Alternatively, these predictions can be interpreted as indexes of endogenous optimum currency area (EOCA indexes) similar to those introduced by Bayoumi and Eichengreen (1997).

The chapter is structured as follows: Section 4.2 presents some stylized facts of the acceding countries from the point of view whether these countries are likely to fulfill the so-called OCA criteria with the European economic monetary union (EMU). Because the available time series is too short to provide a clear picture, the discussion in section 4.3 focuses the OCA endogeneity hypothesis with respect to trade intensity and intra-industry trade. The revealed relation between, on the one hand, the correlation of business cycles, and, on the other hand, the trade variables is applied for the computation of a potential correlation of business cycles (indexes of endogenous optimum currency area) in the CEECs. Section 4.3 concludes the chapter.

4.2   Stylized Facts of the EMU Enlargement from the Point of View of OCA Theory

Since the start of the 1990s the CEECs have aimed at future membership in the European Union. Over more than a decade of economic reform, these countries have largely succeeded in adjusting their economies to market principles. As a result the European Union started membership negotiations with five CEECs in 1998, and extended them to all ten CEECs in 2000. Finally, in 2004 eight CEECs (all CEECs except for Bulgaria and Romania), as well as Malta and Cyprus, joined the European Union.

As part of this enlargement agenda, several CEECs have already expressed their aspiration to join the euro area as soon as possible after accession. Correspondingly, the European Union, including the Eurosystem, has outlined a three-step approach to the monetary integration of the candidate countries from central and eastern Europe (for more details, see Kopits 1999). The first countries (Estonia, Slovenia, and Lithuania in 2004, as well as Cyprus and Latvia in 2005) have already entered the exchange rate mechanism (ERM II) of the European Union, and finally, after the fulfillment of the convergence criteria, they will adopt the euro.

4.2.1   Observed Convergence of Business Cycles in the European Union and the CEECs

Several authors have reported increasing similarities in business cycles between the EU member countries (mainly Germany) and the CEECs since economic reforms were introduced. According to Boone and Maurel (1999), between 55 percent (Poland) and 86 percent (Hungary) of CEECs' cycles (given by detrended unemployment) are explained by German shocks. This figure is lower than the estimate for the

French–German interdependence of business cycles (91 percent) but higher than the estimates for the German influence on Spanish (43 percent) and Italian (18 percent) business cycles. Therefore these authors conclude that the benefits from eventually joining the euro area could outweigh the costs in the CEECs.

Similarly Korhonen (2003) correlated monthly indicators of industrial production in the euro area and nine accession countries (excluding Bulgaria) in Central and Eastern Europe. He used separate VARs for the first difference of the euro area production and production in each of the accession countries, and found that business cycles in the most advanced accession countries (especially Hungary) exhibit a relatively high correlation with the euro area business cycle. This correlation seems to be at least as high as for some small current EMU member countries. Fidrmuc and Korhonen (2003) found similar results for the correlation of supply and demand shocks between transition countries and the euro area.

Since the second half of the 1990s business cycles in several CEECs have become strikingly close to the business cycle of the European Union, as proxied by Germany (see table 4.1). At the beginning of the 1990s the business cycles in the CEECs were determined by the so-called transitional recession. Therefore the correlation of business cycles was low between 1991 and 2001. The recovery in these countries was strongly influenced by the growing exports to the European Union. As a result the EU business cycle has determined the developments in CEECs' economies since the mid-1990s. In particular, the correlations of growth of industrial production between Germany and Hungary (0.83) and Germany and Slovenia (0.86) has been higher than the corresponding correlations of EU countries with Germany (0.52) on average between 1996 and 2001.

However, the period of about six years might be too short to conclude that the business cycles have already become similar. In particular, this period corresponds to only about one full business cycle. Actually the correlations of industrial production in Germany and that in the Czech Republic and Slovakia have remained relatively low. Insofar as the Czech Republic and Slovakia are similar to other CEECs, country-specific shocks may be expected to have had significant effects on these economies. The difference between the Czech Republic and Slovakia, on the one hand, and the remaining CEECs, on the other hand, indicates that asymmetric shocks are still likely in the European Union and the CEECs.

Table 4.1
Similarity of business cycles of selected countries with Germany

	Industrial production		Real gross domestic product	
	1991–2001[a]	1996–2001[a]	1991–2001[a]	1996–2001[a]
Austria	0.79	0.79	0.46	0.79
Belgium	0.33	0.05	0.24	0.05
Finland	0.35	0.85	−0.55	0.85
France	0.86	0.71	0.08	0.71
Greece	0.47	0.46		
Ireland	0.27	0.12	0.19	−0.03
Italy	0.58	0.55	0.19	0.55
Netherlands	0.56	−0.11	0.06	−0.11
Portugal	0.58	0.42	0.12	0.42
Spain	0.80	0.63	0.19	0.63
Denmark	0.69	0.60	−0.02	0.51
Sweden	0.38	0.13	−0.20	0.34
United Kingdom	0.11	0.35	−0.65	0.45
Czech Republic		0.35		0.02[b]
Estonia		0.57		0.43[b]
Hungary	0.35	0.83		0.67[b]
Latvia		0.39		0.41[b]
Lithuania		0.63		0.08[b]
Poland	0.18	0.36		0.18[b]
Slovakia		0.31		−0.29[b]
Slovenia		0.86		0.34[b]
Bulgaria		0.25		0.36[b]
Croatia	0.22	0.40		0.16[b]
Norway	0.09	0.39	0.03	−0.03
Romania	0.08	−0.08		0.03[b]
Switzerland	0.71	0.71	−0.17	0.76
Turkey		0.27	−0.22	0.16

Source: IMF, Vienna Institute for International Economics, own calculations.
Note: The similarity of business cycles is measured by the correlation of detrended indicator of economic activity (fourth difference of logs).
a. Approximate time periods, the actual time periods may differ by about one year due to data availability.
b. Correlation according to Fidrmuc and Korhonen (2003), time period starting between 1995/1996 and 2000.

4.2.2 Trade Integration between the European Union and the CEECs

Since the opening-up of eastern Europe, the importance of EU countries for CEEC trade has increased dramatically. As of 2001 the European Union is the most important trading partner of all CEECs. Trade with EU countries has accounted for between 40 percent (Lithuania) and 75 percent (Hungary) of CEEC total exports. These export shares are comparable to or even higher than intra-EU shares for nearly all EU member countries. On the import side, the predominance of the European Union is only slightly weaker. Furthermore the shares of exports and imports going to and coming from an "enlarged European Union," which is the current member countries plus ten accession countries, are even higher. By this indicator, the enlarged Europe is the most important export market for Slovakia and the Czech Republic, followed by Portugal, the Netherlands, and Austria.

The CEECs are relatively open economies. Exports account for about one-third of GDP in Hungary, and above 40 percent in the Czech Republic, Slovakia, and Slovenia. Thus these countries are relatively more open than nearly all EU countries (see De Grauwe 2003). There are but a few EU countries, including Belgium, the Netherlands, and Ireland, that are significantly more open than the smaller CEECs (export shares between 50 percent and 70 percent of GDP). Only Poland's exports are relatively low at 17 percent of GDP, but this corresponds to the larger size of the Polish economy. Buiter and Grafe (2002) note that the CEECs are also relatively open, if we compare their trade to GDP at purchasing power parities.

From the point of view of the conventional OCA theory, if intra-industry trade accounts for a high share in trade, then, ceteris paribus, business cycles are expected to be more similar across countries. By contrast, increased bilateral trade intensity can lead to the divergence of business cycles if the increase in trade is mainly due to the increased specialization. Therefore intra-industry trade can be used to identify which model is more appropriate for a particular group of countries.

The growth of intra-industry trade, which is observed in intra-EU trade, also dominates the recent East–West trade developments. This would increase net gains from the integration of CEECs into the euro area. According to Fidrmuc (2004, 2005), the shares of intra-industry trade in EU trade with the Czech Republic, Slovenia, and Hungary, as computed by Grubel-Lloyd indexes[2] for three-digit SITC commodity groups, are already comparable to or even slightly larger than in EU trade with, for example, Spain and Sweden (i.e., about 60 percent) in 1998. Poland and Slovakia report somewhat lower levels of intra-industry trade at about 50 percent. These levels are comparable to those of Ireland and Portugal (see figure 4.2). However, the shares of EU intra-industry trade with Estonia, Lithuania, Latvia, Romania, and Bulgaria have still remained slightly below the levels of EU intra-industry trade with Greece and Turkey (35 percent). Nevertheless, the shares of intra-industry trade in CEECs are likely to increase as a part of the accession to the European Union and convergence of income levels.

4.3 Implication of the Optimum Currency Area Theory for the EMU Enlargement

4.3.1 Are Optimum Currency Area Criteria Endogenous?
The theory of optimum currency areas, which was developed by Mundell (1961), McKinnon (1963), and Kenen (1969), has become particularly popular for analyses of the costs and benefits of monetary integration, in particular, with reference to EMU. The basic point of the OCA theory is that countries or regions exposed to symmetric shocks, or possessing mechanisms for the absorption of asymmetric shocks, may find it optimal to adopt a common currency. This stream of literature therefore focuses on assessing the symmetry of output shocks in monetary unions, and/or evaluating the absorption mechanisms, such as labor mobility or fiscal transfers. In general, the stronger any of these linkages (OCA criteria) among countries participating in a currency area are, the more gains may be expected by the participating countries.

Frankel and Rose (1997, 1998) suggest that the OCA criteria are endogenous. Closer trade relations result in a convergence of business cycles. Furthermore similar business cycles create good preconditions for policy integration and the creation of a currency area. However, this view is not universally shared in literature. For example, Krugman (1993) points out that as countries become more integrated, they increasingly specialize. This view is also supported by Eichengreen (1992).

Moreover Kenen (2000) shows in a framework of the Keynesian model that the correlation between the output changes of two countries increases unambiguously with the intensity of trade links between these countries. But this does not necessarily mean that asymmetric

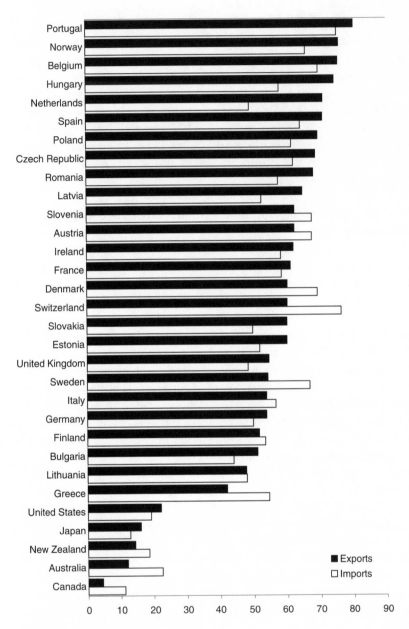

Figure 4.1
Shares of trade with the European Union in 2001 (data from UN World Trade Database).

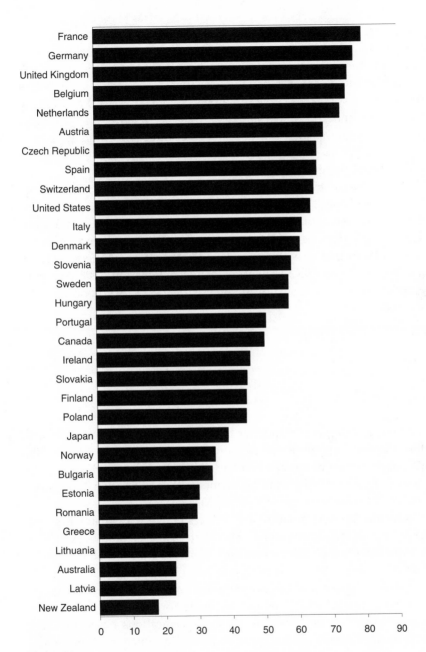

Figure 4.2
Intra-industry trade with the European Union in 1998 (data from Fidrmuc 2005).

shocks are reduced as well. Kose and Yi (2001) also do not find any positive relations between business cycles and trade intensity in a standard international business cycle model. Therefore it is important to keep in mind that it is not trade relation alone which induces the convergence of business cycles in an OCA. Indeed Frankel and Rose's hypothesis underlines that bilateral trade is mainly intra-industry trade, although this indicator does not enter directly their analysis.[3]

4.3.2 Trade Integration and Business Cycles

If intra-industry trade accounts for a high share in bilateral trade, Frankel and Rose (1998) argue that the simple trade intensity increases the convergence of business cycles. They report a significant and positive relation between trade intensity and the correlation of business cycles as measured by various indicators of economic activity in a cross section of OECD countries between 1959 and 1993. For empirical tests, the endogeneity hypothesis of the OCA criteria may be stated as

$$\text{corr}(Q_i, Q_j) = \alpha + \beta \log(TI_{ij}^T),$$

where

$$TI_{ij}^T = \frac{T_{ij}}{T_i + T_j} \tag{1}$$

and where $\text{corr}(Q_i, Q_j)$ stands for the correlation of de-trended (fourth differences of logs) indicator of economic activity and TI denotes the natural logarithm of the bilateral trade intensity between the countries i and j. Trade intensity may be defined either in relation to exports, imports, or trade turnover $(T = X, M, X + M)$.

Industrial production and GDP indexes between 1990 and 1999 are according to the International Financial Statistics of the IMF. The country sample includes Switzerland, Norway, United States, Canada, Australia, New Zealand, Turkey, and Israel in addition to fourteen EU countries (Belgium and Luxembourg are reported as a single region). However, quarterly GDP is not available for Greece, which causes lower number of observations for the specifications based on GDP data than for specifications using industrial production. Trade intensities were computed for 1997, but they do not display significant changes during the 1990s.

Table 4.2 reports several specifications of (1). However, the OLS regression of bilateral economic activity on trade indicators may be

Table 4.2
Trade integration and business cycles

	Industrial production			Real gross domestic product		
	Exports	Imports	Total	Exports	Imports	Total
Constant	0.683	0.686	0.715	0.688	0.681	0.705
	(8.005)	(8.517)	(8.355)	(6.832)	(7.064)	(6.939)
Trade intensity	0.084	0.084	0.091	0.086	0.083	0.090
	(5.378)	(5.632)	(5.683)	(4.655)	(4.780)	(4.782)
Number of observations	253	253	253	231	231	231
SER	0.288	0.286	0.286	0.331	0.329	0.330
Adjusted R^2	0.093	0.104	0.102	0.069	0.080	0.076

Note: The dependent variable is the index of correlation of de-trended indicator of economic activity (fourth difference of logs) between trading partners. Trade intensity is measured as a share of bilateral trade aggregate in total trade aggregates of both countries as indicated by the columns' headers. The instrumental variables in the two-stage OLS include the log of distance, a dummy for geographic adjacency, a dummy for EU-12, the log of aggregate income and the log of income per capita. The country sample includes Switzerland, Norway, United States, Canada, Australia, New Zealand, Turkey, Israel, and the EU countries (only industrial production is available for Greece). Heteroscedasticity-robust t-statistics are in parentheses. Adjusted R^2 and standard errors of regression (SER) are computed using the second-stage residuals.

inappropriate. Countries are likely to orient their monetary policy and fix the exchange rates toward their most important trading partners. The bilateral trade might already reflect the adoption of a common exchange rate policy, and not vice versa.[4] Therefore the regressions have to be instrumented by exogenous determinants of bilateral trade flows. Such instruments are provided by the so-called gravity model including the log of distance between trading partners, a dummy for geographic adjacency, and a dummy for the twelve earlier member states of the European Union,[5] and the aggregate income as well as the income per capita (in logs) of the included countries.

At this stage, trade intensity is revealed to have a significant and positive effect on the correlation of business cycles. This result is robust to the selection of the indicator of economic activity and the particular definition of trade intensities. The business cycles of industrial production seem to be better explained by trade than the business cycles as defined by the correlation of countries' real GDP. This corresponds to the high share of tradables in the manufacturing industry. However, the adjusted coefficient of determination is relatively low for all specifications of (1). As might be expected, the coefficients estimated for trade intensity indicators are slightly higher in the 1990s than in the previous decades as reported by Frankel and Rose (1998). This could indicate that the role of trade relations has increased recently.

4.3.3   Intra-industry Trade and Business Cycles

Equation (1) applies only bilateral trade to explain the similarity of business cycles, although the similarity of trade structure (e.g., the level of intra-industry trade) may be viewed as a major adjustment force inducing the convergence of business cycles between trading partners. Frankel and Rose (1998), Kalemli-Ozcan et al. (2001), and Krugman (1993) use the trade structure arguments in favor also against the endo-geneity hypothesis of OCA criteria. Therefore the relation between the correlation of business cycles, trade integration, and the bilateral level of intra-industry trade is estimated as

$$\mathrm{corr}(Q_i, Q_j) = \alpha + \beta \log(TI_{ij}^T) + \gamma \log(IIT_{ij}), \tag{2}$$

where Q and TI are defined in the same way as in the corresponding formulations of (1). In addition to the previous variables, IIT_{ij} stands for intra-industry trade as measured by the Grubel-Lloyd indexes, which are computed as

$$IIT_t = 1 - \frac{\sum_i |X_{it} - M_{it}|}{\sum_i (X_{it} + M_{it})}, \tag{3}$$

where X and M denote EU's exports and imports by three-digit SITC commodity groups i (as published by the United Nations), respec-tively. This level of disaggregation is more detailed than industry pro-duction used by Imbs (1999) and by Clark and van Wincoop (2001). An index value of 0 shows that there is exclusive inter-industry trade, meaning a complete specialization on different products for each coun-try; an index value of 1 indicates exclusive intra-industry trade.[6] When-ever available, data according to Eurostat are taken. Intra-industry trade at the same level of disaggregation between non-EU countries was computed using the UN World Trade Data. Note that the data according to this classification are not available for earlier periods due to changes in trade statistics.

Equation (2) is again estimated by two-stage OLS. Note that the selected instrumental variables are also highly correlated with intra-industry trade (see Hummels and Levinsohn 1995).[7] In this speci-fication (see table 4.3) the coefficients of intra-industry trade are significant, if estimated for the industrial production, although they

Table 4.3
Intra-industry trade, trade integration, and business cycles

	Industrial production				Real gross domestic product			
	Exports	Imports	Total	Only IIT	Exports	Imports	Total	Only IIT
Constant	0.259	0.468	0.379	0.499	0.444	0.578	0.539	0.476
	(1.598)	(4.325)	(2.576)	(11.934)	(2.361)	(4.381)	(3.221)	(9.636)
Trade intensity	−0.085	−0.011	−0.042		−0.011	0.038	0.022	
	(−1.619)	(−0.323)	(−0.879)		(−0.188)	(0.913)	(0.422)	
Intra-industry trade	0.335	0.207	0.257	0.187	0.195	0.103	0.135	0.175
	(3.597)	(3.043)	(3.047)	(6.554)	(1.812)	(1.304)	(1.457)	(5.324)
Number of observations	253	253	253	253	231	231	231	231
SER	0.280	0.282	0.281	0.281	0.329	0.329	0.329	0.329
Adjusted R^2	0.141	0.130	0.132	0.133	0.078	0.080	0.078	0.082

Note: The dependent variable is the index of correlation of de-trended indicator of economic activity (fourth difference of logs) between trading partners. Trade intensity is measured as a share of bilateral trade aggregate in total trade aggregates of both countries as indicated by the columns' headers. The instrumental variables in the two-stage OLS include the log of distance, a dummy for geographic adjacency, a dummy for EU-12, the log of aggregate income and the log of income per capita. The country sample includes Switzerland, Norway, United States, Canada, Australia, New Zealand, Turkey, Israel, and the EU countries (only industrial production is available for Greece). Heteroscedasticity-robust t-statistics are in parentheses. Adjusted R^2 and standard errors of regression (SER) are computed using the second-stage residuals.

are insignificant (but positive) for two specifications applying real GDP. By contrast, the coefficients of the bilateral trade intensity are close to zero (indeed, they have wrong signs in several specifications) and insignificant for both indicators of economic activity.[8] The revealed pattern is very robust with respect to the choice of instrumental variables and country sample. This indicates that trade intensities have no direct effect on the correlation of business cycles. Therefore TI_{ij} is omitted from the estimated equations,

$$\text{corr}(Q_i, Q_j) = \alpha + \gamma \log(IIT_{ij}), \tag{4}$$

which are reported in the last columns of the two blocks of table 4.3. The coefficients of intra-industry trade are highly significant in both specifications of (4).

As far as the countries with close trade links have high shares of intra-industry trade, the endogeneity hypothesis of OCA criteria is confirmed by (2) and (4). However, table 4.3 shows that the correlation of business cycles of trading partners is not driven by the simple aggregation of shocks, being transferred between the countries via direct trade channels, as argued by Kenen (2000). By contrast to this demand-driven view of an OCA endogeneity, equations (2) and (4) imply that it is the structure of foreign trade, and not the direct effect of bilateral trade, that induces the synchronization of countries' business cycles.

4.3.4 Sensitivity Analyses

Finally, the previous results are very robust with respect to the inclusion of other variables into (2). In particular, the countries wishing to participate in the EMU have tried to increasingly coordinate their economic, fiscal, and monetary policies during the 1990s. Therefore a dummy for the EU countries that qualified for the EMU in 1999 (i.e., the European Union excluding Denmark, Greece, Sweden and the United Kingdom), denoted by EMU, is included. Because neighboring countries are likely to influence each other much more than other countries, a dummy for geographic adjacency, B, is included. Larger countries may also influence the business cycle of smaller countries. Therefore GDP difference, $|Y_i - Y_j|$, is expected to have a positive sign. An augmented version of equation (2) may then be stated as

$$\text{corr}(Q_i, Q_j) = \alpha + \beta \log(TI_{ij}^T) + \gamma \log(IIT_{ij}) + \delta EMU_{ij}$$
$$+ \lambda B_{ij} + \theta \log|Y_i - Y_j|. \tag{5}$$

Table 4.4
Sensitivity analyses

	Industrial production			Real gross domestic product		
	Exports	Imports	Total	Exports	Imports	Total
Constant	−0.327	0.046	−0.214	0.257	0.610	0.484
	(−1.872)	(0.283)	(−1.060)	(1.131)	(3.361)	(2.127)
Trade intensity	−0.185	−0.062	−0.138	−0.068	0.037	0.002
	(−3.891)	(−1.802)	(−2.796)	(−1.085)	(0.953)	(0.041)
Intra-industry trade	0.415	0.220	0.328	0.245	0.081	0.136
	(5.165)	(3.796)	(4.277)	(2.428)	(1.257)	(1.631)
Dummy:	0.231	0.136	0.192	0.095	0.024	0.046
Geographic	(3.083)	(1.910)	(2.540)	(0.968)	(0.260)	(0.477)
adjacency						
Dummy: EMU-11	0.163	0.154	0.164	0.153	0.139	0.145
	(3.950)	(3.760)	(3.947)	(2.722)	(2.533)	(2.608)
GDP difference	0.020	0.022	0.023	−0.011	−0.015	−0.013
	(1.876)	(1.964)	(2.146)	(−0.910)	(−1.179)	(−0.978)
Number of	253	253	253	231	231	231
observations						
SER	0.269	0.275	0.272	0.325	0.325	0.326
Adjusted R^2	0.204	0.172	0.187	0.103	0.101	0.099

Note: The dependent variable is the index of correlation of de-trended indicator of economic activity (fourth difference of logs) between trading partners. Trade intensity is measured as a share of bilateral trade aggregate in total trade aggregates of both countries as indicated by the columns' headers. Trade intensity and intra-industry trade are instrumented by the log of distance, a dummy for geographic adjacency, a dummy for EU-12, the log of aggregate income and the log of income per capita. The country sample includes Switzerland, Norway, United States, Canada, Australia, New Zealand, Turkey, Israel, and the EU countries (only industrial production is available for Greece). Heteroscedasticity-robust t-statistics are in parentheses. Adjusted R^2 and standard errors of regression (SER) are computed using the second-stage residuals.

These variables exhibit the expected signs in nearly all specifications (see table 4.4). Equation (4) shows that institutional changes matter as well. The eleven countries participating in the EMU have had a correlation of business cycles higher by about 0.15 on average during the 1990s. This is relatively high as compared to the sample's mean of 0.25 (for both indicators of the economic activity). This finding thus indicates a positive relation between the monetary as well as fiscal policy and business cycle correlation, although Clark and van Wincoop (2001) could not attribute it to any particular variable (e.g., the development of interest and exchange rates).

However, the results for other additional variables are not very robust. The inclusion of the additional explanatory variables did not improve the goodness of fit either. Therefore equation (5) will not be applied for the prediction used below. Nevertheless, intra-industry trade is positive and significant in nearly all specifications. By contrast, trade intensities have a negative and significant sign in several augmented specifications.

4.3.5 Indexes of Endogenous Optimum Currency Area

The revealed trend to the unification of business cycles in Europe is not surprising. It fully corresponds to the endogeneity of OCA criteria. Therefore the equations estimated above are used to evaluate the potential correlation of business cycles in Germany and the CEECs, given the current integration of these countries and the current level of intra-industry trade (see table 4.5).[9] However, we have to keep in mind that the sensitivity analysis in the previous section indicates that the specifications are not robust enough to be used for standard forecasts. Nevertheless, the out-of-sample predictions can be alternatively interpreted as indexes of endogenous optimum currency area (EOCA indexes) similar to those constructed by Bayoumi and Eichengreen (1997).

A comparison of tables 4.1 and 4.5 shows that the correlations of business cycles in Germany and in other EU countries were on average slightly higher in the 1990s than those predicted by the EOCA indexes. However, this is not so surprising. First, the European Union has made significant progress in the coordination of the economic policy in the member states. As a result of the introduction of the single market in 1992 and the preparations for EMU in this decade, the similarity of business cycles within the EU countries has likely been higher in the 1990s than in the previous decades. Second, Germany was selected as a proxy for the EU because it is known to dominate the European business cycle (see Bayoumi and Eichengreen 1993).

From the various specifications of equation (1), the correlation of industrial production and GDP in Germany and other EU countries is predicted at about 0.37 for both indicators on average. Actually the corresponding correlations predicted for the CEECs (EOCA indexes) are only slightly lower. The Czech Republic, Poland, and Hungary could potentially reach correlations as high as 0.35 on average in the medium run, while the Slovak and Slovene trade is less oriented toward Germany, resulting in a lower predicted correlation of about 0.24 on average.

Table 4.5
Indexes of endogenous optimum currency area of selected countries with Germany

	Industrial production				Real gross domestic product			
	Exports	Imports	Total	Only IIT	Exports	Imports	Total	Only IIT
Austria	0.41	0.44	0.42	0.43	0.40	0.44	0.42	0.41
Belgium	0.44	0.43	0.43	0.43	0.43	0.43	0.43	0.41
Greece	0.26	0.22	0.24	0.24	0.26	0.22	0.24	0.24
Spain	0.40	0.38	0.38	0.41	0.39	0.38	0.38	0.39
Finland	0.28	0.29	0.29	0.34	0.28	0.29	0.28	0.32
France	0.47	0.46	0.46	0.45	0.46	0.46	0.46	0.43
Ireland	0.22	0.30	0.27	0.28	0.21	0.30	0.26	0.27
Italy	0.44	0.44	0.43	0.39	0.44	0.44	0.43	0.37
Netherlands	0.45	0.46	0.44	0.41	0.44	0.45	0.44	0.39
Portugal	0.30	0.30	0.30	0.36	0.29	0.30	0.30	0.35
Denmark	0.34	0.35	0.34	0.38	0.34	0.35	0.34	0.37
Sweden	0.36	0.34	0.35	0.36	0.35	0.34	0.35	0.35
United Kingdom	0.45	0.42	0.43	0.43	0.44	0.42	0.43	0.41
Czech Republic	0.36	0.36	0.36	0.43	0.35	0.36	0.36	0.41
Estonia	0.06	0.06	0.07	0.16	0.06	0.06	0.06	0.15
Hungary	0.33	0.33	0.33	0.38	0.33	0.33	0.32	0.37
Latvia	0.09	0.09	0.10	0.21	0.08	0.09	0.09	0.21
Lithuania	0.14	0.12	0.14	0.20	0.14	0.12	0.13	0.19
Poland	0.35	0.37	0.36	0.33	0.34	0.37	0.35	0.31
Slovakia	0.24	0.27	0.26	0.34	0.24	0.27	0.25	0.33
Slovenia	0.23	0.23	0.23	0.36	0.22	0.23	0.22	0.35
Bulgaria	0.11	0.12	0.12	0.24	0.10	0.12	0.11	0.23
Croatia	0.20	0.15	0.18	0.26	0.19	0.15	0.17	0.25
Norway	0.28	0.35	0.32	0.30	0.27	0.35	0.31	0.29
Romania	0.20	0.21	0.21	0.24	0.20	0.21	0.20	0.23
Switzerland	0.42	0.40	0.41	0.42	0.41	0.40	0.40	0.41
Turkey	0.33	0.31	0.32	0.24	0.33	0.31	0.32	0.24

Notes: Indexes of endogenous optimum currency area are computed according to particular specification of (1) and (4) as indicated by columns' headers.

Similarly equation (4) is used to compute the EOCA indexes for Germany and selected CEECs, which are even higher than the previous figures (see table 4.5). In fact the Czech Republic is predicted to have a higher correlation of industrial production with Germany than all EU countries except for France, although this prediction still remains below the realized levels in several EU countries. The comparison of predicted, or potential, business cycle correlations for selected western and eastern European countries shows small differences between both regions.

4.4   Conclusions

This chapter examined the endogeneity hypothesis of OCA criteria originally introduced by Frankel and Rose (1997, 1998). On the one hand, this issue has significantly influenced the shape of European monetary integration. On the other hand, there is considerable doubt whether there is a causal relationship between trade and business cycles. For example, Krugman (1993) and Eichengreen (1992) argue that integration is likely to support the specialization of participating countries according to the comparative advantage. Krugman finds empirical support for his arguments in the specialization pattern and business cycles of the US regions. Furthermore Kenen (2000) and Kose and Yi (2001) demonstrate that trade links alone do not ensure the convergence of business cycles, if countries are not sufficiently similar.

This chapter addressed the importance of trade structure for the synchronization of business cycles. In particular, intra-industry trade is shown to induce the convergence of business cycles in OECD countries. Furthermore econometric analyses reveal that there is no direct relation between business cycle and trade intensity if regressions are augmented by additional variables. As a result the endogeneity hypothesis of OCA criteria is confirmed, but with respect to intra-industry trade.

This finding is robust to various definitions of trade intensity and different indicators of economic activity for comparisons of business cycles. The sensitivity analysis reveals that the preparation of the EMU has already had positive effects on the synchronization of business cycles in the participating countries in the 1990s.

Finally this chapter addressed a controversial issue of the current enlargement agenda. The future enlargement of the euro area by Central and Eastern European countries has already initiated an intense discussion. The chapter focused on eight acceding countries in central and eastern Europe. On the one hand, the chapter confirms earlier findings, such as that the CEECs have rapidly converged to the EU countries in terms of business cycles and trade integration. In particular, business cycles in several CEECs (Hungary, Slovenia, and to a lesser extent, Poland) have been strongly correlated with the business cycle in Germany since 1993. In this respect it may seem that Hungary, Slovenia, and possibly Poland, not however the Czech Republic and Slovakia, have made headway toward constituting an optimum currency area with the European Union.

On the other hand, the observation period is still too short to conclude that the business cycles have already become similar. In particular, this period has been characterized by only few supply and demand shocks. Furthermore the business cycle in the Czech Republic is not correlated with that in Germany. As the Czech Republic is quite similar to other CEECs, this indicates that country-specific shocks may still have significant effects on these economies.

To shed more light on this ambiguous result, the chapter computed the potential correlation of the business cycle in Germany and in the CEECs using Frankel and Rose's (1998) relation between the degree of trade integration and the convergence of the business cycles of trading partners. These figures may be alternatively interpreted as EOCA indexes, following Bayoumi and Eichengreen (1997). As a result the high degree of trade between the EU countries and the CEECs represents a sound base for business cycle convergence, and thus for a fulfillment of OCA criteria to a comparable degree as by the current EU members in the medium and long run.

Notes

1. Clark and van Wincoop (2001), Kalemli-Ozcan et al. (2001), and Imbs (1999) show that the similarity of production at a relatively high degree of sectoral aggregation has a positive influence on the correlation of business cycles among countries.

2. See equation (3) and the discussion of Grubel-Lloyd indexes below.

3. Fontagné (1999) discusses the relation between intra-industry trade and the symmetry of shocks in a monetary union.

4. Rose (2000) and Frankel and Rose (2000) document positive effects of currency unions and negative effects of exchange rate volatility on bilateral trade.

5. Austria, Finland, and Sweden, which joined the EU in 1995, are excluded here. Nevertheless, the results are largely robust to the exact definition of the dummy variable.

6. One advantage of using the Grubel-Lloyd indexes is their stability over time. For example, Grubel and Lloyd (1975) compute intra-industry trade for a number of countries over a relatively longer period of time. There is a remarkable stability of the ranking of countries by years.

7. The Theil measure of multicolinearity is close to or below 0.1 for all specifications of (2). This indicates that both explanatory variables are not multicolinear. The Theil measure of multicolinearity is defined as the difference between R^2 of the particular specifications of (2) and the incremental contributions to this explanatory power by IT_{ij} and IIT_{ij}, which are computed using the R^2 value for the corresponding specifications of (1) and (4), that is, as $R^2_{(2)} - (R^2_{(2)} - R^2_{(1)}) - (R^2_{(2)} - R^2_{(4)})$. This indicator is zero if all explanatory variables are orthogonal (e.g., see Judge et al. 1988).

8. This result is similar to the finding by Imbs (1999) that the inclusion of additional variables lowers the size of trade integration effects on the correlation of business cycles.

9. These technical assumptions may be viewed as rather conservative because trade with the European Union and the importance of intra-industry trade is likely to increase during the accession to the Union and to the EMU.

References

Bayoumi, T., and B. Eichengreen. 1993. Shocking aspects of European Monetary Unification. In F. Torres and F. Giavazzi, eds., *Growth and Adjustment in the European Monetary Union*. Cambridge: Cambridge University Press, pp. 193–230.

Bayoumi, T., and B. Eichengreen. 1997. Ever closer to heaven? An optimum-currency area index for European countries. *European Economic Review* 41 (3–5): 761–70.

Boone, L., and M. Maurel. 1999. An optimal currency area perspective of the EU enlargement to the CEECs. Discussion Paper 2119. CEPR London.

Buiter, W. H., and C. Grafe. 2002. Central banking and the choice of currency regime in accession countries. Discussion Paper 3184, CEPR London.

Clark, T. E., and E. van Wincoop. 2001. Borders and business cycles. *Journal of International Economics* 55 (1): 59–85.

De Grauwe, 2003. *Economics of Monetary Union*, 5th ed. Oxford: Oxford University Press.

Eichengreen, B. 1992. Should the Maastricht Treaty be saved? Princeton Studies in International Finance 74. International Finance Section, Department of Economics, Princeton University.

Fatás, A. 1997. EMU: Countries or regions? *European Economic Review* 41 (3–5): 753–60.

Fidrmuc, J. 2004. The endogeneity of the optimum currency area criteria, intra-industry trade, and EMU enlargement. *Contemporary Economic Policy* 22 (1): 1–12.

Fidrmuc, J. 2005. Trade structure during accession to the EU. *Post-Communist Economies* 17 (2): 225–34.

Fidrmuc, J., and I. Korhonen. 2003. Similarity of supply and demand shocks between the euro area and the CEECs. *Economic Systems* 27 (3): 373–34.

Fontagné, L. 1999. Endogenous symmetry of shocks in a monetary union. *Open Economies Review* 10 (3): 263–87.

Frankel, J. A., and A. K. Rose. 1997. Is EMU more justifiable ex post than ex ante? *European Economic Review* 41 (3–5): 753–60.

Frankel, J. A., and A. K. Rose. 1998. The endogeneity of the optimum currency area criteria. *Economic Journal* 108 (449): 1009–25.

Frankel, J. A., and A. K. Rose. 2000. Estimating the effect of currency unions on trade and output. Working Paper 7857, NBER.

Grubel, H. G., and P. J. Lloyd. 1975. *Intra-industry Trade: The Theory and Measurement of International Trade in Differentiated Products.* New York: Wiley.

Helpman, E. 1987. Imperfect competition and international trade: Evidence from fourteen industrial countries. *Journal of Japanese and International Economies* 1 (1): 62–81.

Hochreiter, E., and G. Winckler. 1995. The advantages of tying Austria's hands: The success of the hard currency strategy. *European Journal of Political Economy* 11 (1): 83–111.

Hughes Hallett, A., and L. Piscitelli. 2001. The endogenous optimal currency area hypothesis: Will a single currency induce convergence in Europe? Paper Presented at the Royal Economic Society Annual Conference. University of Durham, April 9–11.

Hummels, D., and J. Levinsohn. 1995. Monopolistic competition and international trade: Reconsidering the evidence. *Quarterly Journal of Economics* 110 (3): 799–836.

Imbs, J. 1999. Co-fluctuations. Discussion Paper 2267. CEPR London.

Judge, G., R. C. Hill, W. E. Griffiths, H. Lütkepohl, and T.-C. Lee. 1988. *Introduction to the Theory of Econometrics.* New York: Wiley.

Kalemli-Ozcan, S., B. E. Sørensen, and O. Yosha. 2001. Economic integration industrial specialization, and the asymmetry of macroeconomic fluctuations. *Journal of International Economics* 55 (1): 107–37.

Kenen, P. B. 1969. The theory of optimum currency areas: An eclectic view. In R. A. Mundell and A. K. Swoboda, eds., *Monetary Problems of the International Economy.* Chicago: University of Chicago Press.

Kenen, P. B. 2000. Currency areas, policy domains, and the institutionalization of fixed exchange rates. Discussion Paper 467. London School of Economics, Centre for Economic Performance, London.

Kopits, G. 1999. Implications of EMU for exchange rate policy in Central and Eastern Europe. Working Paper 99/9. IMF, Washington.

Korhonen, I. 2003. Some empirical tests on the integration of economic activity between the euro area and the accession countries: A note. *Economics of Transition* 11 (1): 1–20.

Kose, M. A., and K.-M. Yi. 2001. International trade and business cycles: Is vertical specialization the missing link? *American Economic Review* 91 (2): 371–75.

Kose, M. A., E. S. Prasad, and M. E. Terrones. 2003. How does globalization affect the synchronization of business cycles? *American Economic Review*, forthcoming.

Krugman, P. R. 1993. Lessons of Massachusetts for EMU. In F. Torres and F. Giavazzi, eds., *Adjustment and Growth in the European Monetary Union*. Cambridge: Cambridge University Press and CEPR, pp. 241–61.

Mundell, R. A. 1961. A theory of optimum currency areas. *American Economic Review* 51: 657–65.

McKinnon, R. I. 1963. Optimum currency areas. *American Economic Review* 53: 717–25.

Rose, A. K. 2000. One money, one market: Estimating the effect of common currencies on trade. *Economic Policy: A European Forum* (April): 7–45.

5 Exchange Rate Volatility and the Decline of Employment Growth in the CEE Economies

Ansgar Belke and Ralph Setzer

5.1 Introduction

The transition process from a centrally planned economy to a market economy in Central and Eastern Europe has been accompanied by a large decline in employment. While relative improvements have been recorded in some countries for the last two years, unemployment reduction has still been modest in relation to expectations. At the beginning of the transition process it was widely assumed that the sharp immediate increase in open unemployment would be of a temporary nature only. Most analysts expected that unemployment would soon stop rising and with economic recovery unemployment would level off at a relatively low level (Nesporova 2002). However, employment performance did not improve a great deal in most central and eastern European countries (CEECs in the following), though this was partly due to unfavorable developments in world markets.

This chapter investigates to what extent high exchange rate variability can be made responsible for the negative developments in CEEC labor markets. Although it is widely believed that exchange rate variability reduces welfare, it is difficult to prove this in a formal setting. The problem is that appreciations or depreciations of the exchange rate in response to economic shocks (e.g., preference or technology shocks) generally are welfare improving relative to less exchange rate volatility in face of the same shock. Thus exchange rate swings can smooth out abrupt changes in the terms of trade (Neumeyer 1998). However, the part of exchange rate volatility that is not caused by movements of fundamentals can do harm to an economy in several ways. Previous studies have shown that intra-European exchange rate variability has lowered the volume of trade (see, above all, the impact of exchange rate variability on trade, e.g., the early studies by De

Grauwe 1987 and Sapir and Sekkat 1990), and has increased unemployment and reduced employment opportunities, a finding that had
an important bearing on the evaluation of costs and benefits of EMU
(e.g., see Belke and Gros 2001). More recently Belke and Gros (2002a)
have shown in the context of a project for the European Commission
that exchange rate variability might also have significant negative
effects on labor markets at the global level. Their results indicate that
transatlantic exchange rate variability does have a significant negative
impact on labor markets in the European Union, and possibly also in
the United States. The authors argue that volatility matters because
employment and investment decisions are characterized by some degree of irreversibility in the presence of structural rigidities. Such decisions tend to be discouraged by exchange rate variability, as can be
shown in a variety of economic models. A third category of studies is
related to the emerging markets. Using a dataset for the period 1970 to
2001, Belke and Gros (2002) have investigated the Mercosur countries
Argentina, Brazil, Paraguay, and Uruguay. Their results suggest that
exchange rate and interest rate variability have a significant impact on
investment and employment in these countries. Moreover they find
that economies with relatively closer ties to the United States such as
Brazil show a stronger impact of dollar exchange rate variability.

If similar results can be found for the currencies of the central and
eastern European countries, they warrant a new look at the costs and
benefits of an early adoption of the euro compared with those of introducing the euro at a later stage. The main purpose of this chapter is
thus to provide a sound basis for an (indirect) evaluation of the costs
of the present exchange rate relations of CEEC currencies vis-à-vis
the euro and of the benefits of individual time paths of exchange rate
policies for selected CEECs on their way toward full membership in
the EMU. It is argued that early entry strategies are motivated with an
eye to the benefits resulting from suppressed exchange rate volatility.

The rest of the chapter proceeds as follows: In section 5.2 we derive
a theoretical model to illustrate the negative relationship between exchange rate volatility and employment growth. Section 5.3 defines our
measure of exchange rate variability. Section 5.4 presents and comments the regression results. Here we also check for robustness of
our results with respect to the exclusion of outlier countries with high
exchange rate volatilities (Bulgaria and Romania) and to the use of an
alternative measure of the labor market stance, namely the unemployment rate. Section 5.5 concludes with a discussion of the implications

of our results for the design of future CEEC monetary relations with the eurozone.

5.2   Modeling the Impact of Exchange Rate Volatility on Labor Markets

5.2.1   Motivation

The conventional view of EMU enlargement is to converge first, and durably, and then join. For the eight CEE countries that joined the European Union in May 2004 the time frame for EMU enlargement is thus quite clear: EU admission also formally implies membership in EMU. Initially, however, the new EU members have a right of derogation concerning the introduction of the euro. When can and should derogation be lifted, that is, when should the euro be introduced in these countries? And how can it be ensured that the transition to the euro is smooth? For Estonia, Lithuania, and Slovenia the earliest possible date of entry into the eurozone is 2006, since these countries have started to spend the prescribed two years in the ERM2 system as of the end of June 2004. By contrast, the larger countries Czech Republic, Hungary, and Poland are more skeptical about a rapid adoption of the euro.

Choosing an appropriate exchange rate regime has been a decisive issue for the CEECs since the beginning of the transition process. At the beginning of the 1990s, the main concern of economic policy was to reduce inflation. Consequently many countries sought to use the exchange rate as a nominal anchor by curbing inflation expectations. When having achieved a more advanced stage of transformation, a number of countries moved to more flexible exchange rate arrangements. Today a wide spectrum of different exchange rate regimes continues to coexist—ranging from truly fixed arrangements like the currency board systems in Bulgaria, Estonia, and Lithuania to currency baskets, wide bands, or managed floats in Latvia, Hungary, Slovakia, Slovenia, and Romania to freely floating rates in Poland and Czech Republic where the authorities allow the exchange rate to be determined by market forces. However, the move to flexible exchange rates does not mean a position of *benign neglect* toward the exchange rate. Schnabl (2004) shows that the de facto exchange rate behavior of those exchange rate regimes publicly declared as floating do not always correspond with the announcements. Despite claiming to float the monetary authorities actively intervene in the foreign exchange rate market to increase smoothness of the exchange rate and to avoid serious misalignments.

Similar to other emerging market economies, the reasons for the fear of large exchange rate swings are multiple (Calvo and Reinhart 2000). The traditional channel has been that exchange rate variability might hamper external trade. Recent research by Rose (2000) suggests that two economies that share the same currency trade three times as much than a gravity model of international trade would suggest due to a reduction in uncertainty and transaction costs. Not surprisingly, these strong results have attracted some critique. For instance, Nitsch (2002) has questioned the general applicability of the results by Rose (2000) due to his focus on small and poor countries. Still subsequent contributions (e.g., see Flandreau and Maurel 2001; Engel and Rose 2002; Frankel and Rose 2002) have provided further extensions and have reinforced the argument that lower exchange rate variability reduces uncertainty and risk premia in developing countries, thereby encouraging greater cross-border trade.

In principal, the strong negative impact of exchange rate volatility on foreign trade in emerging economies can be explained by different patterns of trade invoicing. Following McKinnon (1999), primary commodities are primarily dollar invoiced. Since the emerging market economies exports generally have a high primary commodity content, domestic currency prices of their exports will vary proportionally to the exchange rate. Thus large swings in the exchange rate should have a significant impact on foreign trade of these countries, making them more vulnerable to high exchange rate volatility.

Another feature why emerging market economies are on average more intolerant to large exchange rate fluctuations is due to the higher openness of these countries. When imports make up a large share of the domestic consumption basket, the pass-through from exchange rate swings to inflation is much higher. This happens through two channels. First, a devaluation raises the domestic currency price of imported products (which enter the consumer price index). Second, a fall in the value of the domestic currency increases the international price competitiveness of the tradable sector and causes an expenditure switch toward domestic goods, thereby affecting domestic aggregate demand and inflation (Chang and Velasco 2000, p. 74). In most CEECs external trade (imports and exports) accounts for above one-third of GDP; in countries such as Slovenia (67 percent) or Estonia (58 percent) the degree of openness even exceeds 50 percent of GDP. Only Bulgaria

(23 percent), Romania (15 percent), and, due to its larger size, Poland (26 percent) have a somewhat smaller openness index (Buiter and Grafe 2002). Boreiko (2002) demonstrates the importance of trade with EMU countries for the CEECs, relating imports and exports to the eurozone to total imports and exports in 1993 to 2000. His tables show clearly that most of the CEECs have already reached a high share of trade with the eurozone. In some cases—such as Hungary (0.70), Poland (0.67), Slovenia (0.67), and Czech Republic (0.66)—the shares are close to the average of EMU intra-trade (around 0.67 in 1999–2000; see also Belke and Hebler 2002a). The realizations for the remaining CEE countries are lower (Romania: 0.63; Estonia: 0.59; Slovak Republic: 0.54; Latvia: 0.52; Bulgaria: 0.50; Lithuania: 0.46).[1] These differences in openness should be kept in mind for the empirical analysis because they should influence the impact of exchange rate variability on the labor markets in the respective country.

However, studies for Latin America indicate that in emerging markets the analysis of the costs and benefits of regional exchange rate arrangements should not be confined to the impact of stable exchange rates on trade but should be made in terms of overall macroeconomic stability. Capital markets may be an additional source of disturbance. While in developed countries, firms can hedge their exchange rate exposure through a variety of financial instruments, futures markets in transition economies are still relatively illiquid, and tools for hedging the exchange rate risk over a longer time period are simply not available in these countries. As a consequence the idiosyncratic exchange rate risk is likely to be priced in higher interest rates. Thus all exchange rate regimes with a devaluation option will increase the cost of capital and lead to a loss of competitiveness. By contrast, a system where the exchange rate is irrevocably fixed may well lead to lower interest rates and more predictable cost structures (Dornbusch 2001).

How can one illustrate the transmission channel that could account for a negative relationship between exchange rate variability and labor market performance? In the following section we develop a full-fledged model to illustrate a mechanism that explains a negative relationship between exchange rate uncertainty and *job creation*.[2] This model has originally been based on the idea that uncertainty of future earnings raises the "option value of waiting" with decisions which concern *investment projects* in general (Dixit 1989; Belke and Gros 2001). The model, which heavily relies on Belke and Kaas (2002), does not pretend to be close to reality. It is designed to convey the basic idea in a simple way. Moreover our intention is to present a model that allows us to ask whether even a *temporary, short-run* increase in uncertainty can have a strong and lasting impact on employment, and in how far this impact depends on labor market parameters.

5.2.2   Scenario A: Modeling with Binding Contracts

Consider a setup in which there are *three periods* and a *single firm* active in an export-oriented industry that decides on job creation. During the first two periods (called 0 and 1) the firm can open a job, hire a worker, and produce output that is sold in a foreign market in the subsequent periods. If the job is created during period 0, the worker is hired for two periods (0 and 1) to produce output to be sold in periods 1 and 2. If the job is created in period 1, the worker is hired only for period 1 and output is sold in period 2.

To create a job, the firm pays a start-up cost c, which reflects the cost of hiring, training, and provision of job-specific capital. After a job is created, a worker is hired and is paid a wage w above the worker's fallback (or reservation) wage $\underline{w}$ during every period of employment. The fallback wage measures (besides disutility of work) all opportunity income that the worker has to give up by accepting the job. In particular, it includes unemployment benefits, but it might also be positively related to a collective wage set by a trade union or to a minimum wage, both of which should raise the worker's fallback position. In general, we would argue that the fallback wage should be higher in countries that are characterized by generous unemployment benefit systems, by strong trade unions, or by minimum wage legislation.

In every period in which the worker is employed, he produces output to be sold in the following period in a foreign market at domestic price p, which has a certain component p^* (the foreign price) plus a stochastic component e (the exchange rate). We assume that the foreign price is fixed ("pricing to market"), and that the exchange rate follows a random walk. In period 1, the exchange rate e_1 is uniformly distributed between $-\sigma_1$ and $+\sigma_1$. The exchange rate in period 2, e_2, is uniformly distributed between $e_1 - \sigma_2$ and $e_1 + \sigma_2$. An increase in σ_i means an increase in uncertainty, or an increase in the mean preserving spread in period $i = 1, 2$ (σ_i is proportional to the standard deviation of e_i). Uncertainty can be temporary (e.g., if $\sigma_1 > 0$ and $\sigma_2 = 0$) or persistent (if also $\sigma_2 > 0$). As will become apparent soon, however, the variability of the exchange rate during the second period has no influence on the result.

The wage rate w for the job is determined by the (generalized) Nash bargaining solution that maximizes a weighted product of the worker's and the firm's expected net return from the job. We assume that both the firm and the worker are risk-neutral. This assumption implies that risk-sharing issues are of no importance for our analysis. Thus we may assume realistically (but without loss of generality) that the worker and the firm bargain about a fixed wage rate w (which is independent of realizations of the exchange rate) when the worker is hired, so that *the firm bears all the exchange rate risk*. A wage contract that shifts some exchange rate risk to the worker will leave the (unconditional) expected net returns unaffected and therefore have no effect on the job creation decision. Of course, if the firm were risk-averse, the assumption that the firm bears all exchange rate risk would make a postponement of job creation in the presence of uncertainty even more likely.

Consider first the wage bargaining problem for a job created in *period 0*, in which case the worker is hired for two periods. After the job is created (and the job creation cost is sunk), the (unconditional) *expected gross surplus* of this job is equal to $E_0(S_0) = 2p^* - 2\underline{w} = 2\pi$, where $\pi = p^* - \underline{w}$ denotes the expected return of a *filled* job per period (we abstract from discounting). Denoting the bargaining power of the worker by $0 < \beta < 1$, the *firm's net return* from the job created in period 0 is[3]

$$E_0(\Pi_0) = (1 - \beta)E_0(S_0) - c = 2(1 - \beta)\pi - c, \qquad (1)$$

where $E_0(\Pi_0)$ denotes the expected net return and $E_0(S_0)$ the expected gross surplus for a project undertaken in period 0.

In order to make the problem nontrivial, we assume that the expected return from job creation in period 0 is positive, meaning $2(1 - \beta)\pi - c > 0$. Implicit in our model is the assumption that the firm and the worker sign a *binding employment contract for two periods* (0 and 1). Hence job termination is not an option in case the exchange rate turns out to be unfavorable. In period 1 (after realization of the exchange rate) the conditional expected gross surplus from job continuation is $E_1(S_1) = \pi + e_1$, which may be negative if the exchange rate falls below $-\pi < 0$.

If the firm waits until *period 1*, it keeps the option of whether or not to open a job. It will create a job only if the exchange rate realized during period 1 (and so expected for period 2) is above a certain threshold level, or barrier, denoted by b. Given that employment in period 1

yields a return in period 2 only, this profitability barrier is defined by
the condition that the (conditional) expected net return to the firm is
zero:

$$(1 - \beta)(p^* + b - \underline{w}) - c = 0$$

or

$$b = \frac{c}{1 - \beta} + \underline{w} - p^* = \frac{c}{1 - \beta} - \pi. \tag{2}$$

Whenever $e_1 \geq b$, the firm creates a job in period 1, and the conditional expected net return to the firm is $E_1(\Pi_1) = (1 - \beta)(\pi + e_1) -
c \geq 0$. Whenever $e_1 < b$, the firm does not create a job in period 1,
and its return is zero. Hence, whenever both events occur with pos-
itive probabilities (i.e., whenever $\sigma_1 > b > -\sigma_1$),[4] the unconditional expected return of waiting in period 0 is given by

$$E_0(\Pi_1) = \left(\frac{\sigma_1 + b}{2\sigma_1}\right) 0 + \left(\frac{\sigma_1 - b}{2\sigma_1}\right) \left[(1 - \beta)\left(\pi + \frac{\sigma_1 + b}{2}\right) - c\right], \tag{3}$$

where the first element is the probability that it will not be worthwhile
to open a job (in this case the return is zero). The second term represents the product of the probability that it will be worthwhile to open
the job (because the exchange rate is above the barrier) and the average
expected value of the net return to the firm under this outcome. Given
condition (2) this can be rewritten as

$$E_0(\Pi_1) = \frac{(1 - \beta)(\sigma_1 - b)^2}{4\sigma_1}. \tag{4}$$

This is the key result since it implies that an increase in uncertainty
increases the value of waiting, given that equation (4) is an increasing
function of σ_1.[5] As σ_1 increases, it becomes more likely that it is worthwhile to wait until more information is available about the expected return during period 2. The option not to open the job becomes more
valuable with more uncertainty. The higher the variance the higher the
potential losses the firm can avoid and the higher the potential for a
very favorable realization of the exchange rate, with consequently
very high profits. It is clear from (1) and (4) that the firm prefers to
wait if and only if

$$\frac{(1 - \beta)(\sigma_1 - b)^2}{4\sigma_1} > 2(1 - \beta)\pi - c. \tag{5}$$

As the left-hand side is increasing in σ_1, the firm delays job creation if exchange rate uncertainty is large enough. The critical value at which (5) is satisfied with equality can be solved as[6]

$$\sigma_1^* = 3\pi - \frac{c}{1-\beta} + 2\sqrt{\pi\left(\frac{2\pi - c}{1 - \beta}\right)}. \tag{6}$$

Whenever $\sigma_1 > \sigma_1^*$, firms decide to postpone job creation in period 0. Since σ_1^* is increasing in π (and thereby decreasing in the fallback wage $\underline{w}$), decreasing in the cost of job creation c and decreasing in the worker's bargaining power β, we conclude that a strong position of workers in the wage bargain (reflected in a high fallback wage or in the bargaining power parameter) and higher costs of hiring raise the option value of waiting and make a postponement of job creation more likely. Thus *the adverse impact of exchange rate uncertainty on job creation and employment should be stronger if the labor market is characterized by generous unemployment benefit systems, powerful trade unions, minimum wage restrictions, or large hiring costs.* The adverse employment effects of these features have been confirmed empirically in various studies, and there are many other theoretical mechanisms to explain them (e.g., see Nickell 1997). What our simple model shows is that these features also *reinforce* the negative employment effects of contemporaneous and short spikes of exchange rate uncertainty. In sum, we retain *two conclusions* from the model. First, even a *temporary* spike in exchange rate variability can induce firms to wait with their creation of jobs (for exactly this reason the level of the exchange rate at the same time loses explanatory power). Second, the relationship between exchange rate variability and employment should be particularly strong if the labor market is characterized by rigidities that improve the bargaining position of workers. A stronger fallback position of workers raises the contract wage, lowers the net returns to firms, and induces firms to delay job creation in the face of uncertainty.

5.2.3   Scenario B: Modeling without Binding Contracts

Our argument in section 5.2.2 rests on the assumption that workers cannot be fired immediately if the exchange rate turns out to be unfavorable. Hence sunk wage payments are associated with the decision to hire a worker. These sunk costs and, consequently, the impact of uncertainty on job creation become more important if there are high firing costs. However, as we would, even if there are no firing costs and if workers can be laid off at any point in time, exchange rate uncertainty should have a direct impact on job destruction. To illustrate this proposition, consider the scenario of a labor market in which the firm and the worker can sign a contract only for one period and keep the option to terminate the work relationship whenever it becomes unprofitable. In period 1 the conditionally expected surplus of job continuation is $\pi + e_1$, which is positive whenever $e_1 > -\pi$. Hence, whenever uncertainty is large enough ($\sigma_1 > \pi$), there is job destruction in period 1 with probability $(\sigma_1 - \pi)/2\sigma_1$. The (unconditional) expected net return to the firm from a job created in period 0 (and with the option of destruction in period 1) is therefore

$$E_0(\Pi_0) = [(1 - \beta)\pi - c] + \left(\frac{\sigma_1 - \pi}{2\sigma_1}\right)0 + \left(\frac{\sigma_1 + \pi}{2\sigma_1}\right)(1 - \beta)\left(\pi + \frac{\sigma_1 - \pi}{2}\right),$$

(7)

where the first term is the expected return from the job in period 1, whereas the second and third terms represent the expected surplus from the job in period 2 (after destruction or after continuation in period 1) under the assumption $\sigma_1 > \pi$. If $\sigma_1 < \pi$, the job would never be destroyed, and the expected net return is, as before, $2(1 - \beta)\pi - c$. Hence, after rearranging (7), the expected net return from a job created in period 0 can be written as

$$E_0(\Pi_0) = \begin{cases} 2(1 - \beta)\pi - c, & \text{if } \sigma_1 < \pi, \\ (1 - \beta)(\pi + (\sigma_1 + \pi)^2/(4\sigma_1)) - c, & \text{if } \sigma_1 \geq \pi. \end{cases}$$

(8)

On the other hand, if the firm waits until period 1, the (unconditional) expected net return is, as in section 5.2.2,

$$E_0(\Pi_1) = \begin{cases} \max(0, (1 - \beta)\pi - c), & \text{if } \sigma_1 < |\pi - c/(1 - \beta)|, \\ (1 - \beta)(\sigma_1 + \pi - c/(1 - \beta))^2/(4\sigma_1), & \text{if } \sigma_1 \geq |\pi - c/(1 - \beta)|. \end{cases}$$

(9)

It is now easy to see that the firm never delays job creation. First, if $\sigma_1 \leq |\pi - c/(1 - \beta)| < \pi$, the firm never destroys a job in period 1, so we have $E_0(\Pi_0) > E_0(\Pi_1)$. Second, if $\sigma_1 \geq \pi$, the condition $E_0(\Pi_0) > E_0(\Pi_1)$ means that

$$4\sigma_1\left(\pi - \frac{c}{1 - \beta}\right) + (\sigma_1 + \pi)^2 > \left(\sigma_1 + \pi - \frac{c}{1 - \beta}\right)^2,$$

(10)

which turns out to be equivalent to $(2(1 - \beta)\pi - c)(c/(1 - \beta) + 2\sigma_1) > 0$ and which is satisfied because of our assumption $2(1 - \beta)\pi - c > 0$.

Hence the firm does not delay job creation also in this case. Finally, if $|\pi - c/(1 - \beta)| < \sigma_1 < \pi$, the condition $E_0(\Pi_0) > E_0(\Pi_1)$ means that

$$4\sigma_1(2(1 - \beta)\pi - c) - (1 - \beta)\left(\sigma_1 + \pi - \frac{c}{1 - \beta}\right)^2 > 0. \tag{11}$$

But because this inequality is satisfied at the boundaries $\sigma_1 = \pi$ and $\sigma_1 = |\pi - c/(1 - \beta)|$ and because the left-hand side is a concave function of σ_1, the inequality is also satisfied in the interval $|\pi - c/(1 - \beta)| < \sigma_1 < \pi$. Hence firms always prefer to create a job in period zero, so exchange rate uncertainty has no impact on job creation.

However, since there is job destruction with probability $(\sigma_1 - \pi)/(2\sigma_1)$ (whenever $\sigma_1 > \pi$), *the probability of job destruction is increasing in uncertainty.* Hence there is also a negative impact of exchange rate uncertainty on employment in this case. Moreover this effect is more pronounced if the worker's fallback wage is higher (if π is smaller). Therefore the basic conclusions of our model remain valid. Thus, perhaps against common intuition (but as an additional interesting innovation here), we can show that uncertainty does not lead to delays but to spurts in the decision to fire. In contrast to the usual models of investment under uncertainty of the Dixit-Pindyck style, the impacts of increased uncertainty on employment are unambiguously negative and can be directly tested empirically.

5.2.4 Does the Model Apply to the CEEC Labor Markets?

According to our model the relationship between exchange rate variability and employment is particularly strong if the labor market is characterized by rigidities that, for example, improve the bargaining position of workers. Labor markets of most current EU members are widely considered to be rigid enough to function by the mechanism explained in the model. Where do the new EU member countries stand in this respect?

Riboud, Sánchez-Páramo, and Silva-Jáuregui (2002) have assessed the flexibility of labor market institutions in six CEE countries: the Czech Republic, Estonia, Hungary, Poland, Slovakia, and Slovenia.[7] According to their findings based on large-scale indicators for regular contracts, temporary contracts, and collective dismissals, these countries range somewhere *in the middle of the flexibility scale* compared to the OECD economies. They do not reach the levels of flexibility of the United Kingdom, Ireland, or Denmark but exhibit much greater flexibility than the Club Med countries, France and Germany.[8] As regards

Table 5.1
Labor market flexibility in the CEECs: How large are the costs of job creation and the fall-back wage?

	Employment protection legislation[c]				Unemployment insurance		Taxes	
	Regular employment	Temporary employment	Collective dismissals	EPL strictness[d]	Benefit replacement ratio	Benefit duration (months)	Payroll tax rate (%)	Total tax rate (%)
Czech Republic	2.8	0.5	4.3	2.1	50	6	47.5	73.4
Estonia	3.1	1.4	4.1	2.6	10	3–6	33.0	63.3
Hungary	2.1	0.6	3.4	1.7	64	12	44.0	81.5
Poland	2.2	1	3.9	2	40	12–24	48.2	80.0
Slovakia	2.6	1.4	4.4	2.4	60	6–12	50.0	81.0
Slovenia[a]	3.4 (2.9)	2.4 (0.6)	4.8 (4.9)	3.5 (2.3)	63	3–24	38.0	69.1
CEEC average	2.7	1.2	4.1	2.4	48		43.4	74.7
EU average[b]	2.4	2.1	3.2	2.4	60		23.5	53.0
OECD average	2.0	1.7	2.9	2.0	58		19.5	45.4

Source: Hobza (2002) and Riboud et al. (2002).
a. Numbers in brackets refer to the new labor code if approved.
b. EU average without Luxembourg and Greece.
c. 1: minimum protection; 6: maximum protection.

the unemployment insurance systems, the CEECs seem to be less generous than the OECD or EU countries. They also spend less on both passive and active employment policies. In terms of the role of the unions in the wage negotiation process, the new member countries range somewhere in the middle of the OECD countries. They have, however, extremely high payroll and other taxes, which exceed even the highest levels in the European Union. Even more important in our context is the fact that they have strong employment protection legislation.

These results are consistent with findings by Belke and Hebler (2002) and Cazes (2002) who state that Central European countries have adopted labor market institutions, institutional arrangements, and legal frameworks that share many features with present EU member countries. This trend clearly increases job creation costs. It is further supported by the fact that the CEECs are required, prior to their entry

Passive policies		Active policies		Unions			
Percent of GDP	Spending per unemployed	Percent of GDP	Spendng per unemployed	Union density (%)[e]	Union coverage index[f]	Coordination unions	Coordination employers
0.31	0.04	0.19	0.02	42.8	2	1	1
0.08	0.01	0.08	0.01	36.1	2	2	1
0.56	0.06	0.40	0.04	60.0	3	1	2
1.71	0.12	0.49	0.03	33.8	3	2	1
0.54	0.05	0.56	0.05	61.7	3	2	2
0.89	0.11	0.83	0.11	60.0	3	3	3
0.68	0.06	0.42	0.04	49.0			
1.73	0.26	1.16	0.16	44.4			
1.43	0.23	0.92	0.14	39.6			

d. Weighted average of the first three columns.
e. Percentage of salaried workers that belong to a union.
f. 1: less than 25 percent of salaried workers are covered by collective agreements; 2: between 26 and 69 percent are covered; 3: 70 percent or more are covered.

into the European Union, to align their legislation with the *acquis communautaire*, which includes a number of provisions regarding labor market regulations. This kind of legislation has favored employment protection while taxing employers heavily. Hence the transmission channel from exchange rate variability to labor market performance that we have described seems to be relevant in the case of the CEECs as well.

The next step is to address whether different measures of exchange rate volatility—both nominal and real effective volatility vis-à-vis the 31 most important trade partners and the bilateral volatility of the nominal and real euro exchange rate—have any ability to explain the residuals of employment regressions for CEEC economies. So far the literature examining the link between exchange rate variability and labor market performance in emerging markets is rather slim. Hence we begin by presenting and commenting on some initial results.

5.3   Data and Definitions

In order to test empirically for the conjectured impact of exchange rate variability on labor-market performance, we employ a panel of ten Central and Eastern European countries, namely Bulgaria (BG), Czech Republic (CZ), Estonia (EE), Hungary (HU), Latvia (LV), Lithuania (LT), Poland (PL), Romania (RO), Slovak Republic (SK), and Slovenia (SL).

The nominal variability of the currency of each of the ten CEE countries under consideration is measured by taking for each year the standard deviation of the twelve month-to-month changes in the logarithm of its nominal exchange rate against the currencies of their main trade partner countries. The construction of the real variability variable follows an analogous scheme. The nominal exchange rates are deflated with the CPI. The standard deviations based on bilateral rates are then aggregated in one composite measure of exchange rate variability (denoted by VOL below) using the weights that approximate the importance of these currencies in trade with the 31 most important trade partners for the period 1993 to 2002. The average trade weight of CEEC X with country Y (Y = Austria, Belgium, Denmark, Finland, France, Germany, Greece, Ireland, Italy, Netherlands, Portugal, Spain, Sweden, United Kingdom, Bulgaria, Czech Republic, Estonia, Hungary, Latvia, Lithuania, Poland, Romania, Slovakia, Slovenia, Croatia, Belarus, Russia, Ukraine, Switzerland, United States, and Turkey) is calculated as 100 times the exports to country Y plus imports from country Y divided by total exports to the "world" plus total imports from the "world." In our definition, the aggregate "world" corresponds to the sum of countries Y.[9] We did not use the annually changing trade weights because our volatility measure would then change to the same degree as the change in trade pattern varies.

Based on the monthly CPI series for the 30 most important trade partners, the nominal bilateral exchange rates vis-à-vis the US dollar of these countries and the respective trade weights, we calculated for every country the following volatilities of the exchange rate:

• Nominal bilateral exchange rate volatility

• Real bilateral exchange rate volatility

• Effective volatilities of the nominal exchange rate (weighted bilateral volatilities)

• Effective volatilities of the real exchange rate (weighted bilateral volatilities)[10]

It should be emphasized that the first two series refer to the exchange rate volatility "vis-à-vis the euro." This is calculated as the volatility vis-à-vis the DM from 1992:01 until 1998:12, and vis-à-vis the euro from 1999:01. We prefer to aggregate the individual standard deviations instead of using a standard deviation of an average or effective exchange rate because there is extensive evidence that CEEC exporters have priced to market. With an average exchange rate the zloty, for example, could remain constant because the depreciation against the euro would compensate the appreciation against the Bulgarian lewa. Polish firms would not necessarily be indifferent between a situation in which the average exchange rate is constant because the zloty/euro and the zloty/lewa are constant, and another in which the swings in these two bilateral rates just happen to cancel each other out.

We use monthly exchange rates to calculate volatility instead of daily volatility to ensure consistency throughout our entire sample period. Another reason to prefer this measure to shorter term alternatives (e.g., daily variability) was that while the latter might be important for financial actors, they are less relevant for export or employment decisions. The drawback of monthly exchange rates is that we had to use annual data to have a meaningful measure of variability. So we are left with only nine observations for each country.[11]

We use actual as opposed to unanticipated rates, since in order to be consistent with our model described in section 5.2, we assume that the exchange rate follows a random walk. Thus *actual* and unanticipated exchange rate changes should be the same. We feel justified to make this assumption because extensive research based on work by Meese and Rogoff (1983) and Meese (1990) has shown that the random walk model outperforms other standard exchange rate models in out-of-sample forecasting. This still holds even when seemingly relevant economic variables are included.

Our sample covers the period 1992 to 2001 in order to exploit all reliable data information. However, in view of the financial turmoil in the first years of transition, our estimations mostly exclude the year 1992. The average exchange rate variability for each of the ten CEECs under investigation is plotted in figure 5.1 (percentage per month). Peaks occur usually in the year 1998, with the two non–EU acceding countries, Bulgaria and Romania, as clear outliers with high double-digit

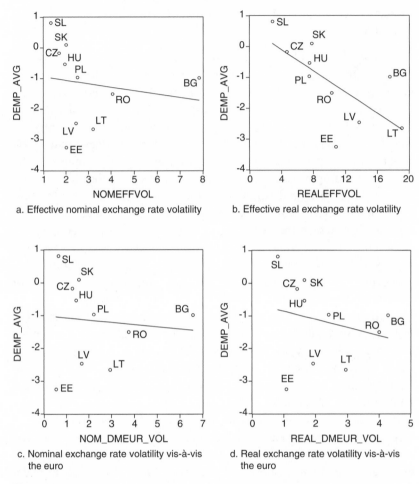

a. Effective nominal exchange rate volatility

b. Effective real exchange rate volatility

c. Nominal exchange rate volatility vis-à-vis the euro

d. Real exchange rate volatility vis-à-vis the euro

Figure 5.1
Employment growth and exchange rate volatility of ten central and eastern European countries from 1992 to 2001.

realizations.[12] Low volatility values typically appear at the end of the sample, especially in 2000 and 2002 when these countries achieved higher internal stability. Effective real volatility decreased for countries that used exchange rate arrangements close to fixed rates but remained high for Poland and Romania, and quite high for Latvia and Lithuania (for a similar observation, see Boreiko 2002, pp. 14ff). In case of the countries with macroeconomic instability and high inflation, an inspection of our data reveals that the variation in the bilateral real exchange rate is large and much higher than nominal exchange rate variability.

Strictly in line with our model we mainly focus our empirical analysis on the impact of exchange rate variability on employment. We use the yearly average of employment in thousands. The existence of a significant unofficial sector in the CEECs should not matter too much for regressions if one uses changes of employment. Moreover data on employment refers only to officially recognized employment, meaning those workers declared to the government and thus subject to social security contributions, income tax, and all labor market regulations. We do not take into account the potentially very large black market or underground economy basically for data availability reasons. The focus on the official labor market is, however, entirely appropriate. In the black market economy the costs of firing are presumably much lower because official employment regulations do not apply. Our model of firing costs therefore applies mainly to official employment, and we can expect volatility to be mainly a deterrent to official employment. Data on (official) employment is usually more accurate than data on unemployment, because the definition of who is looking for work, but unable to find it, changes often. Moreover the geographical coverage of the unemployment statistics changes over time as well. At times the national unemployment data reflect data from one or two major provinces. Employment data, by contrast is usually nationwide because it encompasses all people on the social security registers.

As a cyclical control variable in the employment equations we include the real growth rate of the gross domestic product. The development of wage costs is approximated by the real growth rate of average gross monthly wages. With the exception of Estonia, Latvia, and Lithuania where we used Eurostat and national sources, the data for employment, GDP growth, and wage costs are taken from the CEEC data set compiled by the Vienna Institute for International Economic Studies.

In order to convey a broader picture of the data set and some of the possible correlations, four scatter plots are presented in figure 5.1. It shows for the total economy cross-plots of our measure of employment growth in percent against exchange rate volatility. All variables are averaged over the period 1993 to 2001.

As is evident from the simple scatter plots relating average employment growth (in percent) to the average volatility measure, there is in general a negative relationship between exchange rate volatility and employment in a cross-country view of the CEECs. What matters is that overall the curves are downward sloping (nonvertical and nonhorizontal). Hence we can fit a very preliminary bivariate regression of average employment growth (in percent) on an average of four different measures of exchange rate variability. In all four cases we cannot reject the hypothesis of a negative relationship according to the fitted regression lines. The example of Estonia shows that the introduction of a currency board does not shelter the economy from the negative impact of effective exchange rate variability. The same is true with respect to Latvia, with its exchange rate fixed to the SDRs.

However, we were interested in investigating the validity of our hypothesis more deeply. Our fully specified regressions appear in the next section. We based our formal empirical analysis on tests of nonstationarity of the levels and the first differences of the variables under consideration, namely total economy employment, the different operationalizations of exchange rate volatility, and the real growth rate of average gross monthly wages.[13] The test applied is the first widely used panel data unit root test by Levin and Lin (1992). The results indicate that only (the log of) employment has to be differenced once to become stationary. That is, we estimate panel regressions for employment growth.

Our unit root tests reveal evidence of a stationary behavior of the levels of exchange rate volatility and of real wage growth. Hence we use the employment growth and levels of exchange rate volatility in the following pooled estimations.

5.4 Empirical Model and Results

5.4.1 Empirical Model

Based on our theoretical arguments, we conjecture that controlling for the usual key variables on the labor market,[14] we can show in a cross-country panel analysis of Central and Eastern European countries that exchange rate variability tends to worsen labor market performance. To test for a significant negative relationship between exchange rate variability and labor-market performance, we undertook a fixed effects estimation. This way we could account for different intercepts and hence different natural rates of employment estimated for each CEEC.[15]

In the literature random effects models are sometimes additionally implemented, mainly because fixed effects models and country dummies are costly in terms of lost degrees of freedom. We decided to dispense with such an exercise because our sampled cross-sectional units could not be drawn from a large population. Moreover, following our main argument in section 5.2, there is no reason to assume the country-specific constants in the employment equations as random a priori. Hence random effects models will probably have to be excluded a priori for many richer specifications of the empirical model also from this perspective.

However, for reasons of methodological correctness, we also performed Hausman specification tests to check empirically whether the fixed effects estimation is the correct procedure (against the possible alternative of random effects). For this purpose we computed the Hausman test statistic for testing the null hypothesis of random effects against the alternative hypothesis of fixed effects (Hausman 1978; Stata Corporation 2003, pp. 51ff). We are interested in four specifications according to which employment growth is a function of the real GDP growth rate and one of four different measures of exchange rate variability (effective volatility of nominal and real exchange rates and the nominal and real EXR volatility "vis-à-vis the euro"). We can differentiate between static and dynamic specifications. In our context "dynamic" means the additional inclusion of the growth of employment lagged two periods as an instrument for the lagged endogenous variable. The results, which reveal overwhelming evidence in favor of a fixed effects estimation, are displayed in the table 5.2. Hence we feel that we can legitimately dispense with random effects estimations and focus on fixed effects models.

The empirical model we use can be described by the usual form[16]

$$y_{it} = \alpha_i + x'_{it}\beta_i + \varepsilon_{it}, \tag{12}$$

with y_{it} as the dependent (macroeconomic labor market) variable, x_{it} and β_i as the k-vectors of nonconstant regressors (e.g., exchange rate variability), and the parameters $i = 1, 2, \ldots, N$ for cross-sectional units and $t = 1, 2, \ldots, T$ as the periods for which each cross section is observed. Equation (12) specifies a pooled analysis with common constants α imposed as $\alpha_i = \alpha_j = \alpha$.

Basing the analysis on *levels* of employment as an endogenous lagged variable is problematic for, at least, two reasons. First, employment time series can be plagued by nonstationarity problems (see section 5.3). Second, one has to take account of the well-known problem of endogenous lagged variables in the context of panel analyses (group effects). This is usually achieved by taking first differences, which is a further reason why we conducted our analysis in these terms. Third, the theoretical interest is in the link between the level of exchange rate

Table 5.2
Hausman tests for fixed versus random effects

Measure of EXR variability used	Test statistics	Empirical realization
Static specifications		
Effective volatility of nominal exchange rates	chi-sqr(2)	4.04
	p-value	0.13
Effective volatility of real exchange rates	chi-sqr(2)	11.63
	p-value	0.00
Nominal EXR volatility vis-à-vis the euro	chi-sqr(2)	3.73
	p-value	0.15
Real EXR volatility vis-à-vis the euro	chi-sqr(2)	4.96
	p-value	0.08
Dynamic specifications		
Effective volatility of nominal exchange rates	chi-sqr(2)	17.30
	p-value	0.00
Effective volatility of real exchange rates	chi-sqr(2)	21.13
	p-value	0.00
Nominal EXR volatility vis-à-vis the euro	chi-sqr(2)	11.83
	p-value	0.01
Real EXR volatility vis-à-vis the euro	chi-sqr(2)	18.98
	p-value	0.00

volatility and the *growth* of employment. By this specification a one-time shock in exchange rate volatility results in a permanent reduction of the employment level. This exactly mirrors the central persistence implication of the model, which postulates that even a short-term increase in exchange rate uncertainty leads to less hiring and more firing. The dynamic implications of our specification are thus acceptable for temporary shocks (i.e., spikes) in exchange rate variability, which were emphasized in our model.

In principle, our panel data set need not be applied to a *static* specification (in the following tables this corresponds to the first column for each volatility measure). Especially with respect to the well-known path dependence of employment, it is advisable to also test for *dynamic effects*. In order to capture the speed of adjustment of labor markets, we use the option to include lagged employment variables in the set of regressors throughout this chapter. The corresponding setting with respect to a representative regression equation for one cross section out of the whole system (described by the index *i*) can be written as follows:

$$y_{it} = \alpha_i + x'_{it}\beta_i + \delta y_{i,t-1} + \varepsilon_{it}. \tag{13}$$

However, for estimating our first-order model substantial complications have to be taken into account. Problems can arise because of the heterogeneity of the cross sections in the analysis (Greene 2000, pp. 582ff). The main problem we want to treat here is the correlation of the lagged dependent variable "level of employment" with the disturbance, even if the latter does not exhibit autocorrelation itself. While taking first differences enables us to get rid of heterogeneity (i.e., the group effects), the problem of the correlation between the lagged dependent variable and the disturbance still remains. Moreover a moving-average error term now appears in the specification. However, the resulting model can be treated by a standard application of the instrumental variables approach. The transformed model looks as follows:

$$y_{it} - y_{i,t-1} = (x_{it} - x_{i,t-1})'\beta_i + \delta(y_{i,t-1} - y_{i,t-2}) + (\varepsilon_{it} - \varepsilon_{i,t-1}).\qquad(14)$$

Arellano (1989) and Greene (2000), for instance, recommend using the differences $(y_{i,t-2} - y_{i,t-3})$ or the lagged levels $y_{i,t-2}$ and $y_{i,t-3}$ as instrumental variables for $(y_{i,t-1} - y_{i,t-2})$ in order to derive a simple instrumental variable estimator. The remaining variables can be taken as their own instruments. Arellano (1989) gives some theoretical and empirical support in favor of preferring levels to differences as instruments. As our second step of analysis we therefore implement this procedure within a dynamic framework (in the following tables this corresponds to the second column for each volatility measure). Finally, as a third step we conduct robustness tests by also including variables representing labor-market rigidities. Throughout our regressions we take employment growth as the regressand.

In our regression analysis we apply both the feasible generalized least squares (FGLS) and the seemingly unrelated regression technique (SUR). The FGLS assume the presence of cross-sectional heteroscedasticity and autocorrelation but without correction for contemporaneous correlation. The SUR procedure assumes heteroscedasticity *and* cross-sectional correlation. By this we account for the fact that correlations across countries might become relevant in the case of asymmetric or symmetric shocks to the labor market (contemporaneous correlation; e.g., see Babetski, Boone, and Maurel 2002).

5.4.2 Results
The structure of our presentation of the estimation results is the same for tables 5.3 to 5.5 with the exact specifications of the pooled estimation equations being described in the tables themselves. Half of

the specifications include a lagged endogenous labor-market variable. All specifications contain contemporaneous real GDP growth with or without its lagged value as cyclical control, different measures of exchange rate variability and the estimates of the country-specific constants.[17] The number of lags of the relevant variables was determined by the estimation itself. As in our previous studies, we limited possible lags to a number from 0 to 2 (annual data) and then tested down. Note that the number of observations in each case depends on the variables included and on their lags. The fit of each equation is checked by referring to the R-squared, the F-statistics, and an AR(1) time series test for the autocorrelation of residuals.[18] The latter test for AR(1) residuals is highly recommended by Wooldridge (2002) for dynamic panels, even including lagged endogenous variables. It regresses the dependent variable on the independent variables and the lag of residuals from the original equation. Based on this regression, a standard t-test on the significance of the coefficient of the lagged pool residuals is performed. Under the null hypothesis this coefficient is zero, and thus there is no autocorrelation of the residuals. A nice feature of the statistics computed is that it works whether or not the regressors are strictly exogenous. Our tables for the estimation results display the empirical realization of the t-statistics jointly with the corresponding p-value (denoted as $\hat{t}$). Since the marginal significance level of the F-test of joint significance of all of the slope coefficients is in all cases clearly below 1 percent, the p-value of this test is not explicitly tabulated. However, the degrees of freedom can be easily read off the tables.[19]

Let us first turn to our basic regressions in tables 5.3 (based on the FGLS procedure) and 5.4 (based on SUR estimation) for a sample consisting of all ten CEE countries. It is remarkable that the estimated coefficients measuring the impact of exchange rate volatility on employment growth are mostly significant and always display the expected sign. Our empirical investigations show that exchange rate volatility enters the regression equations with at least one lag. However, in most cases the implementation of even a two-year lag of exchange rate volatility appears superior according to the goodness-of-fit criterion. This corresponds quite nicely with the usual duration of wage contracts in the investigated countries and serves as first evidence of the absence of a reverse causation of the exchange rate volatility by employment growth. As studies for other regions suggest too, the economic impact of exchange rate volatility seems to be *small but nonnegligible*.

The results are in some cases stronger for euro exchange rate volatility than for effective volatility. This may be due to the rather close trade ties of the CEECs with the euro zone. The estimated impact coefficient is larger for nominal than for real volatility in the case of effective exchange rates and the other way round for the bilateral euro exchange rates. The estimated fixed effects exactly mirror the differences in employment growth, as plotted in figure 5.1, with the Baltic states displaying the highest decrease in employment growth. The significance of contemporaneous GDP growth in determining the employment growth is a commonly accepted prior, and it is corroborated by all specifications. The available test statistics point toward correct specifications. In case of our static specifications, the Wooldridge test indicates AR(1) autocorrelation of the pooled residuals. Even if we experiment with different lags of our regressors, the static specifications cannot fully capture the dynamics. Hence we base our conclusions from table 5.4 mainly on the dynamic specifications. All in all, it seems that the ten CEECs are a group too heterogeneous to be characterized by a similarly strong impact of euro exchange rate volatility. Hence we *generalized* the specifications chosen above by estimating a *separate coefficient* of exchange rate volatility for each of the ten CEECs in order to allow for heterogeneity with respect to the impact of volatility. According to our model this heterogeneity might stem from different degrees of labor-market rigidities and/or from different levels of volatility experienced in the past. By allowing for *different volatility coefficients* for each CEEC, we might be able to identify those countries that drive our results. The results from the SUR procedure are reported in table 5.5.[20]

This time the best results in terms of goodness of fit are achieved if exchange rate volatility is included with a one-year lag. However, we found that if also the latter is included with a two-year lag, the estimates of this variable are in most cases significant and display the expected negative signs. For effective volatilities it turns out that employment growth above all in Hungary, Poland, and Slovenia is significantly influenced by effective nominal exchange rate variability. In the case of effective real exchange rate volatility, the pattern changes insofar as now the coefficient of volatility is additionally significant above all for Bulgaria, the Czech Republic, Estonia, and Slovakia in both the static and the dynamic specifications. Furthermore the remaining three countries Latvia, Lithuania, and Romania are also affected by effective exchange rate variability, according to at least one specification. The results do not seem to be driven by the degree of exchange rate

Table 5.3
Impact of exchange rate variability on the growth of employment: FGLS estimates for 10 CEECs (fixed effects)

Regressors	(1)	(2)	(3)	(4)	(5)	(6)	(7)	(8)	(9)	(10)
Instrument for employment growth (−1)		0.10		0.14*				0.25***		0.18*
Real GDP growth rate	0.26**	0.16**	0.21***	0.15**	0.24***	0.20***	0.25***	0.20***	0.27***	0.19***
Measures of exchange rate volatility										
Effective volatility of nominal exchange rate	−0.20** (−2)	−0.14** (−2)			−0.16* (−2)					
Effective volatility of real exchange rate			−0.11*** (−2)	−0.09*** (−2)		−0.06* (−2)				
Volatility of national currency vis-à-vis euro (DM) (nominal exchange rate)							−0.17** (−2)	−0.15* (−2)		
Volatility of national currency vis-à-vis euro (DM) (real exchange rate)									−0.36*** (−2)	−0.34*** (−2)
Common AR error assumed					X	X				

Fixed effects

BG	0.55	0.04	0.59	0.13	0.53	−0.08	−0.00	0.44	0.46	0.94
CZ	−0.73	−0.70	−0.22	−0.42	−0.79	−0.69	−0.83	−0.66	−0.57	−0.34
EE	−3.12	−2.42	−2.15	−1.67	−3.40	−2.90	−3.49	−2.38	−3.02	−2.05
HU	−0.90	0.29	−0.41	0.68	−0.17	0.11	−1.04	−0.15	−0.67	0.27
LT	−2.01	−1.62	−1.09	−0.44	−2.37	−1.51	−2.15	−1.45	−1.61	−0.93
LV	−2.18	−0.58	−0.40	0.32	−0.95	−0.29	−2.39	−1.57	−1.66	−0.91
PL	−1.40	−0.77	−0.90	−0.47	−1.27	−1.10	−1.47	−1.08	−0.91	−0.49
RO	0.48	0.45	0.79	0.80	0.09	−0.12	0.25	0.06	1.19	0.87
SK	−0.55	−1.16	0.13	−0.64	−0.74	−0.42	−0.66	−0.69	−0.42	−0.33
SL	0.32	0.12	0.52	0.17	0.38	0.47	0.20	0.12	0.40	0.44

Weighted statistics

R^2	0.32	0.28	0.32	0.32	0.40	0.43	0.31	0.29	0.37	0.40
F-statistics	2.82	1.66	2.91	2.03	3.11	3.53	2.64	2.90	3.49	3.26
Wooldridge-$\hat{t}$	1.17	1.26	1.21	0.80	—		1.35	1.49	0.59	1.54
(*p*-value)	(0.25)	(0.21)	(0.23)	(0.43)			(0.18)	(0.14)	(0.56)	(0.13)
Total panel observations	78	64	79	64	68	69	78	72	78	72
Sample	1993–2001	1994–2001	1993–2001	1994–2001	1993–2001	1993–2001	1993–2001	1994–2001	1993–2001	1994–2001

Note: The term ($y_{i,t-1} - y_{i,t-2}$) is instrumented by the growth of employment lagged two periods. Numbers in brackets refer to the optimal lag. X denotes the assumption of a common AR error term. *, **, *** indicate significance at the 10 percent, 5 percent, 1 percent level respectively.

Table 5.4
Impact of exchange rate variability on the growth of employment: SUR estimates for 10 CEECs (fixed effects)

Regressors	(1)	(2)	(3)	(4)	(5)	(6)	(7)	(8)	(9)	(10)
Instrument for the growth of employment (−1)		0.06		0.09***				0.05		0.04
Real GDP growth rate	0.19***	0.11***	0.20***	0.11***	0.06***	0.12***	0.17***	0.10***	0.16***	0.09***
Measures of exchange rate volatility										
Effective volatility of nominal exchange rate	−0.20*** (−2)	−0.16*** (−2)			−0.29*** (−2)					
Effective volatility of real exchange rate			−0.08*** (−2)	−0.08*** (−2)		−0.13*** (−2)				
Volatility of national currency vis-à-vis euro (DM) (nominal exchange rate)							−0.16*** (−2)	−0.10*** (−2)		
Volatility of national currency vis-à-vis euro (DM) (real exchange rate)									−0.35*** (−2)	−0.08* (−2)
AR error assumed					X	X				

Fixed effects										
BG	0.60	0.20	0.09	-0.00	1.86	1.40	-0.07	-0.58	0.49	-1.19
CZ	-0.57	0.59	-0.34	-0.41	-0.30	-0.09	-0.70	-0.72	-0.34	-0.73
EE	-2.81	-2.35	-2.43	-1.77	-2.06	-1.71	-3.20	-2.70	-2.57	-2.62
HU	-0.68	0.45	-0.59	0.73	1.10	0.77	-0.85	0.29	-0.35	0.30
LT	-1.74	-1.47	-0.91	-0.49	-1.55	0.40	-1.93	-1.72	-1.22	-1.79
LV	-1.90	-0.46	-1.46	0.27	0.69	0.76	-2.15	-0.72	-1.26	-0.73
PL	-1.06	-0.52	-1.06	-0.33	-0.08	-0.15	-1.17	-0.67	-0.42	-0.66
RO	0.54	0.47	0.48	0.68	0.48	0.81	0.25	0.12	1.25	-0.01
SK	-0.26	-0.96	-0.05	-0.55	0.08	0.50	-0.39	-1.11	0.02	-1.10
SL	0.62	0.36	0.46	0.35	1.29	0.99	0.48	0.27	0.86	0.31
Unweighted statistics										
R^2	0.28	0.25	0.24	0.25	0.11	0.23	0.26	0.22	0.28	0.20
Wooldridge-$\hat{t}$	1.99	1.48	3.08	1.22	—	—	2.66	0.49	1.98	0.33
(p-value)	(0.05)	(0.15)	(0.01)	(0.23)			(0.01)	(0.63)	(0.05)	(0.74)
Total panel observations	78	64	79	64	68	69	78	64	78	64
Sample	1993–2001	1994–2001	1993–2001	1994–2001	1993–2001	1993–2001	1993–2001	1994–2001	1993–2001	1994–2001

Note: The term $(y_{i,t-1} - y_{i,t-2})$ is instrumented by the growth of employment lagged two periods. Numbers in brackets refer to the optimal lag. X denotes the assumption of an AR error term. *, **, *** indicate significance at the 10 percent, 5 percent, 1 percent level respectively.

Table 5.5
Estimations based on cross-sectional specific coefficients of effective exchange rate volatility (SUR, fixed effects)

Regressors	(1)	(2)	(3)	(4)	(5)	(6)	(7)	(8)
Instrument for the growth of employment (−1)		0.07**		0.08***		0.04		0.06
Real GDP growth rate	0.15**	0.08***	0.27***	0.14***	0.11***	0.12***	0.14***	0.09***
Measures of exchange rate volatility								
Effective volatility of nominal exchange rate	X	X						
Effective volatility of real exchange rate			X	X				
Volatility of national currency vis-à-vis euro (DM) (nominal exchange rate)					X	X		
Volatility of national currency vis-à-vis euro (DM) (real exchange rate)							X	X

Country-specific coefficient of exchange rate volatility X lagged one period (if not indicated otherwise)

BG	-0.13*** (-2)	0.04	-0.24***	-0.20***	-0.07** (-2)	0.02	0.19	0.11
CZ	-0.04 (-2)	-0.74***	-0.12**	-0.11*	-0.03 (-2)	-0.38**	-0.70***	-0.42***
EE	-0.06 (-2)	-2.02***	-0.15*	-0.23**	1.29 (-2)	0.63	-1.05***	-0.86***
HU	-2.11*** (-2)	0.74***	0.31**	0.26***	-2.45*** (-2)	-0.35	-2.62***	-0.51*
LT	-0.39** (-2)	-0.15	0.12***	0.07	-0.01 (-2)	-1.61**	-0.75***	-2.74***
LV	-1.19*** (-2)	-0.22	0.12	0.10***	-1.28*** (-2)	-0.82*	-0.31**	-1.09***
PL	-0.39** (-2)	-1.14***	-0.22***	-0.29***	-0.57*** (-2)	-1.22***	-1.27***	-1.29***
RO	-0.07 (-2)	-0.28***	0.04	-0.03	-0.06 (-2)	-0.19***	-0.04	-0.23***
SK	-0.14 (-2)	-0.99***	-0.25***	-0.19***	0.15 (-2)	-0.61**	-0.60*	-0.39
SL	-0.27* (-2)	-1.65***	-1.13***	-0.72***	0.01 (-2)	0.37	0.18	0.31

Table 5.5
(continued)

Regressors	(1)	(2)	(3)	(4)	(5)	(6)	(7)	(8)
Unweighted statistics								
R^2	0.41	0.51	0.51	0.50	0.44	0.34	0.43	0.38
Wooldridge-$\hat{t}$	−0.22	0.25	0.83	1.52	−0.88	0.44	1.30	−0.33
(*p*-value)	(0.83)	(0.80)	(0.41)	(0.14)	(0.39)	(0.66)	(0.20)	(0.74)
Total panel observations	78	65	82	65	78	65	82	65
Sample	1993–2001	1993–2001	1993–2001	1993–2001	1993–2001	1993–2001	1993–2001	1993–2001

Note: The term $(y_{i,t-1} - y_{i,t-2})$ is instrumented by the growth of employment lagged two periods. X denotes volatility for which the country-specific coefficient is estimated. Numbers in brackets refer to the optimal lag. *, **, *** indicate significance at the 10 percent, 5 percent, 1 percent level respectively.

volatility experienced by a single CEEC, since the countries that display persistently higher effective volatility (e.g., Bulgaria, Romania, Latvia, and Lithuania) do not display a bulk of significant coefficients of volatility. Hence we could argue that the often stressed heterogeneity among the CEE countries becomes obvious again, now with respect to the impact of exchange rate volatility.

However, the pattern changes when the bilateral euro volatilities of the CEEC currencies are included. We correlated these results with regard to openness vis-à-vis the eurozone, and it became obvious that the Czech Republic and Hungary whose economies are most open to trade with the eurozone, and strikingly also Poland as the least open CEE country, are among those countries for which the results are most in line with our main hypothesis. These countries are joined by Lithuania and Latvia with four respectively three entries as well. Estonia, Romania, and the Slovak Republic display two entries each. Somewhat surprisingly, Bulgaria, an often cited candidate for euroization, reveals only one entry. Finally, Slovenia does not display any evidence of negative employment impacts of exchange rate variability. However, according to figure 5.1, Slovenia reveals one of the lowest degrees of exchange rate volatility. This may be a good reason why Slovenia's high degrees of openness toward the eurozone and of labor market rigidities do not lead to more significant entries in table 5.5.

Although exchange rate variability in all cases does not influence employment growth contemporaneously but *with a lag*, employment could at least theoretically still have an impact on exchange rate variability. Unfortunately, all efforts to apply an instrument variable approach (including various measures of export demand) were impeded by our inability to find a suitable instrument for exchange rate variability. None of the instruments we tried (inter alia current accounts, short- and long-term interest rates) worked to get significant and plausible results. In other words, there is no reason to interpret exchange rate variability as endogenous.

We are skeptical, in general, about the possibility that exchange rate variability at our high frequency is caused by *slow moving* variables such as labor market rigidities or employment. Indeed, all our attempts to use an IV procedure failed because we were not able to find satisfactory instruments for exchange rate variability. Most of the fundamentals in question, with the possible exception of monetary policy, are much less variable in the short run. A further argument validating our proceedings and our results is that of Rose (1995) and Flood and Rose

(1995). They emphasize that exchange rate volatility is apparently to a large extent as *noise* (and not caused by fundamental variability). It does not make much sense to treat a noise series as endogenous. Finally, variability is a key element of an asset price (i.e., the price of currency options). If it were possible to forecast variability, one could forecast option prices. Could exchange rate variability be caused by shocks? This is also rather unlikely, since it has been difficult, in general, to document any link between exchange rate volatility and fundamentals.[21] Furthermore it is a priori unlikely that the kind of shock that requires a substantial exchange rate adjustment (a fall in export demand) occurs with a monthly frequency.

How large is the effect found in thousands of employed persons? We illustrate the answer based on the example of one of the most consistent countries in our estimations, namely Poland. Given that only one lag of exchange rate variability turned out to be important, one can directly use the t-statistic to check for the significance of the effect. For instance, with respect to the nominal variability of the zloty vis-à-vis the euro (the DM), the value of -0.57 is highly significant in the sense that the probability to find this effect if it does not exist in reality is much lower than even $\alpha = 0.01$ (see column 5 in table 5.5). The point estimate implies that a reduction in the variability measure by one percentage point increases employment growth after one year by 0.57 percent. Given a number of about 13.7 millions of employed Polish persons in 2001 this amounts to about 78,000 employed more. This is a small, but still nonnegligible contribution. The effect would actually be three times as strong if the actual variability was eliminated, given the fact that in 2001 the empirical realization of the euro variability of the zloty against the euro was 3.17 percent, or at least twice as high if one eliminates the average variability (2.37 percent). With an eye on the results for the remaining countries in our sample, we have to conclude that the effects for the CEECs on the whole are definitely smaller but still not negligible. Moreover the results are strikingly similar to those gained for Western Europe and thus seem to be plausible.[22]

5.4.3 Robustness Checks

We first test for the robustness of our results with respect to outliers. Figure 5.1 suggests that the results might mainly be driven by the outliers Romania and Bulgaria. If Romania and Bulgaria, whose currencies are characterized by the relatively highest volatilities, are removed from the sample, the significance levels of our results might decline. In table 5.5 we report country-specific volatility coefficients that might be interpreted as a first and preliminary robustness test for such kind of bias. However, in the following, we additionally report the results for the specifications displayed in tables 5.3 and 5.4, but this time excluding the potential "outlier" countries Bulgaria and Romania from our country sample. The methodology is the same, and the results are summarized in tables 5.6 and 5.7.[23]

As shown in these tables, even when the sample is limited to the eight CEE EU acceding countries, exchange rate volatility has significant negative effects on employment growth. Interestingly the magnitude of the coefficients increases in many cases. Once again, the best-fitting specification is identified by using exchange rate volatility with a two-year lag indicating that past values of exchange rate volatility are important for employment determination. In a few of the SUR estimates the Wooldridge tests report that serial correlation may be an issue. We therefore focus our analysis on the results provided by the FGLS estimates. Here the coefficients of nominal volatilities turn out to be highly significant. For real exchange rates we found significant results for bilateral volatilities but not for effective volatilities. Overall, the coefficients still show the expected sign.

Second, it may be puzzling why only employment and not unemployment figures are used for the econometric investigation, especially since Belke and Gros (2002a) in their investigation of US and euro area employment use both. Moreover some readers might find our argument that unemployment figures are less accurate than employment figures not convincing. Hence we have re-estimated the model with unemployment figures and report the results in tables 5.8 (for the FGLS specification) and 5.9 (for the SUR specification).

Because the unemployment results reveal a pattern similar to that of employment, we will consider in more detail some specific unemployment estimates. The coefficients are mostly significant, and in the FGLS estimates the coefficients always display the expected positive sign, implying that higher exchange rate volatility causes higher unemployment rates. In line with our previous specifications, the results are stronger for real than for nominal bilateral volatilities. This applies to both magnitude and significance level of the coefficients. When considering effective volatilities, no significant difference between the coefficients for real and nominal volatility can be found.

In order to detect potential outliers, we also reran our regression by allowing for different volatility coefficients for each CEEC (table 5.10).

Table 5.6
Impact of exchange rate variability on the growth of employment: FGLS estimates for eight CEECs (fixed effects without Bulgaria and Romania)

Regressors	(1)	(2)	(3)	(4)	(5)	(6)	(7)	(8)	(9)	(10)
Instrument for employment growth (−1)		0.11		0.23***				0.15		0.09
Real GDP growth rate	0.45***	0.38***	0.45***	0.31***	0.43	0.30***	0.44***	0.36***	0.39***	0.35***
Measures of exchange rate volatility										
Effective volatility of nominal exchange rate	−0.46*** (−2)	−0.37** (−2)			−0.37*** (−2)					
Effective volatility of real exchange rate			−0.05 (−2)	−0.04 (−2)		−0.03				
Volatility of national currency vis-à-vis euro (DM) (nominal exchange rate)							−0.54*** (−2)	−0.41** (−2)		
Volatility of national currency vis-à-vis euro (DM) (real exchange rate)									−0.51*** (−2)	−0.49*** (−2)
Common AR error assumed					X	X				

Fixed effects									
CZ	-0.65	-0.62	-1.06	-0.89	-0.73	-1.083	-0.76	-0.70	-0.62	-0.50
EE	-3.20	-2.76	-3.87	-2.52	-3.895	-3.82	-4.09	-3.31	-3.27	-2.77
HU	-0.81	-0.25	-1.61	-0.47	-0.494	-0.58	-0.93	-0.37	-0.73	-0.06
LT	-1.72	-1.55	-2.50	-1.58	-2.369	-1.309	-1.65	-1.43	-1.57	-1.25
LV	-1.98	-1.74	-2.91	-1.83	-1.421	-2.533	-2.16	-1.79	-1.61	-1.25
PL	-1.51	-1.34	-2.49	-1.64	-1.613	-1.844	-1.43	-1.31	-1.05	-0.90
SK	-0.74	-0.87	-1.35	-0.95	-1.033	-1.069	-0.87	-0.93	-0.68	-0.69
SL	0.09	-0.01	-0.72	-0.30	-0.090	-0.076	-0.08	-0.23	-0.09	0.02
Weighted statistics									
R^2	0.51	0.52	0.41	0.49	0.52	0.50	0.52	0.53	0.58	0.60
F-statistics	6.09	5.15	4.12	4.69	4.77	4.54	6.49	5.36	8.14	7.20
Wooldridge-$\hat{t}$	0.84	1.03	-0.55	-0.19	-0.11	0.68	0.02	0.11	0.41	0.56
(*p*-value)	(0.41)	(0.31)	(0.58)	(0.85)	(0.92)	(0.50)	(0.98)	(0.91)	(0.69)	(0.58)
Total panel observations	63	59	64	59	55	56	63	59	63	59
Sample	1993–2001	1994–2001	1993–2001	1994–2001	1993–2001	1993–2001	1993–2001	1994–2001	1993–2001	1994–2001

Note: The term $(y_{i,t-1} - y_{i,t-2})$ is instrumented by the growth of employment lagged two periods. Numbers in brackets refer to the optimal lag. X denotes the assumption of an AR error term. *, **, *** indicate significance at the 10 percent, 5 percent, 1 percent level respectively.

Table 5.7
Impact of exchange rate variability on the growth of employment: SUR estimates for eight CEECs (fixed effects without Bulgaria and Romania)

Regressors	(1)	(2)	(3)	(4)	(5)	(6)	(7)	(8)	(9)	(10)
Instrument for the growth of employment (−1)		−0.02		0.15***				0.09***		0.04*
Real GDP growth rate	0.44***	0.38	0.49***	0.40***	0.25***	0.36***	0.43***	0.34***	0.39***	0.32***
Measures of exchange rate volatility										
Effective volatility of nominal exchange rate	−0.50*** (−2)	−0.52*** (−2)			−0.28***	−0.04***				
Effective volatility of real exchange rate			−0.02 (−2)	−0.02 (−2)						
Volatility of national currency vis-à-vis euro (DM) (nominal exchange rate)							−0.52*** (−2)	−0.49*** (−2)		
Volatility of national currency vis-à-vis euro (DM) (real exchange rate)									−0.42*** (−2)	−0.42*** (−2)
AR error assumed					X	X				

Fixed effects

CZ	-0.55	-0.39	-1.32	-1.22	-0.56	-0.83	-0.76	-0.57	-0.74	-0.58
EE	-3.05	-2.82	-4.43	-3.41	-3.20	-2.17	-4.07	-3.39	-3.41	-2.97
HU	-0.67	0.02	-1.99	-0.99	0.42	-0.54	-0.93	-0.21	-0.91	-0.14
LT	-1.53	-1.28	-3.32	-2.48	-0.16	-1.45	-1.66	-1.23	-1.85	-1.50
LV	-1.80	-1.55	-3.55	-2.68	-2.42	-0.75	-2.17	-1.67	-1.91	-1.53
PL	-1.35	-0.97	-2.94	-2.26	-0.98	-1.75	-1.43	-1.06	-1.30	-0.99
SK	-0.61	-0.57	-1.79	-1.45	-0.58	-1.56	-0.86	-0.74	-0.81	-0.71
SL	0.21	0.37	-1.02	-0.65	0.54	-1.14	-0.07	-0.03	-0.02	0.10

Unweighted statistics

R^2	0.45	0.44	0.37	0.38	0.25	0.26	0.44	0.42	0.44	0.43
Wooldridge-$\hat{t}$	1.10	3.95	-4.17	-4.48	-0.66	-0.43	-1.18	-2.08	-1.21	-1.07
(p-value)	(0.28)	(0.00)	(0.00)	(0.00)	(0.51)	(0.67)	(0.24)	(0.04)	(0.23)	(0.29)
Total panel observations	63	59	64	59	55	51	63	59	63	59
Sample	1993–2001	1994–2001	1993–2001	1994–2001	1993–2001	1994–2001	1993–2001	1994–2001	1993–2001	1994–2001

Note: The term ($y_{i,t-1} - y_{i,t-2}$) is instrumented by the growth of employment lagged two periods. Numbers in brackets refer to the optimal lag. X denotes the assumption of an AR error term. *, **, *** indicate significance at the 10 percent, 5 percent, 1 percent level respectively.

Table 5.8
Impact of exchange rate variability on the change in the unemployment rate: FGLS estimates for ten CEECs (fixed effects)

Regressors	(1)	(2)	(3)	(4)	(5)	(6)	(7)	(8)	(9)	(10)
Instrument for the change in unemployment rate (−1)		−0.25***		−0.12***				−0.04		−0.04
Real GDP growth rate	−0.27***	−0.13***	−0.28***	−0.23***	−0.19***	−0.20***	−0.28***	−0.25***	−0.23***	−0.23***
Measures of exchange rate volatility										
Effective volatility of nominal exchange rate	0.12***	0.07			0.16**					
Effective volatility of real exchange rate			0.08***	0.06**		0.20***				
Volatility of national currency vis-à-vis euro (DM) (nominal exchange rate)							0.08**	0.01		
Volatility of national currency vis-à-vis euro (DM) (real exchange rate)									0.17***	0.07
Common AR error assumed					X	X				

Fixed effects

BG	-0.37	3.04	-0.53	0.75	-0.77	-2.86	0.08	0.36	-0.35	0.07
CZ	0.71	1.65	0.55	1.31	0.55	0.50	1.15	1.22	0.91	1.09
EE	1.42	1.81	0.75	1.39	1.37	1.30	1.66	1.97	1.32	1.82
HU	0.57	2.72	0.26	0.88	0.05	-0.01	0.73	0.13	0.49	-0.03
LT	1.27	3.10	-0.04	1.33	1.64	1.52	1.45	2.08	1.12	1.86
LV	0.76	2.26	-0.05	1.06	0.65	0.58	0.96	1.28	0.68	1.10
PL	1.58	4.09	1.36	2.60	0.96	0.88	1.77	1.61	1.31	1.37
RO	0.02	2.11	-0.28	0.49	-0.45	-0.59	0.26	0.10	-0.26	-0.17
SK	1.56	3.99	1.19	2.67	0.74	0.71	1.72	1.81	1.41	1.65
SL	0.88	3.69	0.76	2.16	0.45	0.40	1.03	0.86	0.68	0.74

Weighted statistics

R^2	0.56	0.48	0.50	0.51	0.38	0.40	0.56	0.45	0.54	0.45
F-statistics	10.30	5.98	7.76	5.92	4.07	4.31	9.70	4.73	9.14	4.67
Total panel observations	101	91	97	81	91	91	97	81	96	81
Sample	1991–2001	1992–2001	1991–2001	1993–2001	1991–2001	1991–2001	1991–2001	1993–2001	1991–2001	1993–2001

Note: The term $(y_{i,t-1} - y_{i,t-2})$ is instrumented by the change of the unemployment rate lagged two periods. Wooldridge-t test points to absence of residual autocorrelation in all cases. X denotes the assumption of a common AR error term. *, **, *** indicate significance at the 10 percent, 5 percent, 1 percent level respectively.

Table 5.9
Impact of exchange rate variability on the change in the unemployment rate: SUR estimates for ten CEECs (fixed effects)

Regressors	(1)	(2)	(3)	(4)	(5)	(6)	(7)	(8)	(9)	(10)
Instrument for the change in unemployment rate (−1)		−0.20***		−0.28***				−0.01		−0.02
Real GDP growth rate	−0.27***	−0.15***	−0.29***	−0.18***	−0.21***	−0.27***	−0.26	−0.25***	−0.25***	−0.25***
Measures of exchange rate volatility										
Effective volatility of nominal exchange rate	0.08***	0.04***			0.14***					
Effective volatility of real exchange rate			0.08***	0.03**		0.10***				
Volatility of national currency vis-à-vis euro (DM) (nominal exchange rate)							0.07	−0.02		
Volatility of national currency vis-à-vis euro (DM) (real exchange rate)									0.10***	−0.03
AR error assumed					X	X				

Fixed effects

BG	0.08	2.62	−0.41	3.41	−0.69	−1.14	0.26	0.51	0.24	0.51
CZ	0.76	1.50	0.61	1.82	0.91	0.75	1.14	1.24	1.04	1.26
EE	1.51	1.81	0.90	1.85	1.76	0.84	1.61	2.01	1.46	2.02
HU	0.66	2.28	0.34	3.06	−0.07	−0.08	0.74	0.17	0.64	0.19
LT	1.38	2.92	0.14	2.93	2.21	0.18	1.45	2.14	1.32	2.17
LV	0.86	2.03	0.08	2.33	0.95	−0.09	0.96	1.32	0.84	1.34
PL	1.70	3.58	1.47	4.64	1.02	1.06	1.76	1.68	1.57	1.71
RO	0.21	1.78	−0.19	2.39	−0.57	−0.63	0.32	0.18	0.11	0.22
SK	1.62	3.42	1.30	5.11	1.01	0.88	1.70	1.82	1.57	1.84
SL	0.95	3.11	0.84	4.26	0.41	0.64	1.01	0.88	0.81	0.90

Unweighted statistics

R^2	0.47	0.34	0.44	0.48	0.21	0.23	0.47		0.49	0.33
Total panel observations	101	91	97	90	86	87	97	81	96	81
Sample	1991–2001	1992–2001	1991–2001	1992–2001	1991–2001	1991–2001	1991–2001	1993–2001	1991–2001	1993–2001

Note: The term $(y_{i,t-1} - y_{i,t-2})$ is instrumented by the change of the unemployment rate lagged two periods. Wooldridge-$\hat{t}$ test points to absence of residual autocorrelation in all cases. X denotes the assumption of an AR error term. *, **, *** indicate significance at the 10 percent, 5 percent, 1 percent level respectively.

Table 5.10
Estimations based on cross-sectional specific coefficients of effective exchange rate volatility (SUR, fixed effects)

Regressors	(1)	(2)	(3)	(4)	(5)	(6)	(7)	(8)
Instrument for the change in unemployment rate (−1)		−0.30***		−0.28***		−0.3***		−0.36***
Real GDP growth rate	−0.18***	−0.13***	−0.31***	−0.19***	−0.17***	−0.15***	−0.23***	−0.11***
Measures of exchange rate volatility								
Effective volatility of nominal exchange rate	X	X						
Effective volatility of real exchange rate			X	X				
Volatility of national currency vis-à-vis euro (DM) (nominal exchange rate)					X	X		
Volatility of national currency vis-à-vis euro (DM) (real exchange rate)							X	X

Country-specific coefficient of exchange rate volatility X

BG	0.09***	-0.01	0.09**	0.02	0.12***	-0.08	0.08***	-0.01
CZ	0.73***	0.74***	0.19***	0.23***	0.73***	0.82***	0.66***	0.82***
EE	-0.36	-0.39*	0.06	-0.03	-0.83***	-0.09	0.24	0.13
HU	0.99***	0.52*	0.10	0.05	1.93***	1.12***	0.42	0.54*
LT	0.04	0.06	0.08	-0.02	0.28	0.54	0.97	1.12**
LV	0.35**	0.54***	0.13***	0.13***	-0.19	-0.62	-0.78***	-0.86**
PL	0.46**	0.12	0.02	-0.07	0.73***	0.35*	0.69***	0.40**
RO	0.45***	0.30***	-0.05	-0.03	0.42***	0.28***	0.33***	0.31***
SK	1.08***	0.98***	0.18***	0.17**	1.46***	1.36***	1.67***	1.73***
SL	0.57***	0.12	0.03	0.04	0.40**	-0.10	-0.01	-0.12
Unweighted statistics								
R^2	0.52	0.60	0.46	0.54	0.58	0.60	0.55	0.62
Total panel observations	96	89	97	90	96	89	97	89
Sample	1991–2001	1992–2001	1991–2001	1992–2001	1991–2001	1992–2001	1991–2001	1992–2001

Note: The term $(y_{i,t-1} - y_{i,t-2})$ is instrumented by the change of the unemployment rate lagged two periods. X denotes volatility for which the country-specific coefficient is estimated. Wooldridge-t test points to absence of residual autocorrelation in all cases. *, **, *** indicate significance at the 10 percent, 5 percent, 1 percent level respectively.

Comparing these results to the employment specification in table 5.5, we see that for some countries the impact of exchange rate volatility on labor market performance is even stronger now. Interestingly in the cases of the Czech Republic and Slovakia the coefficients are highly significant in all specifications. With the exception of nominal bilateral volatilities, Latvia also shows a high degree of significance. By contrast, other countries such as Hungary, Poland, and Slovenia provide poorer results than in the employment specification. Seen on the whole, the results are stronger for euro volatilities than for effective volatilities, a finding that again refers to the CEEC's close trade ties with the eurozone and that may provide an argument for an early entry to the eurozone.

5.5   Summary and Outlook

The results of this chapter suggest that the high degree of exchange rate variability observed from time to time in the CEECs has tangible economic costs. Our earlier studies on intra-EMS, transatlantic, and Mercosur exchange rate variability have already indicated that reductions in exchange rate variability can yield substantial benefits for small open economies. It is fully possible that the same applies for most of the CEECs. It was argued here that this result is due to the fact that all employment decisions have some degree of irreversibility. We investigated both effective and bilateral euro exchange rate variability because we were interested in the costs of exchange rate variability, in general (effective volatilities), and in evaluating one partial benefit of euroization—the elimination of the exchange rate risk—in particular (bilateral volatilities vis-à-vis the euro). Overall, our results are rather strong in that we find that exchange rate variability in many cases has a significant impact on employment growth and on the unemployment rate. Moreover the data confirm the expectation that economies with relatively closer ties with the eurozone, such as Hungary, are more strongly affected by euro exchange rate variability. The estimated impact coefficients were in most of the cases smaller when we pooled all of the ten CEECs. This systematic correlation between openness and strength of impact of exchange rate volatility on trade corresponds to the general finding of the literature: that for emerging markets this channel is much more important.

What are the implications of the results concerning the labor market impact of euro volatility for the debate on exchange rate policy in the CEECs? Given the preliminary character of our analysis, one certainly has to be cautious in terms of policy conclusions. However, fixing exchange rates against the euro should bring significant benefits for these countries. Thus our main result could be read as support for the policy conclusion that the new EU member countries should join the euro area as soon as possible. This reinforces the argument recently put forward by Gros and Hobza (2003), and others, that there is little concrete evidence that the new EU member states will need to undergo a lengthy period of real convergence before joining the euro.

Annex

Data Sources   Oesterreichische Nationalbank (2002, 2002a), Vienna Institute for International Economic Studies (2002), Estonia, Latvia, Lithuania: Eurostat and national sources.

CPI   Index of consumer prices.

GDP   Gross domestic product, real growth rate (percentages).

EMP   Employment in thousand persons (all sectors), annual average.

DEMP   Employment growth in percentages (logarithm)

UNEMP   Unemployment rate in percentages, end of period.

WAGE   Average gross monthly wages, real growth rate (percentage).

XR   Specified national currency (n.c. units) per US dollar, monthly average, nominal, bilateral exchange rates vis-à-vis other countries than the US calculated via cross rates.

XRR   Specified national currency (n.c. units) per US dollar, monthly average, real (deflated with CPI), bilateral exchange rates vis-à-vis other countries than the US calculated via cross rates.

VOLXREFF   Effective volatility of nominal exchange rates (30 bilateral volatilities calculated for each CEEC, effective volatilities were generated by multiplying each of the 30 bilateral volatilities with the respective trade weight).

VOLXRREFF   Effective volatility of real exchange rates (30 bilateral volatilities calculated for each CEEC, effective volatilities were generated by multiplying each of the 30 bilateral volatilities with the respective trade weight).

The following country codes apply throughout the study: BG (Bulgaria), CZ (Czech Republic), EE (Estonia), HU (Hungary), LV (Latvia), LT (Lithuania), PL (Poland), RO (Romania), SK (Slovakia), and SL (Slovenia).

The algorithm to calculate bilateral CEEC exchange rate variability series is as follows (the other EXR variability series are constructed analogously):

```
SMPL 1990.1 2002.12
FOR %EX 'all exchange rates of interest'
  GENR VOL%EX = NA
  FOR !1=0 to 144 STEP 12
  SMPL 1990.1+!1 1990.12+!1
  GENR VOL%EX=SQR(@VAR(D(log(%EX))*100))
  NEXT
NEXT
SMPL 1990.1 2002.12
```

Notes

We thank conference participants at the Euro Area Business Cycle Network (EABCN) Workshop on Business Cycle and Acceding Countries, April 23–24, 2004, in Vienna for valuable comments. We also profited very much from comments by Paul de Grauwe, Daniel Gros, and Gene Liang and an anonymous referee. Jarko Fidrmuc and Thomas Gitzel provided us with valuable data.

1. Numbers are averaged over the period 1999 to 2000 (see Boreiko 2002, p. 14).

2. For a similar model that analyses the effect of exchange rate uncertainty on investment and not explicitly on the labor market, see Belke and Gros (2001).

3. The wage bargain leads to a wage rate maximizing the Nash product $(2w - 2\underline{w}) \cdot \beta(2p^* - 2w)1 - \beta$ whose solution is $w = (1 - \beta)\underline{w} + \beta p^*$. Hence the expected net return for the firm is $2p^* - 2w - c = (1 - \beta)(2p^* - 2\underline{w}) - c$.

4. We do not *a priori* restrict the sign of the barrier b. Hence one of these conditions is automatically satisfied, whereas the other is satisfied only if uncertainty is large enough.

5. Formally this results from the fact that equation (4) is only valid whenever σ_1 exceeds b (otherwise the exchange rate could never exceed the barrier and the firm never creates a job in period 1) and whenever $-\sigma_1$ is lower than b (otherwise, the exchange rate could never fall below the barrier and the firm always creates a job in period 1).

6. The other (smaller) solution to this equation is less than $|b|$ and is therefore not feasible.

7. In order to allow for a comparison with the developed economies, the authors made use of the OECD methodology (OECD 1997, 1999).

8. See our table 5.1 and Riboud et al. (2002, p. 7f). However, in terms of employment protection legislation, Slovenia belongs to those countries with the highest degree of inflexibility. This could change if the new proposed labor code is approved (Boeri and Terrell 2002).

9. It should be noted that trade data for euroland substitute the data for the single euro-zone member countries from 1999 on.

10. In the annex we describe the exact algorithm to calculate bilateral CEEC exchange rate variability series.

11. In principle, one might employ option prices to extract implicit forward-looking volatilities, but option prices are generally available only for the US dollar and sometimes against the DM, and even then only for limited periods.

12. The high exchange rate volatility at the end of the 1990s may be explained by a shift of market expectations due to transmission of uncertainty in the course of the East Asian (1997–98) and Russian (1998) financial crises.

13. The results of unit root tests for the employment protection legislation index are available on request. It should be kept in mind that the artificial and constructed character of these institutional variables can create serious problems for their correct empirical treatment. Hence in cases of doubt about the order of integration we do not rely too much on the numerical results but stick to economic intuition when specifying our regression equations.

14. We do this by allowing for country-specific constants in the employment regressions or by implementing real wage growth or a labor market protection legislation index.

15. Due to the limited availability of data for the CEECs with a maximum of nine annual observations country-specific regressions are not (yet) an option.

16. Dummies for different exchange rate regimes are not included throughout the regressions since the impact of different exchange rate regime on the labor market is exactly the focus of our study.

17. The inclusion of a cyclical control variable can itself be interpreted as a first robustness test. Due to lack of space, the country-specific constants, while interesting for their own are not displayed in the tables.

18. See Wooldridge (2002, p. 176f). Serial correlation should not be present in a model that is supposed to be dynamically complete in the conditional mean. However, in cases where we implement an AR(1) term explicitly into our regression equations, the Wooldridge test is, of course, not conducted for obvious reasons.

19. The numerator degrees of freedom can be calculated as the number of explaining variables less one and the denominator degrees of freedom corresponds to the numbers of observations minus the number of regressors.

20. Those based on FGLS lead to strikingly similar conclusions and are available on request.

21. See Canzoneri, Vallés and Viñals (1996, pp. 2f and 11f), Mélitz (1995, p. 496), and Rose (1994).

22. Belke and Gros (2001), for instance, find for Germany that eliminating intra-European exchange rate variability of 1995 should raise the number of jobs, ceteris paribus, by 200 thousand.

23. The results in tables 5.6 and 5.7 corroborate results of our own work, which limits the country sample to Visegrád countries. In Belke and Setzer (2003), we limit the sample to a rather monolithic group with respect to labor market rigidities, namely the Visegrád Economies Czech Republic, Slovakia, Hungary, and Poland. By this, the potential outliers Romania, Bulgaria, and Slovenia are excluded.

References

Arellano, M. 1989. A note on the Anderson-Hsiao estimator for panel data. *Economics Letters* 31: 337–41.

Babetski, J., L. Boone, and M. Maurel. 2002. Exchange rate regimes and supply shocks asymmetry: The case of the accession countries. CEPR Discussion Paper 3408. London.

Belke, A., and D. Gros. 2001. Real impacts of intra-European exchange rate variability: A case for EMU? *Open Economies Review* 12(3): 231–64.

Belke, A., and D. Gros. 2002. Monetary integration in the southern cone. *North American Journal of Economics and Finance* 13(3): 323–49.

Belke, A., and D. Gros. 2002a. Designing EU–US monetary relations: The impact of exchange rate variability on labor markets on both sides of the Atlantic. *World Economy* 25(6): 789–813.

Belke, A., and M. Hebler. 2002. The new social dimension of the EU: Labor market impacts for the accession countries. *Constitutional Political Economy* 13(4): 313–53.

Belke, A., and L. Kaas. 2002. The impact of exchange rate volatility on labor markets: Europe versus United States. Paper presented at the 2002 Meeting of the European Economic Association. Venice.

Belke, A., and R. Setzer. 2003. Exchange rate variability and labor market performance in the Visegrád countries. *Economics of Planning* 36(2): 153–75.

Boeri, T., and K. Terrell. 2002. Institutional determinants of labor reallocation in transition. *Journal of Economic Perspectives* 16(1): 51–76.

Boreiko, D. 2002. EMU and accession countries—Fuzzy cluster analysis of membership. Paper presented at the Conference on Monetary Union: Theory, EMU Experience, and Prospects for Latin America. Organized by Banco Central de Chile, Oesterreichische Nationalbank, and the University of Vienna. April 14–16, Vienna.

Buiter, W. H., and C. Grafe. 2002. Anchor, float or abandon ship: Exchange rate regimes for the accession countries. *Banca Nazionale del Lavoro Quarterly Review* 221 (June): 1–32.

Calvo, G. A., and C. M. Reinhart. 2000. Fixing for your life. NBER Working Paper 8006. Cambridge, MA.

Canzoneri, M. B., J. Vallés, and J. Viñals. 1996. Do exchange rates move to address national imbalances? CEPR Discussion Paper 1498. London.

Cazes, S. 2002. Do labour market institutions matter in transition economies? An analysis of labor market flexibility in the late nineties. International Institute for Labour Studies Discussion Paper 140.

Chang, R., and A. Velasco. 2000. Exchange rate regimes for developing countries. *American Economic Review* 90(2): 71–75.

De Grauwe, P. 1987. International trade and economic growth in the European monetary system. *European Economic Review* 31: 389–98.

Dixit, A. 1989. Entry and exit decisions under uncertainty. *Journal of Political Economy* 97(3): 620–38.

Dornbusch, R. 2001. Fewer monies better monies: Discussion on exchange rates and the choice of monetary-policy regimes. *American Economic Review* 91: 238–42.

Engel, C., and A. Rose. 2000. Currency Unions and International Integration. CEPR Discussion Paper 2659. London.

Flandreau, M., and M. Maurel. 2001. Monetary union, trade integration, and business cycles in 19th century Europe: Just do it. CEPR Discussion Paper 3087. London.

Flood, R. P., and A. Rose. 1995. Fixing exchange rates: A virtual quest for fundamentals. *Journal of Monetary Economics* 36(1): 3–37.

Frankel, J., and A. Rose. 2002. An estimate of the effect of common currencies on trade and income. *Quarterly Journal of Economics* 117(2): 437–66.

Greene, W. H. 2000. *Econometric Analysis*, 4th ed. Upper Saddle River, NJ: Prentice-Hall.

Gros, D., and A. Hobza. 2003. Exchange rate variability as an OCA criterion: Are the candidates ripe for the Euro? International Center for Economic Growth. Working Paper 23.

Hausman, J. 1978. Specification tests in econometrics. *Econometrica* 46(6): 1251–71.

Hobza, A. 2002. CEE candidate countries on the way to the eurozone. The Hague, WRR Working Document. Centre for European Policy Studies. Brussels.

Lavrac, V. 2003. Dynamics of inclusion of accession countries in the monetary union: Some institutional aspects. Paper presented at the Conference on Institutions in Transition. Organized by the Institute of Macroeconomic Analysis and Development (IMAD), Kranjska Gora, June 12–14, 2003.

Levin, A., and C.-F. Lin. 1992. Unit root tests in panel data: Asymptotic and finite-sample properties. UCSD Department of Economics Discussion Paper 92-23. University of California, San Diego.

McKinnon, R. 1999. The east Asian dollar standard, life after death? Paper prepared for the World Bank Seminar on Rethinking the East Asian Miracle. July.

Meese, R. 1990. Currency fluctuations in the post–Bretton Woods era. *Journal of Economic Perspectives* 4(1): 117–34.

Meese, R., and K. Rogoff. 1983. Empirical exchange rate models of the seventies: Do they fit out of sample? *Journal of International Economics* 14(2): 3–24.

Mélitz, J. 1995. The current impasse in research on optimum currency areas. *European Economic Review* 39: 492–500.

Nesporova, A. 2002. Why unemployment remains so high in Central and Eastern Europe? ILO Employment Paper 43. International Labour Organisation, Geneva.

Neumeyer, P. 1998. Currencies and the allocation of risk: The welfare effects of a monetary union. *American Economic Review* 88: 246–59.

Nickell, S. 1997. Unemployment and labor market rigidities: Europe versus North America. *Journal of Economic Perspectives* 11(3): 55–74.

Nitsch, V. 2002. Honey, I shrunk the currency union effect on trade. *World Economy* 25(4): 457–74.

OECD. 1997, 1999. Organisation for Economic Cooperation and Development. Employment Outlook.

Oesterreichische Nationalbank. 2002. *Focus on Transition*, 1/2002. Vienna.

Oesterreichische Nationalbank. 2002a. *Internal Data Bank*. Vienna.

Riboud, M., C. Sánchez-Páramo, and C. Silva-Jáuregui. 2002. Does eurosclerosis matter? Institutional Reform and Labor Market Performance in Central and Eastern European Countries in the 1990s. World Bank Social Protection Discussion Paper 0202. Washington, DC.

Rose, A. 1994. Exchange rate volatility, monetary policy and capital mobility: Empirical evidence on the holy trinity. NBER Working Paper 4630. Cambridge, MA.

Rose, A. 1995. After the deluge: Do fixed exchange rates allow inter-temporal volatility trade-offs? CEPR Discussion Paper 1240. London.

Rose, A. 2000. One money, one market: Estimating the effect of common currencies on trade. *Economic Policy* 30: 9–48.

Sapir, A., and K. Sekkat. 1990. Exchange rate volatility and international trade. In P. de Grauwe, and L. Papademos, eds., *The European Monetary System in the 1990s*. London: Longman, pp. 182–98.

Schnabl, G. 2004. De jure versus de facto exchange rate stabilization in Central and Eastern Europe. Tuebingen Discussion Paper 269. University of Tuebingen.

Stata Corporation. 2003. *STATA Reference G-M—Statistics, Graphics, Data Management*. College Station, Texas.

Vienna Institute for International Economic Studies. 2002. Countries in Transition 2002. *WIIW Handbook of Statistics*. Vienna.

Wooldridge, J. M. 2002. *Econometric Analysis of Cross-Section and Panel Data*. Cambridge: MIT Press.

6

The Influence of Productivity, Demand, and Regulated Prices on the Real Bilateral Exchange Rates of Four Accession Countries

Ronald MacDonald and
Cezary Wójcik

6.1 Introduction

We examine in this chapter the behavior of the internal price ratios and bilateral real exchange rates of a group of four transitional, EU accession countries, namely Estonia, Hungary, the Slovak Republic, and Slovenia. Such an analysis is of interest because of the recent accession of these countries to the European Union and ultimately to full participation in EMU. The latter requires participation in ERM II for two years, and therefore one of the key issues, perhaps *the* key issue, facing these countries is at what point and at what exchange rate should they enter the euro area. Should they, for example, wait until they have reached a high degree of (real) convergence with respect to key economic indicators, such as inflation or real GDP, or should they enter ERM II contemporaneously with their membership in the European Union?

Some commentators (e.g., see Gros 2001) have argued that real convergence should not be an obstacle to a rapid movement to ERM II and, indeed, full monetary union for the accession countries. The argument is that since convergence is likely to be a supply-side phenomenon, it is unlikely to affect the accession countries' competitiveness (discussed in more detail below). In contrast, others (e.g., see MacDonald 2001) have issued a cautionary note that economic convergence should be addressed prior to participation in EMU. The latter argument is based on how much catching-up the accession countries face, which is very different from the experience of previous accession countries.

The issue of catching-up arises because CEEC accession countries' GDP per capita (calculated using PPP weights) is only around USD

8,638 compared to the current EU average of approximately USD 22,303 (in 1999),[1] implying that the accession countries' per capita GDP would have to grow by about 160 percent to reach the EU level. Of course, catching up with the EU average is the raison d'être for the accession countries' participation in European Union. However, the catching-up process will necessarily have implications for the participating countries' inflation, which in turn can have important implications for competitiveness, especially if a country aims for a rigid locking of its exchange rate. Such inflationary consequences will, of course, also have a significance for the ability of the country to meet the Maastricht criterion for inflation (set at no more than 1.5 percentage points above the average rate of inflation of the three EU member states with the lowest inflation). However, proponents of a relatively fast entry to EMU stress that the inflationary pressures generated by the catching-up process are likely to be benign, because they are viewed as emanating from the supply side in the form of the Balassa-Samuelson effect. Although such supply-side effects are likely to be important for the accession countries, it seems highly likely that demand-side influences will also be important determinants of inflation differentials, and as we will argue in this chapter, such demand-side effects are likely to have a deleterious effect on inflation and competitiveness.

Our main purpose here is to examine econometrically the relative importance of demand- and supply-side effects on the internal price ratios, and CPI-based bilateral real exchange rates, of a group of four accession countries.[2] One of the key novelties in our work is that we build new measures of demand- and supply-side effects. For example, previous studies proxied the Balassa-Samuelson effect using the ratio of output to employment in industry (e.g., see Halpern and Wyplosz 1997, 2001; Égert 2002), and demand-side influences have been captured using GDP per capita and the acceleration of inflation (Halpern and Wyplosz 2001). Here we also use the ratio of output to employment as our chosen measure of productivity, but we build this measure from output and employment in the traded sector. We also use new demand-side factors, namely private and government consumption.

Additionally we attempt to calculate the effect of regulated prices on the internal price ratios and CPI-based real exchange rates of our group of accession countries. Such prices are likely to be important, given that they still have a share of between 13 and 24 percent of the accession countries' consumer goods basket. We try to quantify how important these prices are for real exchange rates relative to the demand and supply influences discussed above.

The outline of the remainder of this chapter is as follows: In section 6.2, we present a motivational overview of the influence of demand- and supply-side effects on real exchange rates and also survey the extant empirical literature on the Balassa-Samuelson effect. In section 6.3 the data set used for our econometric tests is presented, along with our econometric tests. Section 6.4 contains our empirical results. Section 6.5 concludes.

6.2 Catching up and Demand and Supply Influences on Real Exchange Rates

A useful way of thinking about the sources of systematic movements in real exchange rates is to consider the following decomposition of the real exchange rate. As usual, we define the logarithm of the (CPI-based) real exchange rate as

$$q_t \equiv s_t - p_t + p_t^*, \tag{1}$$

where q represents the real exchange rate, s is the nominal exchange rate, p is the overall price measure (the CPI); an asterisk denotes a foreign variable and lowercase letters denote natural logarithms. These overall prices may be decomposed into traded and nontraded components as

$$p_t = \alpha_t p_t^T + (1 - \alpha_t) p_t^{NT}, \tag{2}$$

$$p_t^* = \alpha_t^* p_t^{T*} + (1 - \alpha_t^*) p_t^{NT*}, \tag{2'}$$

where p_t^T denotes the price of traded goods, p_t^{NT} denotes the price of nontraded goods, and the αs denote the share of traded goods in the economy. A similar relationship to (1) may be defined for the price of traded goods as

$$q_t^T \equiv s_t - p_t^T + p_t^{T*}. \tag{3}$$

Using expressions (1) to (3), we may obtain our desired decomposition of the real exchange rate as

$$q_t \equiv q_t^T + q_t^{T,NT}, \tag{4}$$

where $q_t^{NT,T} = (\alpha_t - 1)(p_t^{NT} - p_t^T) - (\alpha_t - 1)(p_t^{NT*} - p_t^{T*})$ is the so-called internal price ratio, the relative price of nontraded to traded goods in the home country relative to the foreign country. What are the factors driving these two components of the real exchange rate? Consider, first, the internal price ratio, $q_t^{T,NT}$.

In the traditional Balassa-Samuelson approach to understanding systematic movements in the real exchange rate (e.g., see De Gregorio, Giovannini, and Wolf 1994) productivity shocks in the traded sector are the key force driving the internal price ratio and, ultimately, the CPI-based real exchange rate. The key assumptions in the Balassa-Samuelson approach are that the law of one price (LOOP) holds and therefore q_t^T is zero, or constant, production technology is Cobb-Douglas, with constant returns to scale, and there is some mechanism equalizing wages between the traded and nontraded sectors. With these assumptions it is then straightforward to demonstrate that a positive shock to total factor productivity in the traded sector raises the average wage in the economy, the relative price of nontraded to traded goods rises, and the CPI-based real exchange rate appreciates. Hence the Balassa-Samuelson prediction is that there should be a positive (negative) relationship between total factor productivity in the traded (nontraded) sector and the CPI-based real exchange rate, and the coefficient should be equal to the share of expenditure on nontraded goods.

A second supply-side influence on the internal price ratio involves relative factor endowments. In the traditional Hecksher-Ohlin two-factor, two-good relative factor endowments model, nontraded (traded) goods are assumed to be relatively labor-intensive (capital-intensive) in production. High per capita income countries are assumed to have a comparative advantage in producing commodities, so the relative price of nontraded goods will be higher in countries with relatively high per capita income.

The influence of demand, of both the public and private sector, on the internal price ratio has been highlighted by Dornbusch (1988), Neary (1988), and Bergstrand (1991). As a country catches up and income rises, demand-side factors can affect the internal price ratio if preferences are nonhomothetic. Usually preferences are thought to be biased in favor of the nontraded good because services are viewed as superior goods. In this case, of course, the demand-side influences would reinforce the supply-side effects, and although this may be thought of as an equilibrium relationship, there may be policy issues in the short to medium run for an accession country wishing to avoid excessive inflationary consequences. The policy implications of demand-side effects are further likely to be more pronounced if preferences are skewed in favor of traded goods.

Starting with Bergstrand (1991), a number of studies have sought to capture both the demand- and supply-side influences on the real exchange rate using GDP per capita. For example, Bergstrand (1991) has demonstrated that over 80 percent of the cross-sectional variation of real exchange rates can be explained by per capita GDP and a constant, and that a 1 percent increase in per capita GDP produces a 0.5 percent increase in the real exchange rate (or the inflation differential). Slok and De Broek (2000) have demonstrated that a similar relationship also holds for the current group of accession countries.

As we have seen, an essential component of the Balassa-Samuelson hypothesis is that the LOOP holds continuously and that q_t^T is constant or zero. However, the broad thrust of the empirical evidence for developed countries is that the LOOP does not hold. This is evident from studies that focus explicitly on testing the LOOP (e.g., see Isard 1977) and also studies that examine the decomposition of the CPI-based real exchange rate. For example, Engel (1993) and Rogers and Jenkins (1995) have shown that for developed countries the variability of q_t^T always dominates the variability of $q_t^{T,NT}$. There are a number of interpretations for this finding, such as the importance of sticky prices (e.g., see Mussa 1986), the pricing-to-market behavior of firms (see Betts and Devereux 1996), the importance of transaction costs in imparting nonlinear adjustment to q_t^T (see Obstfeld and Taylor 1997), or the imperfect substitutability of traded goods across countries (see MacDonald and Ricci 2002). Although all the foregoing arguments seem plausible, the issue of imperfect substitutability seems especially so, given that casual empiricism suggests that goods entering international trade are imperfectly substitutable: a 3 series BMW produced in Germany, for example, is not a perfect substitute for, say, a Ford Mondeo produced in the United Kingdom. Indeed, for white goods such as refrigerators, which appear to be very similar across brands and countries, it is well known that even within Europe such items are highly differentiated to appeal to different tastes in different countries.

Even if q_t^T is the dominant component in explaining real exchange rate variability, this does not necessarily mean that Balassa-Samuelson effects are unimportant. A number of studies have examined the impact of productivity in the traded and nontraded sectors on the real exchange rate. For example, using the OECD sectoral data base to construct measures of total factor productivity (TFP), Chinn and Johnston

(1999) demonstrate for the US dollar bilateral exchange rates of a set of developed countries that the Balassa-Samuelson terms are correctly signed and statistically significant with a point estimate close to 0.8. MacDonald and Ricci (2001) confirm this result for a similar panel of countries.

A number of studies have quantified the Balassa-Samuelson effect, and also demand-side effects, for the current group of accession countries. The first study to estimate the effects of productivity for transitional economies is that of Halpern and Wyplosz (1997), who use a reduced-form approach to capture the effects of productivity and other measures of economic effectiveness on the real exchange rates of a panel of eighty countries (the countries in the panel fall into the following panel groupings: OECD countries, Africa, Southeast Asia, Latin America, and transition economies). Halpern and Wyplosz are able to distinguish among these different groupings using fixed and random effects estimators. The productivity measure is average productivity (i.e., they do not distinguish between productivity in the tradable and nontradable sectors), and this is captured by GDP per worker. Their measure of aggregate average productivity produces a large and significant coefficient, which is shown to be sensitive to the inclusion of regional and country dummies—it declines quite dramatically as such dummies are added in. Conversely, the coefficient on investment in human capital (proxied using secondary school enrollment) rises as the regional and country dummies are introduced. They also find that a 10 percent decline in the size of agriculture relative to industry increases the dollar wage by between 1 and 2 percent. A 10 percent increase in the size of the government raises wages by 3 to 6 percent. This effect is interpreted as measuring the effect of public services and infrastructure on aggregate productivity.

Halpern and Wyplosz (2001) focus more directly on the Balassa-Samuelson effect, using a panel data set for nine transition countries over the period 1991 to 1999. Their measure of productivity in the tradable sector is taken to be the ratio of industry output to employment, while the measure of productivity in the nontradable sector is taken to be the ratio of output to employment in the service sector. Their panel regressions involve regressing the relative price of the service sector to the industry price onto the two productivity measures and the two demand-side proxies, namely PPP-adjusted GDP per capita and the change in the rate of inflation. The productivity terms enter with the correct signs and are both statistically significant. The coefficient on productivity in the industry sector is 0.24; that for the coefficient on productivity in the service sector is −0.18. GDP per capita also entered with a small, though positive, coefficient; the inflation effect did not have a clear-cut impact on the internal price ratio. Halpern and Wyplosz demonstrate that their results are robust to a number of different estimation methods and that the Balassa-Samuleson effect is strongest in a regime of floating exchange rates.

Égert (2002) examines the Balassa-Samuelson effect for the Czech Republic, Hungary, Poland, Slovakia, and Slovenia over the first quarter of 1991 to the second quarter of 2001. The productivity measure used is the ratio of the index of industrial production to employment in that sector (productivity in nontradables is set to zero, since no data are available). As in Halpern and Wyplosz, the industrial sector proxies the traded sector, while the service sector represents the nontraded sector. The relative price of nontraded goods is determined as changes in the price of services relative to the producer price index of final industrial goods. The econometric results are generated using the Johansen cointegration method, on a country-by-country basis, and using panel cointegration tests for the group of countries. Significant and correctly signed productivity effects are reported for this group of countries with respect to both the internal price ratio and also the CPI-based real exchange rate. For the single-country estimates Égert (2002) finds the coefficient on the productivity term to be greater than minus one for the internal price ratio and below minus one when the CPI based real exchange rate is the dependent variable. The panel-based cointegration tests produce coefficients on productivity that are similar to the single-country results.

MacDonald and Wójcik (2004) examine the impact of productivity and demand shocks on the real effective exchange rates of the same group of countries considered in this chapter. They show that the impact of productivity on real effective exchange rates is small, although statistically significant. As we will see, in this chapter we report a much bigger impact for the effect of productivity differentials on bilateral real exchange rates. MacDonald and Wójcik (2004) also find that regulated price effects dominate the effect of productivity on the real effectiveness. MacDonald and Wójcik also calculate the implications of the productivity effects for inflation differentials once the countries participate in the euro and find that these effects are also small.

In this section we have discussed the potential impact demand- and supply-side effects can have on the real exchange rate. We now explore the relationship between these variables for a group of accession countries. Having done so, we then draw out the policy implications of our findings in a concluding section.

6.3 Data Description and Estimation Methods

Our empirical analysis focuses on four accession countries for which good quality productivity data are available. The four countries are Estonia, Hungary, the Slovak Republic, and Slovenia. Other important accession countries, such as the Czech Republic, Poland, and other Baltic countries, are excluded simply because we were unable to obtain comparable data for these countries. Austria serves as the foreign, or numéraire, country. The choice of Austria as numéraire reflects the fact that it is geographically very close to Hungary, Slovenia, and the Slovak Republic (it has a common border with these countries), has close trading links with these countries, and is structurally very similar to the German economy, which is their main trading partner.

The data frequency is quarterly, and the time series dimension differs across countries and variables. However, we have constructed a balanced panel from the individual countries for the first quarter of 1995 to the first quarter of 2001. Apart from the interest rates, all the data are in constant prices and are transformed into a base index with 1995:1Q = 100. All time series, apart from the real interest rates (RIR) and net foreign assets (NFA), have been seasonally adjusted using an X-11 filter, and apart from the interest rates, all data have been transformed by taking natural logarithms. Data on NFA and interest rates are taken from the IMF's International Financial Statistics CD-ROM, while data on Austrian interest rates are sourced from the OeNB. All other data were obtained from the respective central banks or statistical offices.

We use two key dependent variables in our study. The first is the internal price ratio, Lrp100nta, the price index of nontradables relative to the price index of tradables, and the second, lrer, is the real bilateral exchange rate of Austria relative to the accession country's currency. We have constructed this exchange rate such that an increase implies an appreciation of the real exchange rate. In defining tradable and nontradable categories (for prices and productivity), we follow the definitions used in the industrial country literature (e.g., see De Gregorio et al. 1994). For our measure of relative prices, tradables comprises the following categories: food and nonalcoholic beverages, alcoholic beverages and tobacco, clothing and footwear, transport and communication. Nontradables comprises the following categories: housing, household goods, health, recreation and entertainment, and miscellaneous goods and services.[3]

The key independent variable used in our study is productivity in the tradable relative to the nontradable sector. We use labor productivity as a proxy for marginal total factor productivity; it is calculated by dividing value added, or GDP, by employment in the respective sector. We use labor productivity here rather than the theoretically more appropriate total factor productivity, simply because of the lack of availability of the latter. For this measure the tradable sector includes the following categories: agriculture, hunting, and forestry; fishing; mining and quarrying; manufacturing, transport, and communication. The nontradable sector includes the following categories: electricity, gas and water supply; construction; wholesale and retail trade; hotels and restaurants; financial intermediation; real estate, renting, and business activities; public administration and defense; education, health, and social work; and other community social and personal activities.

Due to the lack of more disaggregated data for Hungary, tradables contained mining and quarrying; manufacturing and electricity; and transport, storage, and communications. Nontradables for Hungary comprised construction; trade; repair; hotels and restaurants; financial intermediation and real estate activities; public administration; education, health, and social work; and other community social and personal service activities. For Slovakia, the tradable sector contains agriculture; mining and quarrying; manufacturing and transport; storage and communication. The nontradables, in turn, consist of electricity, gas, and water supply; trade; repair of motor vehicles; and other services.

Our constrained productivity measure is labeled lratna, and the unconstrained measures are lrata (productivity in tradables) and lrana (productivity in nontradables).

The demand-side variables included as explanatory variables are consumption as a proportion of GDP, private consumption as a proportion of GDP, and total consumption as a proportion of GDP. For Slovenia, quarterly data on consumption are only available from 1999.

Therefore, to construct a quarterly series for the period before 1999, we extrapolated the annual values. The final set of explanatory variables involve regulated prices.

As noted above, our empirical tests are conducted for a panel of four countries. Recent developments in the econometrics of panel data sets were sought to address the potential nonstationarity of the series entering the panel. In particular, McKoskey and Kao (1998), Pedroni (1997), and Phillips and Moon (1998) have proposed panel equivalents to the single equation fully modified estimator while McKoskey and Kao (1998) and Mark and Sul (1999) have proposed using a panel dynamic ordinary least squares (DOLS) estimator. Since Kao and Chiang (1999) have demonstrated that the panel DOLS procedure exhibits less bias than the panel ordinary least squares OLS and panel fully modified estimators and Mark and Sul (1999) have emphasized the tractability of the estimator, we employ a panel DOLS estimator for all our regressions.

A version of the panel DOLS estimator that allows for limited heterogeneity in the form of fixed effects is

$$y_{it} = \theta_{1i} + \theta_{2t} + \theta_3 x_{it} + \sum_{j=-p}^{+n} \theta_{4j} \Delta x_{it+j} + \omega_{it}, \tag{5}$$

where y_{it} is a scalar, taken to be either lrpnta or LRER in our application, x_{it} is a vector of explanatory variables, discussed above, with dimension k, θ_{1i} is an individual fixed effect, θ_{2t} is a time effect, θ_3 percent represents a vector of coefficients, p is the maximum lag length, n is the maximum lead length, and ω is a Gaussian vector error process. The leads and lags of the difference terms are included to ensure that the error term is orthogonalized. Our representation of the panel DOLS estimator assumes that the dynamics are the same across individuals.

Our econometric approach involves starting with a baseline specification and making panel regressions of the two relative price terms onto the relative productivity terms. Robustness checks are then performed on these regressions to ensure that any significant effects of productivity do not result from an omitted variable bias. We then go on to explore the influence of demand side effects, and regulated price and distribution effects on the baseline model. We believe that this sequential approach helps clarify the role that each of the key variables have on the relative price terms.

6.4   Empirical Results

6.4.1   The Baseline Model and the Balassa-Samuelson Effect

In this section we consider the effect of the Balassa-Samuelson term on the internal price ratio and on the CPI-based real exchange rate. For example, in the first column of table 6.1 we report results from the panel DOLS regression of the internal price ratio (lrpnta) onto the constrained Balassa-Samuelson effect. The point estimate is correctly signed and strongly significant. The magnitude of the coefficient on the Balassa-Samuelson effect, although numerically below the magnitude of the expenditure share on nontraded goods, is nonetheless insignificantly different from this expenditure share. The unconstrained coefficients reported in column 2 are correctly signed, strongly significant and of a plausible magnitude. The unconstrained estimates show that the coefficient on tradable productivity is much larger than the coefficient on productivity in nontradables, and indeed the hypothesis that they are equal and opposite is clearly rejected. This would seem to be evidence against a Balassa-Samuelson interpretation of the effect of productivity and favor the MacDonald and Ricci (2002) interpretation. Columns 3 and 4 show that the constrained and unconstrained Balassa-Samuelson terms have a much larger effect on the CPI-based real exchange rate (LRER), and in this case the restriction that the coefficients are equal and opposite is not rejected. The importance of the Balassa-Samuelson effect in this regression contrasts sharply with that of MacDonald and Wójcik (2004), who found only a small effect when using real effective exchange rates as the dependent variable.

In columns 5 and 6 we incorporate the constrained and unconstrained Balassa-Samuelson terms into a regression for the CPI-based real exchange rate containing both relative net foreign assets as a proportion of GDP and the real interest differential as explanatory variables. These variables are seen as key variables in explaining systematic movements of real exchange rates (see MacDonald 1999), and we include them here to ensure that the effects of the Balassa-Samuelson effect on the real exchange rate are not spurious. In accordance with theory the coefficients on both NFA and RIR are expected to be positive. Note that coefficients on the unconstrained Balassa-Samuelson terms are similar, in terms of significance and sign, to the regressions where NFA and the real interest differential are not included, whereas the coefficients of the constrained term is larger. The restriction that the coefficients on productivity are equal and

Table 6.1
Basic Balassa-Samuelson model and a robustness check (estimation method: PDOLS)

	Lrpnta	Lrpnta	LRER	LRER	LRER	LRER	LRER	LRER	LRER
NFA/GDP (rnfagdpa)					0.0001 (1.55)	0.0002** (2.00)	0.0003*** (2.92)	0.003*** (3.01)	
Real interest rates (rir)					−0.016*** (3.21)	−0.009 (1.18)	0.005 (0.93)	0.007 (0.048)	
Balassa-Samuelson effect (lratna)	0.41*** (5.79)		0.57*** (3.78)		2.57*** (7.58)				
Productivity in tradables (lrata)		0.51*** (7.45)		2.02*** (6.52)		2.19*** (4.00)			
Productivity in nontradables (lrana)		−0.23* (3.08)		−2.40*** (7.06)		−2.62*** (7.80)			
Testing restrictions on Balassa-Samuelson[a]									
F Test		20.544		1.84		0.995			
Probability		(0.000)		(0.17)		(0.321)			
Adjusted R^2	0.27	0.39	0.13	0.39	0.49	0.50	0.08	0.089	0.02
Number of observations	100	100	100	100	100	100	100	100	100

Note: Estimations are in levels *, **, and ***, statistically significant at 10, 5, and 1 percent levels; absolute t-values in parentheses.
a. Wald test on restrictions: HO: Irata = −Irana.

opposite is also continued. The coefficients on the NFA term are correctly signed (although insignificant in one case), while the coefficients on the real interest rate term are wrongly signed, only one being significant.

The last three columns contain the results from regressing the real exchange rate on various permutations of the two macro variables. The sign, magnitude, and significance of the coefficients on NFA in these regressions are similar to the regressions that include the macro-variables with the Balassa-Samuelson term; the coefficients on the real interest rate terms are insignificantly positive.

The unconstrained estimates of the Balassa-Samuelson effect contrast with that reported in MacDonald and Ricci (2002) for a panel of G7 countries. They found that the coefficient on productivity in the tradable sector was smaller, in absolute terms, than the coefficient on nontradables. In the context of their model, MacDonald and Ricci rationalized this in terms of imperfectly substitutable traded goods and a home expenditure bias. Our finding of such a strong symmetrical productivity effect reflects, we believe, the relative importance of productivity on the evolution of real exchange rates for the transition countries.

6.4.2 Demand-side Variables and the Balassa-Samuelson Effect

The first three columns of table 6.2 explore the effects of adding in the three demand variables—government consumption, private consumption, and total consumption—in addition to the Balassa-Samuelson effect onto the internal price equation. As can be seen, the coefficients on the demand variables are similar across the three equations, each being approximately −0.1. It is noteworthy that the coefficient on the Balassa-Samuelson terms is unaffected by the introduction of the demand-side variables, and it would seem that the two variables coexist and have independent influences on the real exchange rate. Perhaps the most notable feature of the coefficient on the demand-side variables is that they have negative signs. This means they are wrongly signed in terms of the conventional effect referred to in section 6.3. Of course, as we have noted, the conventional (positive) sign presupposes that the law of one price holds. If it does not, and this is likely to be particularly so for the accession countries, then the negative sign is not entirely unexpected, since traded goods are more likely to be regarded as luxury goods in the accession countries than services are, which is the conventional assumption. Clearly, the negative sign has important

Table 6.2
Basic Balassa-Samuelson model: Demand side and a robustness check (estimation method: PDOLS)

	Lrpnta	Lrpnta	Lrpnta	Lrpnta	Lrpnta	Lrpnta	LRER	LRER	LRER	LRER	LRER	LRER
NFA/GDP (rnfangdpa)							0.001 (1.61)	0.001 (1.49)	0.0001 (1.56)	0.0002 (1.55)	0.0002* (1.84)	0.0002* (1.74)
Real interest rates (rir)							−0.015*** (2.81)	−0.016*** (2.96)	−0.016*** (2.90)	−0.013 (1.45)	−0.011 (1.31)	−0.012 (1.40)
Balassa-Samuelson effect (lratna)	0.42*** (5.97)	0.43*** (6.01)	0.51*** (6.59)				2.54*** (7.11)	2.59*** (7.02)	2.57*** (7.04)			
Productivity in tradables (lrata)				0.52*** (7.18)	0.51*** (7.28)	0.51*** (7.26)				2.48*** (3.81)	2.32*** (3.88)	2.40*** (3.19)
Productivity in nontradables (lrana)				−0.21** (2.51)	−0.21** (2.45)	−0.21** (2.46)				−2.58*** (7.11)	−2.65*** (7.10)	−2.62*** (7.08)
Government consumption/GDP (lrgcgdpa)	−0.10** (2.27)			−0.003 (0.06)			0.056 (0.28)			0.15 (0.59)		
Private consumption/GDP (lrpcgdpa)		−0.13** (2.03)			−0.03 (0.46)			0.23 (0.08)			0.13 (0.39)	
Total consumption/GDP (lrtcgdpa)			−0.11* (1.73)			−0.01 (0.28)			0.065 (0.25)			0.19 (0.60)
Wald test[a]												
Chi-square				13.84	15.52	14.48				0.026	0.355	1.844
Probability				0.000	0.000	0.000				0.870	0.552	0.179
Adjusted R^2	0.28	0.27	0.24	0.37	0.37	0.37	0.47	0.47	0.47	0.48	0.48	0.48
Number of observations	100	100	100	100	100	100	100	100	100	100	100	100

Note: Estimations are in levels *, **, and ***, statistically significant at 10, 5, and 1 percent level; absolute t-values in parentheses.
a. Wald test on restrictions: HO: lrata = lrana = (demand variable) = 0.

implications for these countries as they catch up: some of the catching-up, by spilling over into the traded sector, is likely to make that sector uncompetitive.

However, when the demand-side variables are introduced into the internal price equation with the Balassa-Samuelson term unconstrained (columns 4, 5, and 6), the coefficients on the demand-side variables increase and become insignificant. The source of the insignificance of the demand-side variables in the unconstrained regressions seems to stem from the collinearity of the variables. For example, the correlation coefficients between lratna and each of the demand-side variables is around 0.1 in absolute terms; however, when the productivity variables are entered unconstrained, the correlation coefficient between the demand variables and lrana is between 0.4 and 0.5 in absolute terms. Qualitatively the results for the internal price ratio are confirmed in the regressions for the CPI-based real exchange rates. Here the coefficients on productivity, NFA, and the real interest differential remain unchanged as demand-side variables are added in, although the coefficients on the demand-side variables are all insignificant.

In sum, the demand-side variables have a small, significantly negative effect on the internal price ratio and an effect on the CPI-based real exchange rate, which is small and statistically insignificant.

6.4.3   The Balassa-Samuelson Effect and the Wage Effect

As we noted in section 6.3, the key channel through which the Balassa-Samuelson effect influences the overall CPI-based real exchange rate is through wages. Following MacDonald and Ricci (2001), we include wages in our regressions containing the Balassa-Samuelson effect. If wages are indeed the channel through which the Balassa-Samuelson effect operates, then their introduction should make the productivity term(s) insignificant. These results are presented in table 6.3 for both the internal price ratio and the overall CPI-based real exchange rate. The results for both the internal price ration and the overall CPI-based real exchange rate are interesting. Although the coefficients on the productivity terms drop, compared to the regressions where we do not control for the wage, they are still significantly different from zero. This finding is similar to the results reported in MacDonald and Ricci (2001) for the G7 found that the coefficients on productivity in both the traded and nontraded sectors remained statistically significant after the introduction of the wage. However, the results here differ from MacDonald and Ricci (2001), since the coefficient on productivity in

Table 6.3
Introducing the wage effect (estimation method: PDOLS)

	LRPNTA	LRPNTA	LRER	LRER	LRER	LRER
NFA/GDP (rnfangdpa)					0.0001 (1.36)	0.0002** (2.08)
Real interest rates (rir)					−0.02*** (4.89)	0.014** (2.02)
Balassa-Samuelson effect (lratna)	0.33*** (3.47)		1.38*** (3.66)		1.72*** (4.90)	
Productivity in tradables (lrata)		0.45*** (4.76)		1.19*** (3.00)		1.25*** (2.39)
Productivity in nontradables (lrana)		−0.19** (2.06)		−1.77*** (4.48)		−1.73*** (4.92)
Real wage (lrwea)	0.08 (1.58)	0.05 (1.14)	0.63*** (3.07)	0.67*** (3.25)	0.90*** (5.13)	0.90*** (5.04)
Adjusted R^2	0.30	0.42	0.44	0.47	0.63	0.63
Number of observations	100	100	100	100	100	100

Note: Estimations are in levels *, **, and ***, statistically significant at 10, 5, and 1 percent level; absolute t-values in parentheses.

the traded sector remains significantly positive, rather than significantly negative.

6.4.4 The Influence of Regulated Prices

Deregulation of prices has been one of the main components of transition from central planning to market economies. For example, there is considerable empirical evidence that the adjustment of regulated prices played an important role in the inflationary process and in the development of relative prices in the transitional economies throughout the last decade (e.g., see Pujol and Griffith 1998; Wozniak 1998).[4] The cost recovery hypothesis developed by Zavoiko (1995) provides the most influential theoretical justification of this evidence.

Previously the importance of regulated prices in determining relative prices and real exchange rates in these economies were analyzed separately from the Balassa-Samuelson effect. The potential influence of regulated price on the real exchange rate may be considered by using a variant of the decomposition considered in section 6.2. In particular, if we again assume that the price level is a geometric average of tradable and nontradable prices as in (2). By additionally assuming that the weights of regulated prices on the nontradable price index is γ, while the regulated component in tradables is 0 and that there are no regulated prices in Austria, then

$$q_t \equiv (s_t - p_t^T + p_t^{T*}) + (\alpha - 1)[(\gamma p_t^{NT,r} + (1 - \gamma)p_t^{NT,d}) - p_t^T]$$
$$- (\alpha - 1)(p_t^{NT*} - p_t^{T*}), \tag{6}$$

where the r (d) superscript refers to regulated (deregulated) prices. By adding and subtracting the term $(1 - \alpha)\gamma p_t^{NT,d}$ to (6) a similar expression to (4) may be obtained:

$$q_t \equiv (s_t - p_t^T + p_t^{T*}) + (\alpha - 1)(p_t^{NT,d} - p_t^T) + (\alpha - 1)(p_t^{NT,r} - p_t^{NT,d})$$
$$- (\alpha - 1)(p_t^{NT*} - p_t^{T*}). \tag{7}$$

Equation (7) suggests that the cointegrating relationship for the real exchange rate should include the relative price of unregulated nontradable prices to tradable prices, the relative price of regulated nontradable prices to nonregulated nontradable prices, and the relative price of nontradables to tradables in the foreign country. Unfortunately, our data set only allows us to analyze the effects of regulated prices, and not nonregulated prices, and the productivity differential on the real exchange rate. The regulated prices predominately relate to nontraded goods. (Data appendix B contains a representative listing of regulated prices for the Slovak Republic.)

In figure 6.1 we plot the regulated prices alongside the real exchange rates for each of the countries. For Estonia we note that the trend behaviour of the two series is quite similar, while for the other countries it is not at all similar. Table 6.4 reports the main results. Our regulated price term (lrpa)[5] has a (highly) statistically positive effect on the internal price ratio and on the real exchange rate, irrespective of the specification considered. The point coefficient is between 0.14 and 0.16 for the internal price ratio but much higher for overall real exchange rate, ranging from 0.82 to 0.97. Moreover, introducing the regulated price term significantly increases the model's explanatory power, and this would seem to confirm the importance of this variable for the relative price and real exchange rate developments in these countries.

Probably the most striking result of these estimates is that once the regulated price term is introduced into the model, the significance of the Balassa-Samuelson term essentially vanishes. In particular, when regulated prices are introduced into the internal price equation, jointly

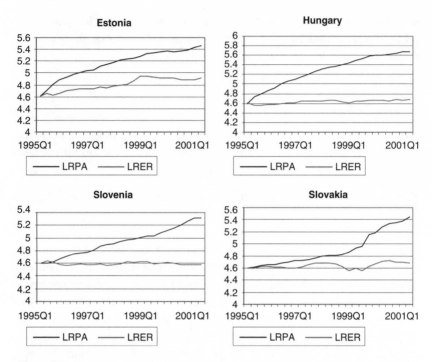

Figure 6.1
Regulated price (LRPA) and real exchange rate (LRER) dynamics in Estonia, Hungary, Slovenia, and Slovakia in 1995Q1 to 2001Q.

with productivity, the constrained Balassa-Samuelson term becomes insignificantly distinguishable from zero. The same holds when we introduce the regulated price term into the macroequation with the real exchange rate as the dependent variable: the constrained Balassa-Samuelson term becomes statistically insignificant. These results are confirmed in the unconstrained case, with the exception of the coefficients on tradables in column 3 and nontradables in column 8, which become smaller compared to the benchmark BS model in table 6.1 while still remaining significant at the 1 percent level.

All in all, our results suggest that the adjustment of regulated prices had an independent and possibly much stronger effect on internal price ratios and on real exchange rates in transitional economies than the Balassa-Samuelson effect did. This finding is important, given the fact that regulated prices still account for a high share of the accession countries' consumer basket, and many prices are still below the cost recovery level.[6]

Table 6.4
Basic Balassa-Samuelson model: Regulated prices and a robustness check (estimation method: PDOLS)

	Lrpnta	Lrpnta	Lrpnta	LRER	LRER	LRER	LRER	LRER	LRER
NFA/GDP (rnfangdpa)				0.0002*** (5.91)	−0.0002*** (4.41)			−0.0002*** (5.96)	
RIR				−0.007*** (3.82)	−0.008*** (2.80)			0.005*** (3.63)	
Balassa-Samuelson effect (lratna)		0.07 (1.05)		0.20 (1.20)		0.09 (0.59)			
Productivity in tradables (lrata)			0.17*** (3.01)		0.26 (1.14)		0.06 (0.42)		
Productivity in nontradables (lrana)			0.10 (1.88)		−0.19 (1.13)		−0.41*** (2.47)		
Regulated prices (lrpa)	0.16*** (11.78)	0.14*** (8.26)	0.14*** (10.56)	0.95*** (20.95)	0.95*** (20.13)	0.82*** (18.74)	0.82*** (20.45)	0.97*** (29.91)	0.84*** (25.88)
Adjusted R^2	0.62	0.62	0.77	0.92	0.93	0.89	0.55	0.93	0.89
Number of observations	100	100	100	100	100	100	100	100	100

Note: Estimations are in levels *, **, and ***, statistically significant at 10, 5, and 1 percent level; absolute t-values in parentheses.

6.4.5 Robustness Checks

We also implemented all of the above-noted tests using a variety of other estimators, such as static OLS and DOLS with a correction for contemporaneous correlation. The application of these different estimators did not change the tenor of our results, and they are therefore not reported here (but are available from the authors on request).

6.5 Concluding Comments

In this chapter we reexamined the effects of productivity differentials and demand on the CPI-based real exchange rates and internal price ratios of a group of four accession countries. In contrast to other empirical studies of CEECs, we use new, and we believe superior, measures of both productivity and demand-side effects for these countries. Our tests were conducted for a panel of four countries: Estonia, Hungary, the Slovak Republic, and Slovenia. Among our main findings are the following: Conditioning real exchange rates and internal price ratios on productivity in the traded and nontraded sectors, and on a number of standard macro variables, we find both productivity terms to be statistically significant and, additionally, to have a much stronger influence on external exchange rates than on internal exchange rates. (This result is in contrast to MacDonald and Wójcik 2004 who did not find this kind of discrepancy using effective, rather than bilateral, exchange rates as a measure of external exchange rates.) The influence of demand-side effects on the two dependent variables (CPI-based real exchange rates and internal price ratios) is weakly negative. Introducing regulated prices into our productivity-based regressions removes the significance of the relative productivity effect and the regulated price effect is significant. In common with MacDonald and Ricci's (2001) study for the G7, we find that productivity in the distribution sector has a significantly positive effect on the internal price ratios of Estonia and Slovenia.

Our results for the effects of productivity on the real exchange rate and internal price ratio contrast with those of Halpern and Wyplosz. In particular, these authors find a much smaller effect of productivity differentials—around half our estimates—on the internal price ratio of a panel of nine transition countries. Halpern and Wyplosz's results for the effects of demand side on the internal price ratio are similar to ours in the sense that they report a small (although positive coefficient) on the demand side effect. The differences between our productivity effects and theirs could reflect the use of a larger panel (unavailable to us because of our chosen measure of productivity) or our use of a different measure of productivity (which we believe is superior to other measures used for transition economies). Our estimated coefficients derived from regressions of the internal price ratio and productivity are similar to Égert (2002) (less than one in absolute terms), but the coefficients on productivity derived from our real exchange rate equations are much smaller, in absolute terms, than Égert's.

We now consider the policy implications of our results for the membership of our group of countries in EMU. Recently some economists (e.g., see Gros 2001) have advocated a relatively rapid movement by the current group of accession countries to full monetary union with the European Union. In this view, catching-up is not deemed to be an important issue with respect to an accession country's competitiveness because it is seen as a purely supply-side phenomenon, and any inflation generated is regarded as benign in the context of a Balassa-Samuelson effect. Our results would seem to offer a cautionary warning to this view, since the inflationary implications of the Balassa-Samuelson effect would seem to be quite large.

For example, using the estimates from the bilateral real exchange rate regressions, we find for the two fast-growing countries in our study, Hungary and Estonia, a Balassa-Samuelson implied inflation differential (against the numéraire country, Austria) of 7.2 percentage points and 7.9 percentage points respectively. For the remaining, slower growing countries we obtain an inflation differential of around 2.3 percentage points for Slovenia and 3.2 percentage points for Slovakia. Clearly, the inflationary implications for the fast-growing countries are inconsistent with the Maastricht criteria, and the inflationary effects would in all likelihood lower the competitiveness of these countries' tradable sectors if they were to participate in the euro prematurely. These inflationary effects are little changed when the effects of the demand side are added in, although the negative coefficient of our demand term suggests that such demand-side effects could have a potentially deleterious effect on competitiveness and therefore should not be neglected. Our inflationary findings are larger than those reported by Halpern and Wyplosz (2001) and in MacDonald and Wójcik (2004) (for effective exchange rates), although they are similar in magnitude to those reported by Égert (2002).

The other main conclusion to stem from our work is that the role of regulated prices has a more significant effect on the real exchange rates and internal price ratios of our group of accession countries than the Balassa-Samuelson effect. Therefore, in future discussions of the European monetary process for accession countries, more weight should be given to the effect of regulated prices. Of course, the interpretation of the effect of regulated prices is not straightforward. If regulated prices have moved from initially low disequilibrium levels to current levels that are close to equilibrium, then past correlations may not offer much guidance to policy makers in the period of runup to monetary union. However, we believe that for our group of accession countries regulated prices are still away from their equilibrium levels, and therefore regulated prices provide information on the determinants of relative prices over and above that contained in the standard demand- and supply-side measures used in this and other studies.[7]

Data Appendix A: Sources, Definitions, and Notation of Variables

The sources of the variables used in this chapter are the IMF's IFS data disc, and where a series is not attainable from this source the authors obtained the data directly from the statistical departments of the central banks of the countries featured in the econometric analysis. (This is the case, for example, for the productivity series.)

Country Mnemonics

ee   Estonia

hu   Hungary

si   Slovenia

sk   Sloval Republic

aa   Austria

Variable Definitions

Prices

Lp100nta   Log of the relative price of nontradable to tradables, seasonally adjusted

Lrpa   Log of regulated prices, seasonally adjusted

Lrpnta   Log of the relative price of nontradable to tradables, relative to the same variable in Austria, seasonally adjusted

Productivity Variables

Latna Log of relative productivity in the tradable to nontradable sectors, seasonally adjusted

Latnas Log of relative productivity in tradable to nontradable sectors, seasonally adjusted, corrected by labor shares

Lata Log of productivity in the tradable sector, seasonally adjusted

Lana Log of productivity in the nontradable sector, seasonally adjusted

Lratnas, Lratna, Lrata, Lrana As above, but all relative to similarly define variables for Austria

Latnoda Log of relative productivity in the tradable to nontradable sectors, calculated without the distribution sector and seasonally adjusted

Latoda Log of productivity in tradable sector, calculated without the distribution sector and seasonally adjusted

Lanoda Log of productivity in the nontradable sector, calculated without the distribution sector and seasonally adjusted

Ladisa Log of productivity in the distribution sector, seasonally adjusted

The traded sector includes the following categories: food and nonalcoholic beverages, alcoholic beverages and tobacco, clothing and footwear, transport, and communication.

The nontradable sector includes the following categories: housing, household goods, health, recreation and entertainment, miscellaneous goods, and services.

Demand Variables

Lgcgdpa Log of government consumption over GDP, seasonally adjusted

Lpcgdpa Log of private consumption over GDP, seasonally adjusted

Ltcgdpa Log of total consumption over GDP, seasonally adjusted

Lcapitaa Log of GDP per capita, seasonally adjusted

Lrgcgdpa, Lrpcgdpa, Lrtcgdpa As above but all relative to similarly defined variables for Austria

Data Appendix B: Items of Regulated Prices for Slovakia

Items with Maximum Prices
Approved by the Ministry of Finance of the SR

- Net rent in rented dwellings
- Water and waste water treatment
- Electricity
- Natural gas for households
- Selected items of medicines and services in health care
- Passenger railway transport
- Passenger bus transport
- Post office services
- Telephone and telegraph services

Approved by local bodies

- City mass transport
- Heat energy for households
- Services connected with housing (cleaning and controlling chimney, sanitary services, etc.)

Items with Subject-Regulated Prices

- Coal and coke
- Selected items of medicines and services in health care
- School and kindergarten boarding
- Social care services

Insurance, Fees

- Statutory insurance of motor vehicles
- Fees for radio and television
- Fees for kindergarten and school education
- Fees for verification of signature in certificates, passport issuing, extract from criminal record, and other fees for legal acts

Notes

We are particularly grateful to Martti Randveer from the Eesti Pank; András Simon from Magyar Nemzeti Bank; Miroslav Beblavy, Tomas Holly, and Mariana Lisa from the National Bank of Slovakia; Uros Čufer and Zemva Mojca from Národná Banka Slovenska; and Andrej Flajs, Karmen Hren, Milena Jankovic, Natasa Zidar, and Bozidara Benedik from the Statistical Office of Slovenia for providing us with the data sets. Many thanks go also to Andreas Nader (OeNB) for excellent statistical help.

1. See MacDonald (2001).

2. In a companion paper (MacDonald and Wójcik 2004) we examine the influence of these factors on the real effective exchange rates of the same group of countries. The results for bilateral exchange rates, reported here, turn out to be dramatically different to those obtained with effective exchange rates.

3. For Hungary tradables contain the category "goods total," namely food and alcoholic beverages, tobacco, clothing and footwear, consumer durable goods, and other goods including motor fuels and lubricants. Nontradables contain the category "services total," namely repairs, clothing and footwear, rent, services for dwellings, household services, personal care and health services, transport services, communication, cultural, educational and entertainment services, gambling, membership, and recreational and other services.

4. Administrative prices still have a share of approximately 13 to 24 percent in the accession countries' consumer basket. See Backé et al. (2002).

5. The definition of the regulated price index differs from country-to-country, depending on the goods that are regulated in each country. All series for regulated prices ware obtained from the respective national banks that construct this measure for their internal analyses.

6. The share of regulated prices in the consumer basket in 2001 was 15 percent in Estonia, 18.5 percent in Hungary, 19.3 percent in the Slovak Republic (value for 2000), and 12.7 percent in Slovenia (value for 2000). See Backé et al. (2002).

7. According to the IMF (2003), recent data confirm that increases in regulated prices continue to exceed increases in other prices. This study also reports that certain regulated prices are still considerably below cost recovery levels.

References

Backé, P., J. Fidrmuc, T. Reininger, and F. Schardax. 2002. Price dynamics in Central and Eastern European EU accession countries. OeNB Working Paper 61.

Betts, C., and M. Devereux. 1996. The exchange rate in a model of pricing to market. *European Economic Review* 40: 1007–21.

Bergstrand, J. H. 1991. Structural determinants of real exchange rates and national price levels: Some empirical evidence. *American Economic Review* (March): 325–34.

Chinn, M., and L. Johnston. 1999. Real exchange rate level, productivity and demand shocks: Evidence from a panel of 14 countries. NBER Discussion Paper 5709.

Clark, P., and R. MacDonald. 1999. Exchange rates and economic fundamentals: A methodological comparison of BEERS and FEERS. In R. MacDonald and J. Stein, eds., *Equilibrium Exchange Rates*. Amsterdam: Kluwer.

Clark, P., and R. MacDonald. 2000. Filtering the BEER: A permanent and transitory decomposition. IMF Working Paper 144.

De Gregorio, J., A. Giovanninni, and H. Worlf. 1994. International evidence on tradeables and nontradables inflation. *European Economic Review* 38: 1225–44.

Dornbusch, R. 1988. Purchasing power parity. In J. Eatwell, M. Milgate, and P. Newman, eds., *The New Palgrave Dictionary of Economics*. London: Macmillan, pp. 1075–85.

Égert, B. 2002. Investigating the Balassa-Samuelson hypothesis in transition: Do we understand what we see. Mimeo.

Engel, C. 1993. Real exchange rates and relative prices: An empirical investigation. *Journal of Monetary Economics* 32: 35–50.

Gros, D. 2001. EMU, the euro and enlargement. In European Commission, *Economic Policy in the Framework of Accession to the European Union and Economic and Monetary Union*.

Halpern, L., and C. Wyplosz. 1997. Equilibrium exchange rates in transition economies international monetary fund. *Staff Papers* 44 (4): 430–61.

Halpern, L., and C. Wyplosz. 2001. Economic transformation and real exchange rates in the 2000s: The Balassa-Samuelson connection. Mimeo.

Helpman, E., and P. Krugman. 1985. *Market Structure and Foreign Trade*. Cambridge: MIT Press.

IMF. 2003. Competitiveness in the Baltics in the run-up to EU accession. IMF Country Report 114, pp. 34–35.

Isard, P. How far can we push the "law of one price"? *American Economic Review* 67 (December): 942–48.

Kao, C., and M.-H. Chiang. 2000. On the estimation and inference of a cointegrated regression in panel data. Mimeo.

Kravis, I., and R. Lipsey. 1983. Toward an explanation of national price levels. *Princeton Studies in International Finance* 52.

Kravis, I., and R. Lipsey. 1988. National price levels and the prices of tradables and nontradables. *American Economic Review* 78: 474–78.

Linder, S. B. 1961. *An Essay on Trade and Transformation*. New York: Wiley.

MacDonald, R. 1999. Exchange rate behaviour: Are fundamentals important? *Economic Journal* 109: F673–91.

MacDonald, R. 2000. Concepts to calculate equilibrium exchange rates: An overview. *Deutsche Bundesbank* 3.

MacDonald, R. 2001. Some exchange rate issues for the new accession countries: Comments and reflections. In European Commission, *Economic Policy in the Framework of Accession to the European Union and Economic and Monetary Union*.

MacDonald, R., and L. Ricci. 2001. PPP and the Balassa Samuelson effect: The role of the distribution sector. International Monetary Fund, Working Paper 38.

MacDonald, R., and L. Ricci. 2002. Purchasing power parity and new trade theory. International Monetary Fund, Working Paper 70.

MacDonald, R., and C. Wójcik. 2004. Catching up: The role of demand, supply and regulated price effects on the real exchange rates of four accession countries. *Economics of Transition* 12(1): 153–79.

McCoskey, S., and C. Kao. 1999. Comparing panel data cointegration tests with an application of the twin deficits problem. Mimeo.

Mark, N., and D. Sul. 2001. Nominal exchange rates and monetary fundamentals: Evidence from a small post–Bretton Woods panel. *Journal of International Economics* 53 (1): 29–52.

Mussa, M. 1986. Nominal exchange rate regimes and the behaviour of real exchange rates: Evidence and implications. *Carnegie-Rochester Conference Series on Public Policy* 26.

Neary, J. P. 1988. Determinants of the equilibrium real exchange rate. *American Economic Review* 78: 210–15.

Obstfeld, M., and A. M. Taylor. 1997. Nonlinear aspects of goods-market arbitrage and adjustment: Hecksher's commodity points revisited. *Journal of Japanese and International Economies* 11: 441–79.

Pedroni, P. 1997. Panel cointegration: Asymptotic and finite sample properties of pooled time series tests with an application to the PPP hypothesis (new results). Mimeo. Indiana University.

Phillips, P., and H. Moon. 1999. Linear regression limit theory for nonstationary panel. *Econometrica* 67 (5): 1057–1111.

Pujol, T., and M. Griffith. 1998. Moderate inflation in Poland: A real story. In C. Cottarelli and G. Szapary, eds., *Moderate Inflation: The Experience of Transition Economics*. Washington, DC: IMF. pp. 197–229.

Rogers, J. H., and M. Jenkins. 1995. Haircuts or hysteresis? Sources of movements in real exchange rates. *Journal of International Economics* 38: 339–60.

Senik, C. 2001. Economic policy and the exchange rate regime in a small open economy (like Lithuania). Mimeo.

Slok, T., and M. De Broek. 2000. Focus on transition economies. *IMF World Economic Outlook* (October).

Svensson, L. 1994. Why exchange rate bands? *Journal of Monetary Economics* 33: 157–99.

Williamson, J. 1985. *The Exchange Rate System*. Washington, DC: Institute for International Economics.

Wozniak, P. 1998. Relative prices and inflation in Poland, 1989–1997: The special role of administered price increases. World Bank Working Paper 1897.

Zavoico, B. 1995. A brief note on the inflationary process in transition economies. International Monetary Fund (July).

7 The EMU Effect on Trade: What's in It for the UK?

Alejandro Micco, Guillermo Ordóñez, and Ernesto Stein

7.1 Introduction

A common question these days, in Europe in general and in Britain in particular, is whether the United Kingdom should join the European monetary union (EMU). The introduction of the single currency in Europe raises issues that are of vital importance to UK interests, whether or not it decides to participate. The decision could potentially have an important impact on trade and on growth, as well as on areas as diverse as financial services, employment, and monetary and fiscal policy.[1]

In the last few years the debate in the United Kingdom regarding EMU has been polarized to an extraordinary degree. For those who oppose the EMU, the idea of participating in the single currency is not merely a dangerous possibility but a disastrous one. For example, Margaret Thatcher insisted that Britain must never join the "doomed" euro in a March 2002 *Times On Line* interview. In particular, Lady Thatcher said that the abolition of the pound "would constitute a major loss of Britain's power to govern herself and thus an unacceptable blow to democracy." She added: "But more, I am convinced that the fundamentals of euroland are irredeemably unsound. The single currency is bound to fail, economically, politically and indeed, socially, though the timing, occasion and consequences are necessarily still unclear." She further noted, "It therefore follows that countries which have not already joined the project would be well-advised to keep out."

Instead, for those who advocate in favor of joining the euro, participation represents not only a good opportunity to improve economic conditions but also an important step toward acquiring an influential role in the process of European Integration. For example, in a December 2001 speech to the European Research Institute in Birmingham,

British Prime Minister Tony Blair referred to the UK "history of missed opportunities." Blair noted, "We vacated a decisive role in shaping the single currency, its timing, the Maastricht convergence criteria and the European Central Bank." He went on to say, "We will not have influence if we only ever see Europe as in opposition to Britain."

At the center of this debate, Chancellor Gordon Brown devised five economic tests that must be met before any decision to join can be made. These tests are:

1. *Convergence test.* Are business cycles and economic structures compatible so that the United Kingdom could live comfortably with euro interest rates on a permanent basis?

2. *Flexibility test.* If problems emerge, is there sufficient flexibility to deal with them?

3. *Investment test.* Would joining EMU create better conditions for firms making long-term decisions to invest in Britain?

4. *Financial services test.* What impact would entry into EMU have on the competitive position of the UK financial services industry, particularly the London wholesale markets?

5. *Growth, stability, and jobs test.* Will joining EMU promote higher growth, stability, and a lasting increase in jobs?[2]

In this chapter we address a different, but related issue: the impact of EMU on trade. The adoption of a common currency could potentially reduce transaction costs in trade among member countries, leading to increased trade flows. The potential increase in trade associated with this reduction in transaction costs was in fact one of the main hopes of the EC Commission as Europe advanced toward monetary unification.

While none of Gordon Brown's five tests deals directly with the issue of trade, we believe that the impact of monetary union on trade may play a role in several of the tests listed above. Take, for example, the convergence test. Although the relationship between trade integration and cycle correlation is in theory ambiguous, there is evidence, drawn from the experience of industrial countries, suggesting that increased trade integration leads to increased cycle correlation. If this is so, monetary union, through its impact on trade, could lead to increased convergence ex post, even if convergence is not high enough to justify UK membership ex ante.[3] Similarly there is ample evidence of complementarities between trade and foreign direct investment (test 3), as well as between trade and financial services (test 4).[4] With regard to the fifth test, Frankel and Rose (2000) have provided evidence of the positive impact that the monetary union, through the trade channel, can have on growth.

The issue of the impact of currency union on trade is not a new one. It is an issue that has been the subject of a large literature, beginning with Rose (2000a), who found that a common currency increased trade among countries by a factor of three. However, most of the empirical literature to date draws its conclusions from the analysis of the currency union experience of very small and poor economies. Thus there are important reasons to believe that the currency union effects discussed in the literature to date may not be the most relevant for the case of the countries in the European Union, since they are so clearly different from previous currency union members in terms of both size and level of development.

An exception is a recent paper by Micco, Stein, and Ordoñez (2003), which, using data on bilateral trade up to 2002, shows that common membership in EMU increases the amount of trade between 8 and 16 percent. Furthermore these authors find no evidence of trade diversion. In this note we expand the exercise of Micco, Stein, and Ordoñez (2003) by looking more closely at the impact EMU would have had on the United Kingdom, had this country become a member of the EMU in 1999. After briefly reviewing the literature on the currency union effect on trade in section 7.2, in section 7.3 we present our empirical methodology and results. Finally, in section 7.4 we conclude.

7.2   Empirical Literature on the Currency Union Effect on Trade[5]

In the last couple of years there has been a growing literature on the impact of common currencies on trade. The first paper to tackle this issue directly was Rose (2000a), who added a currency union dummy to a gravity model of bilateral trade. In order to have enough country pairs with common currencies to allow an estimation of the effect, he included in his sample all the dependencies, territories, colonies, and overseas departments for which the United Nations collects international trade data. This way he put together a sample of 186 countries.[6] Rose found that two countries share a common currency trade over three times as much as do otherwise similar countries with different currencies. In terms of the relevance of this finding for EMU, one important shortcoming is that most currency unions in the sample are either formed by very small or very poor countries (e.g., those in the eastern Caribbean currency area) or by very small or poor countries adopting the currency of larger ones (e.g., Tonga adopting the Australian dollar).

Rose's first study was based on cross-sectional analysis. Therefore the question it answers is whether some countries are sharing a common currency trade more than others. As Glick and Rose (2001) argue, this is not exactly the right question from a policy perspective. What one would want to know, as a policy maker, is the impact of a currency union on those countries that adopt it. In order to answer this question, Glick and Rose (2001) consider the impact of common currency using panel data from 1948 through 1997.[7] Glick and Rose's answer is that adopting currency unions nearly doubles bilateral trade among member countries.[8] Notice, however, that the sample ends in 1997, before the creation of the EMU. Thus, while Glick and Rose treat the right policy question, their answer is relevant mostly for the case of very small and/or poor countries, which are primarily the ones that have had currency unions (or have adopted the currency of others) in their sample.

These controversial findings by Rose and his co-authors were followed by a large number of studies, some of them criticizing their work on methodological grounds, and seeking to "shrink" the currency union effect.[9] Papers worth mentioning, by Rose's critics, are those of Persson (2001) and Tenreyro (2002). Persson argues that the fact that some of the explanatory variables (e.g., country size) may have nonlinear effects, combined with the fact that the selection of country pairs into currency unions is nonrandom (and may depend on those same explanatory variables) biases the results in Rose (2000a). Tenreyro, in turn, emphasizes problems of endogeneity caused by unobservables.

After correcting these problems, both authors find the effect of shared currency on trade to be smaller, on the order of 60 percent. Yet neither author addresses the issue that concerns us because their results are based on the experiences of very small and poor countries.

Two papers that provide some hints about the currency effect on trade in large countries using historical data are Estevadeordal, Frantz, and Taylor (2003) and López-Cordova and Meissner (2003). Both papers look at the experiences of countries during the gold standard, using smaller samples that consist primarily of industrial countries and a small group of large developing countries. Estevadeordal, Frantz, and Taylor, taking data from 1870 through 1939, find that common participation in the gold standard increased trade between 34 and 72 percent, depending on the specification used. López-Córdova and Meissner, taking data from 1870 through 1910, find the gold standard effect to be 60 percent. In addition they find that currency unions double trade, a result that is very similar to that of Glick and Rose (2001).

Another recent paper that has addressed this problem is Rose and van Wincoop (2001). This paper, which is based on a model of bilateral trade developed by Anderson and van Wincoop (2003), estimates the *potential* EMU effect on trade, using data on pre-EMU currency unions. According to the theory, bilateral trade between a pair of countries depends on their bilateral trade barrier *relative* to average trade barriers with all trading partners (i.e., their multilateral trade barrier or "multilateral resistance"). Since reducing barriers vis-à-vis an important trading partner also reduces multilateral resistance, the impact of the currency union on trade should be smaller in the case of countries that are large and proximate. Taking this into consideration, Rose and van Wincoop estimate that the increase in trade for the case of EMU would be of the order of 60 percent. These estimates, however, depend crucially on assumptions made regarding the elasticity of substitution between goods.

A lot has been written on the question of whether the United Kingdom should join EMU.[10] Some papers, such as Artis (2000), analyze the issue from an optimal currency area perspective. Others, such as Mather (2002), have focused on political economy considerations, stressing the political interests of the different actors involved. Yet others, such as Currie (1997) and George (1997), consider a wide variety of aspects to be taken into account. Efforts to measure the potential impact of EMU on British trade, however, have been rather scant.

One of the few attempts to measure the EMU's potential impact on UK trade was by Rose (2000b).[11] In his paper he extrapolates the results of his original cross-sectional gravity equations to the case of the United Kingdom, estimating that "joining EMU might eventually triple the UK's trade with euroland, leading to an overall doubling of British external trade." In addition, extrapolating the results of his paper with Jeff Frankel on the impact of currency unions on trade and growth (2000), Rose estimates that joining the EMU would boost British GDP by 20 percent in the long run. While Rose does not analyze the channels through which the currency union would have such a large effect, he argues "even if we do not know *why* a common currency makes a big difference, it is plausible *that* it does." Rose, however, warns the reader that none of the previous currency unions matched the EMU in terms of size and scope, that data on EMU were still insufficient, that only time would tell what the actual effect of EMU on trade would be, and that in the meantime his estimation results should not be taken too literally.

We now have four years of trade data since the creation of the EMU. For this reason it is now possible to estimate with actual EMU data (rather than pre-EMU data, as in Rose and van Wincoop 2001) the impact of currency union on trade for the specific case of the European monetary union. Likewise it is now possible to look more precisely at the potential impact on a country such as Britain. In a recent paper Micco, Stein, and Ordoñez (2003) estimate the effects of EMU on trade among its members in a direct way. They find that the EMU effect is positive and significant, although much smaller than that suggested by the previous literature. Furthermore they find no evidence that EMU diverts trade away from nonmembers.[12] Given the importance of the issue for the countries in the European Union, and the recent availability of data, it is not surprising that a number of scholars have recently started to work independently on this issue. See, for example, Bun and Klaasen (2002), De Nardis and Vicarelli (2003), and Barr, Breedon, and Miles (2003). These studies arrive at broadly similar results to ours, namely that the Euro's trade impact is positive but modest in size compared to the estimated derived from evidence on other currency unions. In the next section, we present some of the results in Micco, Stein, and Ordoñez (2003), and then extend them to analyze the specific case of the United Kingdom.

7.3   Methodology, Data and Empirical Results

7.3.1   The EMU Effect on Trade

In this section we reproduce some of the results in Micco, Stein, and Ordoñez (2003). While in the previous study we worked with two different samples of countries (developed country sample and EU sample), for our present purposes the EU sample does not have enough country pairs made up of non-EMU countries to study the impact of EMU on the United Kingdom.[13] For this reason it is more convenient to concentrate on the developed country sample, as well as on an extended sample that includes the developed countries plus a group of 18 upper-middle income countries.[14] In order to provide an estimate of the impact of EMU on trade, we first work with a difference-indifference version of the standard gravity model. This methodology allows us to capture the currency union effect in a single estimate, comparing the changes in bilateral trade among EMU (or "treated") country pairs before and after the creation of the monetary union to changes in bilateral trade among non-EMU country pairs, which are used as "controls." In order to address the trade diversion issue, we also compare changes in bilateral trade among country pairs in which only one is a member of EMU with those corresponding to the control group.[15]

Typical variables added to the simplest gravity specification in the empirical trade literature include GDP per capita or population, as well as dummy variables indicating whether the two countries share a common border or a common language, among others. In line with our focus on the "right policy question" discussed in the previous section, in all of our regressions we will use a modified version of the standard gravity model, which relies on panel data and includes country-pair fixed effects (as in Glick and Rose 2001) in order to isolate the time series dimension of the EMU effect on trade, and leave out the cross-sectional variation. Thus time-invariant pair-specific variables such as distance, borders, common language, and colonial links will be subsumed in these country-pair fixed effects. We believe that the use of country-pair fixed effects provides the cleanest benchmark against which to assess the impact of EMU on trade. Against this benchmark, then, we study the impact of EMU on bilateral trade by introducing an additional dummy variable, which takes a value of one when the two countries in the pair belong to the EMU. We call this variable EMU2, indicating that both countries in the pair are part of EMU. Finally we include a dummy variable, which takes a value of one when only one of the two countries in the pair belongs to the EMU. We call this last variable EMU1.

To some extent the inclusion of the country pair dummies addresses potential endogeneity problems that would arise if countries, following the optimal currency area criteria, tend to form currency unions with partners with which they trade a lot. Indeed, as Micco, Stein, and Ordoñez (2003) show, comparison of our results with those obtained when we replace the country-pair fixed effects with the traditional gravity variables suggests that the latter in fact overstates the impact of EMU on trade. It is important to note, however, that the use of country-pair dummies does not completely eliminate the potential for endogeneity. It is possible for countries to join currency unions following a substantial increase in their bilateral trade links. The shorter the period used to estimate the currency union effect, the less severe are the remaining concerns about endogeneity.[16] In any case, if endogeneity were a problem, one would expect to see the increase in trade occurring before the formation of the currency union. These concerns are addressed by looking at the time profile of the impact of currency union on trade.

In addition, as the country-pair dummies subsume also the country fixed effects, they allow us to control for multilateral trade resistance. Anderson and van Wincoop (2003) show that bilateral trade between pair of countries depends on their bilateral trade barrier relative to average trade barriers with all partners. To control for country's multilateral resistance, empirical papers use country fixed effects.[17]

In isolating the impact of the EMU on trade, it is important to control for other factors that may be affecting bilateral trade among the countries in the sample. For this reason we include the following variables as controls: (1) A dummy variable is included that takes a value of one when both countries in the pair belong to the same FTA. (2) A dummy is included for the European Union, which takes a value of one when both countries are EU members (since the impact on trade will be larger than in the more cursory FTAs). (3) An EU trend is included to account for the EU agreement deepening over time (otherwise, we could be attributing to EMU increases in trade that may be due to increases over time). This variable is the negative of the "transposition deficit" computed by the Internal Market Scoreboard, which measures the percentage of EU internal market directives not yet implemented by EU countries.[18] (4) An index of the real exchange rate is created for each of the countries in the pair (in logs) in order to control for valuation effects that may occur as a result of the important swings in the value of the euro experienced immediately following its implementation.[19] (5) The model includes year fixed effects in order to control for the increase in trade flows over time.[20] Thus the baseline model we estimate is the following panel model:

$$\text{Ln } T_{ijt} = \alpha_{ij} + \beta_1 \ln Y_{it} Y_{jt} + \beta_2 FTA_{ijt} + \beta_3 EU_{ijt} + \beta_4 EU \ Trend_{ijt}$$

$$+ \beta_5 EMU2_{ijt} + \beta_6 EMU1_{ijt} + \beta_7 RER_{it} + \beta_8 RER_{jt} + \gamma_t + \varepsilon_{ijt}, \quad (1)$$

where T represents bilateral trade, the α's represent the country-pair fixed effects, the γ's represent the year fixed effects, Y is real GDP, RER is the index of the real exchange rate, and ε_{ijt} is the error term.[21] The first coefficient of interest is β_5, which should be positive and significant if EMU does stimulate trade among its members. The second coefficient of interest is β_6, which should be negative and significant if EMU induces trade diversion.

7.3.2 Data

Following Glick and Rose (2001), our dependent variable is the log of total merchandise trade (exports plus imports) between pairs of countries, in a given year deflated by the US CPI. We work with bilateral trade data from the IMF Direction of Trade Statistics for 1992 to 2002. We use in our analysis two different samples of countries. The first sample includes all 22 industrial countries included in the DOTS dataset (see appendix A for the list of countries). The second extends the sample by including 18 upper middle-income countries.[22] While the second sample has the advantage of the larger size, the first has the appeal that countries are more homogeneous. The developed country sample results in a total of 231 ($22 * 21/2$) country pairs. Out of these, 11 (counting Belgium and Luxembourg as one) have become members of the European monetary union during the period under study. Thus there are 55 country pairs ($11 * 10/2$) that share a common currency, 121 country pairs ($11 * 11$) composed of an EMU member and a non-EMU member, and 55 country pairs of non-EMU members. We exploit this variation to estimate the effect of EMU on trade. This sample of developed countries does not contain observations with zero trade, which saves us the trouble of dealing with this aspect of the gravity model.[23]

Our explanatory variables are taken from different sources. GDP data comes from *World Development Indicators*.[24] The information on the composition of free trade agreements was taken from Frankel (1997) and complemented with data provided by the integration department of the IDB. More details on the definition of the variables used are provided in appendix B.

7.3.3 Empirical Results

The first two columns in table 7.1 present the results of our difference-indifference regressions, using OLS with country-pair dummies in the developed country and extended samples, respectively. In both cases the EMU2 variable is positive and significant, suggesting that the currency union has a positive effect on trade. Compared to the control group (i.e., trade between two non-EMU countries), common membership in EMU increases bilateral trade by nearly 13 percent when we

Table 7.1
Difference-indifference model

Dependent variable: Log of bilateral trade	Ordinary least squares		Median regression	
	OECD developed countries	Extended sample	OECD developed countries	Extended sample
EMU2	0.126	0.046	0.148	0.117
	(0.019)***	(0.023)**	(0.013)***	(0.024)***
EMU1	0.086	0.001	0.095	0.055
	(0.015)***	(0.021)	(0.009)***	(0.011)***
Log of GDP	1.108	0.823	0.999	0.808
	(0.059)***	(0.073)***	(0.031)***	(0.028)***
Free Trade Agreement	−0.008	−0.001	0.003	0.035
	(0.021)	(0.023)	(0.012)	(0.017)**
European Union	0.030	−0.085	0.036	0.006
	(0.022)	(0.025)***	(0.015)**	(0.030)
EU trend	0.000	−0.006	0.000	−0.001
	(0.001)	(0.002)***	(0.001)	(0.002)
Real exchange rate: country 1	−0.220	−0.123	−0.269	−0.226
	(0.045)***	(0.071)*	(0.031)***	(0.028)***
Real exchange rate: country 2	−0.288	−0.339	−0.278	−0.337
	(0.057)***	(0.041)***	(0.034)***	(0.020)***
F Test between EMU2 and EMU1	8.57***	6.63***	25.07***	7.03***
Year dummy	Yes	Yes	Yes	Yes
Country-pair dummy[a]	Yes	Yes	Yes	Yes
Observations	2,541	8,312	2,541	8,312

Source: Micco, Stein, and Ordóñez (2003) and authors' estimation.
Note: Robust standard errors in parentheses. * Significant at 10 percent, ** significant at 5 percent, *** significant at 1 percent.
a. For the case of median regressions we first demean all variables, and then we compute standard quantile regression.

use the developed country sample,[25] and by 5 percent if we use the extended sample. The coefficient for EMU1, namely for the case of country pairs when just one is in EMU, suggests that there is no trade diversion. In the developed country sample this coefficient is actually positive and significant, suggesting that EMU countries also increased trade with nonmembers (by about 9 percent), relative to trade within the control group. In the extended sample the coefficient is also positive but very small, and statistically insignificant. In all cases the EMU2 effect is significantly larger than that of EMU1.[26] Regarding the control variables, it is important to note that the lack of significance on the FTA and EU variables in most specifications does not mean that trade integration does not play a role. For the most part the impact of trade integration on trade is captured by the country-pair fixed effects, at least for the countries that were partners in trade agreements throughout the period.

In the third and fourth columns of table 7.1, we recalculate the previous estimations using median regressions instead of OLS, in both cases controlling for country-pair fixed effects. Unlike OLS, which minimizes the sum of squared errors, median regressions minimize the sum of the absolute value of error terms and therefore are less sensitive to outliers. Reassuringly, the table shows that for the developed sample, both the coefficient for EMU2 and EMU1 are almost identical to our previous estimate using OLS. In the case of the extended sample the EMU2 coefficient becomes 0.12, much closer the one obtained using our developed sample (0.15). This result suggests that the small coefficient for EMU2 in column 2 is driven by extreme observations. The coefficient for EMU1 is positive and significant (0.055) but lower than the one obtained using the developed sample (0.095), suggesting that trade between EMU countries and other developed countries increased more than trade between EMU members and upper middle-income countries.

The fact that EMU increases trade not only among members, but also with nonmembers, is somewhat surprising. The results suggest that EMU may act more as a "trade booster" than just reducing transactions costs among its members.[27] A possible explanation is that the use of the euro, a more liquid currency, makes it easier for member countries to hedge exchange rate risk, even in their transactions vis-à-vis nonmembers. The fact that the coefficient for EMU2 is bigger than that for EMU1 is consistent with the "trade booster" hypothesis: if both countries are in EMU, their bilateral trade flows simply benefit from a double boost. Our results suggest that countries that trade with EMU partners have already obtained some benefits from EMU in the form of increased trade. The size of these benefits will depend on the extent to which they trade with the EMU bloc. For a country like Canada, for which EMU represented around 5 percent of trade (as of 1996), the boost in total trade will be quite small (on the order of 0.3 to 0.5 percent). In contrast, for the United Kingdom, for which EMU members represented 64 percent of total trade prior to 1999, the increase in total trade due to the creation of EMU will be around 4 to 6.5 percent.[28]

A common currency is not simply a reduction in trade barriers within the group, but it reduces transaction costs with outsiders. For example, British households and firms, as heavy traders with the EMU, get some of the same benefits as French households and firms do from the reduction in the number of currencies and units of accounts in the EMU.[29]

While the difference-indifference analysis has the advantage of producing a single estimate for the EMU effect, it does not provide information on whether the jump in trade was abrupt or smooth, whether the trade increased in anticipation of the EMU, or whether the impact is only obvious after a lag. In order to analyze these issues in more detail, we estimated the following panel model:

$$\text{Ln } T_{ijt} = \beta_{ij} + \beta_1 \ln Y_{it}Y_{jt} + \beta_2 FTA_{ijt} + \beta_3 EU_{ijt} + \beta_4 EU \ Trend_{ijt} + \beta_5 RER_{it}$$

$$+ \beta_6 RER_{jt} + \sum_{\tau \in (1992, 2001]} \beta_{7t}I(\tau = t)EMU2B_{ij}$$

$$+ \sum_{\tau \in (1992, 2001]} \beta_{8t}I(\tau = t)EMU1B_{ij} + \gamma_t + \varepsilon_{ijt}, \tag{2}$$

where $I(\tau = t)$ is an indicator function that is one if τ is equal to t and zero otherwise, the rest of the variables are defined as before. The definition of EMU2 in this model is different from its definition in the difference-indifference model. In that case the EMU2 dummy took a value of one only during the years in which the country pair *formally* belonged to EMU. Before 1999 the dummy had a value of zero for all pairs. Here, in contrast, EMU2 takes a value of one for a pair of countries that will be part of EMU, *even before* the formal creation of EMU. For example, EMU2 takes a value of one for the pair Germany-Spain for 1995, though these countries only became part of EMU in 1999. For this reason, while the EMU1 and EMU2 dummies had subscripts *ijt* in the difference-indifference model, they only have subscripts *ij* in this model.[30] The idea is to follow the evolution of trade in these countries over time, and check whether there is a jump around 1999. The interaction of the EMU2 variable with the indicator function discussed above allows us to follow the behavior of trade among the EMU countries year by year. The EMU effect in this specification is not captured directly by the estimated year coefficients (β_τ) for *EMU2*. Rather, it is captured by the jump in these coefficients around the formal creation of the EMU. Similar considerations apply to the EMU1 dummy. As discussed above, the model also includes controls for GDP, FTA, EU trend, and real exchange rate in both countries of the pair.

The results for our developed sample are reported in table 7.2. Figure 7.1 provides a graphical representation of the evolution of the yearly EMU2 and EMU1 coefficients. In both cases there is a noticeable upward jump around the time of the formal creation of EMU, confirming the results of the difference-indifference analysis. What is surprising, however, is that the EMU effect seems to start in 1998, one year before the formal creation of EMU. The most likely explanation for this is that the year 1998 was a pivotal year in the process of monetary unification. Up until 1997, whether the EMU would become a reality was still in doubt, with countries such as Italy and Belgium exceeding the debt convergence criteria set forth in Maastricht, with France inaugurating a socialist government that had promised to focus more on unemployment and less on meeting the convergence criteria, and with Germany complicated by its own unification efforts.[31] In 1998 any lingering concerns regarding the future of EMU were put to rest. On March 25, 1998, the European Commission and the European Monetary Institute published their convergence reports, recommending that 11 countries—Austria, Belgium, Finland, France, Germany, Ireland, Italy, Luxembourg, the Netherlands, Portugal, and Spain—be admitted into the EMU. At the beginning of May the decision was formally announced during a meeting of the heads of state in Brussels, during which the bilateral irrevocable conversion rates were set among the member currencies. This was followed on June 1, 1998, with the official creation of the European central bank.

In addition, to allow us to follow the evolution of the EMU impact over time, the regressions reported in table 7.2 can be used to obtain alternative measures of the EMU impact, which we report in table 7.3. For EMU2, these estimates suggest that the jump in trade among EMU countries is of the order of 15 percent (slightly larger than the OLS results from table 7.1), and statistically significant. For EMU1, the corresponding jump is between 8 and 9 percent. These estimates are obtained from the comparison of the before and after coefficients of the yearly EMU2 and EMU1 variables, leaving out the year 1998.[32] In fact these estimates may have an advantage over the estimates obtained in table 7.1, which may potentially be more tainted by changes in bilateral trade that occurred at the beginning of the sample period, which probably have very little to do with monetary unification. The more compact period in which the yearly coefficients are compared here (e.g., 1996–97 vs. 1999–2000) reduces the chances of having the results contaminated by developments that happened several years before.

Table 7.2
Panel model

Dependent variable: Log of bilateral trade	Developed sample	
	Coefficient	Standard errors
Real GDP	1.096	(0.058)***
Free Trade Agreement	−0.019	(0.020)
EU	−0.023	(0.022)
EU trend	−0.004	(0.001)**
Real exchange rate: country 1	−0.253	(0.045)***
Real exchange rate: country 2	−0.274	(0.057)***
EMU2—1993	−0.031	(0.041)
EMU2—1994	0.060	(0.040)
EMU2—1995	0.093	(0.043)**
EMU2—1996	0.065	(0.041)
EMU2—1997	0.096	(0.042)**
EMU2—1998	**0.189**	**(0.043)*****
EMU2—1999	**0.217**	**(0.040)*****
EMU2—2000	**0.214**	**(0.047)*****
EMU2—2001	**0.263**	**(0.046)*****
EMU2—2002	**0.284**	**(0.051)*****
EMU1—1993	−0.035	(0.039)
EMU1—1994	0.014	(0.037)
EMU1—1995	0.042	(0.040)
EMU1—1996	0.015	(0.037)
EMU1—1997	0.038	(0.039)
EMU1—1998	**0.093**	**(0.039)****
EMU1—1999	**0.103**	**(0.036)*****
EMU1—2000	**0.106**	**(0.040)*****
EMU1—2001	**0.133**	**(0.039)*****
EMU1—2002	**0.138**	**(0.043)*****
Observations	2,541	
Within R^2	0.48	
Year dummies	Yes	
Country-pair dummies	Yes	

Source: Micco, Stein, and Ordoñez (2003).
Note: Robust standard errors in parentheses. * Significant at 10 percent; ** significant at 5 percent; *** significant at 1 percent.

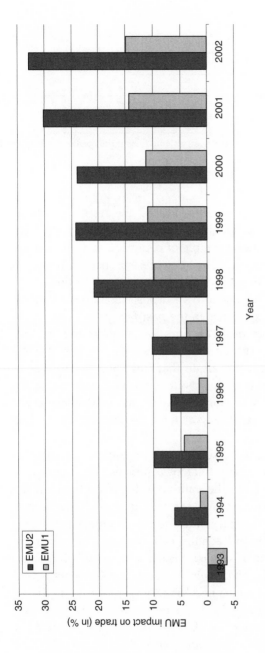

Figure 7.1
EMU effect for developed countries sample: Evolution of EMU2-*year* and EMU1-*year*.

Table 7.3
Alternative measures of the EMU2 and EMU1 impact

	Alternative measures	
	EMU2	EMU1
1999–2000 vs. 1996–1997	14.5***	8.1***
1999–2001 vs. 1995–1997	15.8***	8.6***

Note: *** significant at 1 percent. The impacts are obtained using the coefficients in table 6.2.

7.3.4   UK Analysis

So far we have for the most part reproduced the results in Micco, Stein, and Ordóñez (2003), although with some additional robustness checks (introducing an extended sample of countries, as well as using median regressions). The main goal of the present chapter, however, is to look more closely at the potential impact of the adoption of the euro on the United Kingdom. For this purpose an important question is whether UK trade experience in the past few years is similar to that of other non-EMU countries. This question is interesting because, had the UK trade experienced an evolution similar to that of EMU members, it would be harder to argue that this country missed important trade opportunities by staying out of the monetary union. To answer this question, in this section we extend the models presented above, in order to look more closely at the experience of the United Kingdom.

We expand the difference-indifference model of equation (1) by splitting the EMU1 dummy into two different dummies. The first one is a dummy *EMU1-UK* that takes the value one for trade between the United Kingdom and a country that is formally in EMU.[33] The second dummy (*EMU1–non-UK*) takes the value one for all country pairs composed by an EMU country and a non-EMU country other than the United Kingdom. The key to this exercise is the comparison of the coefficients for *EMU1-UK* and *EMU1–non-UK*. Similar coefficients would suggest that the behavior of the United Kingdom was similar to that of other non-EMU countries. Table 7.4 shows the results of the difference-indifference approach splitting the *EMU1* dummy into *EMU1-UK* and *EMU1–non-UK*. The first two columns use OLS and the other two median regressions, in both cases we control for country-pair fixed effects. We report our results for the developed and extended country samples.

Table 7.4
Difference-indifference model, splitting United Kingdom

Dependent variable: Log of bilateral trade	Ordinary least squares		Median regression	
	OECD developed countries	Extended sample	OECD developed countries	Extended sample
EMU2	0.126	0.047	0.149	0.121
	(0.019)***	(0.023)**	(0.013)***	(0.023)***
EMU1-UK	0.070	0.011	0.107	0.062
	(0.023)***	(0.027)	(0.020)***	(0.043)
EMU1−non-UK	0.088	0.000	0.094	0.054
	(0.016)***	(0.022)	(0.010)***	(0.010)***
Log of GDP	1.107	0.823	1.004	0.810
	(0.059)***	(0.073)***	(0.031)***	(0.027)***
Free Trade Agreement	−0.008	−0.001	0.004	0.036
	(0.021)	(0.023)	(0.012)	(0.017)**
European Union	0.032	−0.086	0.033	0.007
	(0.022)	(0.026)***	(0.015)**	(0.030)
EU trend	0.000	−0.006	−0.000	−0.001
	(0.001)	(0.002)***	(0.001)	(0.002)
Real exchange rate: country 1	−0.228	−0.122	−0.257	−0.227
	(0.048)***	(0.073)*	(0.032)***	(0.027)***
Real exchange rate: country 2	−0.287	−0.339	−0.276	−0.339
	(0.057)***	(0.041)***	(0.034)***	(0.019)***
F Test between EMU2 and EMU1-UK	5.87**	1.60	3.94**	1.72
F Test between EMU2 and EMU1−non-UK	7.39***	6.41***	25.55***	8.32***
F Test between EMU1-UK and EMU1−non-UK	0.63	0.15	0.48	0.09
Year dummy	Yes	Yes	Yes	Yes
Country-pair dummy[a]	Yes	Yes	Yes	Yes
Observations	2,541	8,312	2,541	8,312

Note: Robust standard errors in parentheses. * Significant at 10 percent; ** significant at 5 percent; *** significant at 1 percent.
a. For the case of median regressions we first demean all variables and then we compute standard quantile regression.

The results shown in all columns suggest that the United Kingdom behaved as a typical non-EMU member. Actually, as can be seen in the F-tests reported at the bottom of table 7.3, the *EMU1-UK* coefficient is not statistically different from *EMU1–non-UK*. Furthermore, in the case of the developed country sample, it is also statistically different from the *EMU2* dummy.

From the developed countries sample our analysis suggests that, had the United Kingdom been a part of EMU since 1999, its trade with *all countries* (both those in EMU and those outside of EMU) would have been boosted by around 6 to 7 percent.[34] Using the extended sample, we estimate a boost in trade between 3 and 6 percent, depending on whether we use the OLS or the median regression results. While much smaller than previous estimates by Rose (2000b), our results suggest that joining the euro would lead to sizable gains in trade for the United Kingdom. Around two-thirds of the increase would be associated with trade flows with EMU members.

As in the previous section, it is interesting to follow the evolution of the EMU effect on trade over time, splitting the EMU1 dummy into trade of EMU countries with the United Kingdom, and with the rest of the non-EMU developed world. For this reason we now replicate the model described in equation (2), augmented by splitting the EMU1 dummy into *EMU1d-UK* and *EMU1d–non-UK*, as described above. Results for the developed country sample are presented in table 7.5 and in figure 7.2.

Table 7.5 and figure 7.2 confirm the results of the previous exercise. While the increase for the case of the United Kingdom is slightly larger and has a somewhat different temporal pattern than that for other non-EMU countries, the overall story is quite similar. This is confirmed by the results reported in table 7.6, which presents estimates for EMU2, EMU1-UK and EMU1–non-UK derived from the comparison of the before and after coefficients from table 7.5. The impact of EMU1-UK is of the order of 9 percent, and as discussed above, is slightly larger than that for other developed countries.[35]

The results in table 7.6 suggest that if United Kingdom were in EMU its total trade with would have been boosted by around 7 percent if we consider the two years before and after EMU (row 1), or 8 percent if we consider the three years before and after the EMU (row 2).[36] Had the United Kingdom joined EMU in 1999, this would have led to an increase in total trade in 2000 of around each 44 billion dollars of 2000.[37]

Table 7.5
Panel data analysis, splitting United Kingdom

Dependent variable: Log of bilateral trade		Developed countries, 1992–2002	
		Coefficient	Standard errors
Log GDP		1.097	(0.058)***
Free Trade Agreement		−0.020	(0.021)
European Union		−0.026	(0.023)
EU trend		−0.004	(0.002)**
Real exchange rate: country 1		−0.244	(0.051)***
Real exchange rate: country 2		−0.276	(0.057)***
EMU–EMU	1993	−0.029	(0.041)
	1994	0.062	(0.040)
	1995	0.096	(0.043)**
	1996	0.068	(0.041)*
	1997	0.099	(0.042)**
	1998	**0.193**	**(0.043)***
	1999	**0.221**	**(0.041)***
	2000	**0.217**	**(0.047)***
	2001	**0.266**	**(0.046)***
	2002	**0.287**	**(0.052)***
EMU–UK	1993	−0.023	(0.052)
	1994	0.026	(0.049)
	1995	0.031	(0.051)
	1996	0.038	(0.048)
	1997	0.075	(0.049)
	1998	**0.092**	**(0.052)***
	1999	**0.147**	**(0.050)***
	2000	**0.132**	**(0.054)***
	2001	**0.134**	**(0.056)***
	2002	**0.176**	**(0.060)***
EMU–non-UK	1993	−0.036	(0.040)
	1994	0.013	(0.038)
	1995	0.044	(0.041)
	1996	0.014	(0.038)
	1997	0.036	(0.040)
	1998	**0.094**	**(0.039)***
	1999	**0.099**	**(0.037)***
	2000	**0.105**	**(0.041)***
	2001	**0.133**	**(0.040)***
	2002	**0.135**	**(0.044)***
Year dummy		Yes	
Country-pair dummy		Yes	
Observations		2,541	

Note: Robust standard errors in parentheses. * Significant at 10 percent; ** significant at 5 percent; *** significant at 1 percent.

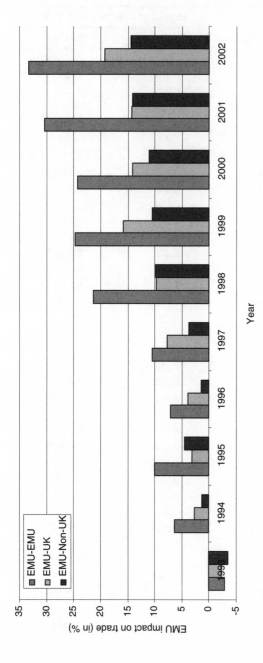

Figure 7.2
EMU effect for developed countries sample with UK split off: Evolution of EMU2-*year* and EMU1-*year*.

Table 7.6
Alternative measures of the EMU2 and EMU1 impact, splitting United Kingdom

	Alternative measures		
	EMU2	EMU1 (UK)	EMU1 (non-UK)
1999–2000 vs. 1996–1997	14.5***	8.7***	8.0***
1999–2001 vs. 1995–1997	15.8***	9.4***	8.4***

Note: *** Significant at 1 percent. The impacts are obtained using the coefficients of column 1 in table 6.5.

7.3.5 Robustness Tests

In this section we check the robustness of our results to alternative estimation methods, and to changes in the country sample. For space considerations, the robustness analysis will focus mainly on the developed country sample.

To see how robust our panel results are, we compute a cross-sectional regression of bilateral trade variation between the period 1995 to 1997 and 1999 to 2001. This specification is robust to any error autocorrelation that our panels could have. The first four columns in table 7.7 present our results using the developed countries sample and the last four the coefficient for the middle-upper income countries sample. The first two columns in each sample present the results using OLS and the other two using median regression. Reassuringly the table shows that for both samples there is an increase in trade among EMU members and among members and nonmembers countries. Depending on the sample and the econometric method we use, the coefficient for EMU2 ranges from 0.19 to 0.28, and from 0.07 to 0.15 for EMU1. Although larger, the estimated coefficients using first differences are not statistically different, at standard confident levels, from the ones estimated in the previous sections. Finally, in all cases UK bilateral trade with EMU member countries seems to behave similarly to the trade of average nonmember countries.

To deal with this potential serial correlation problem, previous studies in this topic, like Micco, Stein, and Ordoñez (2003),[38] estimate a dynamic panel that includes lagged bilateral trade as an independent variable. The authors compute this dynamic model using Arellano and Bond (1991) and considering that EMU started in 1998 instead of 1999, as suggested by the discussion above. The results using this technique are entirely consistent with our previous results. Using the same sample of developed countries, they found similar results.[39]

Table 7.7
Cross-sectional estimation of EMU2 and EMU1 impacts

Dependent variable: Log of bilateral trade	Ordinary least squares		Quantile regression		Ordinary least squares		Quantile regression	
	OECD developed countries	OECD developed countries	OECD developed countries	OECD developed countries	Middle upper income countries	Middle upper income countries	Middle upper income countries	Middle upper income countries
Difference EMU2	0.243 (4.99)***	0.242 (5.07)***	0.264 (4.93)***	0.276 (4.97)***	0.198 (3.61)***	0.187 (3.65)***	0.205 (2.34)**	0.205 (2.12)**
Difference EMU1	0.143 (3.71)***		0.146 (4.58)***		0.065 (1.5)		0.092 (2.98)***	
Difference EMU1-UK		0.14 (2.50)**		0.181 (2.45)**		0.029 (0.42)		0.103 (0.75)
Difference EMU1-non-UK		0.144 (3.56)***		0.137 (4.11)***		0.066 (1.51)		0.093 (2.91)***
Difference log GDP	0.878 (5.75)***	0.877 (5.62)***	0.693 (5.55)***	0.713 (5.51)***	0.775 (4.16)***	0.774 (4.15)***	0.811 (7.47)***	0.808 (7.27)***
Difference Free Trade Agreement					-0.009 (0.09)	-0.009 (0.1)	0.073 (1.11)	0.075 (1.13)
Difference European Union	-0.011 (2.91)**	-0.011 (1.86)*	-0.007 (1.21)	-0.012 (1.6)	-0.017 (3.05)***	-0.016 (2.60)***	-0.009 (0.76)	-0.009 (0.65)
Difference EU trend	-0.372 (3.66)***	-0.375 (3.05)***	-0.426 (3.88)***	-0.367 (2.87)***	-0.541 (3.46)***	-0.546 (3.38)***	-0.42 (4.59)***	-0.413 (4.32)***
Difference Real exchange rate: country 1	-0.533 (2.89)***	-0.534 (2.88)***	-0.304 (2.16)**	-0.25 (1.72)*	-0.538 (5.08)***	-0.538 (5.08)***	-0.392 (6.28)***	-0.39 (6.11)***

Difference Real exchange rate: country 2	−0.244	−0.243	−0.23	−0.246	−0.088	−0.088	−0.19	−0.191
	(4.30)***	(4.21)***	(4.38)***	(4.43)***	(1.23)	(1.21)	(5.50)***	(5.40)***
F Test between EMU2 and EMU1	10.23***	3.53*	8.05***	1.76	12.88***	5.91**	1.89	0.66
F Test between EMU2 and EMU1–non-UK		9.01***		9.08***		12.43***		1.48
F Test between EMU1-UK and EMU1–non-UK		0		0.35		0.4		0.01
R^2	0.36	0.37	0.23	0.23	0.09	0.09	0.09	0.09
Observations	231	231	231	231	762	762	762	762

Note: Robust t-statistics in parentheses. * Significant at 10 percent; ** significant at 5 percent; *** significant at 1 percent.

7.4   Conclusions

In this chapter we used a panel data set that includes the most recent information on bilateral trade to estimate the early effect of the European monetary union on trade. Our data set includes annual bilateral trade from 1992 through 2002 for 22 developed countries, as well as an extended sample that includes a group of 40 upper middle-income countries. During this period 12 European countries formally entered into a currency union. This is a unique event that allows us to study the effect of currency union on trade among a relatively homogenous group of industrial countries.

In Micco, Stein, and Ordoñez (2003) we found that a pair of countries that joined the European monetary union experienced an increase in trade between 10 and 15 percent, depending on the sample used. Furthermore in that study we found that EMU increases trade not only among members but also with nonmembers. The results suggest that EMU may act more as a "trade booster" than just reducing transactions costs among its members. A potential explanation is that the use of the euro, a more liquid currency, makes it easier for member countries to hedge exchange rate risk, even in their transactions vis-à-vis nonmembers. The channels through which EMU matters for trade, however, are not entirely clear, and should be the subject of further research. Regardless of the channel, our results suggest that EMU represented a significant improvement in trade for its member countries. Comparison with the results using the extended sample suggests that the increase of trade between EMU countries and nonmembers is larger for country pairs in which both countries are developed.

In this chapter we analyzed the UK case in particular, trying to isolate its trade experience after the formal creation of EMU. In focusing on the impact on trade alone, we leave out a number of other important considerations that can play a role in the UK decision of whether or not to join the euro. For this reason our results should not be seen as advocating EMU but rather as providing a key piece of the puzzle in the UK-EMU debate. In this regard we found that the United Kingdom behaves as a typical non-EMU developed country. First, due to the EMU "booster effect" on trade, we found that the United Kingdom already benefits significantly from the EMU. The euro already increases UK trade with EMU countries between 8 and 16 percent. Second we estimated that had the United Kingdom joined EMU in 1999, its total in 2000 would have increased by around 7 percent, or 44 billion dollars of 2000, equivalent to 3 percentage points of the UK GDP. This increase in trade is statistically significant, economically important, and probably would have represented an improvement in welfare for the United Kingdom.

Appendix A: Developed Countries Samples

Table 7A.1
List of countries in the developed countries sample

Country	EU country (year of affiliation)	EMU country (year of euro adoption)
Australia		
Austria	1995	1999
Belgium–Luxembourg	1952	1999
Canada		
Denmark	1973	
Finland	1995	1999
France	1952	1999
Germany	1952	1999
Greece	1981	2001
Iceland		
Ireland	1973	1999
Italy	1952	1999
Japan		
New Zealand		
Netherlands	1952	1999
Norway		
Portugal	1986	1999
Spain	1986	1999
Sweden	1995	
Switzerland		
United Kingdom	1973	
United States		

Source: European Union Commission.
Note: Countries affiliated in 1952 created in that year the European Coal and Steel Community (ECSC), which was extended to all economic sectors in 1958, creating the European Community (EC). Formally, the European Union (EU) was created in 1992 when the countries that were part of the EC ratified the Treaty on European Union (Maastricht).

On January 1, 1999, eleven EU member states adopted the euro as their national currency. These countries were selected by the European Council to participate in the European monetary union (EMU) because they had fulfilled the convergence criteria set forth in the Maastricht Treaty.

On June 19, 2000, the EU Council assessed that Greece fulfilled the requirements of the Treaty and approved its accession to the euro area as a twelfth member effective as of January 1, 2000.

Table 7A.2
List of additional countries in the middle-upper income countries sample

Antigua and Barbuda	Malaysia
Argentina	Mexico
Brazil	Panama
Chile	Saudi Arabia
Hong Kong	Singapore
Costa Rica	South Africa
Israel	Turkey
Korea	Uruguay
Kuwait	Venezuela

Appendix B: Data Used in Estimations

Trade   Bilateral trade is measured in millions of dollars and is taken from the *DOTS* (*Direction of Trade Statistics*) published by the IMF. We use the simple average of the bilateral imports and exports declared by both countries (average of these four data samples). For cases where just one of the countries reports bilateral trade, we just take the average of the two available measures. In all cases we use FOB exports and CIF imports. Trade is deflated by the US CPI taken from the IMF International Financial Statistics.

Real GDP   This variable is taken also from the WDI. The WDI converts figures for GDP from constant domestic currencies into US dollars using 1995 official exchange rates. For a few countries where the official exchange rate does not reflect the rate effectively applied to actual foreign exchange transactions, the World Bank use an alternative conversion factor. This information is available only until 2001 in the WDI. GDP was taken from IMF indicators. To calculate the real GDP per capita we divide by the total population in the WDI.

FTAs (Free Trade Agreements)   This dummy takes the value 1 when a country pair belongs to the same free trade area. The data are taken from Frankel (1997) and complemented with data provided by the IDB Integration Department.

EU (European Union)   This is a dummy that takes the value 1 when both countries in a country pair belong to the European Union.

EU Trend (European Union Trend)   This variable is based on the "transposition deficit" data compiled by Internal Market Scoreboard and published in the Web site *http://europa.eu.int/comm/internal_market/*

en/update/score. The transposition deficit measures the percentage of internal market directives, which have not been written into national law, after the deadline for doing so has passed. We multiply this measure by (-1) in order to obtain an increase in the measure as the EU becomes deeper. We used the information corresponding to November of each year.

Real Exchange Rates vis-à-vis USA   This variable is the ratio between the nominal exchange rate of each country vis-à-vis the US dollar and the country's GDP deflator. If we multiplied this index by the US GDP deflator, we would obtain the bilateral real exchange rate vis-à-vis the United States. Since our regressions include time dummies, multiplying our variable by the US GDP deflator would yield identical results.

Notes

We thank Richard Baldwin, Jeff Frankel, Paul Grauwe, Eduardo Levy Yeyati, Ernesto López-Cordova, Jacques Mélitz, Ugo Panizza, Andrew Powell, Andy Rose, and Alan Winters for useful comments and suggestions, and Daniel Leigh for excellent research assistance. We are also grateful to Andy Rose for sharing his data. The opinions in this chapter reflect those of the authors and not necessarily those of the IADB.

1. Currie (1997) discusses the broad impact that the euro could have on the United Kingdom.

2. On June 9, 2003, the United Kingdom made the decision to postpone entry into euro, on the basis of the failure to meet the tests.

3. See Frankel and Rose (1997, 1998). Frankel (2003) analyzes this issue for the specific case of the UK decision. For a discussion of the ambiguous theoretical link between trade and cycle correlation, see Hughes Hallett and Piscitelli (2002).

4. Grosse and Goldberg (1991), Brealey and Kaplanis (1996), Williams (1998), and Galindo et al. (2003) find a positive and significant correlation between proxies of the flow of foreign direct investment in banking and the level of bilateral trade and FDI.

5. This literature review draws heavily on Micco, Stein, and Ordoñez (2003).

6. Within this sample there are over 300 observations for which two countries trade and share a common currency, which allows for the estimation of the currency union effect.

7. The long sample period is crucial in order to have enough country pairs with periods in which they shared currencies and periods in which they did not.

8. Actually the sample used by Glick and Rose includes mostly countries that exited currency unions rather than countries that joined them. In addition these authors do not differentiate countries that formed currency unions from others that simply adopted the currency of another, such as Panama. For a discussion of these issues, as well as an analysis of the difference between the impact of currency unions and the unilateral adoption of the currency of other countries, see Levy Yeyati (2002).

9. The prize for best title among Rose's critics goes to Nitsch (2001), for his paper "Honey, I Shrunk the Currency Union Effect on Trade."

10. A complete survey of this literature exceeds the scope of this chapter.

11. Rose (2000c) made a similar exercise for Sweden and arrives at a similar conclusion that EMU potentially could increase its trade significantly.

12. In fact trade among EMU countries also tends to increase vis-à-vis nonmembers, a result that is consistent with previous evidence provided by Frankel and Rose (2000), who look at the same issue for a much larger sample.

13. In the EU country sample there are only three country pairs conformed by non-EMU countries. Not counting the UK pairs, we would be left with just one pair of non-EMU countries (Denmark-Sweden) from which to identify the EMU effect.

14. The list of countries in each of the samples is included in appendix A.

15. The use of the term "trade diversion" here requires some clarification, since it does not correspond exactly to the concept of trade diversion developed by Viner (1950). In Viner's work, trade diversion involves a geographical shift in the origin of imports for the country that is considering a trade agreement as a result of the preferential treatment, in favor of the partners in the trading bloc and away from the most efficient producers of the goods in question. A currency union could also potentially shift trade away from nonmembers and in favor of members, but unlike the traditional trade diversion case, here there is no distortion involved. In fact it is useful to think about the reduction in transaction costs as akin to a reduction in transportation costs between the currency union members. Despite this, in the rest of the chapter our use of the term trade diversion should be understood as a shift in trade away from nonmembers, since the literature has used the term in this way (e.g., see Frankel and Rose 2000).

16. For this reason we use a relatively short sample, 1992 to 2002.

17. See Rose and van Wincoop (2001), Feenstra (2004), and Anderson and van Wincoop (2003).

18. The use of a linear EU trend yields very similar results.

19. For a discussion justifying the use of these variables, see Micco, Stein, and Ordoñez (2003). The index of the real exchange rate is constructed as the ratio between the country's nominal exchange rate vis-à-vis the US dollar and the country's GDP deflator.

20. Year dummies capture factors such as global changes in transport and telecommunication costs, due for example to changes in oil prices, and increases in security costs after September 11.

21. We do not include GDP per capita in our model because countries populations are almost constant over time, and therefore GDP per capita becomes collinear with our GDP variable and the pairwise fixed effects.

22. The sample does not include any transition economy.

23. In the extended country sample, in contrast, 3 percent of the observations correspond to country pairs with zero trade (268 over 780 × 11). Following Glick and Rose (2001), these observations were dropped from the sample when taking logs of the dependent variable.

24. For some of the upper-middle-income countries GDP data were completed with IMF data.

25. $\text{Exp}(0.126) - 1$.

26. Table 7.1 includes the F-test of the difference between EMU2 and EMU1.

27. We are indebted to Richard Baldwin for suggesting this interpretation of our results.

28. Micco et al. (2003) show that the impact of EMU is fairly widespread among its member countries. They show that the results are robust to exclude one or a group of EMU countries at a time from the sample. In an unreported regression, we show that our results are robust to include a different trend for EMU countries' trade.

29. See Melitz (2003).

30. In this model we leave Greece out of EMU countries because it only joined the monetary union in 2001.

31. These difficulties were reflected in Franco Modigliani's *Financial Times* article of March 14, 1997: "The news that Germany risks failing the exam for admission to economic and monetary union (EMU) has shaken Europe."

32. For example, the first of the four estimates is calculated by averaging the yearly EMU2 coefficients corresponding to 1996 and 1997 in regression 1 (Table 7.2), and doing the same for the years 1999 to 2000. The estimate is simply calculated as

exp(avg coef 96–97 − avg coef 99–00) − 1.

33. As in the difference in difference model of the previous section, this dummy takes a value of zero for all country pairs before the 1999 creation of the EMU.

34. We estimate the increase in trade using UK trade shares in 1995. Using these shares, we compute a 6 percent increase in trade when we use the OLS estimation $[\exp(0.126 - 0.07) - 1] * \text{Export share to EMU} + [\exp(0.088) - 1] * \text{Export share to Non-EMU}$.

35. The difference between EMU1-UK and EMU1–non-UK, however, is not statistically significant.

36. For the case of row 1, we compute the increase of trade for the United Kingdom as the additional increase on trade with EMU countries $(\exp(0.145 - 0.087) - 1)$, multiply by UK export share to EMU countries plus the increase on trade with non-EMU countries $(\exp(0.08) - 1)$, and multiply by their share on UK trade.

37. This number is computed using a ratio trade in goods to GDP of 0.44 and a nominal GDP of 1,415 billion dollars of 2000. For this estimation, trade is computed as the sum of exports plus imports for the whole world (not just for our 22 country sample).

38. Bun and Klaassen (2002) and De Nardis and Vicarelli (2003) use a similar approach to compute the effect of EMU on trade. However, they focus exclusively on EMU 2, and thus do not allow for the possibility of a trade boost effect (or for trade diversion). Compared to the dynamic panel, an advantage of the methodology used in this chapter, in which we follow the impact of EMU over time, is that we do not need to impose a date for the start of the EMU effect, and rather let the data do the talking. In fact the dynamic panel results are quite sensitive to the choice of a starting date. In addition the dynamic panel assumes that the dynamics following the creation of the EMU are exactly the same

as the dynamics following any other shock that affects bilateral trade, such as changes in GDP or in real exchange rates.

39. Using the dynamic panel technique and the sample of developed countries, Micco et al. (2003) found that the increase in trade among EMU members is around 9 percent in the short run, while the effect with non-EMU countries is half as large. The long-run effect among EMU members is 34 percent.

References

Anderson, J., and E. van Wincoop. 2003. Gravity with gravitas: A solution to the border problem. *American Economic Review* 93 (March): 170–92.

Arellano, M., and S. Bond. 1991. Some test of specification for panel data: Monte Carlo evidence and an application to employment equations. *Review of Economic Studies* 58: 277–97.

Artis, M. 2000. Should the UK join EMU? European University Institute. Mimeo.

Barr, D., F. Breedon, and D. Miles. 2003. Life on the outside: Economic conditions and prospects outside euroland. *Economic Policy Panel Meeting*. Photocopy.

Brealey, R., and E. C. Kaplanis. 1996. The determination of foreign banking location. *Journal of International Money and Finance* 15: 577–97.

Bun, M., and F. Klaassen. 2002. Has the euro increased trade? Tinbergen Institute Discussion Paper.

Currie, D. 1997. The pros and cons of EMU. Economic and Monetary Union Team. HM Treasury.

De Nardis, S., and C. Vicarelli. 2003. The impact of the euro on trade. The (early) effect is not so large. European Network of Economic Policy Research Institutes.

Direction of Trade Statistics Database. June 2003. International Monetary Fund.

Estevadeordal, A., B. Frantz, and A. Taylor. 2003. The rise and fall of world trade, 1970–1939. *Quarterly Journal of Economics* 118(2): 359–407.

Frankel, J. 1997. *Regional Trading Blocs in the World Economic System*. Washington, DC: US Institute for International Economics.

Frankel, J. 2003. The UK decision re EMU: Implications of currency blocs for trade and business cycle correlations. In *Submissions on EMU from Leading Academics*. London: H.M. Treasury, pp. 99–109.

Frankel, J., and A. Rose. 1997. Is EMU more justifiable ex post than ex ante. *European Economic Review* 41: 753–60.

Frankel, J., and A. Rose. 1998. The endogeneity of the optimum currency area criteria. *Economic Journal* 108(449): 1009–25.

Frankel, J., and A. Rose. 2000. An estimate of the effect of currency unions on trade and growth. NBER Working Paper 7857.

Feenstra, R. 2004. *Advanced International Trade: Theory and Evidence*. Princeton: Princeton University Press, ch. 5.

Galindo, A., A. Micco, and C. Serra. 2003. Better the evil that you know: Evidence on entry costs faced by foreign banks. Research Department Working Paper 477. Inter-American Development Bank.

George, E. 1997. Speech by the Governor of the Bank of England before the British Chamber of Commerce in Hong Kong on September 23, 1997.

Glick, R., and A. Rose. 2001. Does a currency union affect trade? The time series evidence. NBER Working Paper 8396.

Grosse, R., and L. G. Goldberg. 1991. Foreign bank activity in the United States: An analysis by country of origin. *Journal of Banking and Finance* 15: 1092–1112.

Hughes Hallett, A., and L. Piscitelli. 2002. Does trade integration cause convergence? *Economic Letters* 75: 165–70.

Levy Yeyati, E. 2003. On the impact of a common currency on bilateral trade. *Economic Letters* 79(1): 125–29.

Lopez-Córdova, E., and C. Meissner. 2003. Exchange-rate regimes and international trade: Evidence from the classical gold era. *American Economic Review* 93(1): 344–53.

Mather, J. 2002. The UK and EMU. Public Policy Analysis Lecture 16. Manchester Metropolitan University.

Melitz, J. 2003. Distance, trade, political association and a common currency. Mimeo University of Strathclyde.

Micco, A., E. Stein, and G. Ordoñez. 2003. The Currency union effect on trade: Early evidence from EMU. *Economic Policy* 18: 309–613.

Nitsch, V. 2001. Honey, I shrunk the currency union effect on trade. *World Economy* 25(4): 457–74.

Persson, T. 2001. Currency union and trade: How large is the treatment effect. *Economic Policy* 33: 335–48.

Rose, A. 2000a. One money, one market: Estimating the effect of common currencies on trade. *Economic Policy* 30: 7–46.

Rose, A. 2000b. EMU's potential effect on British trade: A quantitative assessment. Commissioned for *Britain in Europe*. Reprinted in *Wirtschaftspolitische Blätter*.

Rose, A. 2000c. EMU and Swedish trade. Commissioned for *Swedish Employer's Confederation*, 2001.

Rose, A. 2001. Currency union and trade: The effect is large. *Economic Policy* 16: 449–61.

Rose, A. 2002. The effect of common currencies on international trade: Where do we stand. *URL: haas.berkeley.edu/~arose*.

Rose, A., and E. van Wincoop. 2001. National money as a barrier to international trade: The real case for currency union. *American Economic Review* 91(2): 386–90.

Tenreyro, S. 2001. On the causes and consequences of currency union. Mimeo. Harvard University.

Times On Line. March 19, 2002. Interview with Margaret Thatcher by Philip Webster. http://www.timesonline.co.uk/article/0,2-241131,00.html.

Viner, J. 1950. *The Customs Union Issue*. New York: Carnegie Endowment for International Peace.

Williams, B. 1998. Factors affecting the performance of foreign-owned banks in Australia: A cross-sectional study. *Journal of Banking and Finance* 22: 197–219.

World Development Indicators CD ROM (2002). Washington, DC: World Bank.

8

Output Smoothing in EMU and OECD: Can We Forgo the Government Contribution? A Risk-Sharing Approach

Carlos Fonseca Marinheiro

8.1 Introduction

In this chapter I analyze the patterns of output smoothing for euro-area and OECD economies, and I identify the different channels of risk sharing among such countries. I also compare the results obtained with those of the United States. By taking the successful US monetary union as a benchmark, I draw some interesting conclusions on the preparation of the EMU and OECD countries in dealing with asymmetric shocks. When countries give up their independent monetary policies, and the ability to use the exchange rate mechanism, to engage in monetary union, they should be able to smooth out idiosyncratic shocks. If this is not the case, the constitution of the monetary union could be rather costly.

In the United States the federal budget redistributes income among the different states. In Europe, the EMU has no similar tool for doing this, and national fiscal policies are constrained by the Stability and Growth Pact (SGP). Is it possible to successfully run a monetary union without a central (federal) budget or with constrained national fiscal policies? In other words, what is the role of the government sector in smoothing out asymmetric shocks in OECD countries? Could the government sector be replaced by private capital markets to provide risk sharing? These are some of the questions that this study tries to answer.

In Europe the EMU will certainly lead to increased financial integration among euro member countries, and financial markets will be able to contribute to smoothing out shocks in a monetary union. This contribution is made via two different channels. First, individuals resident in a monetary union might share risk through the cross-ownership of assets. If asset portfolios are regionally diversified, their holders are better protected against asymmetric shocks. By holding internationally diversified portfolios, individuals can reduce the exposure of their income and wealth to national idiosyncratic shocks to output, which facilitates consumption smoothing. Second, in a monetary union the economic agents are able to smooth the pattern of aggregated consumption by borrowing or lending internationally. Monetary union increases the depth of the credit market. Thus, if financial markets are sufficiently integrated, these mechanisms could play a crucial role in the smoothing of (asymmetric) business cycles and in the stability of the monetary union.

The financial integration of Europe is still considerably smaller than that of other monetary unions. However, the introduction of the euro in 1999, and the resulting disappearance of exchange rate risk among the twelve EU countries, is leading to increasing financial integration in the euro area. According to the so-called official consensus, the development of euro-area financial markets will help accomplish sufficient risk sharing among EMU members to smooth out asymmetric shocks. The European Commission has put great emphasis on the study of Asdrubali, Sørensen, and Yosha (1996), which concluded that, in the US case the financial markets play a much larger role than federal government transfers as channels of inter-state risk sharing. Such results enabled the Commission to conclude that "in Europe, more integrated capital and credit markets should greatly enhance the capacity of Member States to respond to shocks, as is presently the case for US states."[1] Consequently an analysis will be made here of how the increasing integration of the bond and equity markets in euro area might enhance the potential of risk sharing among member states. In order to do so, the results obtained for euro area will be compared with those of the United States. This analysis is important because increasing risk sharing reduces the pressure exerted on the ECB, and on national fiscal authorities, to deal with shocks concentrated in one or more countries.

In short, this chapter will focus on whether capital markets can replace governments in providing output smoothing for the euro area in the near future. To achieve this, the importance of the different channels of risk sharing in both OECD and EU countries must be quantified, and the smoothing provided by saving broken down into government and private contributions. Moreover this chapter will:

1. Verify whether it is possible to identify a difference in the pattern of output smoothing between the euro-12 countries and the larger OECD

group. More precisely, it will evaluate whether euro-area economies were better prepared in 1999 to enter monetary union than the other countries studied.

2. Assess the impact of the eventual enlargement of the euro area to include the United Kingdom, Sweden, and Denmark.

3. Determine whether the level of government deficit/debt has any impact on the pattern of risk sharing.

4. Compare the patterns of risk sharing in the OECD, in the EU-15, and in euro area using the monetary union of the United States as a benchmark.

5. Study how the pattern of output smoothing has evolved over time. In this regard it will be seen whether or not the degree of stabilization provided by financial markets has increased over time. This analysis will also be helpful in determining how output smoothing is likely to evolve in the near future.

6. Determine whether the size of countries has an effect on risk-sharing patterns.

In order to accomplish these objectives, we will use the international extension of the aforementioned method of Asdrubali et al. (1996), as proposed by Sørensen and Yosha (1998). A panel data estimation will be used for the period 1970 to 1999 for the nineteen OECD economies. The sample considered includes all fifteen EU economies (with the exception of Luxembourg) and the economies of Norway, the United States, Canada, Australia, and Japan.

Compared with previously published literature, this chapter uses a significantly increased sample of data (both in terms of the number of years studied and the number of countries involved) and tests new and interesting hypotheses. More specifically, when compared with the study of Sørensen and Yosha (1998), the results given here have been widened to include the 1990s, and the sample of countries taken has been considerably enlarged from eight EU countries to embrace all the euro area and EU-15 economies except for Luxembourg. Although this is the result of imposing some hypotheses with the purpose off making data from different sources compatible, it enables us to reach more reliable and interesting conclusions concerning the process of European integration. This chapter also tests the above-mentioned hypotheses which, to the best of my knowledge, have not yet been tested in the literature.

8.2   Risk Sharing in a Monetary Union

An optimum currency area (OCA) is an economic unit composed of regions affected symmetrically by disturbances and among which labor and other factors of production flow freely (see Mundell 1961; and McKinnon 1963). Therefore not all monetary unions constitute an OCA. Since the constitution of a monetary union implies the loss of the exchange rate instrument, their member countries become more vulnerable to the effects of asymmetric shocks. Consequently, if the loss of variability of the exchange rate is not offset by a high degree of labor mobility and/or wage flexibility the constitution of the monetary union could be costly in terms of welfare.

Besides labor mobility and wage flexibility there are other mechanisms that provide insurance against temporary asymmetric shocks. Such mechanisms entail some sort of income transfer providing risk sharing, and involve both the public and the private sector. Starting with the public sector, a centralized tax and transfer system (i.e., fiscal federalism within the monetary union) provides a transfer of income to regions that are affected by a negative asymmetric shock. However, if the budgets are not centralized, the national budgets can also provide some insurance: the working of automatic stabilizers means that the deficit of the affected country increases, smoothing the evolution of disposable income. However, as De Grauwe (2003) points out, these transfers are intergenerational and not interregional, implying that increases in consumption relative to output after a negative shock will have to be counterbalanced by a future decrease in consumption relative to output. Moreover this output smoothing provided by the national budget is restricted by the existence of high government deficits.

In addition to public insurance, private insurance can play an important role in risk sharing. By holding regionally diversified portfolios of assets consumers may diversify the geographical source of their income, reducing its exposure to national asymmetric shocks. When a country faces a negative asymmetric shock, the profitability of its firms is negatively affected, which might lead to a reduction in its stock prices. However, the profitability of the other firms of the monetary union is not affected. If a consumer holds a regionally diversified portfolio of assets, his return on such assets does not co-move with the national output but with the average monetary union output. Consequently it is possible to disperse the risk through the financial markets. To the extent to which the monetary union increases the depth of the credit market, it might also be easier for consumers and firms residents in the country negatively affected by the asymmetric shock to borrow against their future incomes, smoothing consumption. Another way of smoothing consumption is through private saving. Consumers of the affected country might decrease their savings in order to maintain their path of consumption.

8.3 Methodology

Different channels of risk sharing will be estimated for the period 1970 to 1999, for a group of nineteen OECD economies, which includes all EU-15 economies (except Luxembourg) along with Norway, Canada, Australia, the United States, and Japan. The main source of data is the OECD national accounts statistics, complemented with other sources, as described in appendix A. I will use the method proposed by Sørensen and Yosha (1998) to identify the different channels for smoothing asymmetric shocks to GDP. This method extends the method proposed by Asdrubali et al. (1996) for the US states, to an international context.

The method permits the identification of four different channels of income and consumption smoothing among different countries or regions:

1. *Factor income*   When there is cross-ownership of productive assets, individuals of one country have claims on the output of other countries, as the national citizens that invested in other countries have the right to the return on that capital. The income derived from these cross-border financial investments will then co-move with the income of other countries. This enables income smoothing through the cross-border ownership of productive assets, and provides insurance against asymmetric shocks that might hit their own national economies.

2. *International transfers*   International transfers smooth income if the net transfers from abroad are larger during idiosyncratic recessions.

3. *Saving and dis-saving*   Intertemporal consumption smoothing can also contribute to intercountry consumption smoothing. Consumers may adjust their savings in response to income shocks, corporations may increase or decrease retained earnings in response to profitability shocks, and government net savings may behave in a countercyclical or procyclical way.

4. *Capital depreciation*   Capital depreciation can contribute to cross-country income smoothing.

The factor income effect is reflected in the national accounts as the difference between gross domestic product (GDP) and gross national product (GNP). Net international transfers are measured as the difference between disposable national income (DNI) and national income (NI).[2] The difference between total consumption and disposable income is total net saving, reflecting consumption smoothing. Capital depreciation is responsible for the difference between GNP and DNI.[3]

The benchmark of the Sørensen and Yosha's (1998) method is full risk sharing. When risk is fully shared within a group of countries, the consumption of a country co-moves with world consumption but does not co-move with country specific shocks (see Arreaza, Sørensen, and Yosha 1998: 8):

$$C_t^i + G_t^i = k^i \text{GDP}_t, \tag{1}$$

where k^i is a country-specific constant representing the fixed proportion claims on world output of country i, t is time, C is private consumption, and G is government consumption.[4] As a result each country's consumption growth is perfectly correlated with world consumption growth. According to Olivei (2000) there are three key assumptions behind full risk sharing with complete markets. First, it is necessary to have perfect capital mobility across countries. Second, asset markets must be complete, to ensure that all idiosyncratic consumption risks are insurable. This requires individuals to have a set of assets available for trade in world capital markets that is sufficiently large to cover all possible future contingencies.[5] Third, each country's output must be tradable in order to allow the trade in assets that involve claims on its domestic output to take place. If a portion of domestic output is nontradable, it is not possible to put international trade claims on it. Consequently it is not possible to diversify the risks arising from fluctuations in nontradable output in international asset markets; such risks must be borne entirely by domestic consumers. For (1) to hold, it is also necessary to assume perfect substitution between private and public consumption, as a well as the exogeneity of GDP shocks. A derivation of this equation can be found in Sørensen and Yosha (1998: 215–17).[6] It should be remembered, however, that the purpose of this method is not to test the hypothesis of full risk sharing but to break down the degree of *observed* (full or partial) risk sharing into several components.

In order to decompose the cross-sectional variance of shocks to GDP, Sørensen and Yosha (1998) take the following identity as their starting point:

$$GDP^i = \frac{GDP^i}{GNP^i} \frac{GNP^i}{NI^i} \frac{NI^i}{DNI^i} \frac{DNI^i}{C^i + G^i} (C^i + G^i), \tag{2}$$

where all variables are measured in per capita real terms,[7] and i is an index of countries; the time index was suppressed. $C + G$ is the total consumption (the sum of private and public consumption).[8] Taking logs and differences, multiplying both sides by $\Delta \log GDP^i$ (minus its mean), and taking the cross-sectional average, leads to the following decomposition of the cross-sectional variance of GDP:

$$
\begin{aligned}
\mathrm{var}\{\Delta\log GDP^i\} = {} & \mathrm{cov}\{\Delta\log GDP^i, \Delta\log GDP^i - \Delta\log GNP^i\} \\
& + \mathrm{cov}\{\Delta\log GDP^i, \Delta\log GNP^i - \Delta\log NI^i\} \\
& + \mathrm{cov}\{\Delta\log GDP^i, \Delta\log NI^i - \Delta\log DNI^i\} \\
& + \mathrm{cov}\{\Delta\log GDP^i, \Delta\log DNI^i - \Delta\log(C^i + G^i)\} \\
& + \mathrm{cov}\{\Delta\log GDP^i, \Delta\log(C^i + G^i)\}.
\end{aligned}
$$

A further division by the variance of $\Delta \log GDP^i$ yields:

$$1 = \beta_f + \beta_d + \beta_\tau + \beta_s + \beta_u. \tag{3}$$

The β coefficients are the coefficient estimates of the following panel regressions:

$$
\begin{aligned}
\Delta\log GDP^i_t - \Delta\log GNP^i_t &= v_{f,t} + \beta_f \,\Delta\log GDP^i_t + u^i_{f,t}, \\
\Delta\log GNP^i_t - \Delta\log NI^i_t &= v_{d,t} + \beta_d \,\Delta\log GDP^i_t + u^i_{d,t}, \\
\Delta\log NI^i_t - \Delta\log DNI^i_t &= v_{\tau,t} + \beta_\tau \,\Delta\log GDP^i_t + u^i_{\tau,t}, \qquad (4) \\
\Delta\log DNI^i_t - \Delta\log(C^i_t + G^i_t) &= v_{s,t} + \beta_s \,\Delta\log GDP^i_t + u^i_{s,t}, \\
\Delta\log(C^i_t + G^i_t) &= v_{u,t} + \beta_u \,\Delta\log GDP^i_t + u^i_{u,t},
\end{aligned}
$$

where the $v_{.,t}$ are time fixed effects. According to Sørensen and Yosha (1998), the inclusion of these time effects is crucial to capturing year-specific impacts on growth rates, meaning the impact of aggregated OECD production. The β coefficients are interpreted as giving the incremental percentage amount of smoothing achieved at each level. β_f captures the amount of smoothing provided by factor income, β_d

gives the amount of smoothing endorsed to capital depreciation flows, β_t captures the international transfers' smoothing, β_s captures the smoothing provided by saving, and finally, β_u gives the percentage of shocks that are left unsmoothed. We will empirically estimate system (4).[9]

The pioneering work of Asdrubali et al. (1996) for the US states identified only three levels of smoothing: capital market, federal government, and the credit market. Hence the degree of detail is greater when different countries are considered. In fact country level data are richer and less prone to measurement errors than US state-level data. For instance, there are no official estimates for the GDP or GNP in the US states. Nevertheless, it is possible to aggregate the more detailed levels of smoothing of the international extension into the three channels obtained for the US states. It is only necessary to further divide the amount of smoothing that occurs via saving (in the international extension) into government saving, corporate saving, and personal saving.[10] The *capital market* smoothing is then the result of the sum of the effects of factor income, capital depreciation, and corporate saving. US *federal government* smoothing (through the federal tax-transfer and grant system) is comparable with income smoothing via international transfers. Finally, US consumption smoothing via *credit markets* corresponds to smoothing through both personal and government saving.

Instead of using the original method of Sørensen and Yosha (1998), we could have used the modified version proposed by Mélitz and Zumer (1999). These authors modified the original model of Asdrubali, Sørensen, and Yosha by adding four additional variables (including openness). They also considered the total amount of shocks left unsmoothed (β_u), to be predetermined, and used a different estimation method. Another crucial difference lay in the interpretation of the beta coefficients. Mélitz and Zumer (1999) started from a different national accounting identity, and consequently identified different channels of risk sharing. However, in order to make our results comparable with previous literature, we decided to use the original method of Sørensen and Yosha (1998).

8.4   Panel Data Estimation Notes

As mentioned above, the estimates used here are based on panel data regressions. Compared with pure cross-sectional or time-series studies, the use of panel data has the advantage of allowing control of individual heterogeneity. Following Baltagi (2001), the general specification of a panel data regression is

$$Y_{it} = \alpha + X'_{it}\beta + u_{it}, \qquad i = 1, \ldots, N; \ t = 1, \ldots, T.$$

The variables have a double subscript, i for the individuals (countries, firms, households, etc.) and t for time. These subscripts reflect the cross-sectional and the time-series dimensions, respectively. The error component disturbances take the following structure:

$$u_{it} = \mu_i + \lambda_t + v_{it},$$

where μ_i stands for the unobservable individual-specific effect, λ_t is the unobservable time effect and v_{it} is the remainder stochastic disturbance term, independently and identically distributed, IID $(0, \sigma_v^2)$.

Either the fixed effects model or the random effects model can be used, depending on the assumptions made on the unobservable components of the error term. In our practical estimation the time fixed effects model will be used. In other words, it will be assumed that λ_t is fixed, μ_i is nil, and v_{it} is stochastic. Furthermore the X_{it} will be assumed to be independent of v_{it} for all i and t.

When using fixed effects, the inference is conditional on the particular set of countries and over the specific time periods observed. Some of the known limitations of the use of time fixed effects are the large loss of degrees of freedom,[11] and the impossibility of estimating the effect of any time-invariant variables, due to the way that the estimators are obtained.[12]

Another possibility would be to estimate the model using random effects. In this case it would be assumed that both μ_i and λ_t were random. This would avoid the loss of degrees of freedom implied by the use of fixed effects, and the inference would pertain to the large population from which the sample was drawn. However, this technique would only be appropriate if we were drawing the N individuals randomly from a large population. Thus it would be necessary to have a representative panel of the whole population about which we were trying to make inferences. This is clearly not the case here, since our sample of nineteen OECD countries comprises roughly the whole population of the developed OECD members. Moreover, as the sample will be split into subsamples, we need our conclusions to be conditional on the particular subsample that is being used. In short, and in this particular case, econometric theory clearly points to the use of the fixed effects model.

When using the fixed effects model, we can choose from using individual fixed effects, time fixed effects, or both. As Sørensen and Yosha (1998: 224–25) point out, the use of time fixed effects is "crucial" in this application, given that they capture year-specific impacts on GDP growth rates, meaning the impact of aggregate OECD GDP. As a result time fixed effects will also be used in my empirical estimates to make them comparable to those of Arreaza et al. (1998) and Sørensen and Yosha (1998) (ASY98 and SY98, respectively).

The system (4) was estimated by SY98 and ASY98 using a two-step generalized least squares (GLS) method (assuming a common AR1 process and allowing for state specific variances of the error terms since GDP is, in general, more volatile for small countries). My empirical estimation will also correct for autocorrelation, but in a different way from that of ASY98: a common AR1 process will not be imposed for all equations.

8.5   Empirical Results for Euro-Area and OECD Countries

My main results use a sample of nineteen OECD economies[13] for the period 1970 to 1999.[14] The presentation of these results begins with a replication of those of ASY98, and is followed by my main results. Then the contribution of saving to smoothing will be divided into private and government components. The influence, if any, of the level of deficit/debt on the smoothing provided by the public and private sectors will also be investigated. Next my results will be compared with those obtained for the US states. Subsequently the way in which the pattern of risk sharing changes when the economy faces more persistent shocks will be analyzed. Finally, the evolution of the pattern of risk sharing over time will be analyzed.

8.5.1   Comparison with ASY98's Results
The presentation of my results begins with a replication (and extension) of those obtained by Arreaza et al. (1998)[15] in table 8.1. Columns 1 and 4 show ASY98 results for eight and eleven EU economies, respectively.[16] Columns 2 and 5 show my replication.

Despite some probable revisions of data, and a slightly different estimation method,[17] results very similar to those of ASY98[18] were obtained. For the 1971 to 1993 period and for the EU-8 sample, the amount of unsmoothed shocks is exactly the same, but there are some small differences in the smoothing composition. For the eleven EU

Table 8.1

Channels of income and consumption spending (%): Replication and extension of the results of ASY (1998, Table 3.1)

	EU-8			EU-11[a]			
	ASY (98)	Own estimate		ASY (98)		Own estimate	
	(1)	(2)	(3)	(4)	(5)	(6)	(7)
	1971–1993	1971–1993	1971–1999	1980–1993	1980–1993	1980–1999	1971–1999
Factor income (β_f)	−1 (1)	0 (0)	−2 (1)	−3 (2)	−4 (1)	−7 (3)	−4 (2)
Capital depreciation (β_d)	−8 (8)	−11 (7)	−11 (8)	−8 (8)	−13 (6)	−14 (7)	−12 (9)
International Transfers (β_t)	3 (2)	2 (1)	2 (2)	5 (3)	4 (3)	4 (3)	2 (2)
Saving (β_s)	50 (10)	53 (10)	54 (11)	37 (7)	42 (6)	48 (7)	54 (13)
Not smoothed (β_u)	56 (14)	56 (11)	58 (13)	69 (14)	70 (11)	70 (13)	60 (15)

Note: Absolute t-statistics in brackets. Arreaza et al. (1998) report standard errors in their tables; thus the corresponding t-statistics for ASY98 were obtained by dividing the coefficient estimate by its standard deviation, ignoring any (nonreported) rescaling. In our estimates we corrected for first-order serial correlation (AR1) using a two-step search procedure in Winrats 5.01. Where necessary, results were rescaled to sum 100 percent. The ASY98's EU-8 sample comprises Austria, Belgium, Denmark, France, Greece, Germany, and the UK.
a. The ASY98 EU-11 sample consists of EU-8 + Italy, Netherlands, and Sweden. It does *not* correspond to the first euro-11 countries.

countries sample and for the period 1980 to 1993, comparing my results (column 5) with original ASY98 results (column 4), I found that the percentage of unsmoothed shocks is roughly the same (70 percent). Regardless of the estimate the large difference in the amount of shocks left unsmoothed in the OECD countries when compared to US states[19] is striking. However, there are some differences in the composition of channels responsible for the smoothing of shocks: capital depreciation and factor income show a more negative dis-smoothing effect in my estimate, which in turn is offset by increased smoothing through saving.

Extending the duration of the EU-8 sample to the end of the 1990s (column 3), has no major effect on the results: factor income is found to destabilize output, while the smoothing provided by saving shows a marginal increase. The overall result is only a small increase in the percentage of unsmoothed shocks (from 56 to 58 percent).

With regard to the sample of eleven European economies, extending the results to 1999 leaves the amount of unsmoothed shocks unaltered. However, there is an increase in the amount of dis-smoothing through factor income (and capital depreciation) that is being compensated for by an increase in smoothing by saving. However, it should also be mentioned that the coefficient of factor income (β_f) is generally estimated with low precision, as reflected in the relatively low t-statistics. Extending the estimation period back to 1971 (i.e., in adding the 1970s to the sample) leads to a drop in the percentage of unsmoothed shocks, which is a result of both a decrease in the dis-smoothing by factor income and capital depreciation and an increase in the smoothing provided by saving. This reflects the fact that the last two decades of the twentieth century were characterized by a lower degree of income smoothing than the extended 1971 to 1999 period: the amount of shocks to income left unsmoothed for the period of 1971 to 1999 (and for EU-11) is 10 percentage points lower than for the 1980 to 1999 period. As I will show later, this is mainly the result of including the first half of the 1990s. Some possible explanations are related to the events that occurred in that period.

The early 1990s were characterized by extraordinary events that particularly affected Europe: first, there was the collapse of the USSR, then German reunification, and in September 1992 the crisis in the European monetary system (EMS).[20] The break up of the USSR had clear negative impact on Nordic countries' (especially Finland's) exports to the former USSR area. Moreover some of the mechanisms advanced by Krugman (1993) might also have played a role. That is, the negative shock to Finland's GDP might have induced an exodus of capital that could have caused an even larger negative variation in such countries' GNP. This might help explain the negative coefficient of factor income smoothing. German reunification, the subsequent tightening of monetary policy throughout Europe, and the EMS crisis could also have lowered the potential for risk sharing.

8.5.2   Main Results

Table 8.2 shows my main results regarding the different channels of risk sharing, divided into different subsamples of countries for the period of 1970 to 1999. Focusing on the results for the whole sample of 19 OECD economies, it can be seen that only 41 percent of shocks to

Table 8.2
Channels of income and consumption spending: Different country samples 1970 to 1999 (%)

	All	Small	EU-15	EU-11	EU-12	Small EU-15	G7	South periphery EU	Core EU
Factor income (β_f)	-2	-1	-1	-1	0	-1	-2	-3	2
	(1)	(1)	(1)	(1)	(0)	(0)	(1)	(1)	(1)
Capital	-7	-7	-7	-7	-7	-8	-8	-3	-11
Depreciation (β_d)	(7)	(6)	(6)	(5)	(6)	(6)	(4)	(1)	(4)
International	-1	-2	-1	-3	-2	-3	2	1	3
Transfers (β_t)	(1)	(2)	(1)	(2)	(2)	(2)	(3)	(0)	(2)
Saving (β_s)	50	52	51	51	53	52	47	41	44
	(15)	(12)	(12)	(9)	(11)	(10)	(9)	(4)	(5)
Not smoothed (β_u)	59	59	59	60	56	59	60	64	62
	(20)	(16)	(16)	(13)	(13)	(14)	(13)	(6)	(7)

Note: AR1 estimation. *EU-11*: First 11 euro countries (with the exception of Luxembourg): Austria, Belgium, Finland, France, Germany, Italy, Ireland, Netherlands, Portugal, and Spain. *EU-12*: EU-11 + Greece. *EU-15*: EU-12 + Denmark, Sweden, and United Kingdom. *G7*: Canada, Germany, France, United Kingdom, Italy, Japan, and United States. *Small countries*: Australia, Austria, Belgium, Denmark, Finland, Greece, Ireland, Netherlands, Norway, Portugal, Spain, and Sweden. *South periphery EU*: Spain, Greece, and Portugal. *Core EU*: Germany, France, Italy, Belgium, and the Netherlands. "All" stands for the whole sample of 19 OECD economies: EU-15 + Australia, Canada, Norway, United States, and Japan. *t*-Statistics are in brackets. Estimates corrected for first-order serial correlation (AR1) using a two-step search procedure in Winrats 5.01. Where necessary, results were rescaled to sum 100 percent.

GDP in these countries were smoothed. The only channel that effectively smoothes income is saving (50 percent), while all other channels that might potentially smooth income are actually leading to income dis-smoothing: factor income flows dis-smoothed output by −2 percent,[21] capital depreciation also has a negative contribution of −7 percent, and international transfers have a nonstatistically significant impact of −1 percent. With the exception of the negative contribution from international transfers, the results are similar to those of ASY98 for the period 1971 to 1993.

The lack of smoothing through *factor income flows* might be interpreted as the result of the absence of significant cross-ownership of productive assets among OECD economies. This result is in line with the usual "home bias" in the composition of portfolios. Moreover the contagious effect in financial markets might also limit risk-sharing benefits from holding an *internationally* diversified portfolio.[22] *International transfers* do not seem to be motivated by income smoothing motivations. In the European Union such transfers are mainly due to the Common Agricultural Policy (CAP), structural funds, and their counterpart—the member states contributions to the EU budget. However, the resources of the EU budget have a ceiling of 1.27 percent of the Union's GNP (the actual figure in 2001 was 1.11 percent of GNP). Consequently the EU budget has a very small influence on EU income, limiting its contribution to the smoothing of output shocks. *Capital depreciation* is responsible for the difference between national income and GNP. Its negative contribution to smoothing may be due in part to how national accounts data is calculated.[23]

As mentioned above, *saving* is the only operative smoothing channel.[24] It is the result of the net saving decisions of households, corporations, and governments. This aggregated figure is subdivided below into government and private contributions. While smoothing via saving does not necessarily require actual cross-country flows of funds, it may involve such flows, given that aggregate consumption smoothing via saving is more difficult in a closed economy (SY98: 227).

In the same table the sample of countries has been divided into different subsamples. As mentioned in the introduction, I wanted to test a set of interesting hypotheses, namely to determine whether the size of a country has any relevance to patterns of output smoothing among countries. Consequently I considered the G7 group of large countries separately from the group of small countries, within which the EU members were also isolated. I also wanted to determine whether EU countries and euro-area economies are in any way different from the larger OECD group. Hence I isolated EU-15 countries, the euro-area economies (both the present 12 members and the first 11 members). Furthermore, and in the spirit of Bayoumi and Eichengreen (1993), the "EU core" and the EU southern "periphery" were also considered.

As for the results regarding the different subsamples, I can state that in general, no major differences are to be found among such groups of countries. In fact the picture for those subsamples does not differ to any great extent from the pattern of risk sharing for the entire sample. There are, however, a few interesting exceptions. The first exception is the positive contribution made by factor income flows to the "core" EU countries, reflecting the impact of the cross-ownership of assets. It could be that individuals in the "core" economies of the European Union hold a more regionally diversified portfolio of assets than the rest of the sample of countries, due to a larger integration of their economies. Another exception is the positive role played by international transfers for the subset of G7 economies, "core" EU countries and the three southern "peripheral" EU countries. However, all these subgroups of countries have larger shocks left unsmoothed (62 percent for the EU "core" against 59 percent for all EU-15). This result is due to the small degree of smoothing through saving, particularly for southern "peripheral" EU countries and for the EU "core," where saving only smoothes respectively 41 and 44 percent of shocks. The EU-15 figure stands at 51 percent.

8.5.3 Contribution Made by Private and Government Sectors to Consumption Smoothing

As mentioned above, the impact of net saving on the smoothing of consumption is the result of the net saving behavior of three sectors: households, corporations and the government. I can only shed light on the question of whether the financial markets can replace the government in the role of smoothing output by discriminating between government and private saving contributions to smoothing. Due to data availability limitations, I am also only going to differentiate between two sectors: the government and the private. In the private sector, contributions are made by both personal saving behavior (households) and corporate behavior. However, according to Sørensen and Yosha's results (1998: 231–32), "personal saving contributes nothing to cross-country consumption smoothing,"[25] which implies that almost all of the reported private saving smoothing is the result of corporate net saving behavior.[26]

ASY98's methodology will be used to estimate such effects. ASY98 were also only able to differentiate between two sectors because of data limitations. Recall that the incremental smoothing provided by total net saving (β_s) is obtained by the regression:

$$\Delta\log \text{DNI}_t^i - \Delta\log(C_t^i + G_t^i) = v_{s,t} + \beta_s \Delta\log \text{GDP}_t^i + u_{s,t}^i$$

To break down the smoothing provided by total net saving further, into private and government saving, I used the following regression:

$$\Delta\log \text{DNI}_t^i - \Delta\log(\text{DNI}_t^i - X_t^i) = v_{x,t} + \beta_{sx} \Delta\log \text{GDP}_t^i + u_{x,t}^i \tag{5}$$

where the generic variable X is either net government saving or net private saving.

Table 8.3 presents the results.[27] In general, the contribution made by the government sector to smoothing is larger than that of the private sector. For the whole OECD-19 sample, the government sector is found to smooth 29 percent of the shocks for the period 1971 to 1999, while the private sector saving behavior was responsible for 21 percent of smoothing. The figures for the EU-15 are very similar (27 and 24 percent, respectively). For these countries the government sector is responsible for more than 50 percent of the smoothing due to saving. Euro-12 countries, however, show a different pattern of smoothing: the private sector (32 percent) contributes more to smoothing than the government (21 percent). The same pattern showing the predominance of private sector saving smoothing is also found in the small-country subsample,

Table 8.3
Decomposition of smoothing provided by total net saving into government and private sectors, 1970 to 1999

	All	EU-15	EU-12	Small	Small EU-12	Small EU-15
Government	29	27	21	25	18	26
	(7)	(6)	(4)	(5)	(3)	(5)
Private	21	24	32	28	37	26
	(4)	(4)	(4)	(4)	(4)	(3)
Total saving (β_s)	50	51	53	52	55	52
	(15)	(12)	(11)	(12)	(9)	(10)

Note: See note to table 8.2 for description of the samples of countries considered, and text for details.

especially for the subset of small euro-area economies. For the latter, the gap between public and private smoothing through saving is the largest of all: private sector saving smoothes 37 percent of the shocks while the government smoothes only 18 percent. The lower degree of risk sharing through the government sector in small countries may be due to the automatic fiscal stabilisers being less effective at smoothing output in relatively small economies (see Marinheiro 2003a: ch. 3).

8.5.4   Consumption Smoothing: High versus Low Deficit Countries

An attempt will now be made to find out whether the contribution made by public sector saving to output smoothing is the same, irrespective of government deficit. According to recent literature, the higher the budget deficit or debt accumulation rises, the lower is the effectiveness of fiscal stabilizers.[28] To test this hypothesis, it is necessary to distinguish high- from low-deficit countries.[29] ASY98 propose to split the sample according to the average deficit over the sample period for each country. They found no evidence that the deficit level affects the amount of consumption smoothing provided by the public, or private, sectors (ASY98: 17). The reason for this lack of evidence is the difference in behavior between the EU and OECD samples. While for the EU sample the authors concluded that the smoothing through the government sector is higher for low-deficit countries, the conclusion is the opposite for the larger OECD group. For the OECD group ASY98 found more smoothing in high-deficit countries. However, it should be mentioned that in their applied work, ASY98 considered net government saving to be equal to the negative of the deficit (ASY98: 17). As a result they rather inappropriately used net saving data to distinguish high- from low-deficit countries instead of using government net lending data. As the formulas in appendix A show, these two measures are only equivalent when government net capital transfers and government consumption of fixed capital are equal to government gross capital formation and government purchases of land and intangible assets, that is, when the capital budget deficit corresponds exactly to government capital consumption.[30]

In table 8.4 the method proposed by ASY98 was used to distinguish such subgroups (but using net government lending data). That is, I considered high-deficit countries to be those that showed, over the period 1970 to 1999, an average deficit above the unweighted average deficit of the whole sample, which was 2.76 percent. As a result the group of high-deficit countries consisted of eleven countries (Australia,

Table 8.4
Decomposition of smoothing provided by total net saving into government and private sectors: High- versus low-deficit countries, using ASY definition

| | 1970–1999 | | | | | | 1980–1993 | | | | 1986–1999 | |
| | All | | EU-15 | | Small | | All | | OECD-17 (SY98) | | All | |
Deficit level →	High	Low	High	Low	High	Low	High	Low	High	Low	High	Low
Government	15	53	12	55	8	55	24	80	40	31	15	81
	(3)	(7)	(2)	(6)	(1)	(5)	(3)	(7)	(7)	(6)	(2)	(7)
Private	37	2	41	-4	49	-1	23	-25	12	6	24	-14
	(5)	(0)	(5)	(0)	(5)	(0)	(2)	(2)	(2)	(2)	(2)	(1)
Total saving (β_s)	52	54	54	51	56	54	47	55	52	37	39	67
	(11)	(12)	(9)	(9)	(9)	(9)	(7)	(7)	(10)	(6)	(5)	(9)

Note: See note to table 8.2 for a description of the samples of countries considered. *High-deficit countries:* Those with an average deficit above the average deficit of the sample (2.76 percent). *Low-deficit countries:* Austria, Germany, Denmark, Finland, France, Japan, Norway, and Sweden. *High-deficit countries:* Australia, Belgium, Canada, Spain, United Kingdom, Greece, Ireland, Italy, Netherlands, Portugal, and United States. The shaded columns regarding OECD-17 are from SY98, table 3.9, p. 32.

Belgium, Canada, Spain, the United Kingdom, Greece, Ireland, Italy, the Netherlands, Portugal, and the United States), and the remaing eight countries consisted of the low-deficit countries (Austria, Germany, Denmark, Finland, France, Japan, Norway, and Sweden).

The empirical results lead clearly to the conclusion that a large government budget deficit does have a negative effect on the amount of consumption smoothing through government net saving. Both for the nineteen OECD countries and the EU-15 economies, the consumption smoothing provided by the government sector is substantially higher for low-deficit countries. For all nineteen OECD economies, government saving smoothes 53 percent of the shocks for low-deficit countries, while for high-deficit countries only 15 percent are smoothed. Even during the ASY98 period of 1980 to 1993, we found no evidence that for OECD countries the smoothing of shocks provided by the government sector is higher for high-deficit countries.[31] Another conclusion drawn from the results is that the amount of private and government smoothing appears to be substitutable: the amount of total net saving smoothing does not differ greatly between high- and low-deficit countries.[32] For low-deficit countries, almost all the smoothing is provided by government saving behavior, while for high-deficit countries, the major provider of consumption smoothing through saving is the private sector.

As for the small countries, they show the same pattern, apart from an unusually low contribution from net government saving to smoothing in high-deficit countries. It should be noted that all the Nordic countries along with Austria are included in the low-deficit–small country subgroup. These are countries that have large fiscal stabilizers, which helps explain the high contribution made by the government sector in this subgroup.

In table 8.5 another method was used to distinguish low-deficit from high-deficit subsamples. The classification of countries was allowed to vary over time. Each year a country was assumed to have a large deficit if its deficit level was substantially above the (unweighted) average budget deficits of the aggregate OECD19 recorded in that year. More precisely, a country was classified as having an "above normal" deficit in year t, when its budget deficit for that period was larger than the average OECD deficit by at least 1 percent. Deficits were defined as "below" in all other cases.

The empirical results show that the "below average" deficit sample benefits from a larger (and statistically significant) contribution from

Table 8.5
Decomposition of smoothing provided by total net saving into government and private sectors: High- versus low-deficit countries, using deficit above/below average definition

| | 1970–1999 | | | | | | 1980–1993 | | 1986–1999 | |
| | All | | EU-15 | | Small | | OECD | | All | |
Deficit level →	Above	Below	Above	Below	Above	Below	Above	Below	Above	Below
Government	19	29	17	26	7	25	24	48	34	40
	(3)	(6)	(2)	(5)	(1)	(4)	(2)	(7)	(3)	(6)
Private	37	18	45	18	60	20	4	5	–4	7
	(3)	(3)	(3)	(3)	(4)	(3)	(0)	(1)	(0)	(1)
Total saving (β_s)	56	46	62	44	67	45	28	53	31	47
	(8)	(13)	(8)	(9)	(7)	(9)	(3)	(10)	(4)	(9)

Note: See note to table 8.2 for a description of the samples of countries considered. Each year a country is classified as being a high-deficit country if its government budget deficit surpasses the (unweighed) average deficit of the whole sample of 19 OECD economies by at least 1 percent.

government saving to output smoothing. This result underscores the previous conclusion that a high deficit leads to a reduction in the amount of smoothing provided by net government saving. Again it was found that for small countries, an "above normal" deficit results in a very small contribution from the government sector to the smoothing of consumption shocks.[33] However, an increase in the contribution from the private sector more than compensates for this decrease. For the whole period 1970 to 1999, it was found that the "above-average" deficit subsample displayed a higher amount of total smoothing provided by saving. But this somewhat unexpected result does not hold for the 1980 to 1993 nor for the 1986 to 1999 subperiods.

8.5.5   Comparison with the US States

It is interesting to compare the results obtained for the above-mentioned group of countries with those obtained for the US states by Asdrubali et al. (1996) (ASY96). For this, I will aggregate my more detailed results into three levels of smoothing: capital market, transfers, and credit market. Capital market smoothing corresponds to the sum of factor income, capital depreciation, and corporate saving smoothing. Using Sørensen and Yosha's conclusion (1998: 231–32) on the nonrelevance of personal saving, in my estimate I assume that the amount of personal saving smoothing is nil. Transfers refer to international transfer smoothing. Credit market smoothing corresponds to smoothing through both personal and government saving.

Table 8.6 shows both the SY98 estimates and my estimates for the period 1981 to 1990. The results for the sample of nineteen OECD economies are reasonably close to the SY98 ones, which related to their more restricted sample of twelve OECD countries. The amount of unsmoothed shocks was found to be similar (62 percent in my estimate, 57 percent in the SY98 sample). However, the smoothing by capital markets was higher in the SY98 estimates (15 percent compared with 8 percent for my sample of countries), and the results for the EU countries were substantially different from those reported in SY98. The unusually low level of credit market smoothing reported by SY98 for their six EU countries (3 percent) was not found with my sample of EU-15 economies. My estimate was much closer to the result reported for the OECD (19 percent). Nevertheless, both in my estimate and in that of SY98, when the OECD and the EU samples are compared, the latter displays a much lower level of smoothing provided by the credit market, which in turn implies a larger amount of unsmoothed shocks.

Table 8.6
Comparison of income and consumption smoothing: EU, OECD, and US states, using SY98 and our own results for the period 1981–1990

	SY98			Own estimate	
	US states	OECD*	EC-6	All	EU-15
Capital markets	48	15	8	8	9
	(12)	(4)	(1)	(0)	(0)
Transfers	14	2	7	3	5
	(14)	(2)	(2)	(2)	(2)
Credit market	19	26	3	27	19
	(2)	(5)	(0)	(4)	(2)
Not smoothed	19	57	82	62	68
	(2)	(11)	(9)	(11)	(8)

Note: See note to table 8.2 for a description of the samples of countries considered. The source of the first three columns is ASY96, table 1, p. 1092. *EC-6*: Belgium, Denmark, Finland, France, Germany, Italy, and United Kingdom. *OECD**: Austria, Belgium, Finland, France, Germany, Italy, Sweden, United Kingdom, United States, Japan, Australia, and Canada. ASY96 report standard errors in their tables, thus the corresponding t-statistics for ASY96 were obtained by dividing the coefficient estimate by its standard deviation, ignoring any (nonreported) rescaling. Capital markets smoothing corresponds to the sum of factor income, capital depreciation, and corporate saving smoothing. Transfers refer to international transfer smoothing. Credit market smoothing corresponds to smoothing through personal and government saving. Our estimate assumes that the amount of personal saving smoothing is nil.

These differences in the smoothing by the credit market channel are due to different government contributions to smoothing. They may also reflect differences in the relative importance of the banking sector, in particular, variations in the importance of relationship lending agreements between continental Europe and the Anglo-Saxon world.

Comparing the results for the US states with those of my estimates for the EU-15, for the period 1981 to 1990, it can be seen that the amount of shocks left unsmoothed is much higher in the European Union than within the US federation (68 percent compared with only 19 percent). This is mainly the result of the enormous difference in the amount of smoothing provided by the capital markets.

Capital markets smooth 48 percent of asymmetric shocks to the US states' GSP, while in the European Union they only smooth 9 percent of the idiosyncratic shocks to GDP.[34] The role of the US federal tax-transfer system in smoothing output (14 percent) is also considerably higher than the contribution of international transfers to smoothing shocks to EU output (5 percent). Interestingly, the amount smoothed by the credit market is exactly the same in both estimates (19 percent).[35] As the credit market smoothing mainly measures the smoothing provided by government saving behavior, it can be concluded that the public sector plays a crucial role in the smoothing of asymmetric shocks in Europe. Sørensen and Yosha (1998) go even further and conclude that the restrictions on national budget deficits imposed by the EU Treaty should be relaxed to allow governments to smooth output shocks. They further maintain that a greater insurance role for the EU budget may be demanded by national governments, until the degree of integration of the EU credit market allows a substantial amount of consumption smoothing via personal saving.[36]

Table 8.7 shows our estimates for the full 1970 to 1999 period together with ASY96's results for the US states for the periods 1964 to 1970 and 1981 to 1990. Also included are updated estimates for the US states for the period 1970 to 1998. These estimates were obtained by using Bent Sørensen's database and econometric program.

For the period 1970 to 1999, our results relative to the three channels of smoothing do not vary substantially for the different subsamples of countries considered. In the OECD the most important channel of output smoothing is the credit market (it represents 29 percent of smoothing achieved by the nineteen OECD economies).[37] Next in importance comes the capital market smoothing (12 percent for the same group). International transfers actually dis-smooth output (−1 percent for OECD19) but are not statistically different from zero.[38] As in table 8.2, the amount of shocks left unsmoothed is around 60 percent for the several subsamples considered. Comparing the small countries with the enlarged group of nineteen OECD economies, the former shows a higher degree of smoothing through the capital markets (19 percent), and somewhat less smoothing through the credit market (25 percent). Overall, the amount of shocks smoothed by the three channels is roughly the same, with the amount of shocks left unsmoothed being 59 percent for both groups of countries. The small euro-area economies display a similar picture to the more extended sample of small OECD countries, showing, however, a higher degree of capital market smoothing (30 percent) and lower smoothing through the credit market. Adding the 3 percent of dis-smoothing provided by the international transfers, we arrive at a total of 55 percent of shocks left unsmoothed.

As for the twelve euro-area countries, they show a level of capital market smoothing of 25 percent, which is higher by 13 percentage

Table 8.7
Comparison of income and consumption smoothing; EU, OECD, and US states 1970 to 1999

	US states 1964–1990	US states 1981–1990	US states 1970–1998	All	EU-15	EU-12	Small	Small EU-12	Small EU-15
Capital markets	39	48	45	12	15	25	19	30	18
	(13)	(12)	(17)	(3)	(3)	(3)	(3)	(4)	(3)
Transfers	13	14	14	−1	−1	−2	−2	−3	−3
	(13)	(14)	(35)	(1)	(1)	(2)	(2)	(2)	(2)
Credit market	23	19	21	29	27	21	25	18	26
	(4)	(2)	(4)	(7)	(6)	(4)	(5)	(3)	(5)
Not smoothed	25	19	20	59	59	56	59	55	59
	(4)	(2)	(4)	(20)	(16)	(13)	(16)	(11)	(14)

Note: See note to table 8.2 for a description of the samples of countries considered. t-Statistics are given in brackets. The source of the two first columns is ASY96, table I and table III (pages 1092 and 1094). ASY96 report standard errors in their tables, thus the corresponding t-statistics for ASY96 were obtained by dividing the coefficient estimate by its standard deviation, ignoring any (non-reported) rescaling. The third column for the United States, is obtained by using Bent Sørensen's database and his econometric program. "Capital market" smoothing corresponds to the sum of factor income, capital depreciation, and corporate saving smoothing. "Transfers" refers to international transfer smoothing. "Credit market" smoothing corresponds to smoothing through personal saving and government saving. Our estimate assumes that the amount of personal saving smoothing is nil.

points (pp) than in the OECD19. However, the degree of risk sharing provided by the credit market (21 percent) is 8 pp below the figure for the whole sample. As a result the total amount of unsmoothed shocks is 56 percent, only 3 percentage points below the figure for the whole sample of nineteen OECD economies. Consequently, from the viewpoint of cross-country risk sharing, it appears that before the period of introduction of the euro (1999), the euro-area economies were not substantially better prepared to embrace monetary union than the rest of the OECD countries considered in our study.

According to our results, an eventual *enlargement of the eurozone* to include the United Kingdom, Denmark, and Sweden (i.e., to all EU-15 members) will lead to a small increase in the amount of unsmoothed shocks (3 pp). This is the result of a smaller capital market contribution to smoothing in these three "nonparticipating" countries (the difference between EU-15 and EU-12 is −10 pp), which is not fully offset by higher credit market smoothing, meaning government-led smoothing (+6 pp).

Comparing the euro area with the federation of the United States, it can be seen that the amount of total risk sharing is considerably lower in the former group of countries, where the amount of shocks left unsmoothed is 56 percent, which compares with only 20 percent for the United States. With regard to the different channels of risk sharing, the credit market smoothing in the EU-12 countries (21 percent) is exactly the same as its equivalent in the United States (in the 1970–1998 period). But the main differences between the two regions lie the amount of risk sharing provided by transfers and by the capital markets. While in the United States the federal government tax and transfers system smoothes 14 percent of the idiosyncratic regional shocks, in the EU-12 such an inter-regional transfer system does not exist. Indeed, international transfers actually dis-smooth output by 2 percent. The amount of risk sharing provided by the capital markets in the euro-area countries (25 percent) is also substantially below (approximately just half) that of the US states (45 percent for the period 1970–1998, and 48 percent for 1981–1990). This is most probably the result of a much lower degree of cross-country ownership of productive assets than in the monetary union of the United States.

If the introduction of the euro leads to capital markets becoming as integrated in the euro area as they were in the US federation in the 1970 to 1998 period, an increase of 20 pp in the amount of risk sharing provided by euro-area capital markets can be expected. Everything else being constant, the amount of shocks unsmoothed is expected to drop to 36 percent in this scenario. However, the total amount of shocks left unsmoothed in the euro area will still be considerably larger than the 20 percent found in the US states, because of the lack of smoothing through international transfers in the euro area. A larger EU central budget might help in this regard. It could also be argued, however, that the Stability and Growth Pact provisions, which constrain the operation of fiscal policy within the EMU, might lead to a reduction in the amount of smoothing provided by the credit markets, which is mainly the result of net government saving smoothing.

8.5.6 Further Results: More Persistent Shocks and Evolution over Time

We next considered some extensions to our main results. The first involves increasing the length of the differencing frequency interval from one to three years of.[39] This makes it possible to analyze the response of the economy to more long-lasting shocks.

When the differencing frequency is increased to three years, the amount of long-lasting, unsmoothed shocks increases considerably: almost three-quarters of all shocks remain unsmoothed (across the whole sample this value rises from 59 to 74 percent).[40] The only operative channel for smoothing output is net saving. For the whole sample of nineteen OECD countries, saving smoothes 35 percent of all shocks at the three-year horizon. Moreover the smoothing effect of saving is almost exclusively due to the public sector (33 percent) while private saving contributes almost nothing to risk sharing (2 percent). In contrast, at the one-year differencing frequency interval the contribution from both sectors was more or less balanced. Hence in times of more persistent shocks only government saving appears to provide effective risk sharing. This is because only the government sector has the ability to resort to borrowing in order to sustain the fall in net savings over a longer period of time.

A second extension of the main results is the analysis of the evolution of the smoothing patterns over time. If we consider just two large subperiods (1971–1985 and 1986–1999), then over these two subperiods the major risk-sharing channels show great stability. However, while the aggregated contribution of saving remains roughly the same, the contribution from government and private saving differs radically between these subperiods. Consequently, at the cost of reducing the degrees of freedom, we opted to consider a half-decade subdivision.

Table 8.8
Channels of income and consumption spending smoothing (%): Evolution over time (EU-12) half-decade subdivision

	EU-12						
	1971– 1974	1975– 1979	1980– 1984	1985– 1989	1990– 1994	1995– 1999	1971– 1999
Factor income (β_f)	0	1	2	3	−14	17	0
	(0)	(0)	(0)	(0)	(2)	(3)	(0)
Capital depreciation (β_d)	−1	−10	−11	2	−11	−5	−7
	(0)	(2)	(2)	(0)	(2)	(1)	(6)
International transfers (β_t)	−4	−11	10	7	0	2	−2
	(1)	(2)	(2)	(1)	(0)	(1)	(2)
Saving (β_s)	59	69	25	23	86	33	53
	(2)	(5)	(2)	(2)	(5)	(2)	(11)
Of which government	15	19	18	24	67	13	21
	(2)	(1)	(0)	(2)	(4)	(1)	(4)
Of which private	44	59	17	−1	18	21	32
	(3)	(4)	(1)	(0)	(1)	(1)	(4)
Not smoothed (β_u)	46	51	73	66	40	53	56
	(2)	(5)	(3)	(4)	(3)	(5)	(13)

Note: See note to table 8.2 for description of the samples of countries considered.

The results for the euro area are given in table 8.8 and show more instability, especially in the 1990s.[41] Particularly notorious is the instability of the factor income estimate. Such instability makes it almost impossible to extrapolate the evolution of this parameter to the near future. Consequently, in our view, it is not possible to claim, as Kalemli-Ozcan et al. (2003) did, that the cross-ownership of productive assets is already playing a decisive role in the euro area, making it similar to the US federation. On the contrary, even for the more recent period of 1995 to 1999, the total amount of idiosyncratic output shocks left unsmoothed is still 5.9 times that of the US states.[42] Moreover it appears that the fiscal tightening in the run-up to the single currency has lead to a fall in the amount of shocks smoothed by government saving behavior.

8.6 Conclusions

We have presented empirical results regarding the patterns of risk sharing for a sample of nineteen OECD economies, which includes all

EU-15 member countries (except Luxembourg), for the period 1970 to 1999 comprising the three decades prior to the introduction of the euro. Following Sørensen and Yosha (1998), we identified four channels of risk sharing: factor income flows, capital depreciation, international transfers and saving. We concluded that the only operative smoothing channel is saving. Total net saving was found to smooth 50 percent of the idiosyncratic shocks to GDP in our nineteen OECD economies, while 59 percent of the shocks remained unsmoothed, causing a shock in consumption. Such an amount of shocks left unsmoothed is considerably higher than the 25 percent found for the US states by Asdrubali et al. (1996) for the period 1964 to 1990.

No substantial differences emerged in the pattern of risk sharing among our different subsets of OECD, small countries, EU-15, and EU-12 economies. The amount of idiosyncratic shocks to GDP left unsmoothed in the euro area was 56 percent, which is very similar to the figure for the whole sample of OECD countries (59 percent). Hence we can conclude that from the risk-sharing point of view, the euro-area countries do not appear to be better prepared to engage in a monetary union than the rest of the other OECD countries.

As the contribution from saving to smoothing may be divided into government and private components, it is possible to ascertain whether the private sector can substitute for the government sector in providing output smoothing. It seems that for the whole sample of OECD countries the government sector contributed more to risk sharing (29 percent) than the private sector (21 percent). However, both small countries and the EU-12 countries, and especially the small EU-12 member states, show a contribution to risk sharing from the private sector that is higher than that provided by the government sector. In the case of small countries, this result may reflect the reduced effectiveness of automatic fiscal stabilisers. Although the contribution from the private sector in euro area (32 percent) is larger than that of the government (21 percent), the contribution from the government is still decisive, especially in smoothing more persistent shocks to output. Nonetheless, fiscal profligacy was found to reduce the contribution to smoothing from the public sector. When high- and low-deficit countries were considered separately, clear evidence was found, contrary to Arreaza et al. (1998), in favor of the hypothesis that a high-deficit level leads to reduced consumption smoothing by the public sector. Such results lead us to conclude that in a successful monetary union it is vital to ensure there is adequate short-term flexibility in fiscal policy, while, at the same time, fiscal discipline in the medium–long term must not be disregarded.

The results for OECD and EU countries were compared with those of Asdrubali et al. (1996) for the US states. According to their updated estimates, for the period 1970 to 1998 in the US states, only 20 percent of idiosyncratic shocks were left unsmoothed. Their results further show that insurance, meaning capital market smoothing (45 percent), is much more important than credit (21 percent) in smoothing regional shocks in the United States. However, the credit channel itself is more important than the net transfers from the central federal government (14 percent). For the EU-12 countries, in the period 1970 to 1999, capital market insurance was found to smooth 25 percent of the shocks to GDP; the credit markets (essentially net government saving) smoothed another 21 percent, while international transfers actually dis-smoothed output (−2 percent). As a result 56 percent of the asymmetric shocks went unsmoothed. Hence, when comparing the US federation with the euro-area countries, some *major differences* emerge. First, the amount of inter-regional shocks left unsmoothed in the euro area (56 percent) is more than twice the equivalent amount in the US federation (20 percent). A second major difference between the EU-12 and the United States is that in the latter there is substantial inter-regional smoothing through the federal government deficit (14 percent). This is absent in the euro-area countries, where there is almost no inter-nation smoothing through the EU central budget (international transfers were found to actually dis-smooth output by −2 percent). In contrast, national government budgets are found to have a decisive smoothing importance in the EU-12. However, the national budgets provide mainly inter-temporal smoothing, rather than direct inter-regional smoothing. Third, the amount of risk sharing provided by the capital markets in the EU-12 is lower (25 percent) than in the United States (45 percent). This lower insurance role is probably the result of the less regionally diversified portfolios of assets among the residents of EU countries in comparison with their US counterparts.[43]

More smoothing is to be expected from market forces due to the functioning of EMU. EMU makes it is easier for countries to borrow internationally (before the introduction of the euro it was easier for individuals to borrow within their own country than for countries to borrow from the rest of the world). In the long run, economic integration favors the holding of property claims across borders, meaning it favors the cross-ownership of productive assets. If the introduction of the euro leads capital markets to become as integrated in the euro area as they were in the US federation in 1970 to 1998, we could expect a gain of 20 pp in the amount of risk sharing provided by euro-area capital markets. Holding everything else constant, the amount of shocks left unsmoothed is expected to drop to 36 percent under this (optimistic) scenario, which is still considerably larger than the 20 percent left unsmoothed in the US states. This outcome could be explained by the already mentioned absence of smoothing through international transfers in the euro area. Therefore a larger EU central budget, with objectives other than the redistribution of structural funds, might help in this regard. It is also possible to argue that the constraints imposed by the European Union Treaty and the Stability and Growth Pact (SGP) on the operation of fiscal policy in EMU, might lead to a reduction in the amount of smoothing provided by the credit markets, which is mainly the result of net government saving smoothing. Some SGP partisans argue that if member countries achieve a balanced budget position over the business cycle, the stability pact provides sufficient room for maneuver. However, this still remains to be proved in practice and is a source of concern.

To sum up, no large differences in the pattern of risk sharing for OECD, EU-15 and euro-area countries were found in our research. Nevertheless, there are considerable differences between the euro area and the successful monetary union of the United States: the euro area shows much lower insurance against asymmetric shocks than the US states. As long as the increasing economic integration in Europe does not lead to a substantial decrease in the incidence of idiosyncratic shocks, such shocks can impose nonnegligible welfare costs. Finally, given the relatively large importance of the public sector in providing risk sharing, especially in smoothing more persistent shocks, it does not seem likely that private capital markets can easily take over the government role of providing a sufficient degree of risk sharing, at least not in the near future.

Appendix: Data Sources

The source of data used in this study was the OECD national accounts, available from the OECD Statistical Compendium 2001, edition 1, for the period 1970 to 1999. However, due to the unavailability of data for certain variables, particularly for certain individual countries, data from other sources was also used, and these data are described below.

Although the resulting data set is the outcome of imposing certain hypotheses to make data from different sources compatible, it does enable us to extend our sample to nineteen OECD economies, including all EU-15 countries (with the exception of Luxembourg). The sample comprises the euro countries (Austria, Belgium, Finland, France, Germany, Italy, Ireland, the Netherlands, Portugal, Spain, and Greece), along with the remaining EU countries (Denmark, Sweden, and the United Kingdom), and the five non-EU countries (Australia, Canada, Norway, United States, and Japan).[44]

Data are expressed in real per capita terms. Net factor income (NFI), national income (NI), and disposable national income (DNI) were deflated using the GDP deflator. Due to the existence of blank values for 1999, we extended the following series using a simple extrapolation based on the last three years: NFI, NI, and DNI for Australia and NI and DNI for Japan.[45]

Classification of Countries

Based on 1995 GDP and purchasing power parities (PPPs), OECD (1999: 192) has classified the members of the organization into two groups: (1) seven major OECD economies (United States, Japan, Germany, France, Italy, United Kingdom, and Canada) and (2) smaller OECD economies (all remaining countries).

Fiscal Data

To break down total net saving data into government and private components, we need data on at least one of those latter variables. Since the OECD national accounts statistics are quite incomplete for both subcomponents, we used data from the OECD Fiscal Positions and Business Cycles database (also available in the OECD Statistical Compendium 2001, edition 1) for government saving. The information below gives the definitions concerning government saving and net government lending:

```
Government gross saving = Total current receipts -
Total current disbursements.

Government net saving = Government gross saving -
Government consumption of fixed capital.

Government net lending = Government gross saving +
Capital transfers received - (Gross capital
```

formation + Capital transfers paid + Purchases of
land and intangible assets) = Government net saving
+ Government consumption of fixed capital + Capital
transfers received - Gross capital formation -
Capital transfers paid - Purchases of land and
intangible assets = Government budget balance.

It can be concluded from an examination of these relationships that
in order to find net government saving, we need data on gross government saving and on government capital consumption. Gross government saving data comes from the variable "savings, government" of
the OECD Fiscal Positions and Business Cycles (FPBC) database, complemented with data from the European Commission (2000b) for
Denmark (1970–1987), United Kingdom (1970–1986), and Ireland
(1970–1976).

The source of net government lending data (also known as the government budget balance) was again the FPBC database, complemented
with data from the European Commission (2000b) on "Government
budget balance" for Denmark (1970), United Kingdom (1970–1977),
Greece (1970–1974), and Ireland (1970–1976).

The source of data regarding *government consumption of fixed capital*
was the "gross saving, consumption of fixed capital government" variable of the FPBC database. Exceptions to this include data relating to
the United Kingdom, Denmark, France, Greece, and Portugal. For the
United Kingdom the source of data was the variable "consumption
fixed capital government" from OECD National Accounts volume II
database. Lack of data for Denmark, France, Greece, and Portugal in
both FPBC and National accounts database forced us to resort to a
proxy. We assumed that the share of government capital consumption
(GKC) in the total capital consumption of a nation (TKC) was directly
linked to the share of public investment (GINV) in the total investment
(TINV), through a moving average of two periods:[46]

$$GKC_t = TKC_t \left(\frac{GINV_t}{TINV_t} + \frac{GINV_{t-1}}{TINV_{t-1}} \right).$$

In order to make the government consumption of fixed capital compatible with the other variables (expressed in real per capita terms), we
used the previous variables expressed as ratios of GDP, and resorted to
the following linking method:

$$\mathrm{gnsav}_t = \frac{\mathrm{GovNetSaving}_t}{\mathrm{GDP}_t},$$

$$\mathrm{NetSav}_{\mathrm{RPC}t} = \frac{\mathrm{gnsav}_t * \mathrm{GDP}_t}{P_t * \mathrm{Pop}_t} = \mathrm{gnsav}_t * \mathrm{GDP}_{\mathrm{RPC}t}.$$

Net government saving as a percentage of GDP was first calculated. Then, assuming, as before, the same deflator for net government saving and GDP (P_t), it was only necessary to multiply net government saving expressed as a percentage of nominal GDP by real per capita GDP ($\mathrm{GDP}_{\mathrm{RPC}}$) to get the real per capita net government saving.

Net private sector saving was then calculated as the difference between total net saving and net government saving.

With regard to the quality of the above-mentioned proxy for government consumption of fixed capital, we took the United States as benchmark and compared the result of the proxy with actual data. The proxy only gave rise to a minor error: the average error for the period 1970 to 1999 being only 0.2 percent of GDP.

Notes

This research is based on my PhD dissertation in Economics at the Catholic University of Leuven. I am extremely grateful to my supervisor, Prof. Paul De Grauwe, for his most helpful comments. I would like also to thank the participants in the CESifo Venice Summer Institute, in particular, Luca Onorante and Jacques Mélitz, for their useful comments. A word of recognition is also due Bent Sørensen for making his data set available and for the GAUSS econometric program used in the US states' calculations. Any errors that may remain are solely my responsibility. This research received financial support from the FCT, under the Sub-programme Science and Technology of the Second Community Support Framework to Portugal.

1. Buti and Sapir (1998: 29).

2. However, in our view, the difference between DNI and NI could involve some degree of smoothing through the government budget, which might give rise to an interaction with net government saving smoothing. Take the example of a tax cut that leads to an increase in disposable household income. If Ricardian equivalence does not hold, increased consumption results. The counterpart of the increased household's disposable income is an increase in government net lending. However, it is not possible to control this second order potential for interaction.

3. Following OECD National Accounts concepts, $\mathrm{GNP} = \mathrm{GDP} + $ net factor inflow to the country; $\mathrm{NI} = \mathrm{GNP} - $ depreciation; $\mathrm{DNI} = \mathrm{NI} + $ net international transfers; and, $C + G = \mathrm{NI} - $ net saving.

4. Sørensen and Yosha (1998: 217) show that under the assumption of logarithm utility, the share of country i's world consumption is the discounted expected share of its future output in world consumption.

5. This implies that a worker should be able to insure his labor income against unemployment and against all other contingencies that might occur Olivei (2000: 4).

6. The derivation is based on the assumption of identical risk averse expected utility maximizer consumers.

7. The consumption deflator was used to deflate all variables, measuring the output and consumption of each country in terms of real consumption within that country.

8. As mentioned in note 3, the variables are defined according to OECD National Account conventions.

9. The purpose of this method is to discover the extent to which asymmetric shocks are smoothed. However, as only temporary shocks should be smoothed, the method ought not to capture permanent shocks. The first difference formulation and the time fixed effects should be sufficient to ensure that outcome. Moreover, Sørensen and Yosha (1998: 225n. 23) check the robustness of their main regressions using Hodrick-Prescott filtered data, reaching very similar results.

10. Corporate saving smoothing essentially captures the effect of retained earnings behaviour. If, when profits fall, the amount of dividends remains more or less the same (due to a reduction in retained earnings), corporations contribute to income smoothing (assuming that individuals do not see through the corporate veil).

11. The estimators are obtained using time or individual dummies.

12. The time-invariant variables "disappear" when the within regression is estimated, which uses deviations from the time average.

13. The sample includes all EU economies (except Luxembourg), along with Norway, Canada, Australia, United States, and Japan.

14. As the estimation requires a calculation of the growth rates, we lose the first observation, thus reducing the sample length to the 1971 to 1999 period.

15. The results of ASY98 have the advantage of being more up-to-date than those of SY98.

16. The sample of eleven EU economies does not correspond to the first 11 euro countries.

17. As already mentioned above, in contrast to ASY98, we do not impose an identical autocorrelation parameter across equations.

18. In general, our results in column 5, for EU-11*, are closer to the ASY98 results represented in column 1 for the OECD than to the ASY98 results for EU-11* (column 4). More specifically, our estimations do not show the low level of smoothing from saving, for EU-11* countries. In fact, for the period 1971 to 1999 the amount of shocks smoothed by saving, and the amount of shocks left unsmoothed, are very similar for both samples of countries.

19. According to ASY96, only 19 percent of shocks to each state GSP were left unsmoothed in the US federation, in the period 1981 to 1990. Hence the amount of risk sharing among OECD and EU countries is substantially inferior to its counterpart in the US states. Section 8.5.5, below, gives a detailed comparison of the results obtained for the OECD and EU countries with the results for the US states.

20. See Gros and Thygesen (1998) for a detailed analysis of the EMS crisis.

21. However, as the low t-statistic indicates, the coefficient on factor income smoothing is not statistically different from zero.

22. In our opinion, the best way to diversify risk in increasingly integrated international financial markets, characterized by ever more correlated returns, is the holding of sector-diversified portfolios.

23. Capital depreciation follows rigid accounting rules, being more or less independent of the business cycle. If, in reality, capital depreciation were affected by the business cycle, we would expect capital depreciation to decrease in recessions (reflecting a lower utilization of productive capacity), leading to a lower volatility of NI with respect to GNP, and thereby to a positive β_d coefficient. However, such events are not likely to be reflected in National Accounts data.

24. Furthermore its coefficients are all statistically significant.

25. SY98 were able to distinguish the three components of saving because they used a more restricted sample of thirteen OECD countries for which detailed data was available.

26. This result is used later to compare our results with those obtained for the US states by ASY96.

27. Following ASY98, no correction for first-order serial correlations was made while estimating the government and private contributions as such a correction was considered to be unjustified.

28. Just see, for example, Perotti (1999) and Artis and Buti (2000).

29. A direct test to see whether the level of public debt has any impact on the amount of risk sharing provided by the government sector was also carried out. The results obtained (not reported here, for brevity) are very similar to those obtained in this section.

30. In other words, and neglecting net capital transfers, this assumption is only true when the amount of government net capital formation is nil. When considering the whole economy, as described by a Solow growth model, zero net capital formation (i.e., capital depreciation equal to capital formation) is only obtained when we assume that the economy is at a steady state with no technical progress and no population growth. These assumptions are very difficult to sustain in the case of industrialized countries; consequently ASY98's simplification might bias their empirical results.

31. To aid comparison, table 8.4 also includes the ASY98 results for the OECD-17 group.

32. In general, the amount of smoothing provided by the private sector is not statistically different from zero for low-deficit countries.

33. This contribution is not statistically different from zero.

34. Moreover the amount of capital market smoothing is not statistically different from zero for the European Union, while it is highly statistically significant for the US states.

35. Both such estimates present a t-statistic of 2.

36. More recently Kalemli-Ozcan, Sørensen, and Yosha (2003) updated the SY98 and ASY98 estimates. However, the new results are not directly comparable to earlier ones as the authors changed the estimation method and limited their study to just the first channel of output smoothing, which is the smoothing that occurs through factor income. They found that factor income makes a positive contribution to smoothing in the more recent period of 1993 to 2000. More precisely, factor income was found to smooth 6 percent of

the shocks to GDP in the EU-14 countries (11 percent in the former EU-8), which compares with 55 percent in the US states. This partial analysis led the authors to change their previous conclusions, reported in SY98, to state that "... the unified Europe is becoming more similar to the union of US states in terms of integration at the macroeconomic level!" (idem: 2). In our opinion, this conclusion might be hasty since it is based on just one channel of smoothing (disregarding the total amount of unsmoothed shocks), and on a very short period of time.

37. It should be remembered that the credit market channel corresponds to the smoothing achieved via government net saving.

38. A comparison of the t-statistics of the ASY96 estimates for the US states with my own estimates for OECD countries shows that for the US states the capital market smoothing and transfers were estimated precisely, while for my sample of international countries higher standard deviations are found. Conversely, my estimates for the credit market channel and for the total amount of unsmoothed shocks show much lower standard deviations than ASY96's estimates for the US states. A similar pattern is apparent in the SY98 estimates (see table 8.6).

39. For example, the variation of GDP is now defined as $(GDP_t - GDP_{t-3})$.

40. Due to space constraints the results are not shown here but are available in Marinheiro (2003b).

41. Further results, including the first two subperiods' division, and a decade division may be found in Marinheiro (2003b).

42. In using Bent Sørensen's econometric program for the US states, I found that only 9% of the inter-regional asymmetric shocks were left unsmoothed in the US for the period 1995 to 1998. The amount of smoothing by the capital market was found to be 48 percent, the transfers smoothed another 11 percent of shocks, and the credit market another 31 percent.

43. Although the comparison of the euro area with the US gives us some very interesting insights, it should be mentioned that this comparison is not perfect. There is, in fact, a little asymmetry in the comparison between these two regions caused by the different methods used to reach the results for the United States and for the European Union. For the latter I split total net saving into government and private saving. This was not done in the US studies, which makes the comparison more difficult.

44. The OECD considered countries to account for 94 to 95 percent of OECD total GDP, as reported in OECD (1999).

45. For Australian NFI the extrapolation was based only on the last two years, due to a change in the growth rate.

46. Investment is defined as gross fixed capital formation, and its source is the OECD National Accounts volume I.

References

Arreaza, A., B. E. Sørensen, and O. Yosha. 1998. Consumption smoothing through fiscal policy in OECD and EU countries. *NBER Working Paper* W6372. (Published in Poterba, J. M., and J. von Hagen, eds. 1999. *Fiscal Institutions and Fiscal Performance*. Chicago: University of Chicago Press, pp. 1959–1980).

Artis, M., and M. Buti. 2000. Close to balance or in surplus: A policy-maker's guide to the implementation of the stability and growth pact. CEPR Discussion Paper 2515.

Asdrubali, P., B. E. Sørensen, and O. Yosha. 1996. Channels for interstate risk sharing: United States 1963–1990. *Quarterly Journal of Economics* 111(4): 1081–1110.

Baltagi, B. H. 2001. *Econometric Analysis of Panel Data*, 2nd ed. Chichester: Wiley.

Bayoumi, T., and B. Eichengreen. 1993. Shocking aspects of European monetary integration. In F. Torres and F. Giavazzi, eds., *Adjustment and Growth in the European Monetary Union*. Cambridge: Cambridge University Press.

Buti, M., and A. Sapir. 1998. *Economic Policy in EMU: A Study by the European Commission Services*. Oxford: Oxford University Press.

De Grauwe, P. 2003. *The Economics of Monetary Integration*, 5th ed. Oxford: Oxford University Press.

Gros, D., and N. Thygesen. 1998. *European Monetary Integration*. Essex: Longman.

Kalemli-Ozcan, S., B. E. Sørensen, and O. Yosha. 2003. Asymmetric shocks in a monetary union: Updated evidence and policy implications for Europe. Preliminary version of the paper prepared for the European Commission, Economic and Financial Affairs, Workshop "Who will own Europe? The internationalization of asset ownership in the EU today and in the future." Brussels, February 27–28. *http://europa.eu.int/comm/economy_finance/events/2003/events_workshop_0203_en.htm.*

Krugman, P. 1993. Lessons of Massachusetts for EMU. *In* F. Torres and F. Giavazzi, eds., *Adjustment and Growth in EMU*. Cambridge: Cambridge University Press, pp. 241–61.

Marinheiro, C. 2003a. EMU and fiscal stabilisation policy: The case of small countries. PhD dissertation. Katholieke Universiteit Leuven.

Marinheiro, C. F. 2003b. Output smoothing in EMU and OECD: Can we forego government contribution? A risk sharing approach. *CESifo Working Paper* 1051. *http://ssrn.com/abstract=460143.*

McKinnon, R. I. 1963. Optimum currency areas. *American Economic Review* 53(4): 717–25.

Mélitz, J., and F. Zumer. 1999. Interregional and International Risk Sharing and Lessons for EMU. *Carnegie-Rochester Series on Public Policy* 51: 149–88.

Mundell, R. A. 1961. A theory of optimum currency areas. *American Economic Review* 51(4): 657–65.

Olivei, G. 2000. Consumption risk-sharing across G-7 countries. *Federal Reserve Bank of Boston, New England Economic Review* (March): 3–14.

Perotti, R. 1999. Fiscal policy in good times and bad. *Quarterly Journal of Economics* (November): 1399–436.

Sørensen, B. E., and O. Yosha. 1998. International risk sharing and European monetary unification. *Journal of International Economics* 45: 211–38.

9   On the Implications of a Unilateral Currency Union for Macroeconomic Volatility

Roberto Duncan

9.1   Introduction

The issue of adopting a unilateral currency union, such as dollarization—defined as one country's official adoption of the currency of another for all commercial and financial transactions[1]—has been widely discussed in recent years. The issue acquired urgency after the Asian crisis, and the effect that had on Latin American countries, and because of the advent of the euro. The debate has ensued in both partially dollarized economies[2] (e.g., Peru, Argentina, and Uruguay) and nondollarized developing economies (Ecuador, Mexico, and Nicaragua[3]) over the low degree of substitution between domestic and dollar-denominated assets.

According to many authors, official dollarization has implications for the main macroeconomic variables (inflation, interest rates, domestic product, investment, financial integration, etc.) and for fiscal and monetary management. Therefore the adoption of official dollarization by a developing economy requires a thorough analysis.

However, before considering this policy change, it is advisable to know what the benefits are of abandoning domestic money unit and adopting the dollar or other "hard currency." If the net benefits are significantly positive, what are the prerequisites that the economy should present, before its dollarization, to maximize those benefits?[4] That is, what is the adequate foreign reserves level? What should be the features or conditions of the financial system? Is it necessary to reform the government's finances? Is it necessary to have total flexibility in the labor market? Should the country be part of a currency union? Is a partially dollarized economy a good candidate for an official dollarization scheme? And, if preconditions were given, how to implement an official dollarization scheme?[5] That is, to what exchange rate level should the economy be dollarized? Will seignorage be shared with the United States?

As can be seen, there are many questions that policy makers and researchers might formulate about this subject. In my opinion, it is still necessary to deepen the discussion on the first question from a theoretical perspective, especially regarding the scarcity of officially dollarized economies and, consequently, the lack of enough data to evaluate their macroeconomic performance.[6] Moreover the advantages of an official dollarization virtually have not been discussed within a general equilibrium framework,[7] especially for partially dollarized economies that are supposed to be good candidates for this kind of regime.

This work seeks to assess the implications of an official dollarization program on the volatility of the main macroeconomic variables of an emerging market economy that faces currency and asset substitution. It seems especially pertinent to study macroeconomic volatility for several reasons. Currently, in the aftermath of international crises—from the Asian to the Argentinean one—emerging market economies have faced significant real instability. Besides, in a world with risk aversion, it is important to study (real and nominal) volatility for a better understanding of economic agents' behavior. Finally, if we consider that central banks take policy decisions about exchange rate regimes based on welfare loss functions that depend generally on output and inflation volatility, then we should consider macroeconomic volatility as a relevant matter.

Thus, for this purpose, I use simple dynamic stochastic general equilibrium models as laboratories to study these issues. Two models are formulated and simulated for a small open economy that faces external (via terms of trade) and domestic (via technological and fiscal and monetary policy) shocks. The first model represents a partially dollarized economy with floating exchange rate that is calibrated for the Peruvian economy. This model is capable of replicating relatively well the main co-movements of the data during the 1992 to 2002 period. The second model represents a fully dollarized economy. Simulation exercises are performed to compare the behavior of key variables (e.g., output, inflation rate, consumption, investment, and fiscal deficit) in both environments. At the end we want to find out what would happen with macroeconomic volatility in Peru, if this economy becomes fully dollarized.

This chapter is organized as follows: Section 9.2 provides a discussion of the arguments for and against full dollarization advanced in the literature. Section 9.3 formulates the dynamic stochastic general equilibrium models. Section 9.4 describes their parameterization and solution, and section 9.5 presents the main findings. Concluding remarks are provided in section 9.6.

9.2 Costs and Benefits of Dollarization

Tables 9.1 and 9.2 show the pros and cons of official dollarization found in the economic literature.

9.2.1 Price Stabilization and Low Inflation

There seems to be a consensus in the literature on that a fully dollarized economy might achieve United States inflation rate (or a similar one) and that this economy could succeed on stabilization programs (a recent example seems to be Ecuador). Edwards and Magendzo (2001) and Edwards (2001a, b) found empirical evidence that supports this viewpoint. They detected that inflation rates have been significantly lower in dollarized nations than in nondollarized ones.

On stabilization and credibility, Goldfajn and Olivares (2000) raise the point that credibility gains due to full dollarization cause less volatility in the domestic inflation rate. Using a dynamic general equilibrium model calibrated for the Mexican economy, Mendoza (2000) concludes that the welfare gain by removing the lack of credibility on stabilization would be from 6 to 10 percent of steady-state consumption level.

However, as Berg and Borensztein (2000) remark, the stability owing to dollarization is itself relative, as the US dollar fluctuates in value against other widely traded currencies.

9.2.2 Loss of Seignorage versus Fiscal Discipline

Savastano (1999) and Mendoza (2002) consider that the main disadvantage of full dollarization is the loss of seignorage. As Berg and Borensztein (2000) point out, the acquisition of the initial stock of domestic money could add an indirect cost for a country that does not have enough foreign reserves to buy up its domestic currency.[8] Calvo (1999a, b) opposes this idea, arguing that partially dollarized economies already suffer loss of seignorage. He argues that a full dollarization scheme could include a pact with United States to share this revenue.

Table 9.1
Benefits of an official dollarization

Authors	Benefits	Observations
Inflation and stabilization		
Savastano (1999)[a]	Promotes price stabilization. Inflation rate would be equal or less than US inflation.	Berg and Borensztein (2000): Stability promised by dollarization is itself relative, given that the US dollar fluctuates in value against other widely traded currencies.
Goldfajn and Olivares (2000)[a]	Credibility gains cause less variability in domestic inflation rate. Helps to achieve the inflation rate convergence to US inflation rate.	
Mendoza (2000)	Welfare gains by removing lack of credibility of stabilization (6.4–9.7 percent of level of consumption).	Based on DGEM calibration estimates.[c]
Edwards and Magendzo (2001)	Inflation has been significantly lower in dollarized nations than in nondollarized ones.[b]	See also Edwards (2001a, b).
Dornbusch (2000)	Gains are inversely proportional to the national money's quality, past, current, and prospective.	
Fiscal policy		
Savastano (1999)[a]	Generate fiscal discipline.	Goldfajn and Olivares (2000): Absence of seignorage does not necessarily imply fiscal discipline.
Chang (2000)[a]	May enhance the credibility of fiscal policy if the government does not choose sound policies.	Edwards (2001a, b): Dollarized countries have had similar fiscal records than nondollarized countries.[b] Sims (2002): It does not automatically generate pressures for greater fiscal responsibility, and may create incentives in the opposite direction.

Interest rates, devaluation, and default risk

Calvo (1999a, b)	Lower level and volatility of domestic interest rates.	Savastano (1999): Interest rates would tend to decrease, but they do not converge totally to international interest rates due to country risk, which would not necessarily decrease. Goldfajn and Olivares (2000): It is not clear whether reduction in domestic interest rates is the consequence of full dollarization or the competitive international banking system (in the case of Panama). Elimination of currency risk does not preclude default risk or the high volatility of sovereign spreads.[b]
Hinds (1999)	Pensions funds and other savings would be protected against devaluation and inflation.	
Schuler (1999)	Less inflation improves the safety of property rights, and thus, this allows less credit risk.	
Berg and Borensztein (2000)	Eliminates the sudden risk of sharp devaluations, and thus reduces risk premium of international borrowing.	
Chang (2000)	May lower country's cost of credit.	Pereyra and Quispe (2002): Spreads actually reflect the perception of country's general features and they will be higher as higher are the macroeconomic, institutional and political soundness.
Panizza et al. (2000)	Virtually eliminates exchange rate risk.	
Dornbusch (2000)	Implies a dramatic decline in interest rates with all attendant benefits.	
Mendoza (2002)	Devaluation risk would be greatly reduced. It can never be fully eliminated because a sovereign nation might always try to reverse the dollarization.	Carrera et al. (2002): Default risk would reduce if economy's real volatility reduces.
Powell and Sturzenegger (2000)	Elimination of currency risk will have significant impact on country risk spreads in Latin American emerging countries.	

Table 9.1
(continued)

Authors	Benefits	Observations
Financial integration and banking system		
Calvo (1999a, b)	Lower probability of external crisis and contagion.	Berg and Borensztein (2000): It does not eliminate the risk of external crises, since investors may flee due to problems of weakness in fiscal position or the soundness of the financial system. It does not reduce the impact of external real shocks.
Schuler (1999)	Contributes to accelerate the consolidation of the banking system and solves its losses because banks at the present do not present currency matching and they are exposed to currency instability.	
Calvo and Reinhart (1999)	It ameliorates (eliminates) the "sudden stop problem."	
Hausmann (1999)	Would expand the menu of financial options open to emerging-market governments and firms, and (therefore) would increase financial stability. Facilitates international integration.	Goldfajn y Olivares (2000): It is not a warranty of instantaneous access to international markets.[b] Sims (2002): It has ambiguous implications for the stability of the financial system, because it reduces range of assets available in trading risk and it leaves the government less able to intervene supportively in financial crises.
Berg and Borensztein (2000), Goldfajn and Olivares (2000)	Increases financial markets efficiency creating long-run instruments and allocating resources in better way than other exchange regimes. May reduce the impact of external confidence shocks.	
Panizza et al. (2000)	Might reduce financial fragility by reducing volatility of key relative prices in the economy, and contributes to the development of banking system.	Based on an empirical analysis for Central American countries.

Mendoza (2000)	Welfare gains from weakening of financial frictions and improved access to global capital markets.	
Mendoza (2002)	Enhanced credibility and reduced informational frictions could result in better access to international capital markets in terms of reduced liquidity coefficients and margin requirements.	Mean: 4.6 percent of consumption, even if policy credibility remains weak. Financial assets and liabilities would be matched in terms of currency denomination.

Trade and current account position

Panizza et al. (2000), Lizano (2000)	Lower transaction costs related to trading goods and assets denominated in different currencies. Reduces uncertainty and risk (exchange rate volatility) in trade and investment; and costs related to the need to deal with multiple currencies.	Based on Optimal Currency Area literature, Mundell (1961) and McKinnon (1963). Edwards (2001a, b): Dollarized countries have not been spared from major current account reversals.[b]
Morandé and Schmidt-Hebbel (2000)	Less market segmentation and higher market integration. Higher international trade due to less currency risk.	Klein (2002): Effect of dollarization on trade with United States is not statistically different from the effect of a fixed dollar exchange rate on trade with United States.

Investment and growth

Savastano (1999)[a]	Larger amounts of investment and growth rates.	Edwards (2001a, b): Panama's case suggests that external shocks result in greater costs in terms of lower investment and growth than nondollarized countries.[b]
Berg and Borensztein (2000)	Higher level of confidence among international investors, more investment and growth. No possibility of sudden capital outflows motivated by fears of devaluation.	
Lizano (2000)	Improves the possibility to attract foreign investors.	

Table 9.1
(continued)

Authors	Benefits	Observations
Mendoza (2002)	Sharp decline in information costs: foreign investors would no longer need to pay for information on the dollarized economy's monetary policy.	Can increase demand elasticity for emerging markets' equity of foreign traders, which limits the size of asset price declines.

a. The author compiles this advantage (sometimes from other authors), but he or she does not necessarily support it.
b. Based on an empirical work.
c. DGEM denotes dynamic general equilibrium model.

Similarly, for Alesina and Barro (2001), this loss is not a social waste but redistribution between the countries. Therefore the United States could return the seignorage to the dollarized country.

In Dornbusch's (2000) view there is an important offset to the loss of seignorage from the reduction in public debt service costs that result from reduced interest rates, and this factor is surely far more significant than the 1 percent or so of GDP in seignorage loss.

On the other hand, Savastano (1999) compiles the idea that one of the benefits of official dollarization is that it generates fiscal discipline owing to the elimination of the possibility of monetary issuance to finance fiscal deficit. Similarly, according to Chang (2000), it has been argued that the loss of seignorage may be beneficial if it forces an otherwise irresponsible government to choose sound policies, enhancing the credibility of the government policy.

In contrast, Goldfajn and Olivares (2000) perform an empirical analysis based on VAR estimates for Panama concluding that the absence of seignorage does not necessarily imply fiscal discipline. Edwards (2001) also finds that dollarized countries have had similar fiscal records than nondollarized countries.

9.2.3   Devaluation Risk, Default Risk, and Interest Rates

Calvo (1999a, b) has defended the idea that full dollarization implies a lower level and volatility of domestic interest rates. Besides, Schuler (1999) states that the lower inflation provoked by full dollarization should improve the safety of property rights and, consequently, reduce the credit risk for an economy. On the contrary, Savastano's (1999) view is that interest rates would tend to decrease but they would not converge totally to international interest rates due to the country risk, which would not necessarily decline. For Goldfajn and Olivares (2000) it is not clear whether the reduction in domestic interest rates is the consequence of full dollarization or the competitive international banking system in the case of Panama.

According to Berg and Borensztein (2000), another argument in favor of dollarization is that it eliminates the sudden risk of sharp devaluations and, thus, reduces the risk premium of international borrowing. Chang (2000) and Powell and Sturzenegger (2000) also consider that the dollarization of an economy may lower the country's credit cost.[9] Mendoza (2002) thinks that devaluation risk would be greatly reduced but never be fully eliminated because a sovereign nation might always try to reverse the dollarization. In that sense

Table 9.2
Costs of an official dollarization

Authors	Costs	Observations
Monetary and exchange rate policy		
Rojas-Suárez (1999)	Loss of nominal exchange rate as an instrument to ameliorate terms-of-trade shocks.	Calvo (1999a, b): The loss of monetary policy is not significant in comparison to its current limited power: emerging economies depend on US monetary policy through the changes of the Treasury Bond rate. Besides, "hyperactivity" by central banks is (in part) the responsible of our crisis.
Berg and Borensztein (2000)[a], Mendoza (2002)	Loss of monetary policy. This is replaced by the US Fed monetary policy. The central bank could not affect money supply of the economy because that results from balance of payments.	Calvo (1999a, b): Instead of nominal exchange rate, prices and wages would adjust to terms-of-trade shocks. Domestic currency depreciation is contractive in emerging economies. Competitivity gains might be achieved through fiscal policy.
Schmitt-Grohé and Uribe (2001a)	The least successful of monetary policies (in the particular case of Mexico). Agents would prefer to give up 0.1–0.3 percent of consumption to have a policy other than dollarization.	Based on the calibration of a model for Mexican economy.
Cooley and Quadrini (1999)	It is not welfare improving because of the lack of long-term monetary policy.	
Lender of last resort		
Berg and Borensztein (2000)	Loss of lender of last resort (LLR) and hence the central bank's response to financial system emergencies. But it should not impede the ability of authorities to provide short-term liquidity to the system or assistance to individual banks in distress.	Calvo (1999a, b): It can be outweigh by a deeper banking integration (between domestic and foreign banks, e.g., Panama) and through the use of contingent external credit lines (e.g., Argentina) in the case of a crisis. Dornbusch (2000): The assumption is that central bank, not the Treasury or the world capital market, is the appropriate lender. Gavin (1999): The central bank could provide liquidity support to local banks if it keeps excess dollar reserves.

Gale and Vives (2002)	Whereas the LLR may impose too little financial discipline, dollarization may impose too much.	
Fiscal policy		
Savastano (1999), Mendoza (2002)	Loss of seignorage.	Calvo (1999a, b): At the present partially dollarized economies suffer loss of seignorage. A full dollarization scheme should include a pact with United States to share seignorage.
Berg and Borensztein (2000)	For a country that does not have enough foreign reserves to buy up its domestic currency, the acquisition of initial stock could add indirect costs.	Dornbusch (2000): There is an important offset to the loss of seignorage from the reduction in public debt service costs that result from reduced interest rates. Alesina and Barro (2001): It is not a social waste, but redistribution between the countries.
Investment and growth		
Goldfajn and Olivares (2000)	The absence of monetary and exchange rate policy might induce larger output volatility (providing fiscal policy is not very countercyclical) in comparison to a flexible exchange rate regime.	Carrera et al. (2002): Real volatility reduction depends on the degree of synchronization between the cycles of the leader and associated country and the effect and relative importance of the trade and financial transmission channels from the leader to the associated country.
Edwards (2001), Edwards and Magendzo (2001)	Dollarized countries have grown at a significantly lower rate than nondollarized countries.[b]	It is due, at least in part, to these countries' difficulties in accommodating external disturbances. There has not been statistical difference in macroeconomic volatility between dollarized and nondollarized economies.
Drew et al. (2001)	Volatility in output and inflation would be greater under a common currency policy environment.	Based on an empirical analysis for New Zealand.

a. The author compiles this advantage (sometimes from other authors), but he or she does not necessarily support it.
b. Based on an empirical work.

Goldfajn and Olivares (2000) consider that the elimination of currency risk does not preclude default risk or the high volatility of sovereign spreads.

9.2.4   Financial Integration and Banking System

It has been contended that dollarization facilitates financial integration and a better performance of the domestic banking system. According to Calvo (1999a, b), dollarization could lower the probability of external crisis and contagion. Schuler (1999) considers that it would contribute to accelerate the consolidation of the banking system and solve its losses because banks—in a partially dollarized economy—do not necessarily present currency matching and are exposed to currency instability. The mechanism exposed by Hausmann (2000) is that dollarization would expand the menu of financial options open to emerging-market governments and firms, and therefore it would increase financial stability. For Panizza et al. (2001), dollarization might reduce financial fragility by reducing the volatility of key relative prices in the economy, and contribute to the development of the banking system.[10] Mendoza (2000) calibrates a dynamic equilibrium model for Mexico and concludes that there could exist a welfare gain (4.6 percent of steady-state consumption level) by improving the access to global capital markets, even if policy credibility remained weak. Mendoza (2002) concludes that the enhanced credibility and reduced informational frictions could result in better access to international capital markets in terms of reduced liquidity coefficients and margin requirements.

On the other hand, Goldfajn and Olivares (2000) think that full dollarization is not a warranty of instantaneous access to international markets. Berg and Borensztein (2000) consider that it does not eliminate the risk of external crises, since investors may flee due to problems of weakness in fiscal position or the soundness of the financial system. For Sims (2002), dollarization has ambiguous implications for the stability of the financial system because it reduces the range of assets available in trading risk and leaves the government less able to intervene supportively in financial crises.

From my viewpoint, mainly in the case of partially dollarized economies, an official dollarization scheme could initially cause important losses for the banking system, since banks receive revenues from currency exchange transactions. For instance, in the 1999 to 2000 period these net earnings are around 2.11 times the net profits of Peruvian banking system.[11] This cost for the private banks can be seen as the counterpart of the benefits for private firms and consumers. In this sense Rojas-Suárez (1999) suggests that one precondition to dollarization is a sound domestic system.

9.2.5 Dollarization, Trade, and Current Account Position

Based on the optimal currency area literature (Mundell 1961; McKinnon 1963), several authors, such as Lizano (2000), consider that a benefit for dollarizing a Latin American economy is the lower transaction cost related to trading goods in different currencies. Similarly, Panniza et al. (2000) remark that a common currency would reduce uncertainty and risk (exchange rate volatility) in trade and investment aside from the cost related to the need to deal with multiple currencies.

Nevertheless, there are some objections to the possible benefits of dollarization on trade and current account positions. For instance, Edwards (2001a, b) found that dollarized countries have not been spared from major current account reversals. Also Klein (2002) found that the effect of dollarization is not (statistically) different from the effect of a fixed exchange rate on trade with the United States.

9.2.6 Investment and Growth

Among the benefits of dollarization, Savastano (1999) cites that dollarization is supposed to promote investment and growth. Berg and Borensztein (2000) think that it might generate a higher level of confidence among international investors and more investment and growth since there is no possibility of sudden capital outflows motivated by fear of devaluation. Besides, Mendoza (2002) contends that it produces a sharp decline in information costs because foreign investors would no longer need to pay for information on the dollarized economy's monetary policy. This effect can also increase the demand elasticity for emerging markets equity by foreign traders.

Nevertheless, there are several objections to these viewpoints. According to Edwards (2001), Panama's case suggests that external shocks result in greater costs in terms of lower investment and growth than nondollarized countries. For Goldfajn and Olivares (2000), the absence of monetary and exchange rate policy might induce larger output volatility in comparison to a flexible exchange rate regime, provided that fiscal policy is not very countercyclical. Through a theoretical model, Carrera et al. (2002) remark that real volatility reductions depend on the degree of synchronization between the cycles of the leader and associated country and the effect and relative importance of the trade and financial transmission channels from the former to the latter.

Edwards (2001) and Edwards and Magendzo (2001) conclude that dollarized countries have grown at a significantly lower rate than nondollarized countries. This is due, at least in part, to these countries' difficulties in accommodating external disturbances. However, the authors also find that there has not been statistical difference in macro-economic volatility between dollarized and nondollarized economies. Finally Drew et al. (2001) find that volatility in output and inflation would be greater under a common currency environment in the case of New Zealand.

9.2.7 Elimination of Monetary or Exchange Rate Policy: A Loss or a Gain?

Berg and Borensztein (2000) emphasize that a dollarized economy would relinquish any possibility of having autonomous monetary and exchange rate policies and that these would be replaced by the US monetary policy. Besides, the central bank would not affect the money supply as it results from the balance of payments. Rojas-Suárez (1999) contends that a cost of dollarization is the loss of the nominal exchange rate as an instrument to ameliorate terms-of-trade shocks. Alesina and Barro (2001) think that if we assume that the domestic monetary policy can commit to a useful countercyclical policy, then the loss of an independent policy will represent a true cost. They conclude that this cost will be higher the less correlated is the business cycle of the client country with that of the anchor.

Calibrating a dynamic general equilibrium model for Mexico, Schmitt-Grohé and Uribe (2001a) conclude that dollarization is the least successful of monetary policies. Agents would prefer to give up from 0.1 to 0.3 percent of consumption to have a policy other than dollarization. A similar finding is the one by Cooley and Quadrini (2001).

Calvo (1999) has some opposite observations to these viewpoints. He remarks that the loss of monetary policy is not significant in comparison to its current limited power since emerging economies already depend on US monetary policy through the changes of the Treasury Bond rate. Latin American economies are subject to contagion effects from developed economies. He finishes stating three ideas. First, instead of the nominal exchange rate, prices and wages would adjust to terms-of-trade shocks. Second, domestic currency depreciation is contractive in emerging economies. Finally, competitivity gains might be achieved through fiscal policy.

It must be mentioned that a dollarization regime does not necessarily imply the full elimination of the monetary policy, even though there would be a drastic reduction of the capacity of the monetary authority to perform its policy. The reasons are the following: (1) the central bank would still have the possibility to issue low-denomination currencies,[12] (2) it could still control the legal reserve requirement rate, and (3) it could apply temporary capital controls to have certain degree of influence on foreign inflows.

9.2.8 Does Dollarization Imply a Loss of the Lender of Last Resort?

Gale and Vives (2002) explain that whereas the function of lender of last resort (LLR) may impose too little financial discipline, dollarization may impose too much. By constraining the central bank's role as LLR, it may be impossible to extend assistance to a distressed bank even in situations where this would be efficient ex ante. On the other hand, Berg and Borensztein (2000) allude to the fact that full dollarization may impair the country's LLR function and hence the central bank's response to financial system emergencies. However, the authors continue, dollarization should not greatly impede the ability of the authorities to provide short-term liquidity to the system or assistance to individual banks in distress. Such facilities are available if the central bank saves funds in advance or secures lines of credit with international banks. Calvo (1999) has also contended that the loss of LLR can be outweighed by deeper banking integration—between domestic and foreign banks, for example, Panama—and the use of contingent external credit lines (e.g., Argentina). Similarly Dornbusch (2000) pointed out that the argument of the loss of LLR is intriguing because it is based on the assumption that the central bank, not the Treasury or the world capital market, is the appropriate lender. Finally, Gavin (1999) considers that the central bank could provide liquidity support to local banks if it keeps excess dollar reserves for this purpose.

9.2.9 Other Costs

According to Bogetic (2000), there is also a cost of converting prices, computer programs, cash registers, and vending machines from domestic currency to the foreign currency chosen. This is a one-time cost that can vary considerably from country to country. Bogetic (2000) also adds that there may be associated legal and financial costs of revising contracts or refinancing. In addition Cohen (2000) mentions that dollarization implies the loss of a vital symbol of national identity.

In summary, the main conclusions of this review are the following. First, there is not a general consensus on the benefits and costs of full dollarization, except on a lower inflation rate. Second, there is a shortage of studies for emerging market economies that face currency and/or asset substitution and that are supposed to be good candidates for a full dollarization scheme. Third, there are virtually no studies that formally evaluate the implications of full dollarization on macroeconomic volatility, especially through a dynamic general equilibrium framework.

9.3   A Simple Theoretical Framework

In this section I formulate the models setting their main characteristics. First, I consider a model capable of representing a small open economy that shows currency and asset substitution with a floating exchange regime, the current regime in Peru. Second, I present a fully dollarized economy model in which the dollar is the only legal tender for commercial and financial transactions. In both cases I obtain first-order conditions and steady-state solutions to compare their implications mainly in terms of macroeconomic volatility. As an application, the first model is calibrated for specific features of the Peruvian economy and the same parameter values will be used to solve the second model.

9.3.1   A Partially Dollarized Economy with Flexible Exchange Rate
The economy has the following features: (1) household's utility is a function of consumption, leisure, and a liquidity service function which depends on real money holdings denominated in both currencies; (2) an interest rate rule followed by the monetary authority and flexible exchange rate; (3) demand for domestic and foreign money (currency substitution), and demand for assets denominated in domestic and foreign currency (asset substitution); (4) constant distortionary taxes and convex costs of price adjustment (price rigidities); (5) two types of good, importables and exportables, thus the economy is small and

open (presence of exogenous terms of trade); (6) presence of technological, fiscal-policy, monetary-policy, foreign-interest rate, and terms-
of-trade shocks.

Households

The economy is populated by an infinitely lived representative agent
that optimizes an utility function, which depends positively on real
private consumption c_t, real domestic money balances m_t, real foreign
money balances m_t^*, and leisure l_t:

$$E_t \left\{ \sum_{t=0}^{\infty} \beta^t u[c_t, l_t, \Phi(m_t, m_t^*)] \right\}, \tag{1}$$

where $E\{.\}$ denotes the mathematical expectation operator conditional
on information available in period t, $0 < \beta < 1$ is the subjective discount factor, and Φ is a liquidity service function, as in McNelis and
Asilis (1992) and Bufman and Leiderman (1992).[13] It is supposed that
the household is endowed each period with one unit of time, which is
divided between leisure, $1 - L_t$, and work, L_t. The functions u and Φ
take the following forms:

$$u(c_t, l_t, \Phi) = \frac{(c_t l_t^\eta)^{1-\sigma}}{1 - \sigma} + \log \Phi(m_t, m_t^*), \tag{2}$$

$$\Phi(m_t, m_t^*) = A_m m_t^\phi m_t^{*1-\phi}, \qquad A_m > 0, \quad 0 < \phi < 1, \tag{3}$$

where $\sigma > 0$ is the intertemporal elasticity of substitution and ϕ represents the share of domestic money on the total amount of money. To
a certain extent the degree of currency substitution is captured by this
parameter. With a progressively lower value of ϕ, currency substitution increases.

The representative household has access to four financial assets: domestic and foreign money, and assets denominated in domestic, b_t,
and foreign currency, b_t^*, which yield the gross interest rates R_t and
R_t^*, respectively. Besides, the household owes physical capital, K_t,
which depreciates at a constant rate, δ, and presents the following law
of motion:[14]

$$K_{t+1} = (1 - \delta)K_t + i_t. \tag{4}$$

There are two goods produced in this economy. The importable good,
y_1, is consumed and produced domestically and also can be imported,

but the exportable good, y_2, is not consumed domestically and supposed to be an endowment.

The household's constraint is given by

$$c_t + i_t + b_t + b_t^* + m_t + m_t^* \leq (1 - \tau)(w_t L_t + r_t K_t + q_t y_2) + T_t + \frac{m_{t-1}}{1 + \pi_t}$$

$$+ \frac{e_t m_{t-1}^*}{1 + \pi_t} + \frac{R_t b_{t-1}}{1 + \pi_t} + \frac{R_t^* e_t b_{t-1}^*}{1 + \pi_t} - \Psi(\pi_t) + D_t, \tag{5}$$

where i_t denotes real investment in period t, τ is the (constant) income tax, w_t denotes real wage, r_t represents real cost of capital, q_t is the relative price of exportables to importables (terms of trade), T_t denotes real lump-sum transfers, π_t is the inflation rate, $\Psi(\pi_t)$ is cost of price adjustment,[15] and D_t are firm profits.

The function $\Psi(\pi_t)$ measures the cost of altering prices and thus represents the degree of price rigidity. It is supposed to be strictly convex in the inflation rate and zero in steady-state equilibrium. Particularly, I will assume that $\Psi(\pi_t) = (\rho_i/2)(\pi_t - \pi_{ss})^2$, where π_{ss} is the steady-state inflation rate.

In a decentralized equilibrium and given the laws of motion (see appendix A), the agent maximizes (1) subject to (2) through (5). Accordingly the first-order conditions are

$$u_c(c_t, l_t, \Phi) = \lambda_t, \tag{6}$$

$$u_m(c_t, l_t, \Phi) = \lambda_t - \beta E_t \left(\frac{\lambda_{t+1}}{1 + \pi_{t+1}} \right), \tag{7}$$

$$u_{m^*}(c_t, l_t, \Phi) = \lambda_t - \beta E_t \left(\frac{\lambda_{t+1} e_{t+1}}{1 + \pi_{t+1}} \right), \tag{8}$$

$$u_L(c_t, l_t, \Phi) = -\lambda_t (1 - \tau) w_t, \tag{9}$$

$$\lambda_t = \beta R_{t+1} E_t \left(\frac{\lambda_{t+1}}{1 + \pi_{t+1}} \right), \tag{10}$$

$$\lambda_t = \beta R_{t+1}^* E_t \left(\frac{\lambda_{t+1} e_{t+1}}{1 + \pi_{t+1}} \right), \tag{11}$$

$$\lambda_t = \beta E_t \lambda_{t+1} [(1 - \tau) r_{t+1} + (1 - \delta)]. \tag{12}$$

Notice that since the bonds are risk-free assets, R_{t+1} and R_{t+1}^* are known in period t; thus they are placed out of the expectation operator.

Firms

The representative firm maximizes its profits given by

$$D_t = y_{1t} - w_t L_t - r_t K_t \tag{13}$$

subject to a returns-to-scale technology:

$$y_{1t} = F(K_t, L_t, z_t) = A_0 K_t^\alpha L_t^{1-\alpha} e^{zt}, \qquad A_0 > 0, \quad 0 < \alpha < 1, \tag{14}$$

where z_t is a technological shock. Thus, given the law of motion of the technological shock, the firm maximizes (13) subject to (14), obtaining standard first-order conditions:

$$F_K(K_t, L_t, z_t) = r_t, \tag{15}$$

$$F_L(K_t, L_t, z_t) = w_t. \tag{16}$$

Public Sector

The baseline monetary policy of this model is an autoregressive interest rate rule á la Taylor:

$$R_{t+1} = (1 - \theta_1)R_0 + \theta_1 R_t + \theta_2(y_t - y_{ss}) + \theta_3(\pi_t - \pi_{ss}) + \varepsilon_{Rt+1}, \tag{17}$$

where y_t is total output, y_{ss} denotes total output in steady state and R_0 corresponds to the long-run or steady-state domestic interest rate. Domestic exogenous monetary shocks are transmitted to inflation rate through equation (10) and reinforced through the interest rate rule (17) provided that θ_2 be positive. Given the existence of price rigidities, these shocks generate an opposite effect on output in the short run because prices cannot adjust thoroughly. However, all monetary shocks do not have real effects in the long run.

On the other hand, fiscal policy consists of an exogenous public-expenditure law of motion:

$$g_t = (1 - \rho_g)g_0 + \rho_g g_{t-1} + \varepsilon_{gt}, \tag{18}$$

where ε_{gt} is a zero-mean shock with variance σ_g^2.

Equilibrium

Market clearing in the economy implies that aggregate demand equals aggregate supply:

$$c_t + i_t + g_t + \Psi(\pi_t) = y_{1t} + q_t y_2. \tag{19}$$

9.3.2 A Fully Dollarized Economy

Consider now a fully dollarized economy with the following characteristics: (1) household's utility function depends on consumption, real money holdings denominated in dollars, and leisure; (2) a fixed exchange rate equal to one and no domestic money as legal tender; (3) consequently loss of monetary policy; (4) demand for bonds denominated in foreign currency; and (5) the remaining assumptions of the partial-dollarization model.

Households

In this framework the infinitely lived agent optimizes an utility function which depends on real private consumption c_t, leisure l_t, and real foreign money balances m_t^*:

$$E_t \left\{ \sum_{t=0}^{\infty} \beta^t u(c_t, l_t, m_t^*) \right\}, \tag{1'}$$

where

$$u(c_t, l_t, m_t^*) = \frac{(c_t l_t^\eta)^{1-\sigma}}{1-\sigma} + \gamma \log m_t^*. \tag{2'}$$

The (new) representative household's constraint is

$$c_t + i_t + b_t^* + m_t^* \le (1-\tau)(w_t L_t + r_t K_t + q_t y_2) + T_t$$

$$+ \frac{m_{t-1}^*}{1+\pi_t} + \frac{R_t^* b_{t-1}^*}{1+\pi_t} - \Psi(\pi_t) + D_t, \tag{3'}$$

where each variable denotes the same as before.

In a decentralized equilibrium, the agent of this officially dollarized economy maximizes $(1')$ subject to $(2')$, $(3')$, and (4). The first-order conditions are, as before, $(6), (7), (9), (10), (12)$, and

$$u_{m*}(c_t, l_t, \Phi) = \lambda_t - \beta E_t \left(\frac{\lambda_{t+1}}{1+\pi_{t+1}} \right), \tag{4'}$$

$$\lambda_t = \beta R_{t+1}^* E_t \left(\frac{\lambda_{t+1}}{1+\pi_{t+1}} \right). \tag{5'}$$

Firms and Public Sector

The problem of the firms is the same as in the partially dollarized economy. For the public sector this is similar to the partially dollarized case, except for the absence of the interest rate rule and, consequently, the capability to perform (countercyclical) monetary policy. Finally, the market-clearing condition (19) is alike in both models.

9.4 Calibration

This section describes the parameterization and solution of the model (in the partially dollarized economy) and the capability of replicating the basic co-movements of the main macroeconomic variables of the actual data.

9.4.1 Parameterization and Method of Solution

I calibrate the first model for the Peruvian economy.[16] I assume three criteria to assign values to each parameter of the models. The first criterion is to use some of the standard parameter values given in previous literature for the Peruvian economy. There are just a few works that attempt to calibrate dynamic equilibrium models for Peruvian data. Table 9.3 summarizes the (quarterly) parameter values and their corresponding criterion of choice. For instance, according to Quiroz et al. (1992), I assume that $\beta = 0.976$ (which implies a real interest rate around 10 percent annually) and $\sigma_z = 0.06$, and according to Bernanke and Gurkaynak (2001), I assume that $\alpha = 0.44$. For simplicity, I set the intertemporal elasticity of substitution $\sigma = 1$ to use a log utility specification.

The second criterion is to estimate the exogenous laws of motion (terms of trade, foreign interest rate, and public expenditures) and a simple Taylor rule for the Peruvian economy using quarterly data for the 1992.1 to 2002.1 period. The results are $\rho_q = 0.88$, $\sigma_q = 0.045$, $\rho_R = 0.93$, $\sigma_{R^*} = 0.007$, $\rho_g = 0.47$, $\sigma_g = 0.055$, $\theta_1 = 0.75$, $\theta_2 = 0.343$, and $\theta_3 = 0.01$.[17]

The third criterion is to find the parameter value necessary to match sample moments of Peruvian data, such as the average share of consumption on GDP, standard deviations of output and inflation, and so on. For example, I calculate the steady-state levels of consumption, investment, public expenditure and exports (as percentage of output) as averages over the sample period (on quarterly basis). Then I match approximately these averages setting $A_0 = 1.35$, $\delta = 0.0375$, $g_0 = 0.225$, and $Y_2 = 3.3$. The actual averages are 73.1, 17.5, 9.4, and 12.8 percent respectively, while steady-state values for the same ratios are 72.6, 18.1, 9.3, and 9.5 percent.

Table 9.3
Parameterization of the models

Parameter	Symbol	Value	Criteria of choice
Subjective discount factor	β	0.976	Calibration of steady-state real interest rate around 10% (annual), using Quiroz et al. (1992)
Intertemporal elasticity of substitution	σ	1	Log utility specification
Utility sensitivity to domestic money (partially dollarized economy)	ϕ	0.47	Calibration of a degree of currency substitution (approximated by share of US\$ demand deposits on total amount of demand deposits in Peruvian banking system) around 59%
Utility sensitivity to dollar money (fully dollarized economy)	γ	0.53	The same as in the partially dollarized model $(1 - \phi = 0.53)$
Utility sensitivity to leisure	η	1	Calibration of steady-state labor: 0.34. This value implies a labor day of 8.2 hours
Capital share	α	0.44	Bernanke and Gurkaynak (2001)
Technological constant	A_0	1.35	Calibration of steady-state share of consumption on GDP around 73%
Technological AR1 coefficient	ρ_z	0.48	Calibration of output volatility
Technological volatility	σ_z	0.06	Quiroz et al. (1992)
Depreciation rate	δ	0.0375	Calibration of steady-state share of investment on GDP around 18%
Cost of price adjustment parameter	ρ_i	2	Calibration of output volatility
Steady-state exportable sector	Y_2	3.3	Calibration of steady-state share of exportable sector on GDP around 12%
Terms-of-trade AR1 coefficient	ρ_q	0.88	OLS estimate (data: 1992.01–2002.01)
Terms-of-trade volatility	σ_q	0.0449	OLS estimate (data: 1992.01–2002.01)
Income tax	τ	0.25	Income taxes (approximately)
Steady-state government expenditure	g_0	0.225	Calibration of steady-state share of government expenditures on GDP: 9.4%

Table 9.3
(continued)

Parameter	Symbol	Value	Criteria of choice
Government AR(1) coefficient	ρ_g	0.47	OLS estimate (data: 1992.01–2002.01)
Government expend. volatility	σ_g	0.055	OLS estimate (data: 1992.01–2002.01)
Foreign interest rate (constant)	R_0^*	$1.1^{(1/4)} - 1$	Calibration of steady-state annual currency depreciation around 3%
AR(1) coefficient	ρ_R	0.93	OLS estimate (data: 1992.01–2002.01)
Foreign interest rate volatility	σ_{R^*}	0.0069	OLS estimate (data: 1992.01–2002.01)
Domestic interest rate (constant)	R_0	$1.13^{(1/4)} - 1$	Calibration of steady-state annual inflation rate around 3%
AR(1) coefficient	θ_1	0.75	OLS estimate (data: 1992.01–2002.01)
Output deviation coefficient	θ_2	0.343	OLS estimate (data: 1992.01–2002.01)
Inflation deviation coefficient	θ_3	0.01	OLS estimate (data: 1992.01–2002.01)
Domestic interest rate volatility	σ_R	0.2	Calibration of inflation rate volatility

Sources: Central Bank of Peru (BCRP), the National Bureau of Statistics of Peru (INEI), and the Superintendency of Banks and Insurance (SBS).
Note: AR(1) denotes first-order autoregression process. All the parameter values are used in both models with the exceptions mentioned in this table. The covariances of the shocks are supposed to be zero. Data from the Peruvian economy are from 1992.01 to 2002.01, except for demand deposits (1993.01–2000.04).

On the other hand, I suppose that $\phi = 0.47$ to match a steady-state degree of currency substitution of 59 percent (approximated by the share of US\$ demand deposits on total amount of demand deposits in the Peruvian banking system in the 1993 to 2000 period),[18] that $\gamma = 1 - \phi$ for the fully dollarized economy to maintain the same effect of foreign currency on utility in both economies, that $\eta = 1$, which implies an employment rate of 34 percent or a labor day of 8.2 hours, that $\tau = 0.25$ to approximate the income tax in Peru, that $R_0 = 3.1$ percent, which implies an annual (nominal) domestic rate of 13 percent and steady-state inflation around 3 percent (close to the inflation target of the Central Bank of Peru), and that $R_0^* = 2.4$ percent, which implies a foreign interest rate of 10 percent and currency depreciation around 3 percent annually.

I also adjust the parameter values to allow the model match the volatilities of real output and inflation rate. The main metrics of comparison were a standard deviation of output around 3.8 percent (quarterly filtered data with deterministic trends) and a standard deviation of inflation rate around 3.6 percent. Therefore I match this metric relatively well using $\rho_z = 0.48$, $\rho_i = 2$, and $\sigma_R = 0.2$.

Finally the solution of the model is achieved using a perturbation method developed by Schmitt-Grohé and Uribe (2001). This method consists of a second order approximation to the policy functions of the dynamic equilibrium model. Once the models were solved, series of 5,000 observations were generated in each case to perform a comparative analysis. To perform an appropriate comparison I calibrate both models to achieve the same steady-state values of the variables that are common to both models.

9.4.2 Evaluation of Predicted Co-movements

For an evaluation of the model's capability of prediction, I contrast the co-movements implied by this to those observed in Peru in the 1992 to 2002 period. I choose this span because Peruvian economy faced a hyperinflation process at the end of the eighties and a stabilization program in 1990, which reduced the inflation rate to a two-digit value since 1992.

Table 9.4 shows the main co-movements of the actual series from the data and the simulated series from the model. In particular, I present standard deviations, autocorrelations, and serial correlations with GDP of key aggregate variables such as GDP, consumption, investment, inflation, and currency depreciation.

The co-movements implied by the model are reasonably consistent with the data. In particular, the model captures well volatility of output and inflation rate, but tends to slightly overpredict the volatility of consumption and investment. Besides, the autocorrelations implied by the model are also positive as in the data, specifically it is almost the same in the case of the inflation rate. In addition the model suggests correctly that consumption, investment, and depreciation are positively correlated with GDP as in the actual data. However, a counterfactual prediction of the model is the correlation between inflation and output. In the model this correlation is positive, while in the data it is close to zero. Nonetheless, this stylized fact might be related to the

Table 9.4
Actual and predicted co-movements from the model

Series	GDP (y_t)	Consumption (c_t)	Investment (i_t)	Inflation (π_t)	Currency depreciation (e_t)
Standard deviation (%)					
Data	3.83	4.38	22.42	3.56	5.64
Model	3.71	6.65	39.87	3.67	3.51
First-order autocorrelation					
Data	0.71	0.66	0.57	0.94	0.74
Model	0.48	0.95	0.48	0.93	0.91
Correlation with GDP					
Data	1.00	0.91	0.79	−0.09	0.33
Model	1.00	0.60	0.97	0.36	0.38

Sources: Central Bank of Peru (BCRP) and the National Bureau of Statistics of Peru (INEI). Period: 1992.01–2002.01.

period of decreasing inflation in the first half of the 1990s and be a consequence of the Peruvian stabilization program. In fact, when I calculate the same statistic for a period of higher price stability, such as 1997 to 2002, I find that the correlation increases to 0.29, which is closer to the prediction of the model. In summary, the overall performance of the model is relatively adequate since it is capable of replicating the main co-movements of the Peruvian data during the period of study.

9.5 Main Results

In this section I use the simulated variables from both the partial dollarization model and the full dollarization model to compare the performances of these schemes in terms of macroeconomic volatility.

9.5.1 Output and Inflation Volatility

Table 9.5 reports statistics of output, consumption and investment series from both models. As can be seen, the fully dollarized economy generates higher real volatility expressed in higher (percent) standard deviations of output and investment series. Particularly, the standard deviation of output increases around 0.3 percent quarterly or 1.2 percent annually (of the one from the partially dollarized economy). This finding is associated with the absence of the (countercyclical) monetary policy that can be endogenously used in the partially dollarized regime to ameliorate real shocks. The lack of this instrument in the fully

Table 9.5
Volatility of the simulated series from the models

| Economy | Standard deviation | | | |
	Output	Con-sumption	Investment	Inflation
Partial dollarization with flexible exchange rate	3.714	6.652	39.868	3.669
Full dollarization	4.000	4.740	42.436	0.336

Note: Series of 5,000 observations were generated in each model.

Table 9.6
Tests for equality of variances between series of each model

Test	Output	Consumption	Investment	Inflation
F-Test	1.160219 (0.0000)	1.963975 (0.0000)	1.132881 (0.0000)	119.4863 (0.0000)
Siegel-Tukey	3.910833 (0.0000)	16.96385 (0.0000)	3.081388 (0.0021)	72.80042 (0.0000)
Bartlett	24.81969 (0.0000)	503.0341 (0.0000)	17.49851 (0.0000)	15359.38 (0.0000)
Levene	21.42369 (0.0000)	406.6401 (0.0000)	14.49606 (0.0001)	6320.006 (0.0000)
Brown-Forsythe	21.36347 (0.0000)	406.8610 (0.0000)	14.03977 (0.0002)	6315.889 (0.0000)

Note: The null hypothesis is the equality of the variances of the variables in each model. For an explanation of the main features of the tests, see *Eviews 4.0 User's Guide* (2000). *p*-Values are in parentheses.

dollarized economy could be causing the higher real volatility, especially in investment and output.

When a test for equality of variances between output series is performed, the null of equality is rejected (see table 9.6), verifying that full dollarization implies higher real volatility. The exception is consumption. This variable shows a statistically significant lower standard deviation in the case of full dollarization, even at 1 percent of significance (see table 9.6). This fact is basically owing to the absence of domestic interest rate in the fully dollarized economy. In other words, the lower interest rate volatility in the fully dollarized economy causes less volatility in consumption.

In a fully dollarized economy, the inflation rate is not only lower in average but also presents lower volatility (see table 9.5). Tests for

Table 9.7
Volatility of the simulated fiscal deficit series from the models

	Standard deviation	
Economy	Fiscal deficit (levels)	Fiscal deficit (as % of output)
Partial dollarization with flexible exchange rate	3.803	0.147
Full dollarization	4.096	0.159

Note: Series of 5,000 observations were generated in each model.

equality of variances confirm this fact. Table 9.6 shows unquestionably that the volatility of the inflation rate in the flexible exchange rate regime is (statistically) different from the one of the fully dollarized regime. This is due to a lower volatility of the foreign interest rate, which is the relevant interest rate for consumption in that economy.

9.5.2 Other Implications: Fiscal Deficit Volatility and Reaction to External Shocks

Fiscal Deficit Volatility
According to the literature review, some authors have contended that full dollarization implies more fiscal discipline. Even though it is quite difficult to define and measure fiscal discipline in the model, I will try to approximate it through the volatility (standard deviation) of the public deficit, defined as the excess of government expenditures over income tax revenues, all expressed in real terms. The estimation of this statistic for both models indicates that a partially dollarized economy with flexible exchange rate implies a lower volatility on fiscal position than a fully dollarized economy (see table 9.7), even when fiscal deficit is measured as a percentage of GDP. This fact is verified through the calculation of tests for equality of variances. The null of equality between fiscal deficit variances from each model is not rejected at conventional levels of significance (see table 9.8). That is, "fiscal discipline" could be higher in a flexible exchange rate regime than a fully dollarized economy. This result can be explained by the fact that output is more volatile and so are income tax revenues.

Output Reaction to External Shocks
Figure 9.1 illustrates the response of a positive terms-of-trade shock (+10 percent of its steady-state value) on total output in both models.

Table 9.8
Tests for equality of variances between fiscal deficit series of each model

Test	Fiscal deficit (levels)	Fiscal deficit (as % of output)
F-Test	1.160031	1.157921
	(0.0000)	(0.0000)
Siegel-Tukey	3.913068	3.891236
	(0.0001)	(0.0001)
Bartlett	24.76560	24.16240
	(0.0000)	(0.0000)
Levene	21.40275	21.13643
	(0.0000)	(0.0000)
Brown-Forsythe	21.32609	21.08675
	(0.0000)	(0.0000)

Note: The null hypothesis is the equality of the variances of the variables in each model. p-Values are in parentheses.

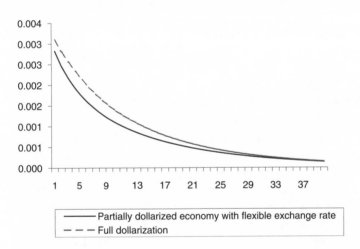

Figure 9.1
Responses of output in both regimes to a positive terms-of-trade shock (over 10 percent of the steady-state value).

Table 9.9
Welfare loss in each economy

χ_1	χ_2	Partial dollariza-tion with flexible exchange rate (1)	Full dollarization (2)	Difference (1) − (2)
0.7	1.7	0.034	0.037	−0.0028
0.6	1.6	0.029	0.032	−0.0022
0.5	1.5	0.025	0.026	−0.0016
0.4	1.4	0.020	0.021	−0.0010
0.3	1.3	0.015	0.016	−0.0004

A transitory increase of terms of trade generates a temporary raise of the exportable production and, consequently, of total output. However, the output response is higher in the fully dollarized economy than in the partially dollarized one. The lack of domestic monetary policy and nominal exchange rate in a full dollarization regime implies that terms-of-trade shocks cause higher output reactions when comparing to the output response from a partially dollarized economy with flexible exchange rate. This finding, joined to the low volatility of inflation rate mentioned before, is not consistent with Calvo's (1999a, b) idea that instead of nominal exchange rate, prices and wages would adjust to terms-of-trade shocks in a fully dollarized economy.

9.5.3 A Welfare Exercise

The change in the utility function from one economy to the other—due to the absence of domestic money in the fully dollarized case—makes unfair any possible welfare comparison between the regimes. Therefore, in order to evaluate the welfare implications of these alternative regimes, I use a simple criterion. Consider a central bank that seeks to minimize an expected social loss function. This function takes the form:

$$L_t = \chi_1 (y_t - y_{ss})^2 + \chi_2 (\pi_t - \pi_{ss})^2. \tag{20}$$

Taking unconditional expectations, the loss function becomes

$$E[L_t] = \chi_1 \, \text{var}(y_t) + \chi_2 \, \text{var}(\pi_t) \tag{21}$$

where $\text{var}(y)$ and $\text{var}(\pi)$ are the unconditional variances of domestic output and inflation, respectively. In particular, following Parrado and Velasco (2002), I begin assuming that the parameters χ_1 and χ_2 take the values of 0.5 and 1.5, respectively. As it can be seen in table 9.9, the flexible exchange rate regime dominates full dollarization for all the values assumed for χ_1 and χ_2.

However, these results must be taken carefully because of some reasons. First, real and nominal volatility in the model are sensitive to the cyclical properties of the monetary policy and the degree of price stickiness, as we will see below. Second, the results of the comparison depend strongly on the values assigned to χ_1 and χ_2. For example, when $\chi_1 = 0.2$ and $\chi_2 = 1.2$ the welfare loss is higher in the first economy. Third, the results of the comparison depend strongly on other possible arguments that can be included in equation (20). For instance, if I supposed that the central bank is concerned about exchange rate fluctuations—remember that the first one is a partially dollarized economy—and I introduced the currency depreciation deviation from steady state with a coefficient of 0.9, the welfare comparison would favor the fully dollarized case.

9.5.4   Sensitivity Analysis

The results presented are not very sensitive to changes in parameter values such as the ones related to the consumer's preferences and firm's technology. Further analysis can be done considering other utility function specifications.

However results are sensitive to the cyclical nature of monetary policy. The countercyclical monetary policy—expressed in an interest rule that depends positively on output deviation from steady state—has a key role. A less countercyclical monetary policy produces less difference on output and inflation volatility between both regimes.[19] Table 9.10 illustrates this idea. The values in each column are the ratios that result from dividing the standard deviation of output (inflation) from the full dollarization regime by the standard deviation of output (inflation) from the flexible exchange rate regime, respectively.

It is verified that in an economy with price rigidities, full dollarization implies higher real volatility due to the loss of a countercyclical monetary policy. Hence the results from section 9.5.1 cannot be generalized especially for economies where monetary policy is acyclical or procyclical.[20]

Finally one of the assumptions of the models presented before is that the government (or the central bank) has enough international reserves (in foreign currency and assets) to satisfy the domestic demand for foreign money. Although this supposition could be at the present realistic for the Peruvian economy, it should not be necessarily the rule for the

Table 9.10
Sensitivity of output and inflation volatilities to the degree of cyclicality of monetary policy

	Output volatility	Inflation volatility
θ_2	Full/partial	Full/partial
0.60	1.13	0.06
0.50	1.11	0.07
0.40	1.09	0.08
0.343	*1.08*	*0.09*
0.20	1.05	0.13
0.10	1.02	0.19
0.00	1.00	0.24

Note: Assumption and results of the baseline model are in italics.

future or for other partially dollarized economies. Further research on this topic should be done considering the absence of this assumption to analyze its implications on macroeconomic volatility.

9.6   Concluding Remarks

The literature review provides some conclusions. First, there is not a general consensus on the benefits and costs of a unilateral currency union except on a lower inflation rate (level and volatility). Second, there is a shortage of studies for emerging market economies that face currency and/or asset substitution and that are supposed to be good candidates for a full dollarization scheme. Third, there are very few studies that formally evaluate the implications of full dollarization on macroeconomic volatility, especially through a dynamic general equilibrium framework.

The results of the simulation exercises suggest, first, that a full dollarization scheme generates (significantly) higher real volatility, especially on investment and output in contrast to a partially dollarized economy with flexible exchange rate regime. This finding is associated to the fact that full dollarization lacks domestic monetary policy, an instrument that can be endogenously used to ameliorate real shocks in an economy with price rigidities. This idea is similar to the one contended by Alesina and Barro (2001). In an economy with flexible prices and/or a central bank with an acyclical monetary policy, real volatility might be virtually the same.

Second, full dollarization implies less inflation volatility. This is due to the absence of a volatile monetary policy that is present in flexible exchange rate regimes and that is replaced by a less volatile (foreign) interest rate. This conclusion is in line with the consensus of the related literature and supported with empirical evidence (Edwards 2001a, b; Edwards and Magendzo 2001).

Third, despite the absence of seignorage, an official dollarization regime tends to cause a more volatile fiscal deficit than a flexible exchange rate. This is closely related to the fact that tax revenues become more volatile, since output is more volatile too and might be seen by economic agents as a symptom of less "fiscal discipline."

Fourth, negative terms-of-trade shocks cause more significant effects on real output in a fully dollarized economy than in an economy with flexible exchange rate. This finding is also consistent with the first conclusion. This finding, joined to the low volatility of inflation rate mentioned before, is not consistent with Calvo's (1999a, b) idea that instead of nominal exchange rate, prices and wages would adjust to terms-of-trade shocks in a fully dollarized economy.

Fifth, a simple welfare exercise assuming a loss function of the central bank shows that the partially dollarized economy with flexible exchange rate dominates full dollarization. Similarly Schmitt-Grohé and Uribe (2001a) and Cooley and Quadrini (2001) found that full dollarization is not a welfare-improving regime compared to other alternatives. Nevertheless, our results must be taken carefully, because volatility in the first model is sensitive to the cyclical properties of the monetary policy and the welfare comparison depends strongly on the specification of the loss function (parameters and determinants).

Finally, if full dollarization causes more real and fiscal volatility, it is very difficult to imagine that dollarization can reduce country risk, as other authors have firmly contended. Thus, although full dollarization (virtually) eliminates devaluation risk it does not necessarily eliminate default risk, because real volatility could be higher and fiscal discipline might be difficult to improve.

Appendix A: Laws of Motion

$$K_{t+1} = (1 - \delta)K_t + i_t, \tag{A1}$$

$$q_t = (1 - \rho_q)q_0 + \rho_q q_{t-1} + \varepsilon_{qt}, \tag{A2}$$

$$R_{t+1} = (1 - \theta_1)R_0 + \theta_1 R_t + \theta_2(y_t - y_{ss}) + \theta_3(\pi_t - \pi_{ss}) + \varepsilon_{Rt+1}, \tag{A3}$$

$$R_{t+1}^* = (1 - \rho_R)R_o^* + \rho_R R_t^* + \varepsilon_{R^*t}, \tag{A4}$$

$$z_t = \rho_z z_{t-1} + \varepsilon_{zt}, \tag{A5}$$

$$g_t = (1 - \rho_g)g_0 + \rho_g g_{t-1} + \varepsilon_{gt}. \tag{A6}$$

In the equations above δ is the depreciation rate; ε_{jt} is a zero-mean shock with variance σ_j^2 for all $j = q, R, R^*, z, g$; $\theta_2 > 0$, $\theta_3 > 0$, and $0 < \theta_1 < 1$; and ρ_i is a parameter between 0 and 1 for all $i = q, R, z, g$.

All the intercepts are positive constants.

Appendix B: Steady-State Equilibrium

In steady state the laws of motion (A2–A6) imply the steady-state value of terms of trade, interest rate denominated in domestic currency, interest rate denominated in foreign currency, technological shock, and government expenditures, correspondingly:

$$q_{ss} = q_0, \tag{B1}$$

$$R_{ss} = R_0, \tag{B2}$$

$$R_{ss}^* = R_0^*, \tag{B3}$$

$$z_{ss} = 0, \tag{B4}$$

$$g_{ss} = g_0. \tag{B5}$$

Substitution of condition (B2) in (10) generates the steady-state inflation rate:

$$\pi_{ss} = \beta R_{ss} - 1. \tag{B6}$$

Using condition (11) and expressions (B4) and (B6), the steady-state rate of depreciation would be

$$e_{ss} = \frac{1 + \pi_{ss}}{\beta R_{ss}^*} - 1. \tag{B7}$$

Equations (4), (5), (6), (9), (12), (16), and (19) yield

$$L_{ss} = \frac{\omega_1 \omega_3 + g_0 - q_0 y_2}{\omega_3(A_1 + \omega_1) - \delta\omega_2}, \tag{B8}$$

where

$$\omega_0 = \left(\frac{\alpha A_0 \beta(1 - \tau)}{1 - \beta(1 - \delta)}\right), \quad \omega_1 = \left(\frac{(1 - \alpha)A_0(1 - \tau)}{\eta}\right),$$

$$\omega_2 = \omega_0^{1/(1-\alpha)}, \quad \omega_3 = \omega_0^{\alpha/(1-\alpha)}$$

Using the expression (B8), equations (6), (9), (16), and rearranging, one obtains an expression for the steady-state consumption that depends on the steady-state employment:

$$c_{ss} = \omega_1 \omega_3 (1 - L_{ss}). \tag{B9}$$

Similarly the steady-state stock of capital can be found with the same equations:

$$K_{ss} = \omega_2 L_{ss}. \tag{B10}$$

With equation (B8) and (B10) one can get the steady-state total production. Finally equations (7), (8), (B2), (B3), and (B9) generate the steady-state money balances in both currencies:

$$m_{ss} = \phi c_{ss} \left(\frac{R_{ss}}{R_{ss} - 1}\right), \tag{B11}$$

$$m_{ss}^* = (1 - \phi)c_{ss} \left(\frac{R_{ss}^*}{R_{ss}^* - 1}\right). \tag{B12}$$

The steady-state values of the variables in the fully dollarized model are the same as the ones in the partially dollarized model. The only difference is that in the former there do not exist expressions like (B2), (B7), and (B11).

Notes

This chapter was previously circulated under the title "Exploring the Implications of Official Dollarization on Macroeconomic Volatility." I thank Rómulo Chumacero, Paul De Grauwe, Claudia Costa Storti, Marc-Andre Letendre, Klaus Schmidt-Hebbel, Alessandro Rebucci, José María Fanelli, Felipe Morandé, Claudia Arguedas, Federico Sturzenegger, an anonymous referee, and the participants at the Meeting on Economics of Chile, the VII Meeting of the Research Network of Central Banks of the Americas, the Fourth Annual Global Development Network (GDN) Conference, the 2003 Econometric Society North American Summer Meeting, the Workshop on Monetary Unions after EMU, and the Latin American Meeting of the Econometric Society for helpful comments and suggestions. The author was working at the Central Bank of Chile at the time this chapter was written. The views expressed herein are those of the author and do not necessarily represent those of the Central Bank of Chile or its Board.

1. Even though official or full dollarization is a specific case of a unilateral currency union, these terms will be used as synonyms along this work.

2. Partially dollarized economies are those that face currency and/or asset substitution between domestic and foreign money.

3. See, for example, Edwards (2001a, p. 249).

4. See, for instance, Eichengreen (2000, 2001), Gruben et al. (2001), and Guidotti and Powell (2002) on this issue.

5. See Gruben et al. (2001) on this point.

6. Remember that the largest officially dollarized economy is Ecuador, which only recently adopted the US dollar in 2000.

7. Exceptions are Cooley and Quadrini (2001) and Schmitt-Grohé and Uribe (2001a) for the case of the Mexican economy.

8. This indirect cost is lower if central bank depreciates the domestic currency before dollarizating the economy.

9. Powell and Sturzenegger (2000) consider that dollarization implies lower country risk especially for highly dollarized economies such as Argentina, Brazil, and Mexico.

10. This conclusion is based on an empirical analysis for Central American countries.

11. Source: Superintendency of Banks and Insurance of Peru.

12. For example, the central banks of Panama and Ecuador still issue low-denomination Balboas and Sucres, respectively.

13. I take from these works the way they model currency substitution through the use of a liquidity service function. The objectives of those papers are different from this because they analyze seignorage and inflation tax issues.

14. I include physical capital in the model mainly because some authors contend that official dollarization has certain implication on investment as seen in the literature review.

15. Similar to Schmitt-Grohé and Uribe (2001a).

16. The Peruvian economy fits very well with the purpose of this chapter, mainly because it is a partially dollarized one and macroeconomic data are available for calibration.

17. I used OLS as method of estimation and Newey-West standard errors consistent with autocorrelation and heteroskedasticity. All the autoregressive parameters are statistically significant at conventional levels, except for the coefficient of inflation in the estimated Taylor rule, that is the reason why I supposed a low value for θ_3.

18. This proxy is more appropriate since it is closely related to the theoretical causes of currency substitution than other bank deposit ratios such as saving or term deposit ratios that tend to capture mainly asset substitution. A discussion on this issue can be found in Duncan (2000, 2001).

19. Alesina and Barro (2001) also contend a similar idea.

20. On the other hand, in an economy with price flexibility, full dollarization does not generate higher real volatility. I also performed a sensitivity analysis considering different degrees of price stickiness (ρ_i) and procyclical/anticyclical fiscal policy. As long as the degree of price stickiness reduces the difference between output volatility from the

flexible exchange rate regime and the one from the fully dollarized regime is lower. In the extreme case when ρ_i is zero, the ratio of the variances becomes unity. This result indicates the important role that also price stickiness plays. The main conclusions remained unchanged in the case of procyclical/anticyclical fiscal policy.

References

Alesina, A., and R. Barro. 2001. Dollarization. *AEA Papers and Proceedings* 91 (2).

Berg, A., and E. Borensztein. 2000. Full dollarization: The pros and cons. IMF Policy Discussion Paper. Washington, DC.

Berg, A., E. Borensztein, and P. Mauro. 2002. An evaluation of monetary regime options for Latin America. Central Bank of Chile: Working Paper 178.

Bernanke, B. S., and R. S. Gürkaynak. 2001. Is growth exogenous? Taking Mankiw, Romer, and Weil seriously. Working Paper w8365. NBER. *Macroeconomics Annual*.

Bloch, C., and J. Chiriaeva. 2002. On dollarization and credibility. Unpublished paper. University of Aarhus.

Bogetic, Z. 2000. Official dollarization: Current experiences and issues. *Cato Journal* 20 (2): 179–213.

Bufman, G., and L. Leiderman. 1992. Simulating an optimizing model of currency substitution. *Revista de Análisis Económico* 7 (1): 109–24.

Calvo, G. 1999a. On Dollarization. Unpublished paper. University of Maryland.

Calvo, G. 1999b. Testimony on full dollarization. Presented before a Joint Hearing of the Subcommittees on Economic Policy and International Trade and Finance. Washington, DC, April 22.

Calvo, G., and C. Reinhart. 1999. When capital inflows come to a sudden stop: Consequences and policy options. Unpublished paper. University of Maryland.

Carrera, J., M. Féliz, D. Panigo, and M. Saavedra. 2002. How does dollarization affect real volatility? A General Methodology for Latin America. Unpublished paper.

Chang, R. 2000. Dollarization: A scorecard. Federal Reserve Bank of Atlanta. *Economic Review* (3): 1–12.

Chang, R., and A. Velasco. 2002. Dollarization: analytical issues. NBER Working Paper 8838.

Cohen, B. 2000. Political dimensions of dollarization. Working Paper. Federal Reserve Bank of Dallas.

Cooley, T., and V. Quadrini. 2001. The costs of losing monetary independence: The case of Mexico. *Journal of Money, Credit, and Banking* 33(2): 370–97.

Dornbusch, R. 2000. Fewer monies, better monies. Unpublished paper.

Drew, A., V. Hall, J. McDermott, and R. St. Clair. 2001. Would adopting the Australian dollar provide superior monetary policy in New Zealand? Reserve Bank of New Zealand Discussion Paper 03.

Du Bois, F., and E. Morón. 1999. Los riesgos y oportunidades de dolarizar la economía Peruana. Unpublished paper.

Duncan, R. 2000. Los procesos de sustitución monetaria y de sustitución de activos en la economía Peruana: 1993–1999. Catholic University of Peru, Undergraduate Dissertation.

Duncan, R. 2001. Histéresis, sustitución monetaria y sustitución de activos: Perú, 1993–1999. *Moneda* XIII (123). Central Bank of Peru.

Edwards, S. 2001a. Dollarization myths and realities. *Journal of Policy Modeling* 23: 249–65.

Edwards, S. 2001b. Dollarization and economic performance: An empirical investigation. NBER Working Paper 8274.

Edwards, S., and I. Magendzo. 2001. Dollarization, inflation and growth. NBER Working Paper 8671.

Eichengreen, B. 2000. When to dollarize? University of California, Berkeley. Unpublished paper.

Eichengreen, B. 2001. What problems can dollarization solve? University of California, Berkeley.

Gale, D., and X. Vives. 2002. Dollarization, bailouts, and the stability of the banking system. *Quarterly Journal of Economics* 117 (2): 467–502.

Gavin, M. 1999. Hearing on official dollarization in Latin America. Prepared testimony before Hearing on Official Dollarization in Latin America. US Senate, Washington, DC.

Goldfajn, I., and G. Olivares. 2000. Is adopting full dollarization the solution? Looking at the evidence. Pontificia Universidade Católica do Rio de Janeiro.

Gruben, W., M. Wynne, C. Zarazaga. 2001. Dollarization and monetary unions: Implementation guidelines. Federal Reserve Bank of Dallas, Working Paper 0201.

Guidotti, P., and A. Powell. 2002. The dollarization debate in Argentina and Latin America. In L. Auernheimer, ed., *International Financial Markets: The Challenge of Globalization.* Chicago: University of Chicago Press.

Hausmann, R. 1999. Should there be five currencies or one hundred and five? CIAO Foreign Policy.

Hinds, M. 1999. Hearing on official dollarization in emerging-market countries. Prepared testimony. Washington, DC. *www.senate.gov/~banking/99_07hrg/071599/hinds.htm.*

Hochreiter, E., K. Schmidt-Hebbel, and G. Winckler. 2002. Monetary unions: European lessons, Latin American prospects. Central Bank of Chile Working Paper 167.

Klein, M. 2002. Dollarization and trade. NBER Working Paper 8879.

Lizano, E. 2000. Dolarización es inevitable para las economías más pequeñas de la región. *www.eldiario.cl.*

McKinnon, R. 1963. Optimum currency areas. *American Economic Review* 53: 717–24.

McNelis, P., and C. Asilis. 1992. A dynamic simulation analysis of currency substitution in an optimizing framework with transactions costs. *Revista de Análisis Económico* 7 (1): 139–52.

Mendoza, E. 2001. The benefits of dollarization when stabilization policy lacks credibility and financial markets are imperfect. *Journal of Money, Credit, and Banking* 33 (2): 440–74.

Mendoza, E. 2002. Why should emerging economies give up national currencies: A case for "institutions substitutions." NBER Working Paper 8950.

Morandé, F., and K. Schmidt-Hebbel. 2000. Esquemas monetarios alternativos: Una evaluación favorable al peso Chileno. *Revista de Economía Chilena* 3(1): 57–84.

Mundell, R. 1961. A theory of optimum currency areas. *American Economic Review* 51: 509–17.

Panizza, U., E. Stein, and E. Talvi. 2000. Measuring costs and benefits of dollarization: An application to Central American and Caribbean countries. Unpublished paper. Washington, DC: Inter-American Development Bank.

Parrado, E., and A. Velasco. 2002. Alternative monetary rules in the open-economy: A welfare-based approach. In N. Loayza and R. Soto, eds., *Inflation Targeting, Design, Performance, Challenges*, vol. 5. Central Bank of Chile: Serie Banca Central, Análisis y Políticas Económicas, pp. 295–343. *www.bcentral.cl/esp/estpub/estudios/bancacentral*.

Pesaran, H., and Y. Shin. 1998. Generalized impulse response analysis in linear multivariate models. *Economic Letters* 58: 17–29.

Pereyra, C., and Z. Quispe. 2002. Es conveniente una dolarización total en una economía parcialmente dolarizada. *Revista de Estudios Económicos* 7. Banco Central de Reserva del Perú.

Powell, A., and F. Sturzenegger. 2000. Dollarization: The link between devaluation and default risk. Business School, Universidad Torcuato Di Tella.

Quiroz, J., F. Bernasconi, R. Chumacero, and C. Revoredo. 1991. Modelos y realidad: Enseñando economía en los noventa. *Revista de Análisis Económico* 6 (2): 79–103.

Rojas-Suárez, L. 1999. Dollarization in Latin America? Prepared Testimony. Prepared testimony before *Hearing on Official Dollarization in Latin America*. US Senate Banking Committee. Washington, DC. *www.senate.gov/~banking/99_07hrg/071599/rojas.htm*.

Savastano, M. 1999. Presentation prepared for the conference "Dolarizar la Economía Peruana: Riesgos y Oportunidades." Lima.

Schmitt-Grohé, S., and M. Uribe. 2001a. Stabilization policy and the costs of dollarization. *Journal of Money, Credit, and Banking*, 33(2): 482–509.

Schmitt-Grohé, S., and M. Uribe. 2001b. Solving dynamic general equilibrium models using a second order approximation to the policy function. Discussion Paper 2963. Centre for Economic Policy Research, London.

Schuler, K. 1999. Presentation prepared for the conference "Dolarizar la Economía Peruana: Riesgos y Oportunidades." Lima.

Sims, C. 2002. Fiscal consequences for Mexico of adopting the dollar. Unpublished paper. Princeton University.

10 Regional Currencies versus Dollarization: Options for Asia and the Americas

Felipe Larraín and José Tavares

10.1 Introduction

In the wake of currency crises in East Asian and other developing countries, there is a new sense of the vulnerability of all developing countries to volatile capital movements.[1] It is not clear whether intermediate exchange rate systems are a sensible policy option. Some developing countries, notably in Latin America, are now explicitly considering options such as official dollarization,[2] while others have opted for floating. In addition the successful transition to a common currency by a wide range of European countries[3] highlights the benefits of fixed parities vis-à-vis trading partners. The moment is thus propitious for an examination of the potential of currency unions versus hard currency pegs.

Before the Asian crisis of 1997 countries in the region relied on unilateral dollar pegs, which could not deal with the asymmetric devaluations in the wake of the fall of the yen.

A common currency in East Asia might have delivered better outcomes as increasing regional trade integration in East Asia (including Japan) suggests. Bayoumi and Mauro (1999) review the case of a currency area in the ASEAN countries and conclude that on economic criteria the ASEAN is only marginally less suited for a regional currency area than Europe was just before Maastricht. The fact that the ASEAN countries have important trade flows with the three major trade areas, the United States, Japan, and Europe, militates against fixing with a particular currency. Low inflation rates, budget deficits, and public debt across the ASEAN, and the rapid adjustment to shocks and levels of intraregional trade similar to Europe, argue for a regional currency reinforced by the high and rising level of trade in manufactures.

Latin American countries such as Ecuador and El Salvador have adopted the US dollar in recent years, while countries in Mercosur discuss the possible future adoption of a common currency, as assessed by Eichengreen (1998). Documenting the high levels of real exchange rate variability within the region, Eichengreen concludes that monetary unification makes sense only as part of a broader integration project that addresses the underlying sources of bilateral volatility.

As for Central America, for most of the past century it has adopted monetary arrangements characterized by the fixing of the nominal exchange rate with relation to the US dollar. The instability of the 1980s led the countries in the region to abandon the peg to the dollar in succession. However, their small economic size and high degree of openness to international trade need to be weighed in any choice of an exchange rate regime. In the past analysts have argued for dollarization[4] as well as for the adoption of a common currency in Central America.[5]

In this chapter we evaluate empirically the options of dollarization and regional currency union in light of the literature on the determinants of real exchange rate volatility. We compute the levels of bilateral integration as well as the determinants of bilateral real exchange rate volatility for the three regions under study—East Asia, South America, and Central America—improving on the existing literature in several ways. First, we provide the first explicit quantitative comparison of dollarization versus regional currency unification for the regions studied, framing previous studies in the appropriate context. Second, our estimation method draws on both time and cross-sectional variation in bilateral data, the former dimension having been largely ignored in the literature. We, however, do not analyze the practical problems inherent to the setting up of a common currency, such as the necessary institutions, their operation and interaction. We recognize the importance of these issues and mention them in passing, but they lie beyond the scope of our analysis.

10.2 Regional Currency Areas versus Dollarization

The seminal contributions in Mundell (1961) and McKinnon (1963), giving rise to the theory of optimal currency areas, remain the focal point for examining currency agreements among countries. According to Mundell, countries or regions that are symmetrically affected by shocks form an optimal currency area. It is not necessary for shocks to be symmetric between countries but only that labor and capital be sufficiently mobile and prices flexible enough to avoid persistent local pockets of unemployment. Any group of countries with a reasonable combination of these three elements—symmetry of shocks, factor mobility, and price flexibility—can benefit from a common currency.[6] In that case nominal exchange rate changes become irrelevant.

What are the benefits of a common currency area? The most conspicuous is the reduction in transaction costs whenever international exchanges of goods, services and capital are involved.[7] These costs are related to fees such as the bid-ask spread and related commission fees that financial institutions charge for foreign currency transactions. Second, in common currency areas there is a concomitant decrease in uncertainty for transactions with in-area foreign partners, and this is likely to foster trade and investment flows. As to the costs of establishing a common currency, they are associated with the loss of autonomy in the conduct of monetary policy. Monetary policy is an important instrument for a prompt response to asymmetric real shocks in the presence of nominal rigidities and imperfectly integrated factor markets. This is because changes in the nominal exchange rate are associated with changes in the real exchange rate.

As opposed to currency union, dollarization implies the simple substitution of a given country's currency by the US dollar.[8] The dollar is a good candidate to perform the functions of means of payment, asset to hold savings, and unit of account given its stable value, and its wide use in international transactions and as reserve currency.[9] Panama, Ecuador, and El Salvador have opted for dollarization,[10] while Guatemala legalized the US dollar in parallel with domestic currency. In addition five US possessions and six other independent countries are officially dollarized.[11] One of the main benefits of dollarization is the decrease in currency risk—if not in country risk—and the resulting convergence between domestic and US inflation and interest rates.[12]

The most conspicuous cost is the loss of an independent monetary policy and control of the lender-of-last-resort function. Given the little relevance of countries considering dollarization in US affairs, their interests as far as monetary policy stance are not likely to be taken into account by federal authorities.[13] The loss of the lender-of-last-resort function drastically limits local authorities in their role as providers of liquidity to the banking system in times of crises, while introducing a moral hazard problem whereby local authorities may lack the incentive to properly monitor it. Furthermore the implied loss of seigniorage revenue may not be irrelevant to the countries in question.[14]

10.3   Regional Currencies versus Dollarization: An Assessment

Different criteria for establishing a currency area have been presented in the literature, and these can be used as a guide to our empirical study.[15] First and foremost, a high level of bilateral trade favors currency unification as the lower transaction costs of a single currency apply to a wider base.[16] The composition of trade flows also matters as countries that export widely different goods are probably subject to asymmetric shocks and more likely to need frequent bilateral exchange rate adjustments.[17] Another criterion for establishing a common currency area is the degree of asymmetry of underlying shocks relative to the flexibility of factor markets. The larger the idiosyncratic country shocks, the more dissimilarity exists between countries and the slower is real adjustment, the less appropriate is the option for a currency area.[18]

Frankel et al. (1998) point to three determinants of the choice of exchange rate regime: credibility, structural characteristics, and commitment to regional integration. Countries that lack fiscal and monetary discipline can fix the exchange rate as a way to import that discipline. The resulting decrease in country risk can lead to benefits through lower interest rates, higher levels of domestic investment and capital inflows.[19]

The institution of a common currency changes the economic relationship among its members in a fundamental way, so one should note the possible problem of endogeneity of the criteria. Bilateral trade makes currency union more beneficial, but adopting a common currency also encourages regional trade flows.[20] Countries may be more suited for a currency area ex post than ex ante if this furthers trade flows, synchronizes output cycles, and changes the responsiveness of prices to exogenous shocks.[21] To assess the level of endogeneity of the common currency criteria, it is also important to acknowledge the credibility issues that this option embodies, such as the governance of a single central bank and the granting (or denying) of escape clauses for members; furthermore the establishment of a single currency involves the problem of institutional and political implementation, widely discussed in the literature.[22]

In this chapter we use a data set comprised of 37 countries in East Asia, western Europe, and North, Central, and South America. The choice of countries in the sample derives from two criteria: the size of the economies and whether they belong to regions where dollarization is a plausible policy choice. The full list of countries is presented in appendix A. For each country pair in the sample we compile a set of indicators of bilateral integration, specific to each country pair and time period:

• Bilateral real exchange rate variability

• Output shock dissimilarity, the degree of correlation of output fluctuations

• Bilateral trade intensity, the share of bilateral trade flows in each country's GDP

• Export similarity, the degree to which two countries rely on similar export products

• Country size, measured as the average of the two countries' absolute GDPs[23]

Each variable is averaged over the periods 1970 to 1979, 1980 to 1989, and 1990 to 1997. The use of different time periods allows us to assess how the feasibility of dollarization versus regional currency unification changes over time, this dimension having been insufficiently explored in the empirical literature on currency areas and dollarization. We acknowledge, however, that while this empirical exercise is straightforward for the 1980s and 1990s, for the 1970s it may be influenced by the collapse of the Bretton Woods arrangement. Our starting point is to compare the decade's average real bilateral exchange rate volatility within each region and between the countries in the region and the United States.

Table 10.1 reports summary statistics of the indicators of bilateral economic integration compiled, by region, for three decades from the 1970s to the 1990s. In appendix A we describe exactly how the indexes of real exchange rate volatility, asymmetry of output shocks, dissimilarity of exports, and intensity of bilateral trade were constructed. Table 10.1 presents, in order, the value of the bilateral indicators when only one of the countries in the country pair belongs to the region, the within-region values (when both countries are in the region) and the same value when one country is in the region and the other is the United States.[24] For the three decades considered, Europe has the lowest values of intra-regional real exchange rate volatility, almost half the level in Asia, a third of Central America's and a fourth of South America's. Our data show that while Europe's level of real exchange rate volatility decreased slightly from a low level in the 1970s, Asia experienced a

Table 10.1
Indicators of bilateral integration

	Real exchange rate volatility			Asymmetry of output shocks			Dissimilarity of exports			Intensity of trade		
	1970s (1)	1980s (2)	1990s (3)	1970s (4)	1980s (5)	1990s (6)	1970s (7)	1980s (8)	1990s (9)	1970s (10)	1980s (11)	1990s (12)
All	0.1218	0.1795	0.1150	0.0330	0.0441	0.0302	11.64	11.48	10.44	0.52	0.61	0.66
All-Europe	0.1139	0.1885	0.1238	0.0315	0.0405	0.0290	12.08	11.49	10.16	0.28	0.28	0.30
Europe	0.0564	0.0558	0.0519	0.0260	0.0193	0.0153	6.69	6.28	5.94	1.38	1.80	1.91
United States–Europe	0.0643	0.1350	0.0988	0.0261	0.0256	0.0188	6.64	6.35	3.87	0.80	1.08	0.98
All-East Asia	0.1215	0.1588	0.1046	0.0320	0.0461	0.0292	12.45	11.79	10.68	0.33	0.41	0.46
East Asia	0.1090	0.0986	0.0578	0.0304	0.0417	0.0233	13.12	11.56	8.27	1.97	2.41	2.76
United States–East Asia	0.0921	0.0696	0.0617	0.0264	0.0399	0.0242	11.58	9.61	6.70	4.16	5.82	6.07
All-South America	0.1494	0.2172	0.1271	0.0369	0.0526	0.0351	12.58	12.96	12.13	0.21	0.22	0.23
South America	0.2024	0.2566	0.1470	0.0418	0.0609	0.0432	11.90	12.11	11.00	0.27	0.34	0.37
United States–South America	0.1321	0.1878	0.0961	0.0382	0.0520	0.0332	13.67	13.95	8.76	2.08	2.43	2.77
All-Central America	0.0947	0.2134	0.1498	0.0323	0.0430	0.0312	11.98	13.08	12.66	0.27	0.24	0.23
Central America	0.0406	0.2028	0.1312	0.0302	0.0372	0.0223	4.25	3.99	4.33	1.24	0.99	0.83
United States–Central America	0.0320	0.1397	0.1067	0.0259	0.0293	0.0239	12.71	13.54	11.16	4.80	4.54	4.33
United States–all countries	0.0876	0.1345	0.0888	0.0297	0.0372	0.0249	10.64	10.27	9.96	2.63	3.24	3.41

Note: All country pairs refer to the sample average: Europe, East Asia, South America, and Central America refer to country pairs where both countries belong to the same region; all-regions refer to the average value for pairs, including a country in the region and one outside; United States–region refers to the pairs comprising the United States and a country in the region. Central America excludes Nicaragua.

dramatic decrease, and in the 1990s has approached European levels of exchange rate volatility. South America and Central America, on the other hand, experienced substantial fluctuations, with an increase in the 1980s and a decrease in the 1990s to levels still substantially higher than Europe's and Asia's.[25] As for the evolution of regional exchange rate volatility versus the US dollar, Asia stands out with the lowest level of volatility, followed by Europe and Central America and, at higher levels, South America. A comparison of exchange rate volatility within the region as compared to volatility versus the dollar in the 1990s allows us to conclude that regional currency unification in Europe seems more feasible than dollarization, while in Asia the dollarization option looked relatively more attractive in the past than it did in the 1990s. As to South and Central America, currencies display lower volatility versus the dollar than among themselves.

Columns 4 through 6 report on the asymmetry of output shocks, where a higher value of the index is associated with more asymmetry, namely lower correlation of output among the countries considered. Europe stands out again for a low degree of output asymmetry, followed by Central America and East Asia. The evolution over time shows a slight decrease in the asymmetry of output shocks in Europe from already low levels in the 1970s. As to the asymmetry of output shocks relative to the US economy, Europe stands out again, followed by Central America, East Asia and South America and the evolution over time parallels that of intra-regional volatility. South America is the only region that has higher intra-regional output asymmetry than asymmetry versus the US output and the difference is significant.[26]

Columns 7 through 9 report on the dissimilarity of export base, a measure of the difference in export structures between the two countries: the larger the index, the more the countries differ as far as their pattern of exports for the eight first SITC codes at one-digit level. Central America comes out as the most homogeneous region, which is not surprising given that these countries share similar specialization patterns in agricultural products and textiles. Central America is also the region that differs the most from the United States in its pattern of specialization. Europe, East Asia, and South America all have patterns of country exports that differ more within than between the region and the United States. Countries in the same region tend to become more similar over time, both within regions and with the United States, which may reflect a general tendency toward diversification as economies grow in income per capita.

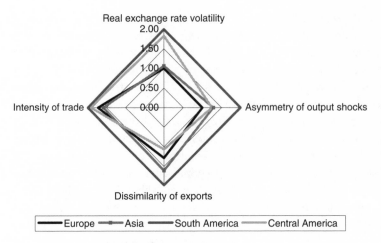

Figure 10.1
Indicators of regional integration (1990s).

Finally the last three columns in table 10.1 present summary statistics for the intensity of bilateral trade, a measure of trade integration. As the level of bilateral trade between two countries increases—as a share of their respective GDPs—the intensity of trade index increases concomitantly. East Asia now stands out as the most integrated set of countries as far as trade while South America is at the other extreme. Trade integration tends to grow over time in all regions, the exception being Central America. As to bilateral trade intensity vis-à-vis the United States, East Asia is the most integrated, now closely followed by Central America. Furthermore all regions tend to trade more with the United States than with its neighbors, the exception being Europe. In the case of the Americas, one should also notice the extremely low absolute levels of regional trade integration.

Figures 10.1 through 10.6 present information on the indicators of integration. The first two figures present the integration indicators in the 1990s for all regions, within regions (figure 10.1) and relative to the United States (figure 10.2). Figures 10.3 through 10.6 compare, for each region, the regional indicators of integration and the same indicators vis-à-vis the United States. In sum, as far as indicators of bilateral integration are concerned, Europe comes out as a deeply integrated group of countries, regardless of the gauge chosen, and European countries are more closely integrated with their neighbors than with the United States. This fact confirms the appropriateness of Europe as a benchmark of a

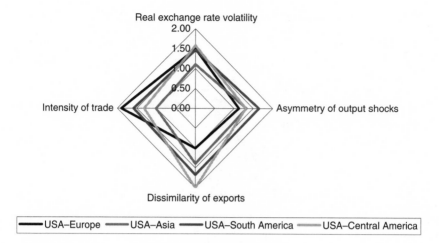

Figure 10.2
Indicators of integration with the US economy (1990s).

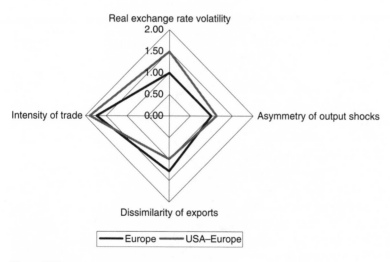

Figure 10.3
Indicators of integration: Europe (1990s).

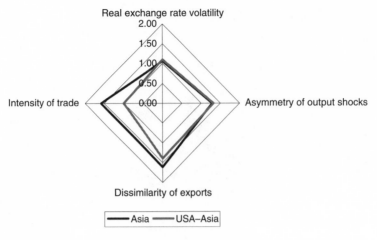

Figure 10.4
Indicators of integration: Asia (1990s).

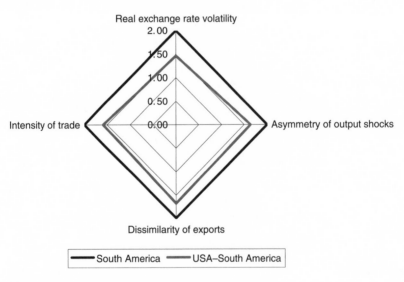

Figure 10.5
Indicators of integration: South America (1990s).

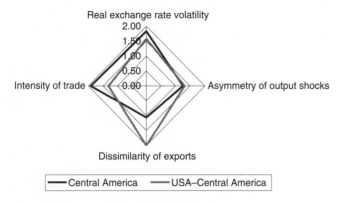

Figure 10.6
Indicators of integration: Central America.

regionally integrated region, against which regional currency unification in other areas is to be assessed.

East Asia as a region has seen remarkable progress in the degree of regional integration over time: real exchange rate volatility, the asymmetry of output shocks, and the degree of export dissimilarity decreased while trade intensity increased. In fact in the 1990s East Asia comes close to European levels of regional integration. While Asia displays levels of regional integration with the United States similar to the regional levels, both South and Central America seem more integrated with the United States than within their region.[27]

We now turn to examining the determinants of bilateral real exchange rate volatility, in particular, how it is affected by the intensity of trade, dissimilarity of exports, and the asymmetry of output shocks. Our data set includes 37 countries for each decade—the 1970s, the 1980s, and the 1990s—including the largest economies in East Asia, South America, and western Europe. The panel estimates determine whether countries in a given region display intra-regional exchange rate volatility or exchange rate volatility versus the dollar that is significantly different from the sample average. In table 10.2 we assess this by including appropriate dummy variables in the panel specification, capturing, respectively, intra-regional observations and bilateral region–US observations. In table 10.3 we estimate the impact of each determining factor on exchange variability versus the dollar or the other regional currencies. This is done by interacting the appropriate dummies with the determining factors (independent variables) in each

Table 10.2
Determinants of bilateral RER volatility: Within-region and against US dollar dummies

	Within-region					Against US dollar			
	All decades (1)	All decades (2)	1970s (3)	1980s (4)	1990s (5)	All decades (6)	1970s (7)	1980s (8)	1990s (9)
Asymmetry of output shocks	1.933** (8.66)	1.774** (7.61)	0.769** (5.06)	3.353** (5.75)	1.575** (10.23)	1.789** (7.58)	0.759** (5.02)	3.509** (5.90)	1.602** (10.33)
Dissimilarity of exports	0.003** (2.66)	0.003** (2.85)	0.000 (−0.18)	0.008** (2.62)	0.002** (3.04)	0.003** (2.37)	−0.001 (−0.74)	0.008** (2.42)	0.001** (2.03)
Intensity of trade	−0.008** (−6.00)	−0.006** (−4.55)	−0.009** (−5.61)	−0.003 (−1.25)	−0.004** (−3.29)	−0.007** (−4.09)	−0.009** (−4.83)	−0.005 (−1.32)	−0.004** (−3.05)
Economic size	−0.009** (−2.82)	−0.004 (−1.35)	0.011** (4.22)	−0.027** (−3.20)	0.009** (5.03)	−0.004 (−1.36)	0.012** (4.23)	−0.028** (−3.30)	0.008** (4.86)
East Asia	—	−0.047** (−5.12)	0.013* (1.63)	−0.118** (−6.86)	−0.038** (−6.93)	−0.040** (−4.17)	0.006 (0.65)	−0.097** (−4.79)	−0.041** (−7.26)
Europe	—	−0.047** (−6.26)	−0.055** (−7.83)	−0.026 (−1.26)	−0.035** (−7.19)	−0.041** (−5.17)	−0.064** (−7.73)	−0.003 (−0.13)	−0.034** (−7.02)
Central America	—	0.148* (1.89)	−0.057** (−4.11)	0.436** (2.38)	0.100** (4.28)	0.116* (1.94)	−0.062** (−5.88)	0.362** (2.53)	0.068** (3.36)
South America	—	0.017** (5.51)	0.090** (2.83)	−0.067** (−1.99)	0.017** (1.31)	0.012 (4.99)	0.075** (2.90)	−0.062** (−0.83)	0.006 (0.83)
Year dummies	Yes	Yes	—	—	—	Yes	—	—	—
Number of observations	2223	2223	741	741	741	2223	741	741	741
R^2	0.18	0.19	0.16	0.18	0.30	0.19	0.17	0.18	0.29

Note: See appendix A for data description. In parentheses we report t-statistics using heteroskedastic-consistent standard errors. ** indicates statistically significant at the 1 percent level and * statistically significant at the 5 percent level. All specifications include a constant, not reported for reasons of parsimony. In columns 2 through 5 region dummies correspond to observations where both countries belong to the designated region; in columns 6 through 9 region dummies refer to bilateral observations where one country belongs to the region and the other is the United States.

specification. Here, a significant coefficient associated with a factor indicates that the factor at stake is more/less important for the pair of countries captured by the dummy than for the typical pair in the sample.

Several notes should be made in order to stress the significance of our results and to suggest future research. First, due to data availability, specially as far as time series are concerned, sticky prices and nominal/real rigidities in local markets could not be measured for a relevant subsample. Second, we do not explicitly control for endogeneity, especially, as far as the possible impact of real exchange rate volatility on trade intensity. Nevertheless, the scope of our analysis is not that of RER volatility determination—in which case endogeneity and simultaneous equations problems should be dealt with—but that of determining significant statistical correlation in order to make assessments on dollarization versus a common currency area as policy options.

Table 10.2 presents estimates of the determinants of real exchange rate volatility for the decades of the analysis, adding dummies for the within-region and US dollar pairs.[28] As can be verified, the higher the degree of asymmetry of output shocks, the higher is bilateral real exchange rate volatility, and the estimates are highly significant, regardless of the decade considered. Second, the more dissimilar the export base is, the higher the exchange rate volatility is, and this variable gains in significance in the 1980s and 1990s. As to the intensity of bilateral trade, as expected, it is negatively associated with the level of exchange rate volatility, significantly so in the 1970s and 1990s. The fourth and last explanatory variable, the size of the economies, has a less clear pattern of association with real exchange rate volatility: whereas larger countries tend to display higher bilateral real exchange volatility in the 1970s and 1990s, the opposite holds for the 1980s.[29] The goodness of fit of the OLS regressions shows that the fit improves over time and is substantially higher in the 1990s than in the 1970s. The sign and significance of the regional dummies tell us how much higher (or lower) is the real exchange rate volatility for each type of country pair, after controlling for its four determinants.[30] East Asia and Europe come out with negative coefficients, indicating lower RER volatility than country characteristics alone would predict. The coefficient on the Central American dummy is negative for the 1970s but positive for the other decades, while South America's coefficient is negative in the 1980s and positive otherwise.[31]

Table 10.3
Determinants of bilateral RER volatility: Regional interactions with determinants

	Within-region				Against US dollar			
	All decades (1)	1970s (2)	1980s (3)	1990s (4)	All decades (5)	1970s (6)	1980s (7)	1990s (8)
Asymmetry of output shocks	1.782**	0.701**	3.155**	1.492**	1.771**	0.666**	3.197**	1.436**
	(7.03)	(4.28)	(5.03)	(8.73)	(6.80)	(4.03)	(4.98)	(8.24)
East Asia	−3.987**	−1.939**	−4.461**	−1.254**	−4.196**	−1.220*	−4.854**	−1.271**
	(−7.02)	(−2.54)	(−4.24)	(−3.64)	(−7.89)	(−1.73)	(−4.70)	(−4.22)
Europe	−0.378	0.062	−2.802**	−0.401	−0.502	0.136	−1.194	−0.125
	(−0.70)	(0.21)	(−3.22)	(−0.91)	(−0.97)	(0.47)	(−1.08)	(−0.29)
Central America	2.311	−0.518**	25.980**	4.224*	1.613	−0.409**	22.319**	4.993**
	(0.83)	(−2.94)	(5.34)	(1.66)	(0.77)	(−2.41)	(6.66)	(2.53)
South America	−0.491	1.861**	−2.192**	0.716	−0.178	2.630**	−2.091**	1.247**
	(−1.04)	(4.27)	(−2.44)	(1.40)	(−0.39)	(6.28)	(−2.40)	(2.63)
Dissimilarity of exports	0.004**	0.000	0.009**	0.002**	0.004**	0.000	0.009**	0.002**
	(2.95)	(0.23)	(2.53)	(3.28)	(2.84)	(−0.38)	(2.62)	(3.16)
East Asia	0.000	0.001	−0.007	−0.002*	0.000	0.003**	−0.010**	−0.002*
	(0.18)	(0.44)	(−1.32)	(−1.68)	(−0.17)	(1.61)	(−2.08)	(−1.88)
Europe	−0.006**	0.001	−0.015**	−0.004**	−0.008**	0.002	−0.018**	−0.004**
	(−2.88)	(0.95)	(−4.36)	(−2.58)	(−3.57)	(1.07)	(−4.27)	(−3.17)
Central America	0.000	−0.001	−0.130	−0.005	0.033	−0.003**	0.049**	−0.001
	(0.001)	(−0.23)	(−1.12)	(−0.43)	(1.60)	(−1.81)	(2.60)	(−0.09)
South America	−0.004*	−0.005	−0.008*	−0.002	−0.005**	−0.004	−0.010**	−0.004*
	(−1.74)	(−1.51)	(−1.67)	(−0.76)	(−2.32)	(−1.30)	(−2.04)	(−1.68)

Intensity of trade	−0.010**	−0.015**	−0.008**	−0.008**	−0.010**	−0.017**	−0.004	−0.009**
	(−5.26)	(−5.65)	(−2.08)	(−6.24)	(−2.86)	(−5.22)	(−0.43)	(−4.98)
East Asia	0.006**	0.010**	0.005	0.008**	0.006	0.011**	0.001	0.008**
	(2.15)	(3.27)	(0.73)	(5.66)	(1.57)	(3.17)	(0.05)	(3.80)
Europe	0.007**	0.013**	0.005	0.006**	0.006	0.015**	−0.001	0.007**
	(2.65)	(4.22)	(1.28)	(3.29)	(1.44)	(4.18)	(−0.10)	(2.94)
Central America	−0.194*	0.014**	−0.373**	−0.055	−0.101**	0.014**	−0.061	−0.009
	(−1.93)	(3.22)	(−2.90)	(−1.41)	(−2.40)	(3.92)	(−1.21)	(−0.69)
South America	0.030*	0.116**	0.022**	0.007	0.001	0.002	0.004	0.002
	(1.80)	(3.69)	(2.64)	(0.46)	(0.18)	(0.12)	(0.29)	(0.52)
Economic size	−0.004	0.012**	0.028**	0.009**	−0.004	0.012**	−0.030**	0.010**
	(−1.14)	(4.25)	(−3.22)	(5.52)	(−1.33)	(4.21)	(−3.53)	(5.98)
East Asia	0.003**	0.002*	0.006*	0.000	0.003**	0.000	0.009**	0.000
	(2.44)	(1.63)	(1.84)	(−0.39)	(3.16)	(−0.13)	(2.80)	(−0.36)
Europe	0.000	−0.003**	0.005**	−0.001	0.001	−0.004**	0.005**	0.000
	(−0.22)	(−4.65)	(2.49)	(−1.06)	(0.77)	(−4.90)	(2.58)	(−1.01)
Central America	0.010	−0.001	−0.002	0.003	0.001	−0.001	−0.041**	−0.001
	(1.01)	(−1.28)	(−0.08)	(0.74)	(0.15)	(−1.23)	(−4.77)	(−0.56)
South America	0.003**	0.002	0.007**	0.000	0.004**	0.001	0.008**	0.000
	(2.26)	(0.94)	(2.04)	(0.22)	(2.49)	(0.46)	(2.48)	(−0.03)
Year dummies	Yes	—	—	—	—	—	—	—
Number of observations	2223	741	741	741	741	741	741	741
R^2	0.21	0.21	0.22	0.32	0.21	0.20	0.24	0.32

Note: See appendix A for data description. In parenthesis, we report t-statistics using heteroskedastic-consistent standard errors. ** indicates statistically significant at the 1 percent level and * statistically significant at the 5 percent level. All specifications include a constant, not reported for reason of parsimony. In columns 1 through 4 region dummies correspond to observations where both countries belong to the designated region; in columns 5 through 8 region dummies refer to bilateral observations where one country belongs to the region and the other is the Untied States. Region names under explanatory variables refer to the interaction between the explanatory variable immediately above and the region dummy.

In table 10.3, columns 1 through 4, we add interactions of each of the regional dummies with the four basic explanatory variables. For example, the asymmetry of output shocks is entered directly and interacted with each of the four regional dummies.[32] The results are to be interpreted so that the coefficient on the asymmetry of output shocks is the sum of the average effect for the sample (first coefficient reported) and its interaction with the respective region dummy.[33] We can verify that for East Asia, an increase in the asymmetry of shocks actually tends to decrease RER volatility. Central America, on the other hand, experiences greater increases in volatility with changes in the asymmetry of output shocks.[34] As for export dissimilarity, there are few differences in its impact across regions and decades. The intensity of bilateral trade has a greater impact on the decrease of RER volatility in Central America than in other regions.

In columns 5 through 8 of table 10.3 we turn to the determinants of bilateral real exchange rate volatility versus the US dollar. Results parallel those in the first four columns of table 10.3. The asymmetry of output shocks in East Asia is actually negatively related to the bilateral RER volatility versus the dollar, while the opposite holds for Central America in the 1980s and 1990s. In sum, asymmetry is a much more important determinant of volatility vis-à-vis the dollar for Central American countries than for the typical pair of countries in the sample. Export dissimilarity is less important in explaining the volatility of European and South American currencies versus the dollar, particularly in the 1980s.

Summing up, we have statistically verified that East Asia and Europe have lower within region volatility and volatility vis-à-vis the dollar than for the representative country in the sample, and these two regions experience a decrease in the levels of RER volatility over time. Central and South America, on the other hand, have periods with lower and higher than predicted levels of volatility. As to the determinants of exchange rate volatility, we find that the asymmetry of output shocks is less important for East Asia than for other regions, while export dissimilarity is less important for Europe and South America. Bilateral trade integration seems to be a particularly important factor in determining exchange rate volatility in Central America. These results hold for both within-region RER volatility and volatility with respect to the US dollar. They suggest that exchange rate arrangements comprising Central American countries should emphasize trade integration, while export dissimilarity is not key for South American countries.

10.4 Conclusion

In this chapter we conducted an empirical examination of the option of dollarization as an alternative to regional currency unification, taking into account the recent literature on the determinants of real exchange rate variability. We presented bilateral indicators of economic integration to assess the relative attractiveness of the two options for East Asia, Central America, and South America. The experience of the European Union is used as a benchmark, given that region's recent option for a regional currency area. We studied the determinants of real exchange rate volatility within each of these regions and between each region and the United States. This way we are able, for the first time, to analyze the degree of within region integration as compared to the degree of integration with the US economy, suggesting which of the two options—dollarization or regional currency area—is most advisable on empirical grounds. On the other hand, it should be noted that in this chapter we did not discuss the issue of credibility nor the costs of setting up the institutions for the two policy options. We acknowledge the relevance of these issues. They lie beyond the scope of our analysis and, as we have pointed out, are extensively dealt with in the literature.

Real exchange rate volatility is lowest for the European Union and highest for South America, with East Asia experiencing a decrease in volatility over time while Central America experienced an increase. With the exception of Europe, all regions experience lower bilateral exchange rate volatility with the United States than with their regional partners. Europe is also, by far, the region with the lowest within-region output shock asymmetry, and the only—with East Asia in the 1990s—for which it is lower than with the United States. Export dissimilarity is lowest for Central America and then for Europe, with East Asia experiencing a substantial decrease since the 1970s. As to the depth of bilateral trade integration, East Asia and then Europe are the most integrated regions, but Europe again stands out as the only region with average within-region trade intensity levels that are higher than average trade intensity with the United States. In sum, as might be expected, Europe stands out as the most deeply integrated region and European countries are more closely integrated within themselves than with the United States. Out of the other three regions, and since the 1970s, East Asia made substantial progress in all indicators of regional integration. In the 1990s Asian intra-regional indicators closely approach those of Europe. As to Central America and South America, these regions stand out for their high levels of integration relative to the United States, higher than the level of integration with their respective regional partners. Both Latin American regions experienced large swings in the degree of integration, with a general decrease in the 1980s and again an increase in the 1990s.

An analysis of the determinants of real exchange rate volatility across regions and time shows that greater asymmetry in output shocks or export patterns and lower levels of bilateral trade are associated with larger fluctuations in real exchange rates. The size of the economy affects exchange rate volatility in a less straightforward way, though there is evidence that smaller countries experience higher exchange rate volatility. When regional dummies are used in addition to the usual determinants of exchange rate volatility, we verify that Europe and East Asia have lower than expected within-region volatility, while Central and South America tend to have higher than expected volatility. The same pattern emerges when we use dummies for each region in relation with the United States.

We find evidence that the asymmetry of output shocks is more important for Central America and less for East Asia than for the typical sample country, and export dissimilarity is less important a factor in determining exchange rate volatility for European countries.

We derive several important messages from our empirical results. First, currency union in Europe was a natural choice given the high degree of intra-regional integration. Second, East Asia has progressively approached European levels of integration, though currency union is not currently an active policy option. Third, Central and South America, display low levels of regional integration, namely relative to the levels of integration with the US economy. Finally, there is evidence that the determinants of real exchange rate volatility differ between regions so that different issues need to be addressed if efforts at currency unification are to be successful. Moreover we find evidence of substantial heterogeneity as to the effects of different factors on real exchange rate volatility, suggesting previous studies in the literature have ignored an important dimension of country experience.

Appendix A: Data

The data set uses information for 39 countries for the period 1970 to 1997. The countries in the sample are the following:

Europe: Belgium-Luxembourg, Denmark, France, Germany, Greece, Ireland, Italy, Netherlands, Portugal, Spain, and the United Kingdom. *Asia*: Hong Kong, Indonesia, Korea, Japan, Malaysia, Philippines, Singapore, and Thailand. *South America*: Argentina, Bolivia, Brazil, Chile, Colombia, Ecuador, Mexico, Peru, Paraguay, Uruguay, and Venezuela. *Central America*: Costa Rica, El Salvador, Guatemala, Honduras, and Nicaragua. *Nafta*: Canada, Mexico, and the United States.

The time periods considered are 1970 to 1979, 1980 to 1989, 1990 to 1997, and 1970 to 1997. In the case of export dissimilarity, trade intensity and country size variables, the last two periods are actually 1990 to 1996 and 1970 to 1996. The variables used in the regression analysis are constructed as follows:

Real Exchange Rate Volatility ($SD(\Delta e_{ij})$)
This variable is calculated as the standard deviation, over each period of time, of the change in the log of the bilateral real exchange rate for countries i and j. The real exchange rate is constructed using consumer price indexes and nominal exchange rate data from the IFS.

Asymmetry of Output Shocks ($SD(\Delta y_i - \Delta y_j)$)
This variable is calculated as the standard deviation, over each period of time, of the difference in the shocks to countries i and j. Output shocks for each country are calculated as annual change in the log of real GDP. The source for real GDP data is the IFS series of GDP. Missing values were completed with national sources or the World Development Indicators from the World Bank.

Dissimilarity of Exports ($DISSIMILARITY_{ij}$)
This variable is calculated adding up, for the eight first SITC codes at one-digit level, the absolute value of the difference between countries i and j of the export shares for each category. Code 9, "Not elsewhere classified, gold and military equipment," was removed from total exports, since in many cases it leads to errors given the size of the items not elsewhere classified. Previous studies in the literature have computed this measure based on four categories only. The mean is

then taken over a period of time. Export shares by SITC are calculated using a combined data set obtained from merging the Feenstra, Lipsey, Bowen data set (1970 to 1992) and the Statistics of Canada data set (1980 to 1996).

Intensity of Trade ($TRADE_{ij}$)

This variable is calculated as the mean, over each period of time, of the average of the two bilateral-export-to-GDP ratios for each pair of countries i and j, that is,

$$\frac{(X_{ij}/GDP_i) + (X_{ji}/GDP_j)}{2}.$$

Bilateral export data come from the data set used for dissimilarity of exports, while GDP data come from World Development Indicators 1998.

Economic Size ($SIZE_{ij}$)

This variable is calculated as the mean, over each period of time, of the average of the GDPs of countries i and j (expressed in logs). The GDP data are in constant dollars and come from the World Development Indicators 1998. For Germany prior to the unification, the data come from IFS.

Notes

This chapter is an extended version of the article "Regional currencies versus dollarization: Options for Asia and the Americas," published in the *Journal of Policy Reform*, March 2003, vol. 6(1), pp. 35–49.

1. The recent increase in capital mobility has brought the benefits of intermediate exchange rate systems into question. Obstfeld and Rogoff (1995) illustrate the difficulties for fixed exchange regimes in a world of high capital mobility, namely the low credibility of central banks under speculative attacks. Eichengreen and Masson (1998) suggest that only very hard pegs and managed floats are likely to survive high levels of capital mobility.

2. See *The Economist* (2002). On the other hand, Larraín and Velasco (2001, 2002) make the case for floating in emerging economies.

3. Micco et al. (2002) have recently uncovered substantial trade effects following the creation of the EMU and the introduction of the Euro.

4. Frankel pointed out that "dollarization probably is a good idea for some countries in Latin America, particularly countries that are quite small and open, let's say, some in Central America." See IMF (1998).

5. This possibility was first raised in Young (1965) and Triffin (1970), the first of which sketches a program for regional monetary unification. On the other hand, Kafka (1973) argued against a currency area in the region, given the poor development of financial institutions and the need to further stabilize fiscal policy choices. Kafka (1973) stated clearly that "Latin America is obviously not an optimum currency area either now or for the foreseeable future. The same is true of its subdivisions, like the Latin American Free Trade Agreement (LAFTA) and, it seems, even the Central American Common Market (CACM). In fact, many Latin American countries are only gradually acquiring the characteristics of optimum currency areas." More recently García, Larraín and Tavares (2001) have assessed the prospects for a common currency in Central America.

6. Bayoumi and Eichengreen (1998) argue that capital mobility may substitute for lack of labor mobility. This is correct only under restrictive conditions. In general, the labor and capital mobility are both necessary.

7. These costs are explicitly mentioned as a benefit of currency union in Mundell (1961), and they were highlighted in the buildup to monetary union in Europe.

8. The policy we refer to in the current paper is that of official dollarization, the monetary regime in which a country formally relinquishes the issue of domestic notes and coins and adopts the dollar as the national currency.

9. Baliño et al. (1999) estimate that deposits in US dollars exceeded 30 percent of broad money in 18 countries, while in 34 others these deposits are significant, at an average level of 16 percent. In another study, Porter and Judson (1996) estimate that 55 to 70 percent of the total amount of dollars issued are held by foreigners, mostly in Latin America and Russia.

10. In Ecuador dollarization was initiated in January 2000 by fixing the local currency to the US dollar, and became full-fledged by September of the same year. The Salvadoran currency began to be phased out in January 2001.

11. These are the Marshall Islands, Micronesia, Palau, Pitcairn Island, Turks and Caicos, and the UK Virgin Islands—all with populations below 125,000.

12. See Larraín and Velasco (2001) for a discussion of these issues.

13. This is further compounded when a dollarized country trades a lot with a non-dollarized neighbor, as the case of Brazil and Argentina illustrates. When Brazil opted for devaluation it forced a dramatic change in the competitiveness of Argentinean exports in Brazil, certainly adding to the Argentinean crisis.

14. See Calvo (1999). For the typical developing economy under responsible monetary management, this may amount to 1 to 2 percent of GDP. Proposals to share the seigniorage between the dollarized economy and the US require the critical acceptance of the United States, which is unlikely given the political overtones of the issue.

15. See Eichengreen and Masson (1998) for a recent survey.

16. The argument goes back to McKinnon (1963) and the optimal currency area theory: major trading partners should keep fixed exchange rates since continuous adjustments of parity are costly, arbitrarily influencing the terms of trade. On the other hand, economies that are more open tend to be vulnerable to external shocks and, in the absence of price flexibility, more dependent on nominal exchange rate adjustments to pursue real adjustments.

17. Kenen (1969) emphasizes this point. Bofinger (1994) states that countries with a more diverse production and export base are less likely to require bilateral exchange rate adjustments.

18. The empirical prediction is thus that the bilateral real exchange rate volatility is lower for pairs of countries whose output shocks are strongly correlated.

19. Other authors have criticized the credibility argument. Tornell and Velasco (1995) argue that flexible exchange rate regimes may actually provide a higher degree of macroeconomic discipline. Whether fixed exchange rates provide more fiscal discipline depends on the government's rate of discount. If only the short term matters for the government, a flexible exchange rate regime may actually provide more discipline. Westbrook and Willet (1999) criticize the credibility argument on different grounds. First, traditional pegs do not always provide sufficient credibility and more credible institutional arrangements may be necessary. Second, pegging to a currency that does not fulfill the optimum currency area criteria would not be a credible move in itself.

20. Lopes and Tavares (2004) assess the relative contributions of currency and trade agreements to bilateral trade intensity. These authors instrument simultaneously for the emergence of both types of bilateral agreement and find no evidence that currency agreements—pegs, bands, or currency unions—matter for bilateral trade, once the impact of trade agreements is accounted for.

21. Currency unions have other dynamic effects. Fatàs (1997) argues that currency unification has opposing effects on the correlation of shocks across countries: while increased regional specialization decreases output shock correlation, the higher intensity of demand linkages and intra-industry trade increases shock correlation. Frankel and Rose (1996a, b) have shown that trade integration and the correlation of country business cycles are mutually reinforcing, whereas Bayoumi and Eichengreen (1998) present evidence that more trade integration leads to lower exchange rate variability. On the labor market front, Marsden (1992) argues that regional integration and the parallel product market integration decrease the market power of firms so that labor markets become more responsive to short-term conditions. The idea is that firms with no market power cannot cushion short-term fluctuations in profitability so that wages have to adjust immediately and thus labor markets respond more directly to economic shocks.

22. See Chang and Velasco (2002), Larrain and Velasco (2001), and Mundell (1997).

23. It is often recommended that small open economies peg their currencies to the currency of the main trading partner. See IMF (1998). Eichengreen and Masson (1998) state that "small countries that trade extensively with large neighbors and/or have large tourism receipts benefit little from an independent monetary policy." Small countries may benefit relatively more from the reduction in transaction costs and uncertainty, as the common currency is a way to bypass the thinness of local exchange markets, avoiding substantial fluctuations.

24. The sample average by indicator and decade and the sample average for bilateral indicators with the US are also reported as benchmarks.

25. Interestingly Central America displayed levels of real exchange variability in the 1970s—a period of substantial efforts toward regional integration—that are actually lower than Europe's for the same decade.

26. Since we are measuring asymmetry of output shocks in terms of decade averages, the significant differences shown in the table remain under alternative measurements of

shocks (e.g., standard deviation from filters) given that averages of ten years show little dispersion in general.

27. In both regions significant macroeconomic imbalances in the 1980s led to lower levels of regional integration and integration versus the US economy in that decade. That has been only partially reversed in the 1990s.

28. The breakdown of the Bretton-Woods monetary system in the early 1970s could unduly influence the results. We reran the specifications in table 10.2 by excluding the first decade and found that the results did not change singificantly.

29. Developing countries—especially in South and Central America—experienced a substantial increase in exchange fluctuations in the 1980s. Since these countries are comparatively small in terms of GDP, the negative coefficient for size in the 1980s may just be capturing the lower volatility of currencies in developed countries of North America and Western Europe.

30. In other words, and assuming the econometric model is appropriately specified, how much two countries in a given region see their bilateral RER volatility increase due to the fact that they are in the same region. The regional dummy measures the impact of all time-unvarying regional characteristics, policy or otherwise, that affect RER volatility.

31. This may seem puzzling given the high degree of RER volatility in South America in the 1980s, the highest in the sample as can be verified in table 10.1. The explanation resides in the fact that the coefficients on the explanatory variables in the 1980s are larger than the same coefficients in the 1970s and 1990s. As South American countries had higher regional levels of output shock asymmetry and export dissimilarity and lower levels of regional trade integration, the higher RER volatility for South America is accounted for by the explanatory variables rather than the regional dummy.

32. The presence in the sample of the United States, Mexico, and Canada assures that there will be no perfect collinearity between these variables.

33. The region names under each explanatory variable name refer to the respective interaction.

34. The US embargo on Nicaragua, with the resulting dramatic drop in output and hyperinflation, accounts in great part for this result.

References

Balino, T., A. Bennett, and E. Borenzstein. 1999. Monetary policy in dollarized economies. IMF Occasional Paper 171, Washington, DC.

Bayoumi, T., and B. Eichengreen. 1998. Exchange rate volatility and intervention: Implications of the theory optimum currency areas. *Journal of International Economics* 45(2): 191–209.

Bayoumi, T., and P. Mauro. 1999. The suitability of ASEAN for a regional currency agreement. IMF Working Paper. Washington, DC.

Bofinger, P. 1994. Is Europe an optimal currency area? In A. Steinherr. ed., *30 Years of European Monetary Integration*, London: Longman.

Chang, R., and A. Velasco. 2002. Dollarization: Analytical issues. NBER Working Paper 8838.

The Economist. 2002. El Salvador learns to love the Greenback. September 28, pp. 34–35.

Eichengreen, B. 1998. Does Mercosur need a single currency? NBER Working Paper 6821.

Eichengreen, B., and P. Masson. 1998. Exit strategies: Policy options for countries seeking greater exchange rate flexibility. IMF Occasional Paper 168. Washington, DC.

Fatás, A. 1997. EMU: Countries or regions? Lessons from the EMS experience. *European Economic Review* 41: 3–5.

Frankel, J. A., and A. Rose. 1998. The endogeneity of the optimum currency area criteria. *Economic Journal* 108 (449): 1009–25.

Frankel, J., and A. Rose. 1996. Economic structure and the decision to adopt a common currency. Working Paper C96/073. University of California, Berkeley, Center for International and Development Economics Research (CIDER).

García-López, C., F. Larraín, and J. Tavares. 2001. Exchange Rate Regimes: Assessing Central Americas's options. In F. Larraín, ed., *Economic Development in Central America*, vol. 1. Cambridge: Harvard University Press.

IMF Economic Forum. 1998. Dollarization: Fad or future for Latin America. Available online at: *http://www.imf.org/external/np/tr/1999/TR990624.htm.* Washington, DC.

Kafka, A. 1973. Optimum currency areas and Latin America. In H. G. Johnson and A. K. Swoboda, eds., *The Economics of Common Currencies. Proceedings of the Madrid Conference on Optimum Currency Areas.* Cambridge: Harvard University Press.

Kenen, P. 1969. The theory of optimum currency areas: An eclectic view. In P. Kenen, ed., *Exchange Rates and the Monetary System: Selected Essays of Peter B. Kenen. Economists of the Twentieth Century Series.* Aldershot: Elgar.

Larraín, F., and A. Velasco. 2001. Exchange-rate policy in emerging market economies: The case for floating. *Princeton Essays in International Finance* 224 (December).

Larraín, F., and A. Velasco. 2002. How should emerging economies float their currencies? *The Economics of Transition* 10 (2): 365–92.

Lopes, J., and J. Tavares. 2004. Trade areas versus currency agreements: Which causes what to economies? Mimeo. Universidade Nova de Lisboa.

Marsden, D. 1992. European integration and the integration of European labour markets. *Labour* 6(1): 3–35.

McKinnon, R. 1963. Optimum currency areas. *American Economic Review* 53(4): 717–25.

Micco, A., E. Stein, and G. Ordoñez. 2002. The currency union effect on trade: Early evidence from the European Union. Mimeo. Inter-American Development Bank.

Mundell, R. 1961. A theory of optimum currency areas. *American Economic Review* 51(4): 509–17.

Mundell, R. 1997. Optimum currency areas. Luncheon speech presented at the Conference on Optimum Currency Areas. Tel-Aviv University. December 5, 1997.

Obstfeld, M., and K. Rogoff. 1995. The mirage of fixed exchange rates. *Journal of Economic Perspectives* 9(4): 73–96.

Porter, R., and R. Judson. 1996. The location of U.S. currency: How much is abroad? *Federal Reserve Bulletin* 82 (October): 883–903.

Tornell, A., and A. Velasco. 1995. Fixed versus flexible exchange rates: Which provides more fiscal discipline? NBER Working Paper 5108.

Triffin, R. 1970. Proyecto para un Fondo Centroamericano de Estabilización. *Revista del Banco Hipotecario de El Salvador*, San Salvador 5(2): 167–82.

Westbrook, J., and T. Willet. 1999. Exchange rates as nominal anchors: An overview of the issues. In R. J. Sweeney, C. G. Wihlborg, and T. Willett, eds., *Exchange-Rate Policies for Emerging Market Economies: Political Economy of Global Interdependence*. Colorado: Westview Press.

Young, J. 1965. Central American Monetary Union, Guatemala. US Department of State, Agency for International Development, Regional Office, Central American and Panama Affairs.

11

An Output Perspective on a Northeast Asia Currency Union

Yin-Wong Cheung and Jude Yuen

11.1 Introduction

The 1997 financial crisis highlights the vulnerability of Asian countries as a group to one country's financial instability. Since then various initiatives and plans on fostering monetary and financial cooperation in the region have been proposed to forestall financial crises. The proposals include improved dialogues, the establishment of central bank swap arrangements (the Chiang Mai Initiative), the idea of an Asian monetary fund, the possibility that currencies collectively peg to the US dollar or a basket of currencies, the creation of an Asian currency unit, and the formation of a currency union.[1] These discussions generate some interests in assessing whether the Asian countries meet the preconditions of an optimum currency area and are suitable for forming a currency union.[2]

This chapter examines the prospect of creating a currency union that consists of China, Japan, and Korea. The formation of a currency union requires deep commitments from its member countries. For instance, member countries have to relinquish their monetary autonomy to use a common single currency. Because China, Japan, and Korea are the three largest economies in East Asia, it is hard to perceive that an effective coordination scheme in the region does not involve these three countries. In Europe the two largest countries, France and Germany, are usually credited for the formation of European monetary union and the launch of the single currency, euro. The Franco–German partnership is deemed to be pivotal for the migration toward the European currency union.[3] Given the European experience, we focus the suitability of an Asian currency union that comprises China, Japan, and Korea.

The standard literature lists a few criteria for countries to constitute an optimum currency area.[4] Business cycle synchronization is one of the major criteria used to evaluate the desirability of a common currency.[5] When business cycles across countries are synchronous, the cost of using a single currency is reduced because there is less need for asymmetric monetary policy responses to common shocks, ceteris paribus. On the other hand, currency union may not be an optimal monetary arrangement when the countries display asynchronous business cycles.[6]

In the literature the contemporaneous correlation of output shocks is commonly used to gauge the degree of business cycle synchronization. Several approaches have been used to derive output shocks for correlation calculation. The results, however, are sensitive to the choice of detrending methods.[7] Bayoumi and Eichengreen (1994) popularize the use of the Blanchard and Quah (1989) decomposition method to measure the size and correlation of output shocks and assert that the supply shock correlation is the relevant measure to evaluate the output shock asymmetry among countries.

Contemporaneous correlation, however, does not necessarily provide a complete picture. The effects of shocks on economies crucially depend on the transmission mechanism within and across them. Divergent monetary or exchange rate policies may deem necessary even in the presence of a high correlation of shocks if the transmission mechanisms are sufficiently different across the countries. On the other hand, a low contemporaneous shock correlation does not exclude the possibility that the economies are in similar phases of a business cycle and do not require different monetary or exchange rate policies. Thus we adopt a *complementary* approach and directly examine comovement patterns of national outputs.

The current exercise assesses output synchronization at both long-run and short-run horizons. First, we investigate whether the national output data tend to move together in the long run. If national output data are drifting apart in the long run, it is impracticable, if not impossible, to pursue a common policy to manage these economies. Thus long-run output co-movement is a basic condition for currency union discussion. Second, we determine whether the countries share short-run cyclical business cycles. After all, most monetary policies are devised to manage transitory shocks. If the countries under consideration share long-run growth trends and short-run economic fluctuations, then a single common currency is a feasible proposition.

The Johansen cointegration approach is used to examine the output comovement pattern. A currency union has implications for interactions among all its member countries that go beyond bilateral relationships. In contrast with the usual bilateral setting embedded in most, if not all, recent studies on currency unions, the cointegration model is a multivariate framework that incorporates interactions between all data series in assessing the output co-movement pattern. Further the error correction specification derived from a cointegration model provides a coherent structure to study output comovements in the long run, effects of deviations from the long-run relationship on short-run variations, and output interactions in the short run. The structure is flexible enough to accommodate various types of data dynamics in the analysis.

The presence of contemporaneous output co-movement is the relevant information when countries have similar and simultaneous responses to a common shock. However, because of structural or institutional differences, countries can display different initial responses to a common shock even though they react similarly to the shock after an initial phase. Thus, in studying short-run cyclical cycles, we consider both "common feature" and "codependence" business cycles—the former type of common business cycles requires countries to be in similar positions throughout a cycle, and the latter type allows countries to behave differently in the initial phase but to be in similar cyclical phases after some initial period. The inclusion of co-dependent business cycles, in addition to common feature ones, alleviates the possibility of understating the degree of output symmetry between countries and the desirability of a currency union.

To offer further insight into the prospect of a currency union in Asia, we quantify the individual countries' potential output losses of establishing one. Since the ideal preconditions of a currency union are rarely fulfilled, there is always a cost for a country to relinquish policy autonomy and join a currency union. The willingness to join is undoubtedly affected by potential costs. Thus, in addition to business cycle synchronization, it is instructive to estimate the individual countries' potential costs of joining a currency union. It is expected that the output cost estimate depends on the characterization of an economy and of shocks affecting it. In this exercise we evaluate output losses using (1) the model in Ghosh and Wolf (1994) to characterize the economy, (2) shocks estimated by three different techniques, and (3) two policy objectives.

The chapter is organized as follows: A brief discussion of the economic interactions, including trade and investment, among the three

Northeast Asia countries is given in the next section. Section 11.3 offers some preliminary analyses on the real per capita GDP data from China, Japan, and Korea. Patterns of output co-movement are studied in section 11.4. The Johansen cointegration test is used to determine the empirical long-run relationship between the output data and the associated error correction model is used to study the links between the long-run and short-run interactions. In the same section, we also investigate the presence of common business cycles using the common feature and codependence tests. Section 11.5 evaluates the output costs of forming a currency union. Using a macro model, the output losses of individual countries and of the three countries as a group are calculated under different shock-identifying schemes and policy objectives. Some concluding remarks are given in section 11.6.

11.2   Recent Developments

What is the prospect of a Northeast Asia economic bloc? As recent as the turn of the millennium, China, Japan, and Korea were not members of any regional economic or trade establishments. Indeed, the discussion on the integration among China, Japan, and Korea is quite recent and scant. Japan and Korea operated mostly within the framework of the General Agreement on Tariffs and Trade and the succeeding World Trade Organization to formulate their trade policies. China only joined the World Trade Organization in December 2001. However, the desire for improved coordination after the 1997 financial crisis offers an incentive for the three Northeast Asian countries—China, Japan, and Korea to cooperate and deepen integration.

   Although a currency union is unlikely to happen immediately, the prospect of enhancing integration among the three countries has drawn certain interest among policy makers and think tanks. For instance, in 2001 the Japanese Cabinet Office published a study that, among other things, examined the prospect of forming a free-trade area encompassing China, Japan, and Korea.[8] The study suggested that while a China–Japan–Korea free-trade area offers a potentially larger economic benefit, a two-country Japan–Korea free-trade area might entail a less painful adjustment process and thus "might be considered as a first step toward a larger free-trade area."[9]

   Possibly the Japanese Cabinet Office's inquiry on a free-trade area consisting of China, Japan, and Korea was a consequence of an initiative that was proposed in November 1999 by officials from these three countries to investigate the prospects of economic cooperation. In November 2000 three research organizations—the Development Research Center of the State Council of China, the National Institute of Research Advancement of Japan, and the Korea Institute for International Economic Policy—formally launched a joint research program on strengthening economic cooperation among China, Japan, and Korea. In the first three years the joint research program focused on trade facilitation (2001), mutual investment among the three countries (2002), and finally, on the economic effects of such a free-trade area among China, Japan, and Korea (2003).[10]

The pace of integration among these three countries was quite fast in recent years. Specifically, the volume of trade among them has experienced astonishing growth along with, albeit slowly, changes in institutional arrangements. With China's WTO accession, further integration is widely anticipated.

As shown in table 11.1, trade among China, Japan, and Korea increased at a faster rate than world trade.[11] Over the last decade the average annual growth rate of the bilateral trade was 14 percent between China and Japan and is 58 percent between China and Korea. In

Table 11.1
China's trade with selected economies (US$mil)

	Year	Japan	Korea
A. Exports	1991	10,252	2,179
	2002	48,483	15,508
Proportion of China's exports	1991	0.142	0.030
	2002	0.149	0.048
Average annual growth rate	1991–2002	13.85	57.06
B. Imports	1991	10,032	1,066
	2002	53,489	28,581
Proportion of China's imports	1991	0.157	0.017
	2002	0.181	0.097
Average annual growth rate	1991–2002	14.41	62.55
C. Total trade with China	1991	20,284	3,245
	2002	101,972	44,089
Proportion of China's trade	1991	0.149	0.024
	2002	0.164	0.071
Average annual growth rate	1991–2002	13.69	57.92

Note: Panel A gives China's exports to Japan and Korea. It also gives these exports as proportions of China's total exports and the average annual growth rates of these exports. Similar information for imports and for total trade is provided in panel B and panel C.

contrast, the world trade grew at an average annual rate of 5.68 percent from 1991 to 2002. Clearly, the trade volume between China and these two countries was nontrivial—the total trade between China and these two countries accounted for 1.16 percent of world trade in 2002. If the trade between Japan and Korea is included, then the trade among these three countries accounted for 1.45 percent of world trade.

After normalizing their diplomatic relationship in 1992, Korea and China have enjoyed rapid growth in bilateral trade—the average annual growth rate exceeded 57 percent. China even overtook the United States as Korea's largest export market in 2003. Japan, on the other hand, was China's large trading partner and accounted for 16.4 percent of China's trade in 2002. The figures underscore the trading intensity between the three Northeast Asian countries. Indeed, China traded more with the other two Northeast Asian countries than with the other two Greater China economies, namely Hong Kong and Taiwan.

The Japanese and Korean foreign direct investments in China were presented in table 11.2. Again, the Japanese and Korean investments in China increased substantially between 1991 and 2002. The average growth rate of investment in China was 23 percent for Japan and 48 percent for Korea. If one excludes Hong Kong and Taiwan, which are known to provide the lion share of foreign direct investment in China, Japan and Korea are two main foreign investors in China.

Both tables 11.1 and 11.2 suggest that China, Japan, and Korea have extensive trade and investment interactions. The trend is likely to persist in the near future. The extensive interactions among these countries provides a good foundation for advancing integration to a higher level.

Table 11.2
Foreign direct investment inflow to China (US$mil)

	Year	Korea	Japan
Inflow to China	1991	119[a]	533
	2002	2721	4190
Proportion of China's FDI	1991	0.01[a]	0.12
	2002	0.05	0.08
Average annual growth rate	1991–2002	48.11[b]	23.14

Note: The foreign direct investment is from Japan and Korea to China.
a. This is the 1992 figure.
b. This is the 1993–2002 figure.

11.3 Data and Preliminary Analyses

The data considered in this study are quarterly real per capita GDPs of China, Japan, and Korea. The data are seasonally adjusted and expressed in logarithms. The sample period is from 1993:IV to 2001:IV. The sample is selected according to the liberalization processes in China and Korea. Specifically, China had a substantially controlled economy before the early 1990s. Extending the data series backward would not yield more information relevant to assessing output integration. The data are retrieved from the CEIC and International Financial Statistics databases. For brevity, the quarterly real per capita GDP data are referred to as GDP or output data henceforth.

As a preliminary analysis, the augmented Dickey-Fuller (ADF) test for a unit root is performed on individual output series. The ADF test is based on the regression equation,

$$\Delta X_{it} = c_i + \tau_i t + \delta_i X_{it-1} + \sum_{j=1}^{p} \alpha_{ij} \Delta X_{it-j} + u_{it}, \tag{1}$$

where X_{it} is the country i's GDP at time t for $i =$ China, Japan, and Korea. Under the unit root hypothesis, $\delta_i = 0$. A trend, a constant, or both, are included if they are significant in the ADF test. The lag parameter (p) is chosen to eliminate serial correlation in the estimated residuals.

The unit root test results of the GDP series and their first differences are reported in table 11.3. The null hypothesis of a unit root is rejected

Table 11.3
Augmented Dickey-Fuller test results

	Levels		First differences	
	Test statistic (lags)	Q(4), Q(8)	Test statistic (lags)	Q(4), Q(8)
China	−2.08 (4)	2.67, 8.87	−8.54* (3)	4.39, 9.04
Japan	−1.56 (3)	0.09, 7.52	−5.14* (2)	0.08, 5.67
Korea	−2.09 (1)	2.70, 9.61	−2.49* (1)	2.44, 4.02

Note: The results of applying the augmented Dickey-Fuller test to the national real per capita GDP data are reported. Lags are selected to remove serial correlation in the estimated residuals and are given in parentheses next to the test statistics. The Box-Ljung statistics based on the first four and first eight serial correlations of the estimated residuals are given under the heading "Q(4) and Q(8)." All the reported Q-statistics are not significant. * indicates significance at the 5 percent level (Cheung and Lai 1995).

not by GDP data but by their first differences. That is, the three output series are difference stationary. The diagnostic Q-statistics indicate that the lag specifications are appropriate, and there is no evidence of serial correlation in the estimated residuals. The inference is consistent with the conventional findings that real per capita GDP data series are unit root processes. Hereafter we treat the GDP series as I(1) processes.

11.4   Common Long-Run and Short-Run Cycles

The I(1) nonstationary property suggests that individual output series tend to drift around without an anchor or steady state. If these output series drift in different directions, then it will be difficult to adopt a common currency and pursue a common monetary policy to manage these economies. In the following subsection, the Johansen (1991) cointegration test is used to test whether these I(1) output series move together in the long run or, technically speaking, whether they have common stochastic trends.

11.4.1   Common Stochastic Trends

The Johansen cointegration test is conducted as follows. Let $\mathbf{X}_t$ be the $n \times 1$ vector containing the three output series ($n = 3$) that can be modeled by a $(p + 1)$th order vector autoregression process:

$$\mathbf{X}_t = \mu + \sum_{i=1}^{p+1} \gamma_i \mathbf{X}_{t-i} + \varepsilon_t, \tag{2}$$

where μ is the intercept term and ε_t is the vector of innovations. The lag parameter p is chosen to set the serial correlation of resulting residuals to zero. The Johansen test statistics are devised from the sample canonical correlations between $\Delta \mathbf{X}_t$ and $\mathbf{X}_{t-p}$, adjusting for all intervening lags. To implement the procedure, we first obtain the least squares residuals from

$$\Delta \mathbf{X}_t = \mu_1 + \sum_{i=1}^{p} \Gamma_i \Delta \mathbf{X}_{t-i} + \varepsilon_{1t}$$

and

$$\mathbf{X}_{t-p} = \mu_2 + \sum_{i=1}^{p} \Gamma_i \Delta \mathbf{X}_{t-i} + \varepsilon_{2t}, \tag{3}$$

where μ_1 and μ_2 are constant vectors. Next we define the matrices $\Omega_{ij} = T^{-1} \sum_t \hat{\varepsilon}_{it} \hat{\varepsilon}'_{jt}$ for $i, j = 1, 2$ and T is the sample size. The Johansen test is based on the eigenvalues, $\lambda_1 \geq \cdots \geq \lambda_n$, of $\Omega_{21} \Omega_{11}^{-1} \Omega_{12}$ with respect to Ω_{22}. λ_i's are the squared canonical correlations between ΔX_t and X_{t-p}, adjusting for all intervening lags. The trace statistic,

$$t_r = -T \sum_{j=r+1}^{n} \ln(1 - \lambda_j), \qquad 0 \leq r \leq n, \tag{4}$$

tests the null hypothesis that there are no more than r cointegrating vectors. For the null hypothesis of r against the alternative of $r+1$ cointegrating vectors, we use the maximum eigenvalue statistic

$$\lambda_{r|r+1} = -T \ln(1 - \lambda_{r+1}). \tag{5}$$

The eigenvectors $v_1, \ldots, v_n$ associated with the eigenvalues $\lambda_1 \geq \cdots \geq \lambda_n$ are the sample estimates of the cointegrating vectors.

The cointegration test results are reported in table 11.4. The lag parameter p is set to 3, which gives insignificant Q-statistics and thus, adequately accounts for the intertemporal dynamics in the data (see table 11.5). Both the trace and maximum eigenvalue statistics reject the hypothesis of no cointegration but not the hypothesis of one cointegrating vector. That is, the output data are cointegrated with one cointegrating vector. The cointegration result implies that even when the individual output series wander randomly over time on their own, they are driven by common stochastic trends and hence have synchronous long-term movements. Despite the differences in output mixes, corporate cultures, and infrastructures, the Johansen test statistics

Table 11.4
Cointegration test results

	Max statistic	Trace statistic
$r = 2$	1.14	1.14
$r = 1$	13.59	14.73
$r = 0$	37.55*	52.28*

Note: The Johansen maximum eigenvalue test and trace test statistics are reported, respectively, under the headings "max statistic" and "trace statistic." The 5 percent level significance is indicated by * (Cheung and Lai 1993). The lag parameter is 3. The estimated cointegrating vector is $(1, 5.39, -2.90)$ with the China coefficient normalized to 1. The chi-square test statistics for the significance of individual cointegrating coefficient estimates are, respectively, 23.32, 20.77, and 33.03. Thus each of the cointegrating coefficient estimates is significant.

Table 11.5
Vector error correction models for output data

	China	Japan	Korea
Constant	0.040*	−0.001	0.004
	(8.729)	(−0.095)	(0.176)
ECT	−0.051*	−0.045	0.123
	(−3.590)	(−1.209)	(1.717)
CH GDP(-1)	−0.696**	−0.192	0.457
	(−4.793)	(−0.500)	(0.623)
CH GDP(-2)	−0.591*	0.069	0.730
	(−4.963)	(0.219)	(1.212)
CH GDP(-3)	−0.597*	−0.195	−0.106
	(−4.475)	(−0.554)	(−0.157)
JP GDP(-1)	0.199**	−0.692*	1.178**
	(1.787)	(−2.359)	(2.094)
JP GDP(-2)	0.079	−0.724*	1.748*
	(0.629)	(−2.178)	(2.745)
JP GDP(-3)	−0.065	−0.314	2.098*
	(−0.491)	(−0.899)	(3.135)
KO GDP(-1)	0.139*	0.225	0.164
	(2.252)	(1.380)	(0.526)
KO GDP(-2)	0.045	0.056	0.018
	(0.773)	(0.366)	(0.062)
KO GDP(-3)	0.000	0.167	−0.558*
	(0.024)	(1.187)	(−2.068)
Adjusted R^2	0.726	0.354	0.513
Q(4)	3.197	1.082	2.267
	(0.525)	(0.897)	(0.687)
Q(8)	5.425	8.672	4.904
	(0.711)	(0.371)	(0.768)

Note: Robust t-statistics are given in parentheses below the parameter estimates. * and ** indicate significant at the 5 and 10 percent levels, respectively. ECT is the error correction term. $Q(p)$ is the Q-statistic calculated from the first p sample autocorrelations with the associated p-value given in the parentheses underneath.

indicate that the output series of China, Japan, and Korea share some common stochastic trends, move in tandem, and do not drift apart in the long run.

The cointegration of output data may be viewed as a necessary condition for forming a currency union. If the output series are not cointegrated, they drift apart in the long run, and it is difficult to effectively manage the three economies using a common monetary policy and a common currency. Thus the cointegration result, which implies the national output data are synchronous in the long run, is supportive of the concept of a China–Japan–Korea currency union.

11.4.2   Vector Error Correction Model

Since the GDP data are cointegrated, a vector error correction model (VECM) is used to examine the interactions between the output growth rates. The VECM is given by

$$\Delta \mathbf{X}_t = \mu + \sum_{i=1}^{p} \Gamma_i \Delta \mathbf{X}_{t-i} + \alpha Z_{t-p-1} + \varepsilon_t, \tag{6}$$

where μ is a vector of constants, Z_{t-p-1} is the error correction term given by $\hat{\beta}' \mathbf{X}_{t-p-1}$, and $\hat{\beta}$ is the estimated cointegrating vector. The responses of output growth to short-term output movements are captured by the Γ_i coefficient matrices. The α coefficient vector reveals the speed of adjustment to the error correction term, which measures deviations from the empirical long-run relationship.

The estimates of (6) are reported in table 11.5. As indicated by the diagnostic Q-statistics, the fitted models are adequate in the sense that the residual estimates display no significant serial correlation. The China equation has the highest adjusted R^2, which is followed by the Korea equation and the Japan equation. A few observations are in order. First, the Chinese growth rate but not the other two is significantly affected by the error correction term. In the trivariate system China is the only country that adjusts to deviations from the empirical long-run output relationship. (Using the Granger causality terminology for the VECM framework [Granger and Lin 1995], Chinese output is Granger caused by the other two economies in the long run.) This result is consistent with the view that China is still at an early development stage and its growth is likely to be sensitive to the external environment.[12] Japan and Korea are relatively matured economies and do not response to the error correction term.

The coefficient estimates of the lagged growth variables, which describe the short-run output interactions among these countries, display a clear pattern. The output variation is transmitted across borders mostly according to the perceived relative economic dominance: China is affected by lagged Japanese and Korean output growth rates, Korea is affected by lagged Japanese growth rates only, and Japan responds only to its own lagged growth. The own lagged growth effect is negative, which is indicative of some kinds of mean-reverting growth dynamics. The cross-country output effect, on the other hand, is predominately positive. The positive spillover effect is a potential source of synchronous movements in these economies. Conceivably a currency union arrangement could exploit the spillover effect and internalize the benefit.

Japan's strong economic influence is directly related to its size and to its massive foreign direct investments in Asia. Despite its recent economic troubles Japan is still the most advanced economy in the region and is considered as one of the locomotives of the Asian and the world economy. Although it is smaller, Korea has a relatively vibrant economy and considerable amount of foreign direct investments in China. The apparent absence of China effects is not surprising. As a newcomer to the stage of the world economy, China is still at its early stage of economic development and exerts a relatively small impact on the other two economies.[13]

11.4.3   Common Feature and Codependent Business Cycles

For the usual conduct of monetary policy, short-run output fluctuations are an prominent concern. When shocks are asymmetric and national business cycles are asynchronous, a common currency and a common monetary policy are ineffectual in combating shocks to the countries and fine-tuning economic activities. Thus business cycle synchronization has significant implications for a common single currency discussion. From the previous subsection, we know that the GDPs of China, Japan, and Korea share long-run cycles. However, there is no direct evidence that these three countries have common business cycles. In this subsection we directly test for the presence of common business cycles.

Output growth correlation patterns are usually employed to gauge cyclical variations in business cycles. Engle and Kozicki (1993) advocate the use of the common feature test to detect common serial correlations and hence common business cycle behavior. The intuition behind the common feature analysis is as follows: Suppose that the elements of $\Delta \mathbf{X}_t$ have a common temporal dynamics. Then, by forming an appropriate linear combination of ΔX_{it}'s, we can eliminate the effect of the common component. Thus the presence of a common cycle, which is routinely measured by serial correlation in the literature, implies the existence of a linear combination of ΔX_{it}'s that is not correlated with the past information set.

Vahid and Engle (1993) devise a procedure to test for common serial correlation cycles in the presence of cointegration. The procedure amounts to finding the sample canonical correlations between $\Delta \mathbf{X}_t$ and $\mathbf{W}(p) \equiv (\Delta \mathbf{X}'_{t-1}, \ldots, \Delta \mathbf{X}'_{t-p}, Z_{t-1})$, where Z_{t-1} is the error correction term. The test statistic for the null hypothesis that there are at least s cofeature vectors is given by

$$C(p,s) = -(T - p - 1) \sum_{j=1}^{s} \ln(1 - \lambda_j), \tag{7}$$

where λ_j is the jth smallest squared canonical correlations between $\Delta \mathbf{X}_t$ and $\mathbf{W}(p)$. The dimension (rank) of the cofeature space is the number of statistically zero-squared canonical correlations. Under the null hypothesis the statistic $C(p,s)$ has a χ^2-distribution with $s^2 + snp + sr - sn$ degrees of freedom.

The concept of a common feature requires that the data respond to shocks simultaneously and are in similar phases throughout a business cycle. Specifically, for countries to share common feature business cycles, the entire time profiles of their reactions to common shocks have to be similar. If countries have different *initial* responses to a given shock, there will be no common feature. Because of country-specific factors including institutional structures and capital/labor input, shocks can initially propagate through countries at uneven speeds and countries can have dissimilar initial responses to shocks. Nonetheless, even with unequal initial responses, the countries can react fully and symmetrically to the shock in later periods. The common feature test will have low power to detect this type of common business cycles because it does not allow for dissimilar initial responses to shocks.

Vahid and Engle (1997) propose the codependence statistic to test for the presence of business cycles in which countries initially have different reactions to shocks but share common cyclical movement after the early phase. Technically a system of time series is said to be codependent if impulse responses of the variables are collinear beyond a certain period. A codependent cycle allows the series to have different initial responses to a shock but requires them to share a common response pattern after the initial stage. The notion of codependence is a generalization of common feature, which requires the variables to have collinear impulse responses for all periods. In fact a common serial correlation feature cycle is a codependent cycle with the initial period (which allows for differential responses) being an empty set. Without restricting the initial effects on the variables, the notion of codependent cycles makes it operationally feasible to model a general class of business cycles. The test statistic for the null hypothesis that there are at least s codependent vectors after the kth period is

$$C(k, p, s) = -(T - p - 1) \sum_{j=1}^{s} \ln\left\{1 - \left[\frac{\lambda_j(k)}{d_j(k)}\right]\right\}, \tag{8}$$

where $\lambda_n(k) \geq \cdots \geq \lambda_1(k)$ are the squared canonical correlations between $\Delta \mathbf{X}_t$ and $\mathbf{W}(k, p) \equiv (\Delta \mathbf{X}'_{t-k-1}, \ldots, \Delta \mathbf{X}'_{t-k-p}, Z_{t-1})$, and $d_j(k)$ is given by

$$d_j(k) = 1 \qquad \text{for } k = 0,$$

and

$$d_j(k) = 1 + 2 \sum_{v=1}^{k} \rho_v(\alpha' \Delta X_t) \rho_v(\gamma' W(k, p)) \qquad \text{for } k \geq 1, \tag{9}$$

where $\rho_v(y_t)$ is the sample autocorrelation of y_t at the vth lag, α and γ are the canonical variates corresponding to $\lambda_j(k)$. Note that when $k = 0$, the codependence test statistic $C(k, p, s)$ is reduced to the common feature test statistic $C(0, p, s) \equiv C(p, s)$. Under the null hypothesis the statistic $C(k, p, s)$ has a χ^2-distribution with $s^2 + snp + sr - sn$ degrees of freedom.

The common feature and codependence test results are given in table 11.6. The common feature test does not reject the hypothesis of $s = 1$ but rejects both the hypotheses of $s = 3$ and $s = 2$. The evidence suggests the presence of one cofeature vector and hence shared business cycles among China, Japan, and Korea. Thus, in addition to common long-term cyclical movements, the three largest Asian economies share common short-term business cycles. As argued earlier, the presence of common business cycles is a key precondition of a currency union.

Table 11.6
Common feature and co-dependence test results

| Null | Common feature test | | Co-dependence test | | |
	Squared canonical correlation	Statistic $C(p,s)$	Squared canonical correlation	Statistic $C(p,k,s)$	Degree of freedom
$S = 1$	0.329	10.390	0.154	3.359	8
$S = 2$	0.532	30.117*	0.427	17.304	18
$S = 3$	0.744	65.584*	0.940	75.308*	30

Note: Under the null hypothesis, the common feature test statistic $C(p,s)$ and the co-dependence statistic $C(p,k,s)$ have an asymptotic χ^2 distribution with $s^2 + snp + sr - sn$ degrees of freedom, where $n = 3$, $p = 3$, and $r = 1$. * indicates significance at the 5 percent level.

On the presence of codependence, results in table 11.6 show that for $k = 1$, the data reject the hypothesis of $s = 3$ but not those of $s = 1$ and $s = 2$. Literally the evidence is for the presence of two codependent vectors and hence for the presence of codependent business cycles. However, we know that a common feature is a special case of codependence, and one cofeature vector was reported. The codependence results should be properly interpreted as evidence of the presence of one codependent vector for common feature business cycles and one for codependent business cycles. That is, in addition to completely synchronized common business cycles, the countries share cycles in which they have differential responses to a common shock in an initial state of three months. After the initial state the national business cycles are synchronous. Apparently the diverse initial responses revealed in table 11.6 do not represent a big negative factor for a currency union proposal.[14] The findings reported in table 11.6 are undeniably a positive evidence for a currency union in the region.

11.5 Potential Output Loss

The output synchronicity results in Section 4 indicate that China, Japan, and Korea are potential candidates of a currency union because their output data move closely together in both the long and short run. The commonality of output variations potentially reduces the costs of adopting a single currency and pursuing a common stabilization policy. While there are benefits of forming a currency union, there are costs too. It is conceived that benefits come at the microeconomic level and are originated from, for example, the gain in economic efficiency, reduction in transaction costs, and elimination of foreign exchange uncertainty. On the other hand, costs are related to macroeconomic management. Joining a currency union implies the monetary authorities have to relinquish policy autonomy and lose the capacity to fine-tune the economy.

11.5.1 The Model

In this subsection we use the Ghosh and Wolf (1994) setting to illustrate the output cost of relinquishing monetary policy autonomy to join a currency union. The model assumes nominal wage rigidity to establish the benefits of autonomous monetary policy. Before joining a currency union, individual countries use their own monetary policies to fine-tune their economies in the presence of adverse shocks to achieve full employment. However, under a currency union arrangement, a common monetary policy is used to combat a unionwide shock, which is a function of shocks to its member countries. Since the currency union shock is not necessarily the same as individual shocks, the pursuant of a common policy does not necessarily achieve full employment as in all member countries and hence induces the output cost of joining a currency union.

Consider the scenario before joining a currency union. Let a country's output be given by

$$Q_t = e^{\theta_t} l_t^{\alpha}, \tag{10}$$

where θ_t is a productivity shock, l_t is labor employed in period t, and $0 < \alpha < 1$ is the labor share. The real wage is equal to the marginal product of labor. The nominal wage rate, w_t, is downward sticky and is based on information available at $t - 1$,

$$\log(w_t) = \log(E_{t-1} p_t) + \log(\alpha) + E_{t-1}\theta_t + (\alpha - 1) \log(\bar{l}), \tag{11}$$

where p_t is the price level, and E_{t-1} is the expectations operator based on information available at time $t - 1$. It is assumed that the wage is set (given the expected price and expected productivity shock) to clear the labor market; thus $\bar{l}$ is the equilibrium employment level.

Since the nominal wage is only rigid downward, the wage rate adjusts to clear the market if the unexpected productivity shock ε_t $(\cong \theta_t - E_{t-1}\theta_t)$ is positive. However, if the unexpected productivity shock ε_t is negative, the wage rate does not move down, and the actual ex post labor demand (l_t) is given by

$$\log(p_t) + \theta_t + (\alpha - 1) \log(l_t) = \log(w_t). \tag{12}$$

Note that l_t does not represent the equilibrium employment level. If the country is not in a currency union, monetary policies can be used to offset the adverse shock and restore labor market equilibrium by setting the price at the level

$$\log(p_t) - \log(E_{t-1}p_t) = -\varepsilon_t. \tag{13}$$

In this case

$$\log(p_t) + \theta_t + (\alpha - 1)\log(\bar{l}) = \log(w_t)$$
$$= \log(E_{t-1}p_t) + E_{t-1}\theta_t + (\alpha - 1)\log(\bar{l}). \tag{14}$$

Now suppose that the country forms a currency union with another country. Let the productivity shock to the currency union be ε_t^c, which is a combination of shocks to the two member countries. Further assume that the currency union's monetary authorities pursue a stabilization policy similar to (13) and set the union's price level (p_t^c) according to

$$\log(p_t^c) - \log(E_{t-1}p_t^c) = -\varepsilon_t^c. \tag{15}$$

When $\varepsilon_t < \varepsilon_t^c$, the policy (15) does not yield full employment for the country under consideration. From (10), (12), and (15), the country's output loss, in percentage term, is given by

$$L_t = 1 - \exp[(\varepsilon_t - \varepsilon_t^c)\alpha/(1 - \alpha)]. \tag{16}$$

See Ghosh and Wolf (1994) for a detailed discussion of the model, interpretations, and caveats. In the following, equation (16) is used to evaluate the nations' output costs of forming a currency union. It should be pointed out that (16) is quite simple and is meant to provide an initial estimate of the cost of joining a currency union.

11.5.2   The Estimated Output Cost

According to equation (16), the output loss of joining a currency union depends on three factors: the shock to the economy ε_t, the shock to the currency union ε_t^c, and the labor share α. To check the robustness of our exercise, we consider ε_t's obtained from three alternative approaches. The vector error correction model in section 11.4 is used to generate the first set of shocks. The Hodrick-Prescott filter gives the second set of shocks. The supply shocks constructed using the Blanchard-Quah method are the third candidate considered in this exercise.

The shock to the currency union ε_t^c is defined in two alternative ways. First, we assume that the monetary authorities in the currency union stipulate the shock to the union as the GDP-weighted average of individual country's shocks. Next, we assume the currency union shock is the simple average of shocks to individual countries. For simplicity we label these two definitions of currency union shocks as the GDP-weighted average shock and the simple average shock hereafter. We also consider the value of the labor share parameter α in the range from 0.3 to 0.7.

Table 11.7 presents the estimates of percentage output losses. A few observations are in order for the results based on the GDP-weighted

Table 11.7
Average output losses in percentages

		GDP weighted average shock			Simple average shock		
		VECM[a]	HP filter[b]	BQ[c]	VECM[a]	HP filter[b]	BQ[c]
$\alpha = 0.7$	China	0.222	0.565	0.213	0.158	0.274	0.164
	Japan	0.079	0.058	0.039	0.651	0.527	0.318
	Korea	1.355	3.185	1.750	1.060	2.228	1.314
	All three[d]	0.110	0.133	0.084	0.639	0.546	0.335
$\alpha = 0.6$	China	0.143	0.365	0.137	0.101	0.176	0.105
	Japan	0.051	0.037	0.025	0.420	0.340	0.205
	Korea	0.887	2.099	1.148	0.691	1.466	0.855
	All three[d]	0.071	0.086	0.054	0.413	0.353	0.216
$\alpha = 0.5$	China	0.195	0.245	0.092	0.068	0.118	0.070
	Japan	0.034	0.025	0.017	0.281	0.228	0.137
	Korea	0.598	1.421	0.774	0.464	0.988	0.575
	All three[d]	0.047	0.058	0.037	0.276	0.236	0.144
$\alpha = 0.4$	China	0.064	0.163	0.061	0.045	0.079	0.047
	Japan	0.023	0.017	0.011	0.188	0.152	0.091
	Korea	0.401	0.957	0.520	0.311	0.664	0.385
	All three[d]	0.032	0.039	0.024	0.184	0.158	0.096
$\alpha = 0.3$	China	0.041	0.105	0.039	0.029	0.051	0.030
	Japan	0.015	0.011	0.007	0.121	0.098	0.059
	Korea	0.259	0.620	0.337	0.200	0.429	0.249
	All three[d]	0.020	0.025	0.016	0.118	0.100	0.062

Note: The average percentage output losses estimated under the assumptions of the currency union shock is given by the GDP weighted average and the simple average of shocks to its member countries are reported. α is the labor share.
a. Output losses derived from shocks estimated from the vector error correction model.
b. Output losses derived from shocks generated from the HP filter.
c. Output losses based on supply shocks estimated from the Blanchard-Quah method.
d. Losses for the three countries as a group.

average shock. First, as indicated by (16), a larger α parameter is associated with a higher percentage of output loss. Intuitively, the output loss in the model is due to the inability to restore the labor market equilibrium. Thus a large labor share implies a large output loss, ceteris paribus. The labor share effect can be quite pronounced. In the case of Korea, when the shocks are computed from the vector error correction model, the output loss increases from 0.6 to 1.35 percent when α increases from 0.5 to 0.7.

Second, the rankings of national output loss estimates are the same across the three shock-estimation methods. Korea always has the largest percentage output loss estimate while Japan has the least. The rankings appear consistent with the way the currency union shock is defined. Because Japan is the largest economy in the group and the currency union shock is defined as a GDP-weighted average shock, the stabilization policy will response more to shocks originated from Japan. Again, consider the case of $\alpha = 0.7$ and the vector error correction model. The output loss estimates are 0.22, 0.08, and 1.35 percent for China, Japan, and Korea, respectively. The Korean estimate is about 17 times larger than the Japanese one.

Even for the simple average currency union shock, Korea tends to have the highest percentage output losses. That is, the large Korean loss is not entirely due to its weight in defining the currency union shock. Further the choices of shock-estimation methods and labor share values have no implication for the relative ranking of national output loss estimates. A possible reason for the result is that shocks to Korea are less similar to those in the other two countries such that the term $(\varepsilon_t - \varepsilon_t^c)$ is always large for Korea.

Third, the output loss estimate appears quite sensitive to the method used to extract the shocks. Among the three shock-estimation methods, the Hodrick-Prescott filter yields the largest output loss estimates for China and Korea, and the vector error correction model tends to give Japan a larger output loss estimate. The variation of loss estimates is quite wide. In the case $\alpha = 0.7$, the Chinese estimates range from 0.21 percent (Blanchard-Quah method) to 0.57 percent (Hodrick-Prescott filter), the Japanese estimates from 0.04 percent (Blanchard-Quah method) to 0.08 percent (vector error correction model), and the Korean estimates from 1.35 percent (vector error correction model) to 3.18 percent (Hodrick-Prescott filter). The results highlight the importance of the shock-estimation method in evaluating output losses of joining a currency union.[15]

Fourth, the percentage of output loss for all three economies as a group is reported in table 11.7. For the cases under consideration the output loss of the group is less than 0.13 percent (Hodrick-Prescott filter and $\alpha = 0.7$). Recall that the output loss is derived under the assumption that individual monetary authorities can perfectly fine-tune their economies, and thus the output loss should be properly interpreted as an upper bound of potential losses. The loss appears small compare with some estimates of the potential benefits of a currency union. For example, in an earlier study (Commission of the European Communities 1990), it is estimated that the cost savings for the European countries to adopt a single currency are between 0.3 to 0.4 percent of the aggregate GDP. The benefit of price convergence, which is a likely consequence of creating a currency union, estimated by Hufbauer et al. (2002) is 0.55 percent of the world GDP. If a common currency for the three Asian countries generates a similar magnitude of savings, then the benefits of forming an Asian currency union will outweigh the estimated output loss.

While the potential gain may offset the potential loss in forming an Asian currency union, there is a re-distribution issue. As evidenced in the table, the output loss of a small country can be quite high. At the same time a small economy is likely to achieve a low level of cost savings from gain in economic efficiency and reduction in transaction costs. Thus, without an appropriate re-distribution scheme, a small economy may not elect to join the union because the cost for it to join the currency union can be higher than the benefit. Obviously there are other (economic and political) factors affecting the decision of joining a currency union. Nonetheless, our discussion offers one perspective to analyze the situation.

The output loss estimates based on the assumption that the currency union shock is the simple average of the shocks to its members are comparable to those based on the GDP-weighted average specification. Specifically, the effects of labor share parameter α and shock-estimation methods on the estimated output losses are qualitatively similar to those derived from the GDP-weighted average shock. However, the use of the simple average shock as the policy target has significant implications for the rankings of output loss estimates. Similar to the previous case, Korea still has the highest output loss estimates. However, in the current case China, instead of Japan, has the lowest loss estimates. Further the Japanese output loss estimates under the simple average shock are higher than those under the GDP-weighted average shock while the opposite is true for the other two countries.

For the three countries as a group, the simple average shock yields output loss estimates that are unambiguously higher than the GDP-weighted average shock does. Indeed, the output loss can go above 0.5 percent of the group output ($\alpha = 0.7$ and vector error correction model). The results strongly suggest that the policy leaning toward the simple average shock, rather than the GDP-weighted average one, leads to a higher level of aggregate output loss. Nonetheless, it is conceivable that, in the absence of re-distribution of gains and losses, Japan with the largest economy in the group would prefer the policy abating the GDP-weighted average shock while the two other countries would favor the one that focuses on the simple average shock.

The output losses in US dollars are presented in the appendix. Comparing the output losses under two different types of currency union shocks, it is obvious that the policy target of the simple average shock imposes a heavier output cost on the three nations as group than the one based on the GDP-weighted average shock. The Japanese output loss under the simple average shock alternative is substantially larger than that under the GDP-weighted average shock. In fact, for all the cases under consideration, Japan has the incentive to pay off the other two countries to reach the policy target of managing the GDP-weighted average shock. Thus, given the relative output gains and losses under these two types of currency union shocks, it is plausible for the common monetary authorities to select the GDP-weighted average shock as the policy target if the countries can compromise and reach a mutually agreeable re-distribution scheme.

Table 11.7 contains output loss estimates for a range of labor share values. Nevertheless, it is instructive to consider the losses corresponding to some "reasonable" estimates of labor shares. To this end we adopt the 1993 to 1996 labor share figures from Harrison (2002) and calculate the corresponding output losses.[16] Specifically, the labor share parameter is set to 0.36 for China, 0.59 for Japan, and 0.49 for Korea.

Table 11.8 presents percentage output losses for specific labor share figures. The estimated loss ranges from 0.038 to 0.138 percent for China, from 0.24 to 0.403 percent for Japan, from 0.446 to 1.367 percent for Korea, and from 0.041 to 0.39 percent for the three countries as a group. Again, the group loss is much smaller when the GDP-weighted average shock, rather than the simple average shock, is considered. Indeed, under the GDP-weighted average shock, the output loss for the group is no larger than 0.073 percent, which is much smaller than the possible gains from using a common currency reported in Commission

Table 11.8
Average output losses in percentages for specific labor shares

	GDP weighted average shock			Simple average shock		
	VECM[a]	HP filter[b]	BQ[c]	VECM[a]	HP filter	BQ[c]
China	0.054	0.138	0.052	0.038	0.066	0.039
Japan	0.049	0.036	0.024	0.403	0.327	0.196
Korea	0.575	1.367	0.745	0.446	0.950	0.553
All three	0.059	0.063	0.041	0.390	0.327	0.199

Note: Estimated average output losses in percentages are computed based on the labor share values: China = 0.36, Japan = 0.59, and Korea = 0.49. For the output losses it is assumed that the currency union monetary authorities respond to the GDP weighted average and to the simple average of shocks to its member countries.
a. Output losses derived from shocks estimated from the vector error correction model.
b. Output losses derived from shocks generated from the HP filter.
c. Output losses based on supply shocks estimated from the Blanchard-Quah method.
d. Losses for the three countries as a group.

of the European Communities (1990) or from price convergence (Hufbauer et al. 2002). The corresponding losses in US dollar values reported in the appendix suggested that with an appropriate redistribution scheme, the countries should select the GDP-weighted average shock as the policy target of the common monetary authorities.

11.6   Concluding Remarks

In this exercise we adopted an output perspective to assess the prospect for China, Japan, and Korea to form a currency union. We found that the three countries have synchronous output movements at both long-run and short-term horizons. Further the estimated output loss appears to be less than the potential benefit from forming a currency union. We also noted that the three countries have considerably intensified their trade and investment interactions since the 1990s. These results are supportive of the idea that China, Japan, and Korea should join forces to form a currency union and promote their common economic interests.[17] The positive inference of an Asian currency union is complementary to some existing studies based on different methodologies.[18]

Although our exercise attempts to offer some insight on the cost of China, Japan, and Korea to form a currency union, the analysis is far from complete. As we showed in section 11.5, the macro model is rather simplistic, and the results are sensitive to, for example, the method used to estimate shocks to the economy.[19] It is fair to state that the estimates are not definitive measures of output losses and should not be taken literally. Instead, one should emphasize the sensitivity of the results to, say, the shock estimation method and the definition of the currency union shock. The sensitivity has significant implications for estimating costs and devising policies in the process of formulating a currency union.

An additional complication is the self-validating nature of an exchange rate regime choice. The implementation of a currency union can induce structural changes that facilitate integration and increase the strength of common business cycles (Corestti and Pesenti 2002; Frankel and Rose 1998; Engel and Rose 2002). The endogeneity of a currency union criterion further complicates the task of estimating costs and benefits. The recent European Union experience also indicates some potential issues on evaluating the costs and benefits of adopting a common currency. For instance, the "imbalance" growth phenomenon—the large countries experience slow growth and small economies experience high growth—was quite unexpected before the adoption of the euro. It has created some tensions in setting the common monetary policy for the union.

It is unrealistic to assume the path to economic integration of China, Japan, and Korea is without impediments. The legacies of war, occupation, and communism remain a reality among the populations of these countries. A consequence of these antagonisms is the aversion to (potential) regional hegemony. Also the cost of adjustment represents another challenge to economic integration. China, Japan, and Korea are at different stages of economic development. While the difference can lead to huge potential gains from trade and integration, it also creates serious problems when these countries have to adjust to external competition. Even without formal steps toward integration, ongoing adjustment to increased import penetration and competition in third markets has already resulted in some political resistance to deeper integration. For instance, agricultural trade is a contentious issue between China and Japan and, to a lesser extent, between China and Korea. Korean products, on the other hand, constitute more than three-quarters of anti-dumping cases investigated by China.[20] Of course, there are concerns that the growing Chinese production capacity will hollow out the manufacturing sectors in other countries and absorb foreign direct investment at the expense of other nations.

There are both economic and noneconomic reasons that the trilateral economic cooperation may run into obstacles. However, recent developments are quite encouraging. For instance, China's willingness to foster trade and economic interactions with her neighboring economies is a positive sign. In the process China presents its growing and booming economy as a benefit and an opportunity rather than a threat to its neighbors. Further China, Japan, and Korea are quite active in promoting and conducting bilateral and multilateral negotiations on trade and financial issues. In addition the rising trend of regionalism (e.g., NAFTA and EU), the shadow of the 1997 financial crisis, and the increasing importance of intra-regional trade still provide incentives to institutionalize the cooperative economic relationship among the Asian countries. It is perceived that the process of economic integration will be long and involved despite the bright promise of closer economic cooperation.

Appendix: The Estimated Output Losses in US Dollars

Table 11A.1
Output losses (US$bil)

		GDP weighted average shock			Simple average shock		
		VECM[a]	HP filter[b]	BQ[c]	VECM[a]	HP filter[b]	BQ[c]
$\alpha = 0.7$	China	0.414	0.985	0.383	0.274	0.490	0.271
	Japan	3.708	2.811	1.732	29.960	25.639	14.275
	Korea	1.293	2.596	1.944	1.018	1.816	1.464
$\alpha = 0.6$	China	0.267	0.636	0.246	0.177	0.316	0.175
	Japan	2.385	1.808	1.114	19.336	16.566	9.199
	Korea	0.845	1.709	1.275	0.663	1.189	0.953
$\alpha = 0.5$	China	0.178	0.426	0.164	0.118	0.211	0.116
	Japan	1.590	1.205	0.742	12.921	11.078	6.142
	Korea	0.569	1.156	0.860	0.445	0.801	0.641
$\alpha = 0.4$	China	0.119	0.284	0.110	0.079	0.141	0.078
	Japan	1.060	0.804	0.495	8.628	7.400	4.099
	Korea	0.382	0.778	0.578	0.298	0.538	0.429
$\alpha = 0.3$	China	0.076	0.183	0.071	0.051	0.090	0.050
	Japan	0.682	0.517	0.318	5.553	4.764	2.637
	Korea	0.247	0.504	0.374	0.193	0.348	0.277

Note: Estimated average output losses are reported under the assumptions that the currency union shock is given by the GDP weighted average and the simple average of the shocks to its member countries. α is the labor share.
a. Output losses derived from shocks estimated from the vector error correction model.
b. Output losses derived from shocks generated from the HP filter.
c. Output losses based on supply shocks estimated from the Blanchard-Quah method.

Table 11A.2
Values of output losses for specific labor shares (US$bil)

	GDP weighted average shock			Simple average shock		
	VECM[a]	HP filter[b]	BQ[c]	VECM[a]	HP filter[b]	BQ[c]
China	0.100	0.240	0.093	0.066	0.119	0.066
Japan	2.288	1.734	1.068	18.555	15.898	8.827
Korea	0.547	1.112	0.827	0.428	0.770	0.616

Note: Estimated average output losses are computed based on the labor share values: China = 0.36, Japan = 0.59, and Korea = 0.49. For the output losses it is assumed that the currency union monetary authorities respond to the GDP weighted average and to the simple average of shocks to its member countries.
a. Output losses derived from shocks estimated from the vector error correction model.
b. Output losses derived from shocks generated from the HP filter.
c. Output losses based on supply shocks estimated from the Blanchard-Quah method.

Notes

The authors thank Hyungdo Ahn, Menzie Chinn, Charles Engel, Paul De Grauwe, Chang-Jae Lee, Yong Hyup Oh, Alejandro Micco, Reinhard Neck, Blanca Sanchez-Robles, Kiril Strahilov, Jose Tavares, and participants of the 2003 Venice Summer Institute Workshop on Monetary Unions after EMU, the seminars at Cheng Kung University, The Hong Kong Institute for Monetary Research, and the Korea Institute for International Economic Policy for their comments and suggestions. Also we thank Desmond Hou for compiling the data. The financial support of faculty research funds of the University of California, Santa Cruz, is gratefully acknowledged.

1. See, for example, Eichengreen (2001) and Wyplosz (2002) for discussions of these proposals and the related references.

2. See, for example, Bayoumi and Mauro (1999), Eichengreen and Bayoumi (1999), Lee, Park, and Shin (2002), McKinnon and Schnabl (2003), and Ng (2002).

3. See, for example, Eijffinger and Haan (2000) and De Grauwe (2000) for a detailed discussion of the European Union.

4. Mundell (1961) is the seminal study on optimal currency areas. Lafrance and St-Amant (1999), for example, offer a recent review of the literature on optimum currency areas.

5. Other criteria include the similarities of trade patterns and levels of economic development, the degree of trade and financial integration, and the mobility of labor markets.

6. McKinnon (2001) refers to Mundell (1973) and points out that, in the presence of risk sharing, asymmetric shocks may not necessarily imply currency union is not desirable.

7. See, for example, Baxter and Stockman (1989), Harvey and Jaeger (1993), and Canova (1998).

8. See Cabinet Office, Government of Japan (2001).

9. Some other studies on the possible China–Japan–Korea economic cooperation are Schott and Goodrich (2001), and Scollay and Gilbert (2001). Cho (2000) offers an

account of the trade between China, Japan, Korea and Southeast Asia countries in the pre-modern time. Nam (2003) provides a detailed account of trade between China and APEC economies.

10. See National Institute for Research Advancement of Japan (2002).

11. The trade data in the table, as those in the other tables, were based on Chinese sources. It is well known that trade data from different national sources differ from each other. However, our discussion is not qualitatively affected by these differences.

12. The discussion in section 11.2 underscores the linkages via trade and investment. China has evolved from a relatively autarkic economy with a trade-to-GDP ratio of 0.11 in 1979 to an economy with a ratio of 0.48 in 2002. In 2002 China's trade-to-GDP ratio is larger than the Japan's one (0.19) and smaller than the Korea's one (0.66). Also exports to Japan and Korea accounted for 20 percent of China's total exports.

13. Although the data did not reveal the Chinese effects, it is conceived that both Japan and Korea are increasingly dependent on China for their exports (e.g., see Williams 2002).

14. McKinnon and Schnabl (2003) use a different approach to assert that the business cycles of East Asia economies are highly synchronized.

15. The result is comparable to the sensitivity of the estimated benefits from free trade derived from different specifications reported in, for example, Brown et al. (2002) and Scollay and Gilbert (2001).

16. Since the China figure is not available, we assume China is a member of Harrison's "bottom-middle" income group.

17. One caveat is that the empirical results are derived from existing data. Given the rapid developments in these countries; especially in China, the future can look very different from what can be inferred from these empirical results.

18. See, for example, Bayoumi and Mauro (1999), Eichengreen and Bayoumi (1999), and Ng (2002).

19. The benefits of forming a currency union are not considered in the current exercise. Further the analysis considers neither the implications of industry-specific shocks nor the cost of resource re-allocation between sectors as a result of joining a currency union. Future analyses of the desirability of an Asian currency union should consider the benefit factors together with other possible costs.

20. See *Korea Times* (2003). Between November 1996 and July 2003, 18 of the 23 cases investigated by China are related to Korean products.

References

Baxter, M., and A. C. Stockman. 1989. Business cycles and the exchange-rate regime: Some international evidence. *Journal of Monetary Economics* 23: 377–400.

Bayoumi, T., and B. J. Eichengreen. 1994. One money or many? Analyzing the prospects of monetary unification in various parts of the world. *Princeton Studies in International Finance 76*.

Bayoumi, T., and P. Mauro. 1999. The suitability of ASEAN for a regional currency arrangement. IMF Working Paper 99-162.

Blanchard, O. J., and D. Quah. 1989. The dynamic effects of demand and supply disturbances. *American Economic Review* 79: 655–73.

Brown, D. K., A. V. Deardorff, and R. M. Stern. 2002. CGE modeling and analysis of multilateral and regional negotiating options. In R. M. Stern, ed., *Issues and options for U.S.— Japan trade policies*. Ann Arbor: University of Michigan Press, pp. 23–65.

Cabinet Office, Government of Japan. 2002. Annual Report on the Japanese Economy and Public Finance, 2001–2002. *http://www5.cao.go.jp/zenbun/wp-e/wp-je02/wp-je02-00301.html*.

Canova, F. 1998. Detrending and business cycle facts. *Journal of Monetary Economics* 41: 475–512.

Cheung, Y.-W., and K. S. Lai. 1993. Finite sample sizes of Johansen's likelihood ratio tests for cointegration. *Oxford Bulletin of Economics and Statistics* 55: 313–28.

Cheung, Y.-W., and K. S. Lai. 1995. Lag order and critical values for the augmented Dickey-Fuller test. *Journal of Business and Economic Statistics* 13: 277–80.

Cho, H.-G. 2000. The trade between China, Japan, Korea and Southeast Asia in the 14th century through the 17th century period. *International Area Review* 3: 67–107.

Commission of the European Communities. 1990. One market, one money. *European Economy* 44. Office for Official Publications of the European Communities.

Corestti, G., and P. Pesenti. 2002. Self-validating optimum currency areas. Manuscript. Presented before 2002 SCIII Conference. UCSC.

De Grauwe, P. 2000. *The Economics of Monetary Union*, 4th ed. New York: Oxford University Press.

Eichengreen, B. J., and T. Bayoumi. 1999. Is Asia an optimum currency area? Can it become one? Regional, global and historical perspectives on Asian monetary relations. In S. Collignon, J. Pisani-Ferry, and Y. C. Park, eds., *Exchange Rate Policies in Emerging Asian Countries*. London and New York: Routledge, pp. 347–66.

Eichengreen, B. J. 2001. Hanging together? On Monetary and Financial Cooperation in Asia. Manuscript. University of California, Berkeley.

Eijffinger, S. C. W., and J. de Haan. 2000. *European monetary and fiscal policy*. New York: Oxford University Press.

Engel, C., and A. K. Rose. 2002. Currency unions and international integration. *Journal of Money Credit and Banking* 34: 1067–89.

Engle, R. F., and S. Kozicki. 1993. Testing for common features. *Journal of Business and Economics Statistics* 11: 369–79.

Frankel, J. A., and A. K. Rose. 1998. The endogeneity of the optimum currency area criteria. *Economic Journal* 108: 1009–25.

Ghosh, A. R., and H. C. Wolf. 1994. How many monies? A genetic approach to finding optimum currency areas. NBER Working Paper 4805.

Granger, C. W. J., and J.-L. Lin. 1995. Causality in the long run. *Econometric Theory* 11: 530–36.

Harrison, A. E. 2002. Has globalization eroded labor's shares? Some cross-country evidence. Manuscript. University of California, Berkeley.

Harvey, A. C., and A. Jaeger. 1993. Detrending, stylized facts and the business cycle. *Journal of Applied Econometrics* 8: 231–47.

Hernandez, L., and P. Montiel. 2001. Post-crisis exchange rate policy in five Asian countries: Filling in the "Hollow Middle"? IMF Working Paper 01/170.

Hufbauer, G. C., E. Wada, and T. Warren. 2002. *The Benefits of Price Convergence: Speculative Calculations*. Policy Analyses in International Economics 63. Washington: Institute for International Economics.

Johansen, S. 1991. Estimation and hypothesis testing of cointegration vectors in Gaussian vector autoregressive models. *Econometrica* 59: 1551–81.

Johansen, S., and K. Juselius. 1990. Maximum likelihood estimation and inference on cointegration—With applications to the demand for money. *Oxford Bulletin of Economics and Statistics* 52: 169–210.

Lafrance, R., and P. St-Amant. 1999. Optimum currency areas: A review of the recent literature. Bank of Canada Working Paper 99-16.

Lee, J.-W., Y. C. Park, and K. Shin. 2002. A currency union in East Asia. Manuscript. Korea University.

McKinnon, R. I. 2001. Optimum currency areas and key currencies: Mundell I versus Mundell II. Manuscript. Stanford University.

McKinnon, R. I., and G. Schnabl. 2003. Synchronized business cycles in East Asia and fluctuations in the yen/dollar exchange rate. *World Economy* 26: 1067–88.

Mundell, R. A. 1961. A theory of optimum currency areas. *American Economic Review* 51: 657–65.

Mundell, R. A. 1973. Uncommon arguments for common currencies. In H. G. Johnson and A. K. Swoboda, eds., *The Economics of Common Currencies*. London: Allen and Unwin, pp. 114–32.

National Institute for Research Advancement of Japan. 2002. Report and joint policy recommendations on strengthening economic cooperation among China, Japan and Korea in 2002. Presented before Trilateral Summit Meeting held in Phnom Penh on November 4, 2002. *http://www.nira.go.jp/newse/paper/joint2/report.html*.

Nam, S.-Y. 2003. *Trade Structure and Complementarity among APEC Member Economies*. APEC Study Series 03-01. Korea: KIEP.

Ng, T. H. 2002. Should the Southeast Asian countries form a currency union? *Developing Economies* 40: 113–34.

Schott, J. J., and B. Goodrich. 2001. Economic integration in Northeast Asia. Presented before 2001 KIEP/KEI/CKS Conference on The Challenges of Reconciliation and Reform in Korea. Los Angeles, CA.

Scollay, R., and J. P. Gilbert. 2001. *New Regional Trading Arrangement in the Asia Pacific*. Policy Analyses in International Economics 63. Washington: Institute for International Economics.

Vahid, F., and R. F. Engle. 1993. Common trends and common cycles. *Journal of Applied Econometrics* 8: 341–60.

Vahid, F., and R. F. Engle. 1997. Codependent Cycles. *Journal of Econometrics* 80: 199–221.

Williams, M. 2002. A Japanese recovery reliant on China. *Wall Street Journal*, October 25, 2002.

Wyplosz, C. 2002. A monetary union in Asia? Some European lessons. In D. Gruen and J. Simon, eds., *Future Directions for Monetary Policies in East Asia*. Reserve Bank of Australia, pp. 124–55.

12

Have a Break, Have a … National Currency: When Do Monetary Unions Fall Apart?

Volker Nitsch

12.1 Introduction

In recent years monetary integration has become fashionable again. Twelve European countries have formed a monetary union, giving up their national currencies for the euro. Other countries have dollarized, adopting the currency of another country on a unilateral basis. After some decades in which almost all countries, except for some small and geographically remote territories, strongly preferred to have their own monies, more than two-thirds of the sovereign countries in the world are either considering to abandon their national money or already have done so.[1]

One of the main reasons for the countries' growing willingness to enter a currency union is the credibility of these arrangements. In contrast to other hard currency pegs (e.g., fixed exchange rates or currency boards), the abandonment of a country's own currency is often assumed to be permanent; it cannot be easily reversed and thus appears to be a more serious commitment than any other fixed-rate regime. For Europeans, the use of a common currency implies a degree of integration that goes much beyond the elimination of exchange rate volatility. For dollarized countries, the adoption of another country's currency means that monetary policy is delegated directly to a foreign authority.

Historically, however, dissolutions of currency unions are not unusual. Glick and Rose (2002) even find that for the period from 1948 through 1997 currency union exits clearly outnumber currency union entries. Of the 146 regime transitions (for which they have data), there were 130 switches out of but only 16 switches into currency unions.

In this chapter, I examine why some monetary unions fall apart, while others remain in existence for a long period of time. In particular,

I ask when does a country leave a currency union. By comparing the behavior of countries in currency unions shortly before their dissolution with that of sustained currency unions, I am able to identify potential causes of currency union breakups.[2] My empirical results suggest that departures from a currency union tend to occur when there is a large inflation differential among member countries, when the currency union involves a country that is relatively closed to international trade and trade flows fall, and when there is a change in political status of a member. In general, however, macroeconomic factors have only little predictive power for currency union dissolutions.

This chapter adds to an already large and again rapidly growing literature on currency unions. Most of the recent (empirical) studies, however, explore the degree of integration in currency unions relative to countries *with different national monies*. Rose and Engel (2002), for instance, measure several economic characteristics for currency union members and compare them to noncurrency union countries. Alesina, Barro, and Tenreyro (2002) rank country pairs by their degree of integration and attempt to identify optimal currency areas. Here, however, I focus exclusively on *existing* currency unions, which then may or may not have been sustained; countries with separate currencies are ignored.

This chapter is also related (and close in style) to the rich empirical literature on the determinants of changes in exchange rate regimes. Turbulences in foreign exchange markets (e.g., regime transitions and currency crashes) have attracted much attention, and numerous studies attempt to link these episodes to macroeconomic and political variables. Examples include Eichengreen, Rose, and Wyplosz (1995), Frankel and Rose (1996), and Kaminsky and Reinhart (1999); Kaminsky, Lizondo, and Reinhart (1998) provide a survey. To my knowledge, however, there is no study that focuses on the breakups of currency unions.

The chapter is organized as follows: Section 12.2 provides some analytical background. Section 12.3 describes the data and their characteristics, followed by a presentation of the results of multivariate analyses in section 12.4. After presenting some more illustrative details in section 12.5, the chapter ends with a brief summary (section 12.6).

12.2 Background

The large theoretical literature on fixed exchange rates offers at least two different analytical frameworks that may help explain why countries leave a currency union. The first is based on Mundell's (1961) concept of an optimum currency area. This concept emphasizes the costs and benefits of monetary integration and argues that the (net) gains from sharing a single currency increase with the degree of economic integration. The dissolution of a currency union can then be viewed as evidence that the members were not part of an optimum currency area; the benefits of using the same money (e.g., lower transaction costs in trading goods and services) were (ex post) smaller than the costs (e.g., the loss of an independent monetary policy). In empirical work, typically four criteria (or a subset) are examined to identify an optimum currency area: the intensity of trade, the symmetry of shocks and cycles, the degree of labor mobility, and the mechanism of fiscal transfers. For dissolved currency unions then, I would expect to find, based on these criteria, a lower degree of integration than for sustained unions.

The alternative framework is provided by the literature on currency crises and speculative attacks. The idea here is that a country may be forced to leave a currency union even if the currency union members generally exhibit the desirable degree of economic integration. Of course, the credibility of the commitment to use the same money makes members of a currency union less vulnerable (and maybe even immune) to a speculative attack. However, similar to other fixed exchange rate arrangements, inconsistencies between domestic economic fundamentals and the exchange rate commitment may arise. Poor policies, for instance, can rapidly increase the costs of monetary integration so that, at some point, a country may decide that it is no longer willing to bear these costs; Chang and Velasco (2002) provide a recent formalization of this time inconsistency problem. To identify empirically when a currency link becomes unsustainable, the literature on currency crises has used a large variety of indicators; Kaminsky et al.'s (1998) summary of 28 selected studies lists alone 105 indicators.[3] It follows that also a much broader set of macroeconomic and financial variables may be relevant in explaining currency union breakups.

A third (intuitively plausible) view is that currency union dissolutions are mainly the result of changes in the political status of a territory; many departures from a currency union link indeed occurred when a colony gained independence and subsequently left the currency area of the former colonizer.[4] Most recently the breakup of federations in Eastern Europe (the Soviet Union, Yugoslavia, and Czechoslovakia) has illustrated the importance of political ties for monetary integration; the dissolution of the political union was also accompanied by a dissolution of the monetary union.[5] This view then implies that currency union exits are largely unrelated to economic fundamentals.

In the empirical analysis, I try to account for these different explanations. Based on the literature on optimum currency areas, I examine the intensity of the ties between currency union members. In particular, I enter explanatory variables not only in absolute levels or rates of change (reflecting the economic conditions in a country) but also relative to the same variable in a partner country using the same currency; this allows to identify the effect of asymmetries and differentials on the likelihood of currency union breakup. Similar to other empirical studies on transitions in the exchange rate regime, I also explore the impact of a wide range of potential indicators. The list of variables can be broadly grouped into five categories and also includes a measure of change in the political status; the remaining groups are (1) macroeconomic indicators, (2) financial variables, (3) fiscal measures, and (4) openness variables. The next section describes the data set in more detail.

12.3 Data

The data used in this chapter come essentially from two sources. Most of the data are obtained from Glick and Rose (2002); they have compiled a data set of macroeconomic variables for 217 countries and territories, covering the period from 1948 through 1997 on an annual basis. This data set has, for my purposes, several useful features. First, it is extremely comprehensive; the data set covers most of the postwar period and virtually all political entities in the world (countries, territories, colonies, dependencies, etc.). Assembled in pairwise form, it comprises more than 400,000 observations although there are many observations missing.[6] Second, the data are extracted from standard sources such as the World Bank's *World Development Indicators* or the IMF's *International Financial Statistics*; they have been checked and corrected for mistakes. Finally, and most notably, the data set contains information on whether a pair of countries shares the same currency. Based on this currency union dummy, I construct a binary variable for a breakup of the currency union in the following year that will serve as regressand in my analysis (as a robustness check, I also construct a dummy variable for currency union breakup in one of the following three years). More details are discussed in Glick and Rose (2002).

In the actual implementation, I extract a subset from this large panel data set, containing the observations of currency union pairs. This leaves 4,625 observations for 245 currency unions (or, more precisely, country pairs in a currency union) of which 128 are dissolved during the sample period; the currency unions and the exits are tabulated in the appendix to the working paper version. Figure 12.1 displays the distribution of observations over time. While the number of observations has a slight tendency to increase over time (mostly due to a better availability of data), currency union exits most often occured in the 1960s and 1970s.[7] Some of these currency union dissolutions are related so that the observations probably should not be treated as independent observations.

To this data set, I add a number of other macroeconomic and financial variables, taken from Rose and Engel (2002). This data set covers a broad set of indicators typically employed in empirical studies on currency crises. Rose and Engel have used these variables to characterize currency unions, I utilize them to characterize currency union exits. In particular, I apply all of their macroeconomic, financial, fiscal, and openness variables.[8] The exact list of variables is in table 12.1 which also shows some descriptive statistics.

12.4   Results

12.4.1   Univariate Evidence
In table 12.1, I report separate means and standard deviations for sustained currency unions (defined to exist for at least the next three years) and dissolved currency union links.[9] This allows me to compare (in univariate fashion) the average behavior of the variable of interest for broken and nonbroken currency unions. I also include a p-value for a t-test of equality of means; differences in means that are statistically significant at the 5 percent level are in bold.

I begin with macroeconomic variables. The first two lines of table 12.1 display the results for real GDP growth. They show that the minimum growth rate[10] for each country pair averages about 0.5 percent for a typical (sustained) currency union, which is on average only slightly below this level (0.3 percent) in the three years before a currency union dissolution but falls to −1.3 percent in the year immediately preceding the break. The results also indicate that a currency union exit is often preceded by a (negative) idiosyncratic shock to one of the members. Broken currency unions display a considerably larger difference in pairwise growth rates than sustained currency unions

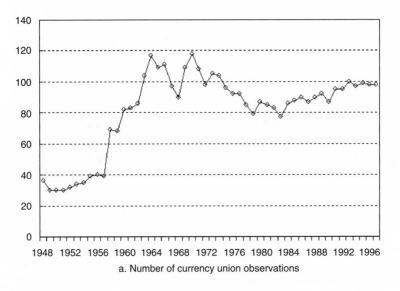

a. Number of currency union observations

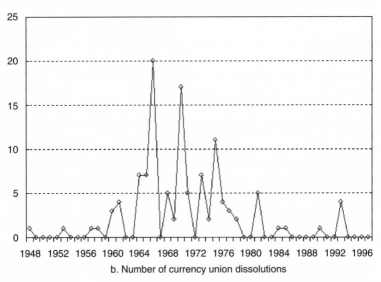

b. Number of currency union dissolutions

Figure 12.1
Description of the data.

(although the deviation just misses statistical significance at the 5 percent level). This is consistent with the literature on optimum currency areas where countries whose business cycles are imperfectly synchronized with those of others benefit the most from the potential stabilization of a *national* monetary policy.

The results for other macroeconomic variables confirm this finding. Broken currency unions are characterized by a particularly large difference in the members' GDP per capita. This differential is a crude indication of a large asymmetry in shocks and cycles but may also support the hypothesis that many currency union exits followed decolonization. Also consumption growth varies widely in dissolved currency unions shortly before the break.

The most convincing piece of evidence, however, is the economically and statistically large difference in the behavior of inflation between sustained and broken currency unions. Country pairs in dissolved currency unions tend to have a much higher rate of inflation and display also a much larger difference in inflation rates than country pairs in sustained currency unions. Moreover the deviation from a typical currency union pair seems to accelerate during the run-up to the currency union break. The average (maximum) rate of inflation increases from 12.3 percent in the three years before a break to 16.6 percent immediately before the break (compared with 9.1 percent in tranquil, non-break periods); the inflation differential rises from 7.1 to 11 percentage points (compared with 4.5 percentage points in periods of tranquillity).

Next I consider financial variables; these variables often feature prominently in studies of banking and exchange rate crises (e.g., see Kaminsky and Reinhart 1999). Most of the measures show statistically significant differences across financial systems in dissolved currency unions relative to sustained ones. For instance, the ratio of M2 to GDP, a measure of financial depth, varies by about 12 percentage points in the run-up to a regime switch compared with an average of less than 9 percentage points in sustained currency unions. There is no clear evidence, however, that the absolute values of these variables (neither in levels nor in growth rates) differ substantially across broken and sustained currency unions. While banking and exchange rate crises have been typically linked to rapid growth in credit and monetary aggregates, there is no measurable difference in the M2 to GDP ratio (or its growth rate), and also the interest rate spread (defined as the lending rate minus LIBOR) is no different (although this result may suffer from the small number of observations). The exceptions are the credit

Table 12.1
Descriptive statistics

	Sustained			Three years before break				One year before break			
	Number observed	Mean	Standard deviation	Number observed	Mean	Standard deviation	Test of equivalence (p-value)	Number observed	Mean	Standard deviation	Test of equivalence (p-value)
A. Macroeconomic variables											
Real GDP growth (%)											
Minimum, pairwise	2,603	0.5	8.2	237	0.3	5.8	0.77	83	−1.3	6.5	0.05
Difference, pairwise	2,603	7.4	10.6	237	8.8	14.2	0.05	83	8.4	6.5	0.36
Real GDP per capita ($)											
Minimum, pairwise	1,036	1,818	2,710	20	1,554	764	0.66	10	1,359	689	0.59
Difference, pairwise	1,036	1,495	2,568	20	4,386	6,171	0.00	10	3,243	5,807	0.04
Private consumption growth (%)											
Minimum, pairwise	1,603	−1.8	8.5	115	−1.3	7.0	0.47	45	−2.0	6.8	0.93
Difference, pairwise	1,603	10.3	10.9	115	10.0	8.8	0.78	45	13.8	10.5	0.04
Total consumption growth (%)											
Minimum, pairwise	1,510	−1.3	7.1	64	−1.1	7.0	0.82	25	−2.5	7.6	0.40
Difference, pairwise	1,510	8.9	9.0	64	10.2	7.6	0.24	25	13.7	8.5	0.01
Inflation (%)											
Maximum, pairwise	1,419	9.1	8.2	129	12.3	14.7	0.00	45	16.6	22.1	0.00
Difference, pairwise	1,419	4.5	4.5	129	7.1	13.5	0.00	45	11.0	21.2	0.00

B. Financial variables

M2/GDP (%)											
Maximum, pairwise	1,558	31.1	16.5	51	31.7	16.7	0.80	22	33.4	16.4	0.51
Difference, pairwise	1,558	8.8	8.3	**51**	**12.1**	**13.2**	**0.01**	**22**	**12.8**	**12.8**	**0.03**
M2/GDP growth (%)											
Minimum, pairwise	1,398	−2.8	8.2	41	−3.7	9.4	0.49	13	−3.7	14.4	0.71
Difference, pairwise	1,398	9.7	9.0	**41**	8.8	9.6	0.54	**13**	13.8	14.4	0.10
Interest rate spread (%)											
Maximum, pairwise	956	5.0	4.4	12	5.1	4.6	0.99	5	4.8	4.3	0.91
Difference, pairwise	956	1.3	1.5	**12**	**3.4**	**3.0**	**0.00**	**5**	**3.3**	**2.2**	**0.00**
Credit to private sector (%GDP)											
Maximum, pairwise	1,586	31.9	18.2	60	37.7	23.2	0.02	28	37.7	23.2	0.09
Difference, pairwise	1,586	12.4	12.9	**60**	**19.5**	**18.5**	**0.00**	**28**	**20.6**	**18.6**	**0.00**
Credit to private sector growth (%)											
Minimum, pairwise	1,425	−6.3	14.1	45	−2.9	12.0	0.11	15	−5.7	14.8	0.89
Difference, pairwise	1,425	14.8	14.2	**45**	**26.1**	**94.0**	**0.00**	**15**	**59.7**	**160**	**0.00**
Domestic banking credit (%GDP)											
Maximum, pairwise	1,584	37.9	23.0	60	45.8	27.2	0.01	28	47.2	26.7	0.04
Difference, pairwise	1,584	15.2	22.0	60	20.5	22.2	0.07	**28**	23.1	22.9	0.06
Domestic banking credit growth (%)											
Minimum, pairwise	1,423	−5.3	13.1	45	−3.1	16.6	0.27	15	−6.2	24.2	0.77
Difference, pairwise	1,423	17.7	19.2	**45**	**29.1**	**75.0**	**0.00**	**15**	**54.0**	**128**	**0.00**

Table 12.1
(continued)

	Sustained			Three years before break				One year before break			
	Number observed	Mean	Standard deviation	Number observed	Mean	Standard deviation	Test of equivalence (p-value)	Number observed	Mean	Standard deviation	Test of equivalence (p-value)
C. Fiscal variables											
Current revenue (%GDP)											
Maximum, pairwise	302	23.7	6.9	22	22.7	6.5	0.53	5	23.0	6.7	0.83
Difference, pairwise	302	7.6	5.8	22	6.7	5.5	0.47	5	6.2	5.2	0.59
Tax revenue (%GDP)											
Maximum, pairwise	353	20.1	4.7	25	20.0	5.0	0.88	6	20.2	5.3	0.97
Difference, pairwise	353	5.5	4.3	25	6.0	3.7	0.60	6	5.9	3.7	0.84
Trade taxes (%revenues)											
Maximum, pairwise	340	38.8	12.8	**34**	**34.2**	**14.0**	**0.05**	10	34.0	15.3	0.25
Difference, pairwise	340	17.9	15.2	34	22.3	13.8	0.11	10	25.1	13.3	0.14
Expenditures (%GDP)											
Maximum, pairwise	313	30.0	8.9	18	30.9	8.6	0.68	6	32.5	11.4	0.50
Difference, pairwise	313	10.0	8.3	18	10.6	5.6	0.78	6	12.9	6.7	0.39
Budget deficit (%GDP)											
Maximum, pairwise	286	-0.8	2.3	**18**	**-2.1**	**2.5**	**0.03**	6	-1.2	2.6	0.70
Difference, pairwise	286	4.9	5.5	18	2.7	1.7	0.09	6	3.6	1.4	0.56
Central government debt (%GDP)											
Maximum, pairwise	61	47.8	34.2	7	23.4	15.9	0.07	3	29.9	8.5	0.37
Difference, pairwise	61	20.7	25.4	7	8.9	6.4	0.23	3	14.1	5.4	0.65

D. Openness variables

Current account (%GDP)											
Minimum, pairwise	1,188	−11.4	9.6	36	−9.0	5.2	0.14	15	−7.6	5.2	0.13
Difference, pairwise	1,188	7.9	9.2	36	5.2	3.8	0.08	15	5.3	4.2	0.27
Exports/GDP (%)											
Maximum, pairwise	1,971	39.1	16.3	151	36.5	19.4	0.05	**58**	**34.7**	**17.7**	**0.04**
Difference, pairwise	1,971	16.9	13.7	151	18.3	14.8	0.22	58	16.9	14.0	0.99
Export growth (%)											
Minimum, pairwise	1,442	−3.5	12.2	63	−4.8	13.7	0.42	**25**	**−11.6**	**14.0**	**0.00**
Difference, pairwise	1,442	17.5	17.4	63	21.4	23.7	0.09	**25**	**27.8**	**26.4**	**0.00**
Export duties (%exports)											
Maximum, pairwise	280	4.3	3.2	**19**	**15.7**	**14.4**	**0.00**	4	**23.5**	**12.4**	**0.00**
Difference, pairwise	280	2.6	2.9	**19**	**13.1**	**13.5**	**0.00**	4	**18.6**	**11.0**	**0.00**
Imports/GDP (%)											
Maximum, pairwise	1,971	46.0	20.3	**151**	**39.4**	**20.5**	**0.00**	**58**	**38.0**	**19.0**	**0.00**
Difference, pairwise	1,971	16.0	16.2	151	17.2	16.0	0.39	58	16.6	14.9	0.78
Import growth (%)											
Minimum, pairwise	1,442	−4.0	11.4	**63**	**−7.1**	**15.0**	**0.03**	**25**	**−15.6**	**17.7**	**0.00**
Difference, pairwise	1,442	16.0	15.6	**63**	**26.3**	**24.8**	**0.00**	**25**	**31.4**	**20.6**	**0.00**
Import duties (%imports)											
Maximum, pairwise	326	22.2	7.0	**30**	**15.1**	**6.5**	**0.00**	8	**11.7**	**6.3**	**0.00**
Difference, pairwise	326	8.5	6.9	30	6.1	4.9	0.07	8	6.9	6.9	0.52
Trade/GDP (%)											
Maximum, pairwise	1,011	38.7	44.6	20	26.0	18.3	0.21	10	21.8	7.7	0.23
Difference, pairwise	1,011	21.7	41.0	20	13.2	17.7	0.36	10	9.2	7.3	0.34
Gross FDI (%GDP)											
Maximum, pairwise	859	2.0	3.0	20	1.0	0.7	0.14	10	0.7	0.5	0.18
Difference, pairwise	859	1.4	2.4	20	0.9	0.6	0.37	10	0.6	0.4	0.30

Table 12.1
(continued)

	Sustained			Three years before break				One year before break			
	Number observed	Mean	Standard deviation	Number observed	Mean	Standard deviation	Test of equivalence (p-value)	Number observed	Mean	Standard deviation	Test of equivalence (p-value)
Gross Private Capital Flows (%GDP)											
Maximum, pairwise	865	17.4	43.6	20	10.0	5.2	0.44	10	8.4	3.9	0.51
Difference, pairwise	865	12.5	43.1	20	4.2	4.0	0.39	10	4.2	4.0	0.54
Bilateral trade growth (%)	3,393	1.2	26.3	289	-0.7	12.3	0.22	102	-1.2	18.5	0.37
E. Institutional variable											
Change in political union											
Dummy	3,531	0.01	0.12	**301**	**0.05**	0.22	**0.00**	**105**	**0.05**	0.21	**0.00**

Notes: "Sustained" currency unions are defined to exist for at least the following three years. The *p*-values refer to a comparison of means between broken and sustained unions; differences significant at the 5 percent level are in bold.

measures that show a pattern consistent with the theory; dissolved currency unions tend to involve countries with a particularly large domestic credit/GDP ratio (well above the ratio recorded for tranquil periods) so that the dissolution of the currency link may be the result of a boom (and bust cycle) in domestic lending.

For fiscal measures, I can only rarely reject the null of no difference in the behavior of these variables between countries that keep a currency union link and countries that depart from a common currency, but (again) many observations are missing. The only notable difference is in budget deficits; countries that leave a currency union tend to have less budgetary discipline.

Turning to openness indicators, there are at least three noteworthy observations. First, the behavior of current account balances does not vary substantially between broken and sustained currency unions.[11] If anything, the current account deficits are smaller before a break and there are smaller differences in pairwise current account balances. Second, countries in dissolved currency unions tend to be less open (as measured by both the exports-to-GDP and the imports-to-GDP ratios), and they also experience a considerable decline in trade prior the break (as measured by both exports and imports growth). This decline in trade, however, is mostly confined to one of the currency union members; there is a large differential in trade growth across broken currency unions. There is also no significant decline in bilateral trade. Third, countries that exit a currency union receive on average smaller capital inflows (relative to GDP), but the difference to tranquil periods is not statistically significant.

Finally, a measure refers to the decolonization hypothesis that (in the past) currency union dissolutions mainly occurred when a colony gained independence and subsequently left the currency area of its former colonizer. As shown in the table, there is some evidence for the intuition. The mean of a dummy on a change in political status is larger for dissolved currency unions than for sustained ones and the difference is statistically highly significant. The average value of 0.05, however, indicates that switches in political status preceded only about one-twentieth of the exchange rate regime transitions in the sample.[12]

12.4.2 Multivariate Results

The preceding comparisons are univariate. I now turn to multivariate analysis. More precisely, I estimate multinomial logit models (by maximum likelihood), linking a binary variable of currency union dissolution to a set of explanatory regressors. As noted above, I employ two measures of currency union exit: a binary variable that is defined as unity if the currency union link is dissolved in the following year (and zero, otherwise), and a binary variable that is defined as unity if the link is broken in one of the next three years.

My exact empirical strategy is dictated by the limited availability of macroeconomic data, which often reduces the number of usable observations. Combining the effects of the variables together into a single model would reduce sample size dramatically. Therefore I apply a two-step procedure.

In a first step, I estimate a baseline regression that includes only a small set of potentially important explanatory variables. In particular, I use as standard regressors: GDP growth, inflation, bilateral trade growth and change in political union. This specification is not the result of extensive pre-testing. Rather, it ensures that, on the one hand, a broad range of potential explanations for the break-up of currency unions is covered, while, on the other hand, the cost of lost observations is minimized. In a later stage, I add the remaining variables to this fixed set of controls, one at a time.[13]

The benchmark results are reported in the first column of table 12.2. Results are tabulated for a currency union dissolution in the following

Table 12.2
Baseline results

	(1)	(2)	(3)
Real GDP growth, minimum	−0.039	−0.027**	
	(−1.614)	(−1.798)	
Real GDP growth, difference	0.014	0.001	
	(0.807)	(0.082)	
Inflation, maximum	0.014		0.018
	(0.721)		(0.939)
Inflation, difference	0.094*		0.074*
	(3.006)		(2.611)
Bilateral trade growth	−0.001	−0.003	−0.001
	(−0.137)	(−0.838)	(−0.211)
Change in political union, dummy	0.404	0.993**	0.455
	(0.384)	(1.855)	(0.439)
Number of observations	1,449	2,840	1,548
McFadden R^2	0.06	0.01	0.06

Notes: Multinomial logit estimation. z-Statistics are in parentheses. Constant not reported. Explanatory variables refer to the year before the currency union dissolution.
* and ** denote significant at the 5 and 10 percent levels, respectively.

year; results are similar for a break in the following three years. Since logit coefficients are not easily interpretable, I am particularly interested in the direction of the link. Associated z-statistics which test the null hypothesis of no effect are in brackets.

The estimates are not especially encouraging in the sense that there do not appear to be tight links between currency union dissolutions and their posited determinants. As shown, only one variable has a statistically significant coefficient, the pairwise difference in inflation. The positive coefficient implies that a large difference in inflation performance across currency union members is associated with a significant increase in the likelihood of a currency union dissolution, holding all else constant.[14] All the other variables have correctly signed, but insignificant coefficients, though some (like the minimum GDP growth rate) are close to significance. This somewhat weak result is not too surprising, however, given the large number of failed attempts to link exchange rates (in general) and currency crises (in particular) to macroeconomic fundamentals. Eichengreen et al. (1995, pp. 254–55), for instance, summarize their detailed analysis of causes and consequences of foreign exchange market turbulences by noting that "regime transitions such as exchange rate flotations ... are difficult to distinguish systematically from periods of tranquillity ... [so that] there do not appear to be clear early warning signals which precede changes in exchange rate regimes."

In the remaining columns of table 12.2, I report the results of two alternative specifications. Dropping the inflation measures almost doubles the number of observations and (slightly) raises the statistical significance of the coefficients on real GDP growth and on a change in political union, but the coefficients remain insignificant on the conventional 5 percent level of confidence. The benchmark results are basically unaffected when measures of GDP growth are dropped.

Table 12.3 performs the extensions. In the upper half of the table, I report the results for the baseline variables. More specifically, I tabulate the range of the estimated coefficients, the maximum/minimum absolute value of the z-statistics and the number of times in which the coefficient enters a regression statistically significantly (at the 5 percent level).

Although the estimates vary substantially across specifications, the results are generally reassuring. As before, the inflation differential has the most precisely estimated impact on the likelihood of a currency

Table 12.3
Extensions

Baseline variables		Maximum coefficient	Minimum coefficient	Maximum $\|z\|$-Statistic	Minimum $\|z\|$-Statistic	Number significant
Real GDP	Minimum	0.024	−1.169	2.47	0.12	5
growth	Difference	0.103	−0.229	2.62	0.01	2
Inflation	Maximum	0.423	−0.049	2.31	0.03	3
	Difference	0.455	0.036	3.03	0.29	15
Bilateral trade growth	Pairwise	0.015	−0.061	1.01	0.03	0
Change in political union	Dummy	6.218	−33.035	3.10	0.00	6

Additional variables		Coefficient	z-Statistic	Mc-Fadden R^2	Number observed	Number cu breaks
A. Macroeconomic variables						
Real GDP per	Minimum	−0.009	−1.87	0.82	695	6
capita	Difference	0.002	1.86			
Private	Minimum	0.003	0.07	0.11	1,104	25
consumption growth	Difference	−0.053	−1.81			
Total	Minimum	0.041	0.86	0.20	941	15
consumption growth	Difference	−0.027	−0.74			
B. Financial variables						
M2/GDP	Maximum	0.040	1.68	0.20	1,071	14
	Difference	0.038	1.22			
M2/GDP	Minimum	0.060	1.53	0.09	972	9
growth	Difference	−0.002	−0.04			
Interest rate	Maximum	−0.058	−0.46	0.13	682	4
spread	Difference	**0.440**	**2.30**			
Credit to private	Maximum	0.002	0.09	0.13	1,100	18
sector	Difference	0.041	1.66			
Credit to private	Minimum	0.011	0.57	0.10	999	11
sector growth	Difference	0.013	1.83			
Domestic	Maximum	0.019	1.27	0.11	1,099	18
banking credit	Difference	0.011	0.56			
Domestic	Minimum	0.003	0.14	0.10	997	11
banking credit growth	Difference	**0.014**	**2.25**			

Table 12.3
(continued)

Baseline variables		Maximum coefficient	Minimum coefficient	Maximum $|z|$-Statistic	Minimum $|z|$-Statistic	Number significant
C. Fiscal variables						
Current revenue	Maximum	0.097	1.08	0.14	265	4
	Difference	−0.197	−1.37			
Tax revenue	Maximum	0.031	0.29	0.12	315	5
	Difference	−0.044	−0.33			
Trade taxes	Maximum	**−0.246**	**−2.42**	0.29	303	7
	Difference	**0.209**	**2.18**			
Expenditures	Maximum	0.066	0.85	0.20	285	5
	Difference	0.035	0.47			
Budget deficit	Maximum	−0.100	−0.43	0.20	261	5
	Difference	0.001	0.01			
Central government debt	Maximum	−0.642	−1.04	0.66	62	3
	Difference	0.871	0.98			
D. Openness variables						
Current account	Minimum	0.007	0.10	0.39	846	10
	Difference	−0.226	−1.93			
Exports/GDP	Maximum	**−0.041**	**−2.13**	0.10	1,273	32
	Difference	0.025	1.17			
Export growth	Minimum	−0.037	−1.70	0.18	953	14
	Difference	−0.013	−0.72			
Export duties	Maximum	0.245	1.77	0.51	291	4
	Difference	−0.070	−0.50			
Imports/GDP	Maximum	**−0.078**	**−3.66**	0.14	1,273	32
	Difference	**0.083**	**3.84**			
Import growth	Minimum	**−0.065**	**−2.16**	0.23	953	14
	Difference	0.020	1.35			
Import duties	Maximum	**−0.488**	**−2.66**	0.36	279	6
	Difference	**0.373**	**2.11**			
Trade/GDP	Maximum	−0.017	−0.19	0.59	677	6
	Difference	−0.148	−1.31			
Gross FDI	Maximum	−0.548	−0.28	0.51	612	6
	Difference	0.490	0.24			
Gross private capital flows	Maximum	0.156	0.68	0.65	616	6
	Difference	−0.887	−1.69			

Notes: Multinomial logit estimation. The six baseline variables (and an unreported constant) are included in all regressions. Additional variables are (pairwise) entered as seventh/eighth regressor; coefficients significant at the 5 percent level are in bold. For the baseline variables the minimum and maximum absolute values of the z-statistic in any of the regressions are reported, and the number of cases in which the variable is significant at the 5 percent level. Explanatory variables refer to the year before the currency union dissolution.

union dissolution; a large difference in inflation performance is consistently strongly and significantly associated with the incidence of a currency union break.[15] In some specifications, also other baseline variables have significant coefficients, notably the dummy on a change in political union (which enters significantly in about one-fourth of the regressions).[16] Thus there is some evidence that a split in political union is often quickly followed by currency union dissolution.

In the lower half of the table the results for the other (additionally entered) variables are shown. Broadly speaking, the results from univariate analyses are confirmed. The coefficients on per capita income take on the expected sign but just miss statistical significance. Similarly financial measures are often just little below conventional significance levels; only a large difference in the interest rate spread is significantly associated with a higher probability of a currency union, perhaps in anticipation of this event. Fiscal measures are, as before, mostly insignificant (including the budget deficit), while a small degree of openness (especially in one of the countries) and low trade growth both coincide with an increased probability of a currency union dissolution.

To summarize, with the possible exception of inflation differentials, there are only few clearly significant links between macroeconomic fundamentals and currency union dissolutions.[17] On the positive side, trade openness appears to matter. Currency unions that include countries which trade only very little (as a share of GDP) are likely to dissolve, especially at a time when the countries experience a decline in external trade.[18] Also changes in political status appear to be important. A breakup in political union is often accompanied by a breakup of the currency link. On the negative side, there is little evidence that the co-movement of output and the symmetry of shocks has a measurable effect on the sustainability of a currency union. Similarly fiscal aspects that play an important role in the design of the European monetary union (in the form of the stability and growth pact) have no predictive power for currency union dissolution.

12.5   More Details

The previous results are derived from a large sample of very diverse experiences. For many economic variables, differences between broken and sustained currency unions are masked by large variances; economic conditions often vary considerably across currency union break-

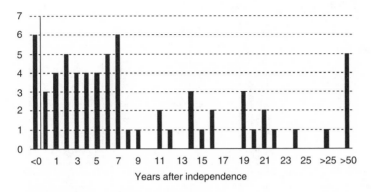

Figure 12.2
Currency union dissolutions and political independence. The columns give the number of switches out of a currency union over the years following political independence. The total sample comprises 69 currency union dissolutions; four of these exits involve still dependent territories.

ups.[19] In this section, I therefore present some more illustrative details of the data set.

A large fraction of the currency unions in the sample are country pairs in which a dependent territory uses the currency of the colonizing country; these currency union links were often dissolved after the colonies gained independence. However, while many of these countries established a national central bank immediately after (or even before) independence, the date when the peg was given up varies markedly. Figure 12.2 plots a histogram of the time period between political independence and currency union exit. Excluding transitive cases, the sample comprises 69 currency union dissolutions. Of these 69 exits, four involve still existing dependencies (Bermuda, Djibouti, Reunion, and St. Pierre and Miquelon); another five links were dissolved before the territory gained independence (the Bahamas, Brunei Darussalam, Qatar, Vanuatu, and Zimbabwe). The remaining 60 cases spread over time, with about two-thirds of the exits (37 cases) occurring within ten years after political independence. Examples for long-lasting currency unions between sovereign nations include the link of the Irish pound to the British pound and the peg of the Malagasy franc to the French franc.[20]

Figures 12.3 and 12.4 present some case study evidence for economic measures for which I find significant differences between broken and sustained currency unions. Figure 12.3 focuses on the inflation differential. The figure provides eight time-series plots of the difference

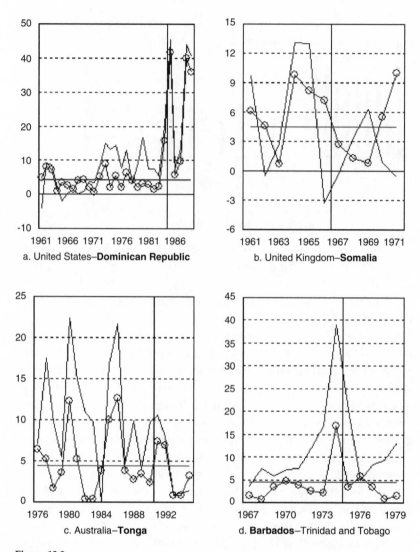

a. United States–**Dominican Republic**

b. United Kingdom–**Somalia**

c. Australia–**Tonga**

d. **Barbados**–Trinidad and Tobago

Figure 12.3
Inflation differentials for selected country pairs. The inflation rate is for the country
(given in boldface) that leaves the currency union. The year of currency union exit is
marked by the vertical line. The circled line shows the inflation differential for each country pair, and the horizontal line the average inflation differential for the sustained currency unions.

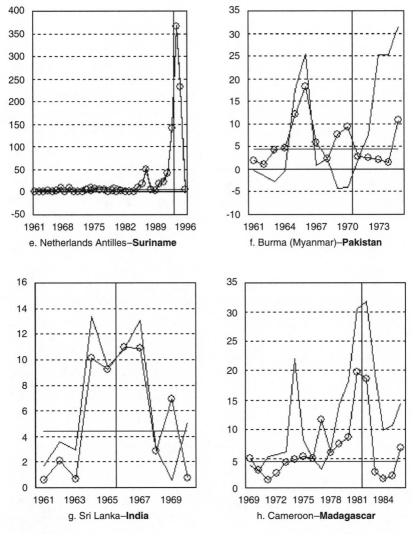

e. Netherlands Antilles–**Suriname**

f. Burma (Myanmar)–**Pakistan**

g. Sri Lanka–**India**

h. Cameroon–**Madagascar**

Figure 12.3
(continued)

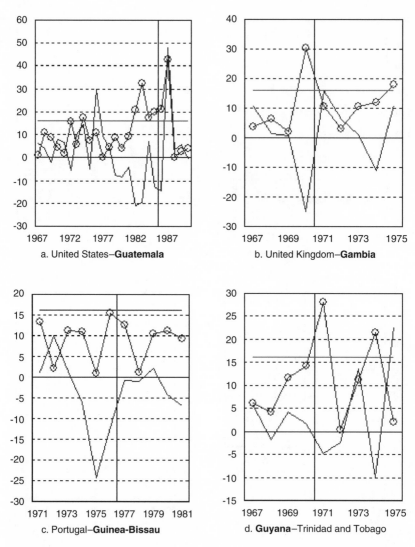

Figure 12.4
Import growth differentials for selected country pairs. The import growth rate is for the country (given in boldface) that leaves the currency union. The year of currency union exit is marked by the vertical line. The circled line shows the import growth differential for each country pair, and the horizontal line the average import growth differential for the sustained currency unions.

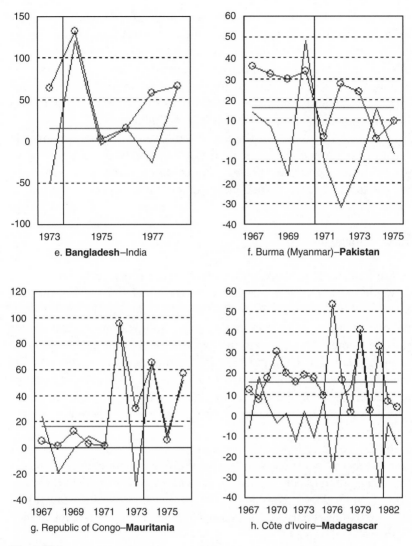

Figure 12.4
(continued)

in national inflation rates before (and immediately after) currency union dissolution (an event marked with a vertical line). As the graphs clearly show, broken currency unions tend to display considerable differences in consumer price inflation before exit, often sizably above the average for sustained currency unions (marked with a horizontal line). Further it is mainly the country that leaves the union that experiences high inflation, often caused by severe fiscal imbalances.

Figure 12.4 provides analogues for differences in import growth. Illustrating previous regression results, large differences in import growth often preceded currency union dissolutions, with especially the departing country experiencing a sometimes dramatic decline in trade.

12.6 Conclusions

A growing number of countries are actively considering whether to abandon its national currency and enter a monetary union. The motives for the adoption of a foreign currency (which implies the loss of some national independence and sovereignty) range from the desire for closer economic integration to the introduction of external discipline.

Since sharing a common currency comes not only with benefits but also with some costs, much of the literature on currency unions focuses on the pros and cons of monetary integration. Many empirical studies discuss this trade-off in the context of proposed monetary unions.

In this chapter, I followed another route. In particular, I searched for stylized facts associated with the breakup of currency unions, since a characterization of currency union exits allows one to answer the question of when does a common currency link become unsustainable. I examined annual data for 245 country pairs that share the same money from 1948 through 1997.

I found that a large inflation differential between currency union members is consistently associated with a high likelihood of a currency union dissolution; an obvious extension would be to search for potential causes of this divergence in inflation performance. Many departures from a currency union link have also occurred when a political union is dissolved. Somewhat surprisingly, neither asymmetries in output nor fiscal variables appear to matter for a typical break of a currency union.

Notes

I thank Graziella Bertocchi, Benjamin Cohen, Charles Goodhart, Jacques Mélitz, Barbara Pistoresi, Andrew Rose, Kiril Strahilov, an anonymous referee, and participants at the CEPR conference on "Macroeconomics and Economic Geography," the CESifo Venice Summer Institute workshop on "Monetary Unions after EMU," the 2002 meeting of the European Trade Study Group, the 2003 meeting of the Verein fuer Socialpolitik, and the Humboldt University Macro seminar for helpful comments.

1. Alesina and Barro (2001, p. 381) note that "roughly 60 small countries or territories [of the 193 independent countries] have for some time been members of currency unions or have used a large country's money," including the 15-member CFA franc zone in Africa and the 7-member eastern Caribbean currency area. In terms of GDP, however, this group of countries (excluding anchor countries) makes up less than 1 percent of world GDP. If one adds to this list the 12-member European monetary union, the accession countries in Europe, the countries in West Africa, Southern Africa and the Arab gulf region that have declared their intention to form a currency union as well as the Latin American countries that seriously consider dollarization, the number of countries without a national currency is easily doubled and the combined GDP is increased by several orders of magnitude.

2. In future work I intend to explore the (short-term) macroeconomic effects of currency union dissolutions.

3. Kaminsky et al. (1998, p. 2) conclude: "The results indicate that an effective warning system [of currency crises] should consider a broad variety of indicators, since currency crises seem to usually be preceded by a broad range of economic problems."

4. Bomberger (2002) argues that the decline in trade after currency union dissolution is mainly the result of a reorientation of trade flows after former colonies gained independence rather than reflecting the change in the currency union status.

5. As Goodhart (1995, p. 449) puts it: "Political, not economic, events have caused the monetary changes in Central and Eastern Europe; economic considerations, although important, have been secondary."

6. For instance, Glick and Rose's sample includes only observations for country pairs with positive bilateral trade.

7. None of the results changes when the analysis is confined to this period.

8. I ignore their measures of educational attainment and geographic remoteness.

9. For broken currency union links, I tabulate the results for the period up to three years prior the break and the (one) year immediately preceding the break. The motivation is that an exit from a currency union (i.e., the introduction and circulation of a country's own new national money) may require some time for preparations (e.g., the establishment of a central bank, the design and printing of banknotes). Therefore economic conditions a few years before a currency union dissolution may be more relevant in explaining this event than the situation shortly before the break. As shown in the table, however, there are only minor differences in the results.

10. The minimum growth rate is the lower value in GDP growth for each country pair/year observation.

11. Eichengreen et al. (1995) report similar findings for currency crises.

12. Another promising approach would be to divide the sample of currency unions by the reasons for their initial adoption. One might expect that while political factors would be of overwhelming importance for the breakup of colonial and federal country currency unions, economic factors would play a large role in the dissolution of voluntarily adopted currency unions. I am grateful to Charles Goodhart for pointing this out to me.

13. Juhn and Mauro (2002) follow a similar approach.

14. Barro (1996, pp. 65–68) argues that prior colonial status (by colonizer) may be an useful instrument for inflation.

15. The inflation differential is the only baseline variable that does not change sign in any of the perturbations.

16. If significant, coefficients have the expected sign.

17. I have performed extensive robustness checks. For instance, I have used probit models, split the sample into pre- and post-1975, excluded politically motivated currency union breakups (i.e., when a colony gained independence), and distinguished between membership in bilateral and multilateral arrangements. In all of these cases the estimates were basically identical with the baseline results. As expected, economic factors appear to be somewhat stronger for currency union dissolutions unrelated to political events, and multilateral arrangements seem to be more robust. There is also some evidence that the (pairwise) minimum GDP growth rate might have an effect.

18. Additionally controlling for country size has no measurable effect.

19. This result basically confirms the findings of Cohen (2001). After examining seven case studies, Cohen concludes (like Goodhart) that economic variables (or organizational characteristics) are only second order issues; the sustainability of currency unions primarily depends on the "political will." However, while giving up a currency union is ultimately a political decision (as is the decision to establish or join a monetary union), my regression results show that economic issues are not completely irrelevant.

20. Ireland departed from its sterling link in 1979, 58 years after independence from the United Kingdom. Madagascar was a member of the French franc zone from independence in 1960 until 1973. After withdrawal in 1973, the Malagasy franc remained pegged to the French franc for another nine years until April 2, 1982.

References

Alesina, A., and R. J. Barro. 2001. Dollarization. *American Economic Review* 91 (May): 381–85.

Alesina, A., and R. J. Barro. 2002. Currency unions. *Quarterly Journal of Economics* 67 (May): 409–36.

Alesina, A., R. J. Barro, and S. Tenreyro. 2002. Optimal currency areas. In *Macroeconomics Annual* 17: 301–45.

Barro, R. J. 1996. Determinants of economic growth: A cross-country empirical study. NBER Working Paper 5698.

Bomberger, W. A. 2002. Decolonization and estimates of the time series effect of currency unions. University of Florida.

Chang, R., and A. Velasco. 2002. Dollarization: Analytical issues. NBER Working Paper 8838.

Cohen, B. J. 2001. Beyond EMU: The problem of sustainability. In B. J. Eichengreen and J. A. Frieden, eds., *The Political Economy of European Monetary Unification*, 2nd ed. Boulder: Westview Press.

Eichengreen, B., A. K. Rose, and C. Wyplosz. 1995. Exchange market mayhem: The antecedents and aftermath of speculative attacks. *Economic Policy* 21 (October): 251–312.

Frankel, J. A., and A. K. Rose. 1996. Currency crashes in emerging markets: An empirical treatment. *Journal of International Economics* 41 (November): 351–66.

Glick, R., and A. K. Rose. 2002. Does a currency union affect trade? The time-series evidence. *European Economic Review* 46 (June): 1125–51.

Goodhart, C. A. E. 1995. The political economy of monetary union. In P. B. Kenen, ed., *Understanding Independence*. Princeton: Princeton University Press.

Juhn, G., and P. Mauro. 2002. Long-run determinants of exchange rate regimes: A simple sensitivity analysis. IMF Working Paper 02/104.

Kaminsky, G. L., S. Lizondo, and C. M. Reinhart. 1998. Leading indicators of currency crises. *IMF Staff Papers* 45 (March): 1–48.

Kaminsky, G. L., and C. M. Reinhart. 1999. The twin crises: The causes of banking and balance-of-payments problems. *American Economic Review* 89 (June): 473–500.

Mundell, R. A. 1961. A theory of optimum currency areas. *American Economic Review* 51 (September): 657–65.

Rose, A. K., and C. Engel. 2002. Currency unions and international integration. *Journal of Money, Credit, and Banking* 34 (August): 804–26.

Index

Accession countries. *See* CEEC accession countries

Acquis communautaire, 50n.2, 89

ADF (augmented Dickey-Fuller) test, 295

Argentina
as partially dollarized, 225
and trade with Brazil, 283n.13
variability of exchange and interest rate in, 78

ASEAN countries, currency area in, 263

Asia. *See also* East Asia; Northeast Asia currency union
and regional exchange rate volatility, 269
and trade integration, 273

Asian financial crisis (1997), 263, 289, 312
as economic integration incentive, 312
and unilateral currency union, 225

Asymmetric shocks. *See* Shocks, asymmetric

Augmented Dickey-Fuller (ADF) test, 295

Australia, in study of smoothing of shocks, 191, 203

Austria
and exchange rate study, 134
as low-deficit country, 205

Balassa-Samuelson (BS) effect or approach
and inflation, 2, 3, 22, 128, 147
key assumptions of, 130
and real exchange rates, 8, 23, 131, 132–33, 137–44

Banking system, and dollarization, 236–37

Belgium, as high-deficit country, 205

Benefits and costs. *See* Costs and benefits

Bilateral integration, and dollarization analysis, 267

Binding contracts, in modeling of exchange rate variability and unemployment, 82–87

Black market, and model of exchange rate variability and unemployment, 93

Blair, Tony, 156

Blanchard-Quah method, 305, 307

Booster effect on trade (trade booster), EMU as, 165, 178

Brazil
in trade with Argentina, 283n.13
variability of exchange and interest rate in, 78

Bretton Woods, collapse of, 267, 285n.28

Brown, Gordon, 156

Budget deficits. *See* Deficit, government

Bulgaria. *See also* Central and Eastern European countries
currency board regime in, 11, 20, 45, 79
EMU trade of, 81
exchange rate variability and unemployment in, 90, 99, 107, 108, 109
as expected member, 17
inflation in, 27n.10
openness of, 80–81

Business cycle convergence
in EU countries, 70
between EU members and CEECs, 57–59
and intra-industry trade, 66–68, 72
and monetary or fiscal policy, 69
and trade intensity, 55–56, 64–66, 68, 72

Business cycles
codependent (Northeast Asia currency union analysis), 300–303
"common feature" and "codependence," 291

Business cycle synchronization, 290
and currency union dissolution, 325

Canada
  EMU trade with, 165
  in study of smoothing of shocks, 191, 205
Capital depreciation
  and business cycle, 221n.23
  as channel of income and consumption
    smoothing, 191, 192, 197, 198, 200, 214
Capital inflows, and currency union
    dissolution, 331
Capital markets
  and exchange rate risk, 81
  risk sharing in, 211
  as smoothing channel, 194, 207, 208, 209,
    215
Catching up
  inflation from, 147
  issue of, 127–28, 147
CEEC accession countries, 127. *See also*
    Central and Eastern European countries
  Balassa-Samuelson and demand-side
    effects on, 132
  and convergence, 127
  and full monetary union, 147
  GDPs of, 127–28
  and real exchange rate, 127, 128–29, 131–
    48
  regulated prices in, 144
CEECs. *See* Central and Eastern European
    countries
Central America. *See also* Latin America
  and dissimilarities of export base, 269
  dollarization of, 264, 283n.4
  and dollarization analysis, 264, 279
  and output-shock asymmetry, 269
  and real exchange rate volatility, 264,
    278, 279, 280
  and regional exchange rate volatility, 269
  and trade integration, 270, 273, 279, 280
Central bank, 41–42
  and bureaucracy theory, 51n.9
  and inflation, 41, 42, 43, 46, 51n.10
Central bank, common, 41–42
  and asymmetric shocks, 47
  and inflation in high-distortion countries,
    44
  and inflation in low-distortion countries,
    46
Central bank, European. *See* European
    central bank
Central and Eastern European countries
    (CEECs). *See also* CEEC accession
    countries; *specific countries*

as converging to EU countries, 73
EMU trade of, 81
EU members' business cycles
    convergence with, 57–59
and euro introduction, 56, 57
EU trade integration with, 60–61
and exchange rate relations or regime, 78,
    79
and industrial production correlation
    with Germany, 70
labor markets of (exchange rate
    variability and unemployment), 87–120
openness of, 80–81
unemployment in, 77
Chiang Mai Initiative, 289
China, 300
  and labor share values, 309
  and Northeast Asia currency union, 5,
    289, 292, 299–300, 307, 310, 311 (*see also*
    Northeast Asia currency union)
  trade of with Japan and Korea, 293–94
China–Japan–Korea free-trade area,
    prospect of, 292
Codependent business cycles, in Northeast
    Asia currency union analysis, 300–303
Cointegration model or test, 133, 290–91,
    296–97
Common Agricultural Policy (CAP), 200
Common central bank. *See* Central bank,
    common
Common currency (common currency
    area). *See also* Optimal currency areas,
    theory of; Regional currency
  in ASEAN countries, 263
  benefits and costs of, 55, 265
  criteria for, 266, 289–90
  practical problems inherent in, 264
Contracts, in modeling of exchange rate
    variability and unemployment, 82–87
Convergence. *See also* Business cycle
    convergence
  and accession countries, 13, 127
  question of need for, 121
Convergence criteria, Maastricht. *See*
    Maastricht criteria for entry
Convergence gap, 9, 25
Convergence test, in UK–EMU debate, 156
Cost recovery hypothesis, 142
Costs and benefits
  of common currency or monetary union,
    55, 265, 291, 303–304, 314n.9
  of dollarization, 227–40, 265

of hard currency, 225
Countercyclical monetary policy, 254, 256
Country credit, and dollarization, 256
Country risk, dollarization as decrease in, 265
Country size, and output smoothing, 189, 200–201
Credibility, and exchange rate regime, 266, 284n.19
Credit/GDP ratio, and currency union dissolution, 331
Credit market
in smoothing of EMU business cycles, 188, 190–91, 207, 208–209, 212, 216, 222n.37
in US consumption smoothing, 194, 207, 208–209, 215
Credit risk, and full dollarization, 233
Crises. *See* Currency crises
Currency area. *See* Common currency
Currency board
in EU enlargement model, 11–12
and full euroization, 45
Currency crises
and dollarization, 236
and exit from currency union, 321
Currency risk, dollarization as decrease in, 265
Currency union. *See* Monetary union(s)
Currency union, Northeast Asia. *See* Northeast Asia currency union
Currency union dissolution. *See* Monetary union dissolution
Current account position (balances)
and currency union dissolution, 331
and dollarization, 237
Czechoslovakia, breakup of, 321–22
Czech Republic. *See also* Central and Eastern European countries
Balassa-Samuelson effect for, 133
and correlation of industrial production with Germany, 70, 72
EMU trade of, 81
and endogeneity hypothesis of OCA criteria, 56
and euro adoption, 79
exchange rate regime in, 79
exchange rate variability and unemployment in, 90, 99, 107, 120
flexibility of labor market institutions in, 87
and German business cycles, 58, 73

Decolonization, and currency union dissolution, 325, 331, 337
Default risk, and dollarization, 233, 236
Deficit, government
and accession countries, 33
and consumption smoothing, 203–207, 214
and currency union dissolution, 331, 336
and risk sharing, 189
Denmark
as eurozone entrant, 189, 211
as low-deficit country, 205
Derogation, right of (introduction of euro), 79
Devaluation risk, and dollarization, 233, 236
Developed countries, and law of one price, 131
Developing countries, currency crises in, 263
Difference-indifference analysis, 160–61, 166, 167
Dixit-Pindyck model, 87
Dollarization, 225–26, 263, 265, 319
as alternative monetary union, 4–5
costs and benefits of, 227–40, 265
vs. regional currency areas, 264–65, 279–81
vs. regional currency areas (assessment), 266–79
vs. regional currency areas (data used), 281–82
seriousness of, 319
Dollarization models
and fiscal deficit volatility (comparison), 251, 256
with fully dollarized economy, 244–45, 255–56
and macroeconomic volatility (comparison), 249–53, 255
of partially dollarized economy with flexible exchange rates, 240–43, 245–49
sensitivity analysis of, 254–55, 256, 259, 260n.20
and terms-of-trade shocks (comparison), 251, 253, 256
welfare exercise on, 253–54, 256

East Asia. *See also* Asia
currency crises in, 263
and dissimilarities of export base, 269
and dollarization analysis, 264, 279

East Asia (cont.)
and monetary union, 2, 4, 5
and output-shock asymmetry, 269
and real exchange rate volatility, 264,
278, 279, 280
and trade integration, 270, 273, 280
and trade intensity, 270, 280
East Asian currency union. See Northeast
Asia currency union
Eastern Europe. See CEEC accession
countries; Central and Eastern
European countries
Economic distortions
and structural reforms, 32
and unemployment, 36
Ecuador, and dollarization, 225, 227, 263,
265
El Salvador, and dollarization, 263, 265
Emerging market economies
and exchange rate fluctuations, 80
instability of, 226
Employment. See at Labor market
EMU effect on trade, 156–57, 160, 178
data from study of, 163, 180–81
empirical results from study of, 163–69
methodology in study of, 160–63
in UK case, 157, 159–60, 165, 170–77,
178–79
EMU (European Monetary Union)
enlargement
conditions for achievement of, 46–48
conventional view of, 79
current member states as benefiting from,
49
and influences on real exchange rate and
internal price ratios, 147
and monetary policy, 39–42
and monetary union, 31
and optimum currency area (OCA)
theory (implications), 61–72
and optimum currency area (OCA)
theory (stylized facts), 57–61
polarization instead of convergence from,
32, 49
and smoothing of shocks, 215–16
United Kingdom, Sweden, and Denmark
in, 189, 211
EMU enlargement and structural reform,
31–32, 48–50
and effect of monetary union on
structural reform, 42–45, 46, 48–50
and monetary policy, 39–42

and need for structural reform, 33–36
and resistance to reforms, 36, 38–39, 46
Endogeneity hypothesis of optimum
currency (OCA) criteria, 3, 55–56, 61, 64,
68, 72–73
Endogenous lagged variables problem, 95
Endogenous optimum currency area,
indexes of, 70–72
Enlargement phase of EU enlargement
model, 8, 14–17
EOCA indexes, 70, 72, 73
Equality of treatment principle, 7
Estonia. See also Central and eastern
European countries
Balassa-Samuelson implied inflation
differential for, 147
currency board regime in, 11, 20, 45, 79,
94
and EMU membership, 147
EMU trade of, 81
and endogeneity hypothesis of OCA
criteria, 56
eurozone entry of, 79
in exchange rate mechanism II (ERM II),
27n.4
exchange rate variability and
unemployment in, 90, 99, 107
flexibility of labor market institutions in,
87
openness of, 80
real exchange rates and internal price
ratios of, 127, 134, 143, 146
EU enlargement model, 7–9, 25–26
and currency board, 11–12
and fiscal issues, 26
and independent monetary policy, 9–11
inflation in, 8, 10–11, 12, 14, 15, 16, 20, 22,
23, 25, 26
numerical exercise on, 17–25
numerical exercise on (alternative),
27n.12
phases of: pre-Maastricht, 8, 20–21
phases of: Maastricht, 8, 13, 21, 25
phases of: enlarged monetary union, 8,
14–17, 21–25, 26
and positive effects of enlargement, 26
Euro
and dollarization debate, 225
early vs. late adoption of (CEECs), 78
and exchange rate risk, 165, 178, 188
Franco-German partnership as key to,
289

introduction of as milestone, 1
from monetary union, 319
right of derogation on, 79
savings from adoption of, 308
Thatcher on, 155
Euro area. *See* Eurozone
Euroization
benefits and costs of, 45
elimination of exchange rate risk from,
120
and Maastricht Treaty, 51n.14
Europe. *See also specific countries*
currency union in, 280
and dissimilarities of export base, 269
financial integration of, 188
and output-shock asymmetry, 269
real exchange rate volatility of, 267, 278–
79, 279, 280
and regional exchange rate volatility,
269
and trade integration, 270, 273, 280
European central bank (ECB)
creation of, 167
risk sharing as help for, 188
European Monetary Union. *See also at*
EMU
and *acquis communautaire*, 50n.2
as changing economists' outlook, 2
Franco-German partnership as key to,
289
1998 as pivotal year for, 167
seriousness of, 319
trade increases from, 4
and UK–EMU debate, 155–56
European Union. *See also* EU enlargement
model
CEEC trade integration with, 60–61
Exchange rate variability and labor
markets in, 78
European Union Treaty, 216
Eurozone (euro area)
enlargement of (CEECs), 2–3, 72–73, 79
enlargement of (future), 211
Exchange rate, flexible, and inflation (vs.
currency board regime), 12
Exchange rate, nominal, in EU
enlargement model, 11
Exchange rate, real
appreciation of (catching-up countries),
27n.3
Balassa-Samuelson approach to
systematic movements in, 130

decomposition of, 129
in EU enlargement model, 21
influences on (four CEEC accession
countries), 127, 128–29, 131–48
variability of (dollarization analysis),
267–69, 273–81
vis-à-vis USA, 181
volatility of, 281
Exchange rate mechanism (ERM II), 57,
79, 127
Exchange rate policy, dollarization as
eliminating, 238–39
Exchange rate regime, and CEECs, 79
determinants of, 266, 320
Exchange rate regime choice, self-
validating nature of, 311
Exchange rate shocks. *See* Shocks,
exchange rate
Exchange rate variability, and trade, 80,
120
Exchange rate variability and
unemployment, 77–78
characteristics leading to adverse impact,
85
data and definitions on, 90–94
empirical model and results on, 94–120
and employment vs. unemployment
data, 109
and irreversibility of employment
decisions, 83, 120
modeling of, 79–89

Factor income, as channel of income and
consumption smoothing, 191, 192, 197,
198, 200, 214
Fallback wage, 82, 85
Federal government (US), as smoothing
channel, 194
Feldstein-Horioka puzzle, 4
Financial integration, and dollarization,
236–37
Financial services test, in UK-EMU debate,
156
Financial variables, and currency union
exit, 325, 336
Finland
as low-deficit country, 205
and USSR collapse, 198
Fiscal deficit volatility, in dollarization
model, 251, 256
Fiscal discipline, and dollarization, 227,
233

Fiscal policy, and business cycle
convergence, 69
Flexibility of labor force, and CEECs, 87
Flexibility test, in UK–EMU debate, 156
Foreign trade in emerging economies, and
exchange rate volatility, 80
France
and correlation of industrial production
with Germany, 72
and German shocks, 57
as low-deficit country, 205
reforms turned back in, 40
Frankel-Rose hypothesis, 3, 55, 56, 64, 72
Full euroization, 45

GDP growth, and monetary union
dissolution, 323
GDP per capita, and currency union
dissolution, 325
General Agreement on Tariffs and Trade,
Japan and Korea in, 292
Germany
and correlations of business cycles, 57–
58, 73
and correlations of growth of industrial
production, 58, 70
and industrial production of other EU
countries, 70, 72, 73
as low-deficit country, 205
reforms turned back in, 40
Gold standard, and trade, 158–59
Government deficit/debt
and consumption smoothing, 203–207,
214
and currency union dissolution, 331, 336
and risk sharing, 189
Government role, in smoothing shocks,
187, 190, 202–203, 214, 216
Gravity model of international trade, 65,
80
difference-indifference version of, 160–61,
166, 167
Greece, as high-deficit country, 205
Growth
and dollarization, 237–38
GDP (and monetary union dissolution),
323
trade, 60–61, 331, 336
Growth, stability and jobs test, in UK–
EMU debate, 156
Grubel-Lloyd indexes, 66
Guatemala, dollarization in, 265

Hard currency pegs, 45, 319
benefits of adopting, 225
vs. currency unions, 263
Hausman specification tests, 95
Hiring costs, and effect of exchange rate
uncertainty on job creation, 85
Hodrick-Prescott filter, 305, 307
Hungary. See also Central and Eastern
European countries
Balassa-Samuelson effect for, 133
Balassa-Samuelson implied inflation
differential for, 147
and correlation of industrial production
with Germany, 70
and EMU membership, 147
EMU trade of, 81
and endogeneity hypothesis of OCA
criteria, 56
and euro adoption, 79
EU trade of, 60
exchange rate regime in, 79
exchange rate variability and
unemployment in, 90, 99, 107, 120
flexibility of labor market institutions in,
87
and German shocks, 57
and optimum currency area, 73
real exchange rates and internal price
ratios of, 127, 134, 146
tradables and nontradables in, 135,
151n.3

Idiosyncratic shocks. See Shocks,
idiosyncratic
"Imbalance" growth phenomenon, 311
Imperfect substitutability, 131
Income per capita, and currency union
dissolution, 336
Independent monetary policy, in EU
enlargement model, 9–11
Inflation
and admittance to union, 31
and catching-up process of accession
countries, 128, 147
and central bank, 41, 42, 43, 46, 51n.10
and currency (monetary) union
dissolution, 6, 325, 333, 336, 337, 342
and dollarization, 227, 240, 256
in EU enlargement model, 8, 10–11, 12,
14, 15, 16, 19, 20, 22, 23, 25, 26
and eurozone enlargement, 2, 3
and exchange rate, 79, 80

and high distortions country, 44
influence of enlargement on, 43–44, 46, 47, 48
and monetary union dissolution, 320
and unilateral currency union, 255
Inflation volatility, in dollarization models, 249
Insurance mechanisms, with monetary union, 4
Integration, bilateral, and dollarization analysis, 267
Interest rates
  and dollarization, 233, 236
  and exchange rate risks, 81
Internal price ratios. *See* Price ratios, internal
International transfers, as channel of income and consumption smoothing, 191, 192, 200, 207, 209, 211, 212, 214, 215
Intra-industry trade, 60–61, 64
  and business cycles, 66–68, 72
  and OCA criteria, 72
Investment, and dollarization, 237–38
Investment projects, and uncertainty of future earnings, 81
Investment test, in UK–EMU debate, 156
Ireland
  in currency union with Britain, 337
  as high-deficit country, 205
Italy
  and German shocks, 57
  as high-deficit country, 205
  reforms turned back in, 40

Japan, 300
  and labor share values, 309
  as low-deficit country, 205
  and Northeast Asia currency union, 5, 289, 292, 299–300, 307, 309, 310, 311 (*see also* Northeast Asia currency union)
  in study of smoothing of shocks, 191
  trade of with China and Korea, 293–94
Japan–Korea free-trade area, prospect of, 292
Job creation, and exchange rate uncertainty, 81
Johansen cointegration method, 133, 290–91, 296–97

Korea, 300
  and labor share values, 309

and Northeast Asia currency union, 5, 289, 292, 299–300, 307, 310, 311 (*see also* Northeast Asia currency union)
trade of with China and Japan, 293–94

Labor market(s), of CEECs (exchange rate variability and unemployment), 79–120
characteristics leading to adverse impact, 85
and employment vs. unemployment data, 109
and fallback wage, 8, 85
and flexibility, 87
and irreversibility of employment decisions, 83, 120
Labor market policy, employed insiders as benefiting from, 38
Labor market reforms
  and eurozone enlargement, 2–3
  and monetary union, 32
Labor market regulations
  as enlargement preparation, 33
  reform of needed (EU-15), 36, 38–39 (*see also* Structural reform and EMU enlargement)
Latin America. *See also* Central America; South America
  and dollarization, 225, 263
  and monetary union, 2, 4–5
  and regional exchange rate arrangements, 81
Latvia. *See also* Central and Eastern European countries
  EMU trade of, 81
  and endogeneity hypothesis of OCA criteria, 56
  exchange rate regime of, 20, 79, 94
  exchange rate variability and unemployment in, 90, 92, 99, 107, 120
Law of one price (LOOP), 130, 131
Laws of motion (dollarization model), 242, 256–57
Lender of last resort
  and dollarization, 239, 265
  and "hard peg," 45
Lithuania. *See also* Central and Eastern European countries
  currency board regime in, 11, 20, 79
  EMU trade of, 81
  and endogeneity hypothesis of OCA criteria, 56
  eurozone entry of, 79

Lithuania (cont.)
  EU trade of, 60
  in exchange rate mechanism II (ERM II),
    27n.4
  exchange rate variability and
    unemployment in, 90, 92, 99, 107
Luxembourg, and study of smoothing of
  shocks, 191

Maastricht criteria for entry, 31, 49
  and entry of Central European countries,
    3, 57
  and new members, 13
  and 1998 as pivotal year, 167
Maastricht phase of EU enlargement
  model, 8, 13
Mercosur countries
  common currency for, 263–264
  and exchange rate or interest rate
    variability, 78, 120
Mexico, and dollarization, 225, 236
Minimum wage restriction, and effect of
  exchange rate uncertainty on job
  creation, 85
Monetarist counterrevolution, 1
Monetary integration, 319
  for Europe, 1 (see also European
    Monetary Union)
  and optimum currency area, 321
  and trade intensity, 55
Monetary policy
  and asymmetric real shocks, 265
  and business cycle convergence, 69
  dollarization as eliminating, 238–39, 265
  and dollarization-model sensitivity, 254,
    255, 256
  and structural distortions, 48–49
Monetary unification, in broader
  integration project, 264
Monetary (currency) union(s), 342. See also
  Regional currency
  costs and benefits of, 291, 303–304,
    314n.19
  dynamic effects of, 266, 284n.21
  in East Asia, 280
  and experts' advice, 1–2
  in Europe, 1–2, 280 (see also EMU
    enlargement; European Monetary
    Union)
  exits from vs. entries into, 319 (see also
    Monetary union dissolution)
  and government role in smoothing of
    shocks, 187

vs. hard currency pegs, 263
insurance mechanisms with, 4
and labor market reforms, 32
in Latin America and East Asia, 2, 4–5
  (see also Dollarization; Northeast Asia
  currency union)
membership of, 343n.1
and OCA, 190
questions about (CESifo Venice
  conference), 2
risk sharing in, 190–191
short-term flexibility and long-term
  rigidity in, 214–15
between sovereign nations (long-lasting),
  337
and trade, 3–4, 157, 157–160
unilateral, 225, 255 (see also Dollarization)
Monetary union, Northeast Asia. See
  Northeast Asia currency union
Monetary union dissolution, 5–6, 319–20,
  342
  analytical frameworks on, 320–22
  causal factors in, 323–36
  causal factors in (illustrative details),
    336–42
  data in study of, 322–23
  and inflation, 6, 325, 333, 336, 337, 342
Montenegro, full euroization in, 45
Mundell, Robert, 1, 264

National identity, dollarization as loss of,
  240
Netherlands, as high-deficit, 205
New members (NMs), 7. See also EU
  enlargement model
Nicaragua, as nondollarized developing
  economy, 225
Nontradables, 149
  for measure of relative prices, 135,
    151n.3
Northeast Asia currency union, 5, 289,
  292–94, 310–12
  and common long- and short-run cycles,
    296–303
  data and preliminary analyses in study
    on, 295–96
  potential output loss from, 303–10, 312–
    13
Norway, in study of smoothing of shocks,
  191, 205

Official consensus, 188
Optimal currency areas, theory of, 1

and currency agreements among
  countries, 264
and dissolution of monetary unions, 5–6
and EMU enlargement (implications),
  61–72
and EMU enlargement (stylized facts),
  57–61
and exit from currency union, 321
and UK–EMU debate, 159
Optimum currency area, 190
Hungary, Slovenia, and possibly Poland
  in, 73
Optimum currency area (OCA) criteria,
  289–90
endogeneity hypothesis on, 3, 55–56, 61,
  64, 68, 72–73
endogenous (indexes of), 70–72
Output reaction to external shocks, in
  dollarization model, 251, 253, 256
Output synchronization, and Northeast
  Asia currency union, 290–91 (see also
  Northeast Asia currency union)
Output smoothing. See Smoothing of
  shocks in EMU and OECD
Output volatility, in dollarization models,
  249

Panama, and dollarization, 237, 265
Paraguay, variability of exchange and
  interest rate in, 78
Partially dollarized economies, 225, 240–
  43, 245–49, 259n.2. See also Dollarization
  models
Peru, and dollarization, 225, 226, 240, 245,
  247, 248, 249, 259n.16
Poland. See also Central and Eastern
  European countries
Balassa-Samuelson effect for, 133
and correlation of industrial production
  with Germany, 70
and endogeneity hypothesis of OCA
  criteria, 56
and euro adoption, 79
exchange rate regime in, 79
exchange rate variability and
  unemployment in, 90, 92, 99, 107, 108,
  120
flexibility of labor market institutions in,
  87
and German shocks, 57
openness of, 81
and optimum currency area, 73
and real exchange rate appreciation, 23

Political change, and currency union
  dissolution, 336, 342
Pre-Maastricht phase of EU enlargement
  model, 8, 20–21
Price ratios, internal, 129–130
influences on (four CEEC accession
  countries), 127, 128–29, 130–31, 134,
  137, 141, 143–44,146–48
and real exchange rates, 134
Prices, regulated. See Regulated prices
Price stability principle, 7. See also
  Inflation
Price stabilization, and dollarization, 227
Private insurance, in risk sharing, 190
Productivity
and internal price ratios, 146
measure of, 128
and real exchange rates, 132–33, 135, 137,
  139, 146
Public sector, in smoothing of shocks, 190.
  See also Government role

Re-distribution issue, in Asian currency
  union, 308, 309
Regional currency
for ASEAN countries, 263
vs. dollarization, 264–65, 279–81
vs. dollarization (assessment), 266–79
vs. dollarization (data used), 281–82
Regionalism, 312
Regulated prices
and internal price ratios or CPI-based
  real exchange rates, 128–29, 147–48
and real exchange rate, 142–44
Relative weight question, and common
  monetary policy, 44
Reservation (fallback) wage, 82, 85
Right of derogation (introduction of euro),
  79
Risk sharing
assumptions behind, 192
in eurozone, 4
in monetary union, 190–91
patterns of, 189
private insurance in, 190
and size of countries, 189, 200–201
and smoothing of shocks in EU and
  OECD, 187–88, 213–16
and smoothing of shocks in EU and
  OECD (comparison with US states),
  207–12, 215, 216, 222n.43
and smoothing of shocks in EU and
  OECD (data sources), 216–19

Risk sharing (cont.)
and smoothing of shocks in EU and
OECD (empirical results), 196–13
and smoothing of shocks in EU and
OECD (methodology of study of), 191–
94
and smoothing of shocks in EU and
OECD (panel data estimation notes),
194–96
by US financial markets, 188
Romania. *See also* Central and Eastern
European countries
EMU trade of, 81
exchange rate regime in, 79
exchange rate variability and
unemployment in, 90, 92, 99, 107, 108,
109
as expected member, 17
openness of, 81
Rose, Andy, 3

Saving, private, smoothing consumption
through, 191
Saving and dis-saving, as channel of
income and consumption smoothing,
191, 192, 197, 198, 200, 201, 212, 214
Seignorage, and dollarization, 226, 227,
233, 256, 265
Shocks
and codependence statistic, 301–302,
303
common, 51n.6
correlation of, 290
in currency-union model, 304–307, 311
endogeneity of, 25
and exchange rate volatility, 77, 108
and optimal currency area, 264–65
smoothing of (EMU), 187–89 (*see also*
Smoothing of shocks in EMU and
OECD)
transmission mechanism crucial for, 290
Shocks, asymmetric, 58
and bilateral integration, 269
and business-cycle correlation, 55
calculation of, 281
and currency union exit, 325
insurance mechanisms for, 4, 190
and OCA theory, 61
and real exchange rate volatility, 275,
278, 280
and remaining outside EMU, 32
smoothing of, 187, 188

Shocks, exchange rate
in EU enlargement model, 16
real, 25
Shocks, idiosyncratic, 214
and monetary union exit, 323
smoothing of, 187
Shocks, supply
country-specific, 25
in EU enlargement model, 12, 13, 17, 21
Shocks, symmetric
and OCA theory, 61
supply, 23
Shocks, terms-of-trade (and dollarization),
238, 251, 253, 256
Single currency, 7. *See also* Common
currency
Size of country, and output smoothing,
189, 200–201
Slovakia (Slovak Republic). *See also*
Central and Eastern European countries
Balassa-Samuelson effect for, 133
Balassa-Samuelson implied inflation
differential for, 147
and correlation of industrial production
with Germany, 70
and EMU membership, 147
EMU trade of, 81
and endogeneity hypothesis of OCA
criteria, 56
exchange rate regime in, 79
exchange rate variability and
unemployment in, 90, 99, 107, 120
flexibility of labor market institutions in,
87
and German business cycles, 58
items of regulated prices for, 150
real exchange rates and internal price
ratios of, 127, 134, 146
tradables and nontradables in, 135
Slovenia. *See also* Central and Eastern
European countries
Balassa-Samuelson effect for, 133
Balassa-Samuelson implied inflation
differential for, 147
and correlation of industrial production
with Germany, 70
and EMU membership, 147
EMU trade of, 81
eurozone entry of, 79
exchange rate regime in, 79
exchange rate variability and
unemployment in, 90, 99, 107, 120

flexibility of labor market institutions in, 87
openness of, 80, 81
and optimum currency area, 73
real exchange rates and internal price ratios of, 127, 134, 146
Smoothing of shocks in EMU and OECD, 4
by government, 187, 190, 202–203, 214, 216
by private sector, 187–88, 190, 201–203, 214, 216
and risk sharing, 187–88, 213–16
and risk sharing (comparison with US states), 207–12, 215, 216, 222n.43
and risk sharing (data sources), 216–19
and risk sharing (empirical results), 196–213
and risk sharing (methodology in study of), 191–94
and risk sharing (panel data estimation notes), 194–96
South America. See also Latin America
and dissimilarities of export base, 269
and dollarization analysis, 264, 279
and output-shock asymmetry, 269
and real exchange rate volatility, 264, 278–79, 279, 280
and regional exchange rate volatility, 269
and trade integration, 270, 273, 280
South Korea. See Korea
Soviet Union, breakup of, 321–22
Spain
and German shocks, 57
as high-deficit country, 205
Speculative attacks, and exit from currency union, 321
Spillovers of reform policies, from monetary union, 43, 44, 49
Stability and Growth Pact (SGP), 187, 212, 216
and currency union dissolution, 336
Steady-state equilibrium (dollarization model), 257–58
Structural distortions, and monetary policy, 48–49
Structural reform and EMU enlargement, 31–32, 48–50
and conditions for enlargement, 46–48
and monetary policy, 39–42
and need for structural reforms, 33–36

and reforms under autonomy and under monetary union, 42–45
and resistance to reforms, 36, 38–39
Substitutability, imperfect, 131
Supply shocks. See Shocks, supply
Sweden
and eurozone (EMU), 50n.2, 189, 211
as low-deficit country, 205
Symmetric shocks. See Shocks, symmetric

Tax systems, of accession countries, 33
Terms of trade, and exchange rate swings, 77
Terms-of-trade shocks, and dollarization, 238, 251, 253, 256
Thatcher, Margaret, 155
Tradables, 149
for measure of relative prices, 135, 151n.3
Trade
and currency union, 157, 157–60
and dollarization, 237 (see also Dollarization)
Trade, EMU effect on. See EMU effect on trade
Trade booster, EMU as, 165, 178
Trade diversion, 161, 182n.15
Trade flows, and monetary union, 3–4
Trade growth
and currency union dissolution, 331, 336
intra-industry, 60–61
Trade integration
and cycle correlation, 156
and dissolved currency unions, 321
in dollarization analysis, 270–73, 279–80
Trade intensity
and business cycle convergence, 55–56, 64–66, 68, 72
calculation of, 282
in dollarization analysis, 267, 270
and real exchange rate volatility, 275
Trade openness
of CEECs, 80–81
and currency union dissolution, 336
of Slovenia, 107
Trade unions, and effect of exchange rate uncertainty on job creation, 85
Transaction costs
and common currency, 55, 166, 265, 266
and EMU impact on trade, 156
and law of one price, 131
and small nation in currency union, 308

Transitional recession, 58
Transition from planned to market
  economy
  in Central and Eastern Europe, 77
  and price deregulation, 142
Transition process of entry into eurozone,
  for Central European countries, 3
Transposition deficit, 162

UK–EMU debate, 155–56, 159
  and Brown's economic tests, 156
  and EMU impact on trade, 159–60
  and UK trade experience, 178–79
Underground economy
  in accession countries, 33
  and model of exchange rate variability
  and unemployment, 93
Unemployment, and distortions in labor
  market, 36
Unemployment benefit systems, and effect
  of exchange rate uncertainty on job
  creation, 85
Unemployment and exchange rate. *See*
  Exchange rate variability and
  unemployment
Unilateral currency union, 225, 255. *See
  also* Dollarization
United Kingdom
  EMU effect on trade of, 157, 159–60, 165,
  170–77, 178–79
  as eurozone entrant, 189, 211
  as high-deficit country, 205
  and UK–EMU debate, 155–56, 159–60,
  178–79
United States
  exchange rate variability and labor
  markets in, 78
  federal budget redistribution in, 187
  federal government as smoothing
  channel in, 194
  as high-deficit country, 205
  insurance mechanisms in, 4
  smoothing of shocks by markets in,
  188
  smoothing of shocks among states of,
  191, 194, 207–12, 215
Uruguay
  as partially dollarized, 225
  variability of exchange and interest rate
  in, 78
USSR, collapse of, 198

Vector error correction model, in
  Northeast Asia currency union analysis,
  299–300, 305
Volatility, macroeconomic, 226

Wage effect, on real exchange rate, 141–42
Werner report (1970), 2
Wooldridge test, 99, 109
World Trade Organization, Japan and
  Korea in, 292

Yugoslavia, breakup of, 321–22. *See also*
  Slovenia